Scholarly Publishing

The Electronic Frontier

D0164624

Scholarly Publishing

The Electronic Frontier

edited by
Robin P. Peek
Gregory B. Newby

The MIT Press
Cambridge, Massachusetts
London, England

Published in conjunction with the American Society for Information Science (ASIS).

This book was set in Sabon by The MIT Press and printed and bound in the United States of America.

Library of Congress Cataloging-in-Publication Data

Scholarly publishing: the electronic frontier/edited by Robin P. Peek, Gregory B. Newby
   p.   cm.
   Includes bibliographical references and index.
   ISBN 0-262-16157-5 (hc : alk. paper)
   1. Scholarly publishing—United States—Data processing. 2. Electronic publishing—United States. 3. Scholarly periodicals—United States—Data processing. I. Peek, Robin P. II. Newby, Gregory B.
Z479.S366   1996
070.5'0285—dc20   95-35556
                                      CIP

Contents

Foreword

James E. Rush

Much has been said and written about electronic publishing and its actual and anticipated effects on various segments of society (that is, on human beings in the global context). This book addresses the issues related to electronic publishing as it may affect one segment of society: academe. Although this is a narrow segment of society, it is important, because a preponderance of what is written and communicated about our world comes from the academic community. In fact, much of the publishing industry is devoted to scholarly communication.

The present debate about the benefits and disadvantages of electronic publishing, especially as it relates to the academic world, focuses on a number of important issues, among which are

intellectual property: who owns the ideas, concepts, theories, experimental data, facts, and opinions that authors record in speeches, articles, books, and other forms of publication (see Branscomb 1994, for example)?

economic property: who invests in the publishing process and who has a right to profit from such investment?

ethical conduct: does electronic publishing foster and encourage plagiarism and worse, or is ethical conduct indifferent to technological change?

egalitarianism or elitism: does electronic publishing favor the favored, or does it enhance equality of access and use, thereby bearing the potential for improvement in the general condition of humankind?

academic legitimacy: does an electronic publication have the merit accorded to the same information in print on paper?

librarianship: what is the role of the library in collecting, organizing, providing access to, and archiving electronic publications?

other societal implications: e.g., education, employment, the nature of work and the work place, general quality of life.

Many secondary issues are also of concern to various constituencies, but I do not believe they are central to the debate at this time.

Actually, the debate is about change and the likely consequences of change for every individual. I doubt that the debate about the changes that are being wrought by the application of modern computer and communication technologies is any more or less contentious, or founded more on opinion rather than fact, than similar debates occasioned by the introduction in earlier times of other technologies (e.g., the printing press, the steam engine, the Jacquard loom, electricity, telephony, or nuclear energy). Everyone who has any significant stake in the publishing business is concerned about his or her fortunes—whether those fortunes are measured in monetary, social, or cultural terms—both during the transition from traditional publishing to electronic publishing and in the electronic publishing world thereafter.

I believe that it is important, as we carry on the present debate, to recall that electronic publishing is not a new phenomenon. On the contrary, electronic publications have been with us since the early 1960s at least (e.g., *Chemical Titles* was first published by the Chemical Abstracts Service in both print and electronic form in 1961). Since that time, many publications have been issued in electronic form. They have often been referred to as databases rather than publications, but publications they are.

Today a sizable number of books, reference works, conference proceedings, journals, and other types of publications are created on, and issued in a form suitable for use with, a computer. The term *electronic publication* generally means just that, a publication in a form suitable for use with a computer. Technically, these publications exist in the form of magnetic fields on some magnetizable medium, or in the form of physical, chemical, or magnetic transformations of some medium that are detectable by means of light (a laser beam). It is the apparatus that permits humans to access and read the publications that is electronic.

As I have already stated, the heart of the debate is about change. Some would have us believe that the publishing industry is undergoing radical change. I agree that the changes we are witnessing are profound when judged from a historical perspective. Many of the issues have been debated for years, however, and are as important in traditional publishing as they are in electronic publishing. Regardless, humans have survived profound changes before, and we will do so again. I believe that change is never truly radical but, rather, is gradual and accelerates as it nears culmination.[1] Nevertheless, perception of change depends on the individual. Each of us may be differently affected by the rapidity of change and by our awareness that change is indeed occurring.

Perhaps the most daunting aspect of change is the inability of the individual, organization, or even nation to exercise any significant degree of control over it. These entities may catalyze change, but they cannot effectively control change once it is set in motion.

The changes occurring in the business of publishing illustrate both these principles—the gradual pace of change and our inability to control it—quite clearly. Electronic publishing is not a sudden discovery, if it may be called a discovery at all. Soon after computers (no sudden discovery either) came into existence, people began to consider how the computer could be applied to myriad aspects of human experience, from numerical calculations to natural language translation. The creation and publication of data in a form manipulable by computer did not escape the notice of early computer users. Vannevar Bush (1945) is generally credited with an early vision of the use of computers in support of scholarly work, and Hans Peter Luhn (1958) demonstrated the use of computers for creating abstracts and indexes of textual works in the late 1950s. Advances necessary for producing electronic publications have been made over the past 40 years, and we now have most of the tools necessary to make the transition from print-on-paper to electronic publishing without having to relinquish any of the advantages of the former to achieve the latter.

In short, changes in the publishing industry that are now being debated began many years ago and have been gaining momentum ever since. That the publishing industry is being transformed is both undeniable and inevitable. That the academic community is being transformed, at least in part because of changes in the publishing industry, is also undeniable and inevitable. Those organizations and industries that support the academic community (among others) and the publishing industry are undeniably being transformed by electronic publishing, and the transformations are inescapable. At the same time, the condition in which these organizations and industries may find themselves (if they continue to exist at all) is by no means clear. That is the root of the anxieties we are experiencing.

There are many interesting and important issues to be considered during the transition to electronic publishing. These issues are worthy of our best effort to resolve them for the benefit of future generations. Unfortunately, the current debate about electronic publishing often seems to be carried on by people who have no historical perspective of the matter. That is dangerous ground upon which to stand.

What is really of concern to most people in the transition to electronic publishing is the likely effect that the changes will have on them. I am no less concerned about these changes, but my concerns are largely related to the organizations I serve (I have labored in academe, but I am not an academic) and their likely future as affected by electronic publishing.

As president of the American Society for Information Science (ASIS), I am concerned about the society's publishing program and how electronic publishing may affect it and the society's future. The ASIS Board of Directors, the ASIS Publications Committee, various task forces, and ASIS staff have all been working to move the society into the world of electronic publishing but at the same time have devoted considerable thought and discussion to the issues that we believe are central concerns of the society with respect to such a transition.

For example, we believe that ASIS should take a position of leadership in the move to electronic publishing. This book is timely in its examination of many of the issues on which the electronic publishing debate focuses. Yet it is a print-on-paper publication, which can hardly allow ASIS to claim leadership in electronic publishing.

ASIS is also concerned with all the same matters as other publishers (e.g., Denning and Rous 1995), including protection of intellectual property, maintenance of the integrity of society publications in the networked world, assessment of the financial consequences of electronic publishing (projections of revenues and costs are not at all clear), and the effect of electronic publishing (or its absence) on society membership and on the stature of ASIS as a professional society.

We in ASIS realize that it is possible to produce electronic publications that not only have the appearance of print-on-paper publications but that exhibit other beneficial properties as well. At the same time we realize that there remain many people (society members or otherwise) who do not have the computer systems necessary to access such publications, even though they may have the need or desire to do so. On the one hand, if ASIS were to introduce enhanced electronic publications, would we disenfranchise society members whom we serve? On the other hand, if ASIS publications were offered in the form of plain ASCII text, would the stature of the society as a leading proponent of information science be diminished? Of course many other factors must be weighed, and choices must be made. Most of these factors and choices are addressed in this volume, so I need not belabor the point.

As executive director of PALINET (a nonprofit library service organization), my concerns about electronic publishing relate to the needs and abilities of member libraries to adopt and adapt to the technologies, operating procedures, and practices necessary to make such publications available to their clientele (many of whom are academics). PALINET deals with the producers and suppliers of electronic publications, on one hand, and, on the other, with the libraries and information centers that make these publications available to and accessible by the public.

Libraries have been on the forefront of the evolution toward electronic publishing, having transformed much of their operations and services to admit significant computer support. For the past 30 years or so, the library has been where a researcher or scholar could most readily gain access to electronic data (publications). Libraries have been quick to adopt CD-ROM technology and thus offer their clientele access to the rapidly growing array of publications distributed on this medium. Libraries have for many years offered electronic finding tools to their clients, and the use of computer systems for accessing library catalogs (themselves a form of electronic publication), performing interlibrary loans, and managing library operations has become de rigueur for a great many libraries, and will ultimately be so for all.

Nevertheless, libraries must face some real problems associated with the acquisition, use, archiving, and management of electronic publications. Again, chapters in this book address many of these problems. Libraries must find effective solutions if they are to continue their long-standing role as the repositories (in whatever form) and trustees of the recorded knowledge of humankind.

Perhaps the greatest uncertainty, and thus the most debate, centers on the consequences that electronic publishing may have on the author, who is the originator of most that is published. With the tools available today, it is possible for almost anyone to be both an author and a publisher. As noted in several chapters in this volume, a growing number of authors are, in fact, self-publishing via the Internet. This raises concerns about quality control (largely implemented today through peer review), proprietary rights (e.g., does the principle of a "work for hire" become meaningless?), and the overall economics of publishing (in many present cases, the entire cost of production and distribution is borne by the author's employer, but no revenue is gained through the distribution of the author's work). For academics, electronic publishing also opens for reexamination and reevaluation the contribution of their writings to their condition and standing within the institution, as well as to the institution as a whole.

Academics may express concern about the relative merits of electronic and print-on-paper publications with respect to academic standing, tenure, and evaluation by peers, but more deep-seated issues are now being discussed. For example, what is the contribution of publishing to the institution's mission? Why should the granting of tenure to a faculty member be more heavily determined by publications than by teaching? Why should tenure be granted at all? What are the economic interests of the institution with respect to the publishing of the works of its faculty? What control does or should an academic institution exercise over the works published by or for those in its employ? How will electronic publishing by or for academics affect the reputation of the academic institution (hence its ability to attract students, faculty, staff, grants, endowments, etc.)?

How will the uncertainties associated with the change to electronic publishing be resolved? Only time will tell. All of us who are interested in this change and the likely futures it may generate must devote considerable energy and intelligent thought to the matter. For although we cannot control change, we should be able to channel and direct it to some degree.

A number of the papers in this volume discuss ways in which we can attempt to channel changes in the publishing industry. In essence these papers focus on issues of control (or guidance, at least). But this volume also contains papers whose authors, like myself, take a more utopian view (to borrow from Kling and Lamb, this volume) of the consequences of changes in the publishing industry. I believe, like K. E. Drexler (1991), that electronic publishing will not only transform publishing for the good of society but will hasten the evolution of knowledge and enable us to learn to deal with one another and with our environment in more intelligent and beneficial ways.

N. Postman (1992), in contrast, takes the antiutopian view, considering technological change to be suspect at best, and potentially far worse for most of humankind (see also Crawford and Gorman 1995). Such a gloomy view of the future does not seem to me to fit into the long history of human existence. To be sure, every technological advance has been misused (or worse) by segments of the population, but I believe that in the long term humanity has benefited far more than it has suffered from such advances. The fact that some people use fire with malicious intent does not diminish the value of fire for humanity as a whole. The same may be said for almost any technological advance. Certainly we have caused irreparable damage to the planet and its inhabitants, but we have not yet destroyed it, and I believe (with the positivists) that we shall not.

Electronic publishing has the potential to support great advances in the dissemination and use of information and education, as well as to foster a more equitable, beneficial relationship among people and between humankind and the planet on which we live. Let this volume serve to inform and direct the debate about how electronic publishing will shape our future, and how we can help to channel and guide the changes now taking place.

References

Branscomb, A. W. (1994). *Who Owns Information? From Privacy to Public Access*. New York: Basic Books.

Bush, V. (1945). "As We May Think." *Atlantic Monthly* 176: 101–108.

Crawford, W., and M. Gorman. (1995). *Future Libraries: Dreams, Madness, and Reality*. Chicago, Ill.: American Library Association.

Denning, P. J., and B. Rous. (1995). "The ACM Electronic Publishing Plan." *Communications of the ACM* 38, no. 4: 97–109.

Drexler, K. E. (1991). "Hypertext Publishing and the Evolution of Knowledge." *Social Intelligence* 1, no. 2: 87–120.

Kling, R., and R. Lamb (this volume). "How Genres of Analysis Shape the Character of Alternative Visions for Electronic Publishing and Digital Libraries."

Luhn, H. P. (1958). "The Automatic Creation of Literature Abstracts." *IBM Journal of Research and Development* 2: 159–165.

Postman, N. (1992). *Technopoly: The Surrender of Culture to Technology*. New York: Alfred A. Knopf.

Note

1. Change usually occurs in fits and starts until its nature and direction become clear enough that momentum can be established, after which the pace of change accelerates to a culmination (but not an end).

Introduction

Gregory B. Newby and Robin P. Peek

This book investigates the future of scholarly electronic publishing. Because of electronic publishing, we will never know what would have happened if traditional paper-based scholarly publishing, now strained by production volumes and costs, remained the sole basis for scholarly communication. Electronic publishing is now viable, as demonstrated in these pages. Communication, production, authoring, and distribution technologies have created an environment where the question is not, Should we change the nature of publishing? but What will the nature of scholarly publishing be, and how should we help to shape it?

The chapters in this book explore the social and organizational issues associated with this critical transitional time when the foundations for the future are being developed. There are many paths that scholarly publishing might take as it enters the twenty-first century, from a complete overhaul of the system as we know it to a gradual retrenching where much remains the same except that paper is no longer the medium for communication. In the mid-1990s, we have an opportunity for critical debate on the implications of various possible futures for scholarly publishing. That debate is found in these pages.

Scholarly publishing evolved from centuries of development resulting in mechanisms for ensuring both quality and exclusion control for the formal collective knowledge contained in published materials. The various components of these mechanisms—scholarly review; editorial processes; the cost, delay, and process of typesetting and distribution, and so forth—combine to decide which scholarly views will be retained for the ages, and in what venues.

Electronic scholarly publishing is not necessarily bound by any traditions. Instead of focusing primarily on journals and monographs, various forms of network-based publishing, optical storage media, and multimedia create new possibilities. Perhaps at no other time in the history of higher education has the academic community been faced with an issue that so fundamentally tugs at the historical roots of how academia has gone about its individual and collective business. The nature of social discourse and organizational structure may be significantly altered as publishing moves from a print-based paradigm to an electronic one.

The issues raised by the change to electronic publishing are complicated. Sweeping statements about new editorial processes, production schemes, and distribution channels do not easily translate into practical and achievable objectives that will meet the needs of consumers. The stakes are high: the quality, integrity, and future of the academic knowledge base lie in the balance.

This book is divided into two parts, "The Impact of Electronic Publishing on Scholarly Life" and "The New Challenges." The first section discusses changes that are occurring and will occur in the role of publishing for scholarly life. The second part introduces some of the principal issues that do not exist, or that exist very differently, in traditional paper-based scholarly publishing.

Although these chapters focus on scholarly publishing, many of the issues are also pertinent to popular publishing, business, entertainment, and interpersonal communication. The authors of the chapters anticipating many changes to society and to day-to-day communication that go beyond the academic arena. A brief outline of the chapters in the book, and an introduction to the authors, follows.

Robin Peek is assistant professor in the Graduate School of Library and Information Science at Simmons College. In "Scholarly Publishing, Facing the New Frontiers," she starts the discussion. Rather than anticipating great changes in the nature of scholarly publishing, she provides a notion of a changed medium within a publishing institution that remains largely the same. She has written and taught about the various aspects of higher education as it evolves because of the forces of the electronic age. She edited a "Perspectives" issue of the *Journal of the American Society for Information Science* on the subject of electronic publishing.

In "How Genres of Analysis Shape the Character of Alternative Visions for Electronic Publishing and Digital Libraries" Rob Kling and Roberta Lamb present a theoretical and philosophical framework from which to consider the role of technology in electronic publishing and other areas of life. They examine the assumptions underlying utopian and antiutopian approaches to genres of social analysis related to technology. Rob Kling is professor of Information and Computer Science at the University of California, Irvine (UCI). He also holds professorial appointments in the Center for Research on Information Technology and Organizations and in the Graduate School of Management at UCI. He is coauthor of *Computers and Politics: High Technology in American Local Governments,* coeditor of *Post Suburban California: The Transformation of Postwar Orange County,* and writer and editor of the 1995 edition of *Computerization and Controversy: Value Conflict and Social Choices.* His research has been published in more than 85 journal articles and book chapters. Roberta Lamb is a doctoral student of Information and Computer Science at UCI. As a member of CORPS (Computing, Organizations, Policy and Society), her research has focused on the usability aspects of online databases and external information resources in the corporate sector. Roberta is a faculty lecturer at California State University, Fullerton, where she teaches a graduate course in database theory and architecture. She is also a manager of Technical Development for an Irvine-based client/server applications development firm.

Robert J. Silverman writes of changes for the producers of academic knowledge in "The Impact of Electronic Publishing on the Academic Community." He anticipates that authors will be required to be increasingly public, and to engage a wider audience in their scholarly debates. As scholarly communication evolves toward a discourse model, he says, the nature of evaluation for academic performance and contribution must necessarily change. He provides a new understanding of the meaning and variety of the academic community. Silverman is the founder and editor of the *Journal of Higher Education.*

Jean-Claude Guédon is a professor in the Departement de littérature comparée at the Université de Montréal. He founded and directed the refereed electronic journal *Surfaces,* which started publication in 1991 and was edited by Bill Readings until his untimely death in 1993. Guédon's chapter, "The Seminar, the Encyclopedia, and the Eco-Museum as Possible Future Forms of Electronic Publishing," describes the foundation of printed periodicals and discusses their relation to the development of intellectual societies and fields of inquiry. Guédon also investigates the effects of electronic publishing on the nature of intellectual society and scholarly communication.

"Tragic Loss or Good Riddance? The Impending Demise of Traditional Scholarly Journals," by Andrew M. Odlyzko, is a condensed version of a larger work. In this chapter Odlyzko examines the growth of publishing in mathematics and extrapolates cost and size, concluding that it will be reasonable to store and distribute the entire literature of mathematics in electronic form. He anticipates growth of peer-review systems and ongoing commentary through an electronic database of papers. Odlyzko is head of the Mathematics of Communication and Computer Systems Department at AT&T Bell Laboratories and is also adjunct professor in the Faculty of Mathematics at University of Waterloo. His professional interests include computational complexity, cryptography, number theory, combinatorics, coding theory, analysis, and probability theory. He is the author of about 140 scientific papers and serves on more than a dozen editorial boards.

In "Implementing Peer Review on the Net: Scientific Quality Control in Scholarly Electronic Journals" Stevan Harnad relates his experiences with and predictions for network-based scholarly journals and general communication. He anticipates some of the same arguments made with respect to general publishing in Rothman's chapter. Harnad is professor of psychology and director of the Cognitive Sciences Centre at the University of Southampton in the United Kingdom. He is founder and editor of *Behavioral and Brain Sciences,* a paper journal published by Cambridge University Press, and *PSYCOLOQUY*, a peer-reviewed electronic journal sponsored by the American Psychological Association. Harnad's research is on categorization and neural networks and on perception, cognition, and language in general. He has written numerous articles on these subjects and has edited and contributed to several books.

Harnad's chapter is the last in the first part of the book, in which the groundwork, history, and current efforts in scholarly electronic publishing are presented. The first chapter in the second part, where conclusions and predictions are drawn for the near future, is by Brian Hayes. In "The Economic Quandary of the Electronic Publisher" Hayes presents a summary and overview of current electronic journals, with a focus on their challenges from disparate readership, lack of institutional support, and varying editorial policies. Hayes is a writer and editor who specializes in topics related to computer science and information technology. He launched the "Computer Recreations" column at *Scientific American* (where he was associate editor for some years) and now writes the "Computing Science" column for *American Scientist* (where he was editor until 1993). His chapter appeared in a somewhat different form in *American Scientist*.

Clifford A. Lynch, in "Integrity Issues in Electronic Publishing," argues that issues of integrity are often overstated. He maintains that integrity is also an issue for print resources and is not as different for electronic resources as is often stated. Lynch believes that such issues as authentication and immediate availability of electronic works are more important for electronic publishing than integrity. Lynch is the 1995–1996 president of the American Society for Information Science and the director for library automation at the University of California, Office of the President.

In "The University Press in the Electronic Future" Lisa Freeman argues for a continuing role of university presses in the world of electronic publishing. Through the 1990s, producing electronic materials will be more time consuming and expensive than producing traditional paper materials, and university presses are positioned to meet these increased demands. Freeman has been director of the University of Minnesota Press since 1990. Prior to her arrival in Minnesota, she worked for the now-defunct British publisher Allen & Unwin and for Sage Publications. She is chair of the Association of American University Presses' Electronic Caucus and has been involved in electronic publishing since 1992.

The past, present, and future of networked communication is presented by Ira H. Fuchs in "Network Information Is Not Free." Fuchs presents cost structures for BITNET and the Internet, and extrapolates the expenses of new forms of communication—including electronic publishing—as they come into play. As vice president for Computing and Information Technology at Princeton University, Fuchs is responsible for the overall management of the university's academic and administrative computing services, electronic communications, media, and printing. He founded CREN (formerly BITNET), a nonprofit organization with more than five hundred institutional members, and he now serves as its president and CEO.

"University Libraries and Scholarly Communication" by Ann Okerson is a synopsis of a study prepared for the Andrew W. Mellon Foundation. The first part of the synopsis presents a state-of-the-art view of the expenditures for various types of libraries. The increasing costs of serials—primarily journals and monographs—is highlighted. The second part looks toward the role of electronic publishing in collection development for academic libraries. Okerson is director of the Office of Scientific and Academic Publishing for the Association of Research Libraries. In 1993 she was named the American Library

Association "Bowker Serials Librarian of the Year" and, for the second time, was given the ALA/Blackwell "Best Article in Serials, Acquisitions, or Collections Development" award. She has been a frequent contributor to many publications in both paper and electronic formats. She serves on several editorial boards, including that of *Ejournal* (an electronic scholarly journal).

L. W. Hurtado presents a vision of cooperation for the future in "A Consortium for Refereed Electronic Journals." He proposes for electronic journals an analog to the "Good Housekeeping" seal—a consortium to create standards and act proactively. He then argues for the consortium to be academic, not based on commercial or other enterprises. Hurtado is professor of religion at the University of Manitoba, Winnipeg. His research is in the field of Christian origins. He is the author of three books, is the editor or coeditor of two others, and has written numerous articles in journals, reference works, and books. In 1991 he convened an ad hoc group to consider his proposal to organize the (first) International Conference on Refereed Electronic Journals, which was held in Winnipeg on October 1–2, 1993.

Marlene Manoff's chapter is called "Revolutionary or Regressive: The Politics of Electronic Collection Development." From the perspective of an academic librarian, she argues that we have not given sufficient consideration to the ways in which new technology may improve, constrain, or alter the process of scholarly research. Looking at Internet tools and CD-ROM resources in libraries, she shows how computerization promotes or privileges certain kinds of research. She questions whether this technology serves some disciplines less well than others and whether it tends to marginalize certain kinds of scholarship. Manoff is collection manager in the Massachusetts Institute of Technology Humanities Library. She has taught literature and women's studies at MIT and collection development at the Graduate School of Library and Information Science at Simmons College. She has chaired two MIT Library task forces on electronic journals whose reports have been published in *Serials Review*. Manoff has also written about the politics of collection development.

In "Traditional Publishers and Electronic Journals" Janet Fisher analyzes the scholarly publishing process and provides insight into how this process might be changed as a result of electronic publishing. Fisher is associate director for journals publishing at MIT Press, which publishes 30 scholarly journals in a wide range of disciplines. Prior to joining MIT, she held various positions in the University of Texas Press Journals Department. She is currently a member of the Board of Directors of the AAUP (Association of American University Presses), a member of NASIG (North American Serials Interest Group), and on the Journal Committee of the Professional and Scholarly Publishing Division of the AAP (Association of American Publishers).

Fytton Rowland, in "Electronic Journals: The Need for Management," justifies the continued role of publishers in the electronic age. He argues for a continuing need for professionals and technical specialists in preparing, copyediting, and presenting works, among other tasks. Rowland is a research fellow in the Department of Information and Library Studies at the University of Technology in Loughborough, England. Previously he was publications production manager of the Royal Society of Chemistry, a learned-society publisher in the United Kingdom.

"The Challenges of Electronic Texts in the Library: Bibliographic Control and Access," by Rebecca S. Guenther, explains the leadership role that she believes must be taken, and is being taken, by the Library of Congress. She describes the transition of cataloging rules for electronic materials and presents the various projects under way. Guenther is senior MARC standards specialist in the Network Development and MARC Standards Office at the Library of Congress. Her responsibilities include work on national and international library automation standards, including USMARC bibliographic, authority, classification, holdings, and community information formats, and USMARC code lists for languages, countries, and geographic areas. She has also been involved in accommodating online information resources into USMARC formats and developing a system for the conversion of Library of Congress Classification into USMARC classification records. This chapter was originally presented as a paper at the 1992 Data Processing Clinic at the Graduate School of Library and Information Science at the University of Illinois at Urbana-Champaign and appeared in the proceedings of that conference.

Brian Kahin's chapter, "Scholarly Communication in the Network Environment: Issues of Principle, Policy, and Practice" treats the larger issue of scholarly communication, of which publishing is a part. He discusses legal issues, especially copyright. Most rules for the copyright of nonelectronic materials seem to apply to electronic ones, but new ways of doing collaborative work invite struggles over issues such as derivative works, prepublication, and so on. Kahin, an attorney, is director of the Information Infrastructure Project in the Science, Technology, and Public Policy Program at Harvard's John F. Kennedy School of Government, where his research centers on legal, institutional, and policy issues in the development of new communications and information environments. He also teaches a Kennedy School seminar on information technology, law, and public policy.

Patrice Lyons writes of copyright law in "Where Electronic Publications and Television Programs Are Really Computer Programs." She addresses public performance rights of computer programs and the applicability of copyright law to programs and the data they contain or produce. She also introduces issues of copyright for electronically stored, generated, or transmitted works. Lyons was formerly a partner at Haley, Bader & Potts and is now in private practice at her firm, Law Offices of Patrice Lyons, Chartered. She has served as a legal officer in the copyright division of UNESCO in Paris (1971–1987). Her practice is geared toward the variety of copyright and trademark issues that affect the communications, computer, and entertainment industries.

The closing chapter in the volume is "Teleread: A Virtual Central Database without 'Big Brother,'" by David H. Rothman, a former poverty-beat reporter who has written five technology-related books and coauthored a sixth. Rothman wants to reduce the cost of knowledge for both the elite and the nonelite. The chapter draws on many of the concepts presented in other sections of this book to create an optimistic and cooperative outlook for a future with flexibility for all types of publishing. This chapter addresses continued access to electronic materials and optimistically predicts a centralized database with central funding, but with openings for private commercial ventures and commercial publishing.

One of the most important questions addressed by the chapters in this book is, How do we get from where we are to where we are going? Our intent in creating the volume is to bring together leading authors from a range of disciplines and professions. The broad cross-section of authors demonstrates the variety of stockholders involved in the transition to electronic publishing. The authors were asked to emphasize the issues and opposing views critical to debate over the next ten years while foundations for electronic publishing are being laid. The ideas, predictions, and concerns expressed here are more than the views of speculators— they come directly from individuals and organizations who are actively engaged in shaping the future of electronic publishing. Perhaps a future volume on electronic publishing will take place using the new media, to provide hindsight on the perspectives presented by the authors.

I

The Impact of Electronic Publishing on Scholarly Life

1

Scholarly Publishing, Facing the New Frontiers

Robin P. Peek

In the United States there are ongoing heated debates regarding how the U.S. health care system needs to change to better serve the population. Meanwhile, a transition to electronic forms of scholarly publishing is occurring. Although the stakes are different, there are similarities between these two issues. We need to decide how, or if, the computer should ultimately transform the manner of scholarly communication by "publishing" individual and collective works. Both debates cause great anticipation and anxiety because changing a system that we rely on and know means to give up something has always existed for something new. Like debates about health care reform, debates about a digitized form of publishing consider the real potential savings and whether anyone should profit. Questions arise about changing who is in charge, evaluating the roles and tasks performed, and determining qualifications needed. In discussions about publishing, much like health care, the issues are complex, and few truly comprehend the difficulties and challenges associated with transforming the existing system.

Technology often moves faster than society is prepared to deal with the changes. In 1993 a historical turning point occurred as both the Internet and multimedia entered the mainstream of American life. This development caused the publishing industry to seriously begin contemplating its future. Scholarly publishers are engaged in a volatile and heated debate about their role, particularly the role of the scholarly journal. Not only are other options technologically viable, but the financial pressures of maintaining and supporting scholarly journals are increasingly acute. Another critical issue in these debates is the great discontinuities of technological access and prowess, which vary considerably across colleges and disciplines. For every faculty member with a state-of-the-art computer, others (and we do not know how many) are still using a wheezing five-year-old computer or do not have a computer at all. For every faculty member with Mosaic (an interface for the World-Wide Web), others have only e-mail, and still others have no Internet connectivity at all. Then there are those faculty and administrators who simply do not care for computing technology. This discrepancy is critical because the viability of digitized publishing seems greater when viewed using a first-rate monitor with excellent graphics, speed, and storage rather than using a low-end machine.

Despite these discontinuities, these debates must go on today with even greater fervor than they have in the past. At no other time in the history of scholarly publishing have the social structures and organizational patterns of creating and maintaining the scholarly word had such serious examination by numerous scholars, librarians, administrators, and publishers. The debate needs to broaden, however, to encompass even more of the stakeholders than just the current participants. Although a variety of efforts underway show the potential of electronic publishing, these efforts are piecemeal when viewed collectively. The experiments may be also be fragile due to the degree that external, and often temporary, funding sources support them. These early projects prove the potential of the medium, but the final products of the endeavors have not yet achieved the status of the common currency of exchange for academic scholarship. There is still much work to be done to find the approach that will liberate scholarly words from the confines of the paper container and still ensure fairness, justice, and quality.

The digitalization of the scholarly word appears inevitable, but the timing is uncertain. Although an environment in which journals are universally electronic may seem far into the future, the foundations laid now will be critical to the evolution of this environment. When everything we have come to know, understand, and expect from scholarly publishing is called into question, the challenge of creating a framework that will be accepted by stakeholders becomes clear.

When Paper Was Essential to Scholarly Communication

There was a time when using journals to allow scholars to communicate was logical and reasonable. The founders of the first scholarly journals, however, would no doubt be surprised at how the journal has changed. Over time, the concept of scholars using a journal to communicate with peers has subtly but radically been transformed. Part of this change can be credited to technological advancement and structural changes in the academic reward system. Papers in early journals were really works-in-progress, with future monographs being considered the final stage, or the "published work." In modern times the journal is, for many disciplines, the final destiny of a scholar's published work, and thus the fundamental purpose of the journal has significantly changed. In no small measure, scholarly communication has changed to become publishing.

The traditional roots of scholarly communication and the idea of the invisible college originated in the 1640s. A group of scholars who met regularly at Oxford University decided to name their group the Invisible College (they later renamed it the Royal Society). As the group grew, the society had difficulties communicating with all who would like to participate owing to the natural inhibitions of the existing technologies. Because they lacked telephones, fax machines, photocopiers, and typewriters, collective communication was not an easy task. Conferences and meetings were held by the Royal Society, but the difficulties and finances of traveling to central locations for conferences limited participation. Travel was a vastly more time-consuming, if not hazardous, venture.

The private letter, which had historically served as the key vehicle for communication between scholars, had been manageable when the number of practicing scholars was few. The notion of college educators engaging in professional research would not evolve for a long time to come, and many scholars who were performing research were doing so on a volunteer basis. But as the number of scholars grew larger, private letters became too cumbersome, so the journal became the suitable means to exchange letters on a broader and more efficient scale. In 1665 the Royal Society began publishing the first scholarly journal, *Philosophical Transactions of the Royal Society of London,* which provided scholars the opportunity to exchange letters widely. Yet the early journals were few in number and they were not seen as the ultimate destination of a scholar's work.

Journals became an important fixture in the scholarly landscape because they brought the members of the invisible college into a singular forum. These journals also provided an effective means of archiving scholarly exchanges. They became known as scholarly communication and were the means to bring together the invisible college, as Ziman noted in 1976: "They [the members of the college] are bound together by the communication of information and knowledge. Science depends heavily upon the printed word for two reasons. It is essential to keep a permanent public record of results, observations, calculations, theories etc. It is also necessary to provide opportunities for criticism, refutation and further refinement of facts" (p. 90).

Today, of course, technology provides many ways for scholars to communicate easily. Increased ease of travel has made attending professional conferences far more feasible, and, for many scholars, attending conferences is a routine event. Typically the conferences generate their own bound editions of "works in progress," which perhaps are more like the early scholarly journals than contemporary journals. Electronic mail and electronic mailing lists provide a means of communicating that early scholars did not imagine. Even scholars who do not have access to networked communications can use the telephone and fax machines to simplify their exchanges.

The fundamental purposes of publishing in a journal have shifted considerably. The popularity of the monograph as a final publication has declined in many disciplines, and the journal has emerged as more than a communication device. Today the journal is deeply entrenched in the academic reward system as the appropriate place to publish. In addition, the publishing of journals has significantly shifted from academic societies to publishers, both nonprofit and for-profit, creating an elaborate hierarchy of publishers. It is from these publication houses that the legitimacy and stature not only of an individual journal but of an academic discipline or subdiscipline are ranked, as Paul and Matasar (1993) observed: "In order for a new discipline to attain legitimacy, it is extremely helpful if a scholarly journal emerges to represent the discipline. . . . If such a journal does not emerge, or if journals seemingly representative of the field do not have academic credibility, then the development and institutionalization of the field can be delayed or even thwarted" (p. 171).

Paper is not a flexible publishing medium, and its requirements have naturally limited what could be done. Without a viable alternative, the norms and mechanisms of scholarly publishing have persisted. Disciplines differ greatly in such things as the role of journals, the editorial practices, and the appropriate economics, factors that further complicate a shift from paper to a paperless environment. H. L. Mencken often noted that every complex problem had a simple solution—and it was invariably wrong. There is probably no simple solution to the problem of changing the manner in which scholarly publishing is conducted.

Paper has served us fairly well over the years. Before an acceptable alternative was available there was little reason to give serious discussion to abandoning it as a vehicle. This poses a particularly vexing problem for academics, because there is not the usual literature to cite and re-cite in dealing with this issue.

A Less Than Perfect World

Scholars publish for several reasons, some of which are practical, such as promotion and tenure. Other reasons have different returns. Scholars may desire a certain immortality in print, hoping their words will outlive them and survive for future generations of scholars. The promotion and tenure decision makers are perhaps the most critical and most unpredictable part of the scholarly publication process, although they will not be discussed in this chapter.

A scholar wants people to read his or her work. For a work to be read, it must be found. Once the journal containing the scholar's paper is published, the scholar wishes the paper to be found by other members of his or her own invisible college. If the other members subscribe to the journal in question, they are probably going to encounter the paper when the journal arrives in the mail. But if the library, not the members, subscribe to the journal, the members will encounter the paper only if they make a pilgrimage to the library.

Casual encounters are problematic means of locating a journal, particularly in the long term. Therefore, researchers rely on the indexing and abstracting publishing services to provide the all-important pointers to scholarly papers. The sheer act of publishing in a journal, however, does not mean that the paper will be picked up by one of these services, because inclusion in an index is not automatic. This was the case in the early 1990s for the *Online Journal of Clinical Trials* (*OJCT*), published by the American Association for the Advancement of Science (AAAS) Press, which also publishes the weekly journal *Science*. Patricia Morgan, director of publications at AAAS Press, had concerns about getting researchers to submit quality work. The *Chronicle of Higher Education* noted that "a new journal in an unorthodox format that could be read only on a computer screen was not thought to be the place to publish papers that might lead to tenure, promotion, better salaries, and more grant money" (Wilson 1994, p. A23).

The *OJCT* lost credibility by not being indexed in *Index Medicus* (on paper) and *Medline* (electronic), the key indexing services for medical research. After a difficult year, the *OJCT* was accepted by the National Library of Medicine for inclusion in these two sources. Patricia Morgan described this action as critical to the survival of the journal: "I don't know, to be blunt, how much longer we could have gone one without being in Medline. Now we're expecting a jump in submission and a jump in circulation" (quoted in Wilson 1994).

Inclusion of a journal into an indexing service does not guarantee that a journal is indexed cover-to-cover, although that is the most common approach. Some indexing services, such as the *Cumulative Index to Journals in Education,* published by the Educational Resources Information Clearinghouse, have a specified set of journal titles, and papers from each issue are selected for inclusion. So it is entirely possible that only one paper from a journal be granted an indexed "pointer." The only means to know if this is the case with an indexing service is by examining the lists that identify whether the contents of a journal are picked up entirely or selectively.

Indexing services are also inhibited by the limitations of their paper container. Because the printed indexes cannot have an infinite size, decisions are rendered regarding which journals to include. Consequently each service has to maintain a set of standards for inclusion. These standards may be objective, for example, requiring that the journal be publishing regularly for one year. More subjective determinations may also be made, for example, deciding that the journal is of a suitable quality.

So through either searching an index or database, finding a reference on a bibliography, or getting a recommendation from an electronic mailing list, the scholar locates a reference. Next he or she must secure the paper itself, which can be a formidable task. If the scholar, or anyone in his or her peer group, does not have a subscription to the journal, then the next hope is that the library subscribes to the journal. But subscribing to the journal does not ensure that the library will have the paper. If our scholar happens to seek the paper in the summer, he or she could find that journals from the past year have been sent to the bindery. Or the scholar may find that the paper has been torn out of the journal by a vandal. Or worse, the journal is missing. Worse still, the whole bound year is missing.

At this point our seeking scholar can hope that the library also purchases the journal title in a microfilm version. Although our scholar may be thrilled to discover that the library has the title in microfilm, he or she is no doubt less than thrilled that this means using the microfilm readers.

If the library does not have the journal, the scholar has perhaps one last hope: interlibrary loan. Because of budgetary problems, resource sharing between libraries has become normative. If our scholar is fortunate, the library can locate the journal at another library that shares with it. If not, the scholar may have to try to visit a library that has the journal and that will allow him or her to use the journal at that location. If a cooperative library is available, the scholar will receive a photocopy of the paper. Because of the increasing reliance on interlibrary loan, many scholars will see only the paper, not the journal in its entirety. Of course, this is the case if the scholar is the one who does the seeking; for many professors, an assistant does the seeking.

Over time the finding of a paper becomes more difficult. Despite its appearance, paper is not a perfect storage medium. While generating an illusion of permanence, it eventually deteriorates. Modern journals have an even shorter life span than earlier journals because of "advances" in paper production. Although alkaline or acid-free paper has a life expectancy of five hundred to one thousand years (depending on the quality of the paper), most of the publishing world relies on paper containing acid, which burns the paper over time, causing it to become yellow and brittle, and eventually to decay into dust. According to Madeline Davis, "The knowledge of our country is crumbling just sitting there" (Brown 1985, p. 591). Preserving paper is an expensive undertaking, so libraries must ultimately decide which materials to save and which to let deteriorate. This is a particular challenge for scholarly journals because generally they are not circulating items, so librarians cannot tell if a particular issue of a journal has been used once, ten times, hundreds of times, or never.

It is unlikely that academia will continue with the present system. In this system libraries purchase and store paper that may never be read. Then they bind the journal, perhaps purchasing it again in microfilm, all of which can cost more than the original journal subscription. Then they spend even more money to house the title and maintain it until, in the not-so-distant future, the paper is about to crumble in their hands, and then they decide whether to spend more money to preserve it. When many college budgets are being reduced by state legislatures, sagging enrollments, or diminishing research grants, seeking a more cost-effective approach seems a logical thing to do. But is academia ready to change? And how much should it change?

The Unusual World of Scholarly Publishing

Publishing in paper requires presses, people who know what to do with those presses, the resources to purchase paper, ink, postage, salaries, and so forth. To recoup the expenses, there has to be a market, and for scholarly journals the market is often very small. This is only one way that scholarly journals are set apart from mainstream publishing.

Publishers must contend with the reality that scholars, referees, and often editors are not paid for their contributions to learned journals. Therefore editors and publishers do not have the ability to control or manage behavior. There is no means of knowing if the upcoming year will have 500 submissions or 50 and if the submissions will all come in January and June or will be nicely distributed over the year. A referee may return the paper promptly or may place the paper in the "to do" stack, where it may linger for weeks. So editors and publishers cannot know what each month or quarter will bring. The best plan is thus to maintain a "backlog" that ensures a steady production flow. This, of course, extends the delay before the paper becomes available to the scholarly community. In a worse scenario, the journal must wait until there are enough papers, which also delays the release of the scholar's work. Such delays can be particularly irritating in the scholarly community because a scholar hopes that he or she will be the one who "got there first." Unfortunately, publishing in paper is a slow, sometimes painfully drawn-out affair. Hayes (1989) reported a three-year delay from the completion of a conference to final publication of the proceedings. Speed of publication, which has long been a problem, seems increasingly problematic in a world of instant communication. In a culture where getting things out first is so important, delays of months or a year (or even longer) seem almost absurd when a message sent to a an electronic mailing list can travel the globe in a matter of seconds.

Delay is caused by the fundamental design of a paper publication and the norms of journals being published in a pattern. If a journal claims to a subscriber that it is published monthly, twelve editions must appear each year. Academia sometimes has some interesting twists on this theme. In the nonacademic world the expectation is that a weekly subscription will indeed come weekly. In the academic world it is entirely possible that the spring edition of a particular journal will arrive with the first winter snows.

As an information container, the scholarly journal is quite rigid in its requirements. A publisher cannot add just half a page, or three pages, to a journal; the publisher must add four pages. So all the papers, all the content, must fit within those parameters. Each addition costs money, so scholars may be forced to limit the size of their work. Finally, all papers have to be ready for processing at one time, so a delay in one paper can hold up the rest.

Publishers must also contend with the curious economic realities of the journal marketplace. A journal's primary market may be a professional association whose membership receives the journal by default as part of membership dues. Other journals are so expensive that the market is primarily, if not exclusively, the academic library. This case is particularly troubling for the publisher, who has no way of knowing how many people use the journal either in person, by photocopy, or by interlibrary loan. A single journal subscription could be supporting five different institutions, four of which the publisher receives no revenue from.

Scholarly publishing maintains an unusual economic model. Although the authors are not paid and the editors are often not paid, the scholars and libraries buy back the works from the publishers, although the works have been essentially subsidized by the academic institution, who paid the salaries of the authors in the first place. In the world of scholarly publishing there are two kinds of publishers, nonprofit and for-profit. For-profit publishers find that "scientific and professional publishing has become one of the most profitable—and competitive" areas (Graham 1992, p. 21).

Publishing in paper has not been perfect, and an electronic alternative may not be able to solve all the problems inherent in scholarly publishing. The task of creating an acceptable alternative to this system, however, may fall to the for-profit publishers, who have the resources (and the motivation) to create their vision of electronic publishing and scholarship. The nonprofit publishers may not be able to develop an alternate model because they may lack the resources to fully develop a test product that will not in turn lose a great deal of revenue.

Publishers starting journals have used the stature of their presses to establish the authority of the journal. Whether for-profit or nonprofit, each publishing house has its place in the hierarchy of prestige. Rawlins (1993), discussing electronic books, argues that publishers' need for a good reputation increases, not decreases, in an electronic environment: "As the number of books published per day mushrooms, the value of the publsher's editors and their reputation will increase. The publisher functions as a stamp of approval, a selector, and a collator. Soon there will be a whole new procession—people who find things, or know who to ask.

Perhaps they will be called ferrets. For those who want to rummage for themselves, there will be another new profession—people who arrange things. Perhaps they will be called mapmakers. And everyone will need people who select things—perhaps they will be called filters" (p. 479).

If Rawlins is correct about publishers, then the simplest path is to let the publishers make the move to electronic journals as subtly and gracefully as possible. Let them build the software engine for electronic editorial work and develop solutions for the finding tools and distribution methods. The publishers can ease the way by producing titles concurrently in print and electronic form. Once the electronic version is acceptable and users are at ease with it, publishers can drop the print version entirely. Academia would not have to worry about a thing; it would just keep writing out the checks, not only to the publisher but to support the technology infrastructure, the printers, and the paper. This may be the best avenue, but other options should be seriously explored first.

The new visions of scholarly publishing have a dominant theme: the exclusion of publishers, particularly commercial presses. One model calls for the creation of the "Scholarly Communication System," which would abandon the traditional scholarly journal and its publishers and return the responsibility of publishing to the universities (Rogers and Hurt 1989). To evaluate this and other models, we must first identify the needs and desires of the users. The traditional means of conducting scholarly publishing is academia's own creation, a direct reflection of the values and beliefs maintained by its membership (Peek 1994). If commercial publishers, or perhaps all publishers, are removed, what will replace the existing hierarchy? A particular journal is "good" because it is published by a particular publishing house, and the reward system dictates that scholars should try to publish their work in a good journal. If you remove the publisher's reputation from the journal, is the journal still a good journal? Will academia still provide rewards for publishing in it? Who will decide which journals or which papers will get good pointers? Academia will need to contend with the loss of the existing mechanisms for quality control if alternative models are embraced.

Facing the "Q" Question

Tackling the problem of the scholarly journal is no minor matter, particularly for an environment that is tradition bound. Even more problematic is that academia is not one culture but many cultures, each with its own norms, values, and limitations. We must ask whether these cultures will be willing to face what Lanham (1993) calls the "Q" question: "What I have called the 'Q' question emerges every time technology changes in some basic way. In each case, we have to ask ourselves, 'what are we trying to protect? The old technology itself or what it carries for us, does to us?'" (p. 154).

Scholarly publishing has been part of the academic landscape for more than three hundred years. Although the role of the journal has shifted from that of a communication exchange to a final publishing destination, the fundamental assumption has been that the manner in which things have been done in the past is the way things should be done for all time. Previous attempts at altering the existing formula or format have not been particularly successful (Peek and Burstyn 1989). In spite of debates about the volume of work produced, the review processes, and the quality of work produced in some journals, the realities, complexities, and finances of print publication appeared to leave little room for sweeping reform. Now that those barriers have been removed and the apparent logic of moving to an electronic alternative is evident, how much reform are the various academic cultures prepared to embrace? Changing the existing structure could well mean changing the quality control system that in turn means changing the reward system.

The notion of a unified academic community is an idealistic one because of the way colleges, universities, and disciplines are divided on such matters as mission, economics, and political structure (Birnbaum 1989). Because of this variety, there is no singular macromodel for what is good scholarship and what it means to be a productive scholar.

This discussion becomes even more complicated when colleges and universities in less technologically developed nations are considered. These institutions may use the scholarly output of more technologically advanced colleges and universities but are not yet advanced enough, and may not be for some time to come, even to consider offering electronic alternatives to their scholars. It is unlikely that the shifting paradigm will wait until electronic access is universal, if such a condition ever exists.

So we face the challenge of finding a cost-effective distribution system that will enhance the quality of the knowledge base and not potentially harm it. We must question the information container, what we do with the container, and perhaps even the contents of the container. This means that we may have to give something up, change our behaviors, or question our traditions. Jerry Campbell (1993), university librarian and vice provost for computing at Duke University, argued, "We should be willing to sacrifice any organizational model or specific practice in order to better carry out our mission" (p. 560).

The debate is still young and needs to broaden its scope, even in the period of discontinuities mentioned earlier in this chapter. How much academia is willing to change is yet unknown. The growth of electronic journals over the Internet shows that at least some scholars find the Internet an acceptable place to publish and to subscribe. Although these journals still remain outside the mainstream of academia, signs show that they are slowly being invited in. Does this signify a willingness to consider another vision of publishing?

Someday digitized publication will be the scholarly norm, not because it is the "high-tech" thing to do but because it is the logical thing to do. We may experience a relatively seamless transition as the publishers create models that work for them and preserve the existing infrastructure and all the players. Alternatively the change may be complex and problematic, with experiments that work and others that fail. This is a rare and wonderful time to examine the future of the scholarly journal but may not be a large window of opportunity to effect real change.

Situations with great potential for change have always been the fodder for grand and lofty visions. It is easy to become seduced into believing that technology is the fix for the ills of scholarly publishing. Technology alone, however, may bring opportunity for change but may not force change itself. Attempts to transform academic culture evoke tensions and fears caused not by discomfort created by the sheer act of change but by the possibility that the final outcome will not be positive. As we face this challenge, we must remember that change has equal opportunity to improve a situation and to make it worse.

References

Birnbaum, R. (1989). *How Colleges Work*. San Francisco: Jossey-Bass.

Brown, J. W. (1985). "The Once and Future Book: The Preservation Crisis." *Wilson Library Bulletin* (May): 591–596.

Campbell, J. D. (1993). "Choosing to Have a Future." *American Libraries* (June): 560–566.

Graham, G. (1992). "The Relationship between Publishers and Academics." *Scholarly Publishing* 24, no. 1: 13–23.

Hayes, R. M. (1989). "Who Should Be in Control?" In *Desktop Publishing in the University*, edited by J. N. Burstyn. Syracuse, N.Y.: Syracuse University Press, pp. 25–33.

Lanham, R. A. (1993). *The Electronic Word: Democracy, Technology, and the Arts*. Chicago: University of Chicago Press.

Paul, K., and A. Matasar. (1993). "Business and Society: The Field and the Journal." *Scholarly Publishing* 24, no. 3 (April): 171–182.

Peek, R. (1994). "The Scholarly Publishing Matrix Confronts an Electronic World: A New World Order or This World Revisited." In *The Eleventh International Conference on Technology and Education,* vol. 1, ed. M. Thomes, T. Sechrest, and N. Estes. London: University of London.

Peek, R. P., and J. N. Burstyn. (1989). "In Pursuit of Improved Scholarly Communications." In *Desktop Publishing in the University,* ed. by J. N. Burstyn. Syracuse, N.Y.: Syracuse University Press, pp. 99–120.

Rawlins, G. J. E. (1993). "Publishing over the Next Decade." *Journal of the American Society for Information Science* 44, no. 8: 474–479.

Rogers, S. J., and C. S. Hurt. (1989). "How Scholarly Communication Should Work in the 21st Century." *Chronicle of Higher Education* (October 18): A56.

Wilson, D. L. (1994). "A Journal's Big Break." *Chronicle of Higher Education* (January 26): p. A23.

Ziman, J. (1976) *The Force of Knowledge.* Cambridge: Cambridge University Press.

2

Analyzing Alternate Visions of Electronic Publishing and Digital Libraries

Rob Kling and Roberta Lamb

Controversies about Computerization

There is a fundamental change in the world of scholarly publishing and libraries as they shift from paper-based to electronic formats. This change has been popularized, in part, by the Clinton administration of the U.S. government, which has made digital libraries a cornerstone of the emerging vision of an advanced National Information Infrastructure (IITF 1994). Today, few prolific academic authors employ a typewriter. Although nearly all academic journal articles and books are now produced in electronic form, most are printed on paper for sale or distribution to their readers. Images of electronic publishing and digital libraries both draw on ways that an author's keystrokes (and thoughts) can be rapidly transmitted to potential readers without the mediation of paper formats, even with significant editorial structuring and filtering. They also suggest ways of expanding the scope of scholarly discourse, by using diverse electronic forums to support active dialogues and debate.

Numerous bibliographic sources are available in searchable electronic forms, and some abstracting services provide the full electronic text of selected articles. But the electronic journals (e-journals) available through the Internet come closest to fitting the image of direct communication between authors of systematic studies and their readers. E-journals have appeared in diverse fields, from avant-garde cultural studies to medicine and even medieval studies.

Librarians observe many practical problems when academics try to work flexibly with today's e-journals (Entlich 1993). They might be rapidly disseminated and searched online, but in many work places e-journal articles are hard to read unless they are printed on paper. Most seriously, publishing exclusively in electronic formats has yet to become legitimate in research universities (Lougee 1994). Furthermore, few university libraries have explicit collection development policies that enable them to archive specific e-journals systematically.

Enthusiasts portray current limitations—such as restrained means of representation (for example, the predominance of ASCII text), uneven access to necessary computing equipment, and contested academic legitimacy—as relatively minor practical problems of a transitional period. When analysts examine electronic publishing and digital libraries in a longer time frame—beyond a 10- or 20-year transitional period—they rely on a few common forms (genres) of analysis. This chapter examines the structure of these genres and some alternatives.

Technologically utopian analyses dominate popular discourse and are commonplace in discussions of future developments in professional communication. Empirically oriented accounts that examine the ways in which faculty and students actually work with computing are much less common and are also less commonly read by scholars, computer and information professionals, and policymakers. These empirical analyses are relatively subtle, portraying an ambiguous world, and have less rhetorical power to capture the imagination of readers than utopian scenarios. Even though they are more scientific, empirically anchored studies don't appeal to many scientists and professionals. It is ironic that computing—often portrayed as an instrument of knowledge—is primarily the subject of discourses whose claims are most suspect. Conversely, the discourses whose claims as valid knowledge are strongest seem to have much less appeal in the mass media and technological communities.

The debates about scholarship and electronic publishing contain allusions and assumptions that are common themes in debates about computerization. Positive economic benefits are predicted to accrue to educators and universities. Exponential rates of acceleration in access to information are predicted to occur. Advocates expect the number of publications to skyrocket, and scholarly works to be more widely available. Electronic publishing seems to have immense benefits—in providing economic payoffs to university presses, in making many academic practices more convenient and thereby increasing productivity, and in improving the diffusion of knowledge by reducing barriers between authors and readers. Selected economic and legal issues dominate the debates about computerization of other domains (Dunlop and Kling 1991); however, the economic or legal role of computerization is not the only area of concern. Other areas that are directly affected by efforts to promote and establish electronic publishing and digital libraries but that are not commonly dealt with have become controversial:

Scholarship. How easily can electronic publishing give scholars rapid access to wider audiences? Does it help scholars, as readers, access a wider variety of materials that are more up-to-date? Can the quality of information be adequately maintained as academic publications transit to electronic formats? Is electronic publishing likely to modify the criteria for academic career advancement and their ties to publication in paper-based journals?

Intellectual property rights. What are the risks to electronic publishers from unlimited distribution without proper compensation? Will mitigation of these risks lead to a redefinition of property or to litigious constraints on the flow of academic information?

Education. To what extent can electronic formats of information give students the intellectual and motivational advantages of one-on-one tutoring in an economical way? What drawbacks might there be in the widespread use of online information in the curriculum?

Knowledge. How might the prevalence of digital information resources alter the institutionally legitimized instances of knowledge? Will the development of new institutions alter the nature of knowledge? What do the knowledge boundaries of a definable search space determine?

Work life. Is computerization likely to improve or degrade the quality of jobs for scholars, researchers, educators, administrators, and librarians? How do different approaches to designing and distributing electronic publications alter the character and quality of jobs? Can the computer and telecommunications components of an electronic publishing environment improve the flexibility of work by enabling employed people to work at home part- or full-time?

Social equity. To what extent are electronic libraries and electronic publications more usable by faculty and students with funds to buy services and adjunct computer equipment? To what extent do electronic publications and digital libraries enhance or diminish the tendency of our society to foster an underclass of functionally illiterate and disenfranchised people?

Employment. How does electronic publishing alter the structure of labor markets and occupations? What is the potential for increase or elimination of jobs for librarians and educators? Do the skill mixes for computer-oriented work help create a lower class with fewer jobs and more barriers to improving their situations?

Gender biases. Professional positions held largely by women (i. e., librarians and K-12 educators) are more likely to be eliminated by the introduction of electronic approaches to information management and education, and men are more likely to be in the professional positions of specifying the requirements for, and designing, computer-based electronic publishing systems. Will this division continue, and with what effect?

These controversial issues, like many social problems, are being discussed by groups with diverse viewpoints. Each group attempts to frame the discussion in a way that reflects and promotes its social interests (Mauss 1975). The debates overlap but sometimes have very distinct characteristics. Even within the university, the concerns that the library science community has about maintaining the knowledge archive differ fundamentally from those of other scholarly communities, such as the community of the humanities. Librarians may care greatly about cataloging procedures; the procedures are ontological acts that they perform to establish the importance of an information item. Humanists, in contrast, may view these acts as completely irrelevant. Computer scientists may not even be aware of these debates. A markedly romantic provincialism has often dominated the communications of the academic computer science community as it has speculated on the potential applications of virtual reality, artificial intelligence, computer-integrated manufacturing, computer-supported cooperative work technologies, and now electronic publishing technologies and digital libraries (see Hillis 1992; Kurzweil 1990). This discourse is useful in that it provides the larger goals and visions that move industries and societies into new domains, but it does not encourage reflection or debate on the controversies raised by the introduction of technology and on the potential for negative social impacts or environmental side effects. It promotes a belief that the future is "safe" and that the possibilities of historical analogy with previous technological introductions can be ignored.

Where the debates are engaged, polarized discussions often ensue (Dunlop and Kling 1991). In this chapter we examine key social assumptions implicit within analyses of computerization with focus on the popular, professional, and scholarly literature that describes computerization, characterizes computer use, and portrays the resultant social changes. This literature can be usefully segmented into five genres: utopian, antiutopian, social realism, social theory, and analytical reduction. Table 2.1 provides a comparison of the ways in which these genres address such issues as the role of technology in social change and the problems caused by technological development.

Assumptions about Technological Change and Progress

Unstated but critical assumptions that underlie social analyses of computerization frame our understanding of the popular, professional, and scholarly literature in which authors claim to describe the nature of computerization, the character of computer use, and the social choices and changes that result from computerization. A large fraction of the literature about computing describes emerging technologies and the ways in which they can expand the limits of the possible. Faster and smaller computers can make it easier for people to access information in a wider variety of places. Richer display devices can help people communicate more readily with computerized systems through pictures and text. High-speed networks can link computer systems together in ways only dreamed of in 1970. The remarkable improvements in the capabilities of equipment generate breathless excitement in researchers, developers, and entrepreneurs, and in the battalions of journalists who document these events in newspapers and magazines.

Some authors enchant us with images of new electronic publishing technologies that offer thrilling possibilities for manipulating large amounts of information rapidly with little effort—technologies to enhance control, create insights, search for information, and facilitate cooperative work. Fewer authors examine a darker social vision in which any likely form of computerization will amplify human misery—a vision in which people sacrifice their freedom and privacy to businesses and government agencies, people become dependent on complex technologies they don't comprehend, and sometimes entire social groups are denied access to crucial, enabling information technologies. Both kinds of stories often reflect the conventions of utopian and antiutopian writing, which limit what they authors can or will say, and which circumscribe the kinds of themes they can effectively examine. Authors relate stories about changes in technology and social life with various analytical and rhetorical strategies (Kling and Iacono 1988, 1991).

Even though writings address social forms that the authors suggest are likely, tacit conventions preclude their discussing important social relationships that are also likely. A genre refers to any body of work that is characterized by a set of conventions. The works that we readily identify as romantic comedies, impressionist paintings, horror films, newspaper editorials, and popular movie reviews are constructed with a set of conventions that make them readily intelligible and accessible.

Table 2.1.
Key characteristics for genres of discourse about computerization

	Utopianism		Empirically anchored genres		
	Technological utopianism	Antiutopianism	Social realism	Social theory	Analytical reduction
Typical evidence	Scenarios	Scenarios	Fine-grained ethnography of specific groups and places	Logical abstraction from empirical evidence	Empirical data examined in terms of a few well-defined categories
Time orientation	Future, treated as discontinuous from past	Future	Present/past	Present/past	Present/past
Role of technology in social change (necessity of effects)	Critical enabler of a good social order	Critical instrument for oppression and social demise	No special role. Usually not a uniquely important catalyst/enabler of social change	No special role. Usually not a uniquely important catalyst/enabler of social change	No special role. Usually not a uniquely important catalyst/enabler of social change
Problems caused by technological development	Few, largely resolvable by new technologies	Important unresolvable social conflicts or other problems exacerbated by some technological developments	No single position	No single position	No single position

Table 2.1. (continued)

	Utopianism		Empirically anchored genres		
	Technological utopianism	Antiutopianism	Social realism	Social theory	Analytical reduction
Conflict	Sustained social conflict is rare aside from bounded legitimate conflict	Intense social conflict is a key feature of the changed social order	Conflict between different social groups is "natural," but the nature of specific conflicts (i.e., coalitions, tactics, outcomes) depends on data	Theories vary, but most organizational-level or social scale theories acknowledge and theorize about power differentials	Conflict may be ignored or examined
Distribution of knowledge to effectively use and understand key technologies	Skills/knowledge available or easily obtainable	Skills/knowledge often unequally distributed. Some groups/classes disadvantaged (and exploited (and exploited) by relative ignorance.	No a priori position, depends upon specific data. Analyst may or may not explicitly examine skill/knowledge	Theories vary. Only a few organizational-level or social scale theories acknowledge and theorize about skill/knowledge differentials	No a priori position, depends upon specific data. Analyst may or may not explicitly examine skill/knowledge

Authors and artists who work wholly within the conventions of a genre are limited in the kinds of themes that they can effectively examine. For example, authors of romantic comedies usually have trouble exploring boredom and the sustained negotiations that people conduct to live day-to-day. Scholars have examined how literary formulas shape fiction (Cawelti 1976), journalistic conventions shape newsmaking (Tuchman 1978; Campbell 1991), and academic conventions shape scholarship (McCloskey 1990; Van Maanen 1988).

These conceptions of genre formulas as epistemological envelopes extend into the realm of writing that is putatively nonfictional, writing that authors position as telling us truths about the world of computerization "out there" and beyond the author's imagination. Many social analyses of computing are written with genre conventions that limit the kinds of ideas that can be readily examined. Conventions make works more easily intelligible. Yet scholars and professionals who read these social analyses are often unaware of how works are crafted within the conventions of specific genres and how these conventions limit, as well as facilitate, analysis and debate.

The utopian and antiutopian genres of social analysis are about 500 years old and predate the social sciences by about 350 years. Authors who work within these genres examine certain kind of social possibilities and usually move quite freely beyond the technologies one finds in use today and beyond social relations that are commonplace today. Utopian tales are devised to stimulate hope in future possibilities and antiutopian tales are devised to stimulate anger at horrible possibilities. Technological utopianism is particularly influential in North America, so appreciating its epistemology helps us to understand an important aspect of North American thought.

A different set of investigative strategies and genres is based on examining existing computerized systems as they are used in real social settings. These investigations and genres of writing rest on the empiricist's faith that by examining the world as it is, we can learn something important about the worlds that might be. We will examine three major genres that depend on empirical observation: social realism, social theory, and analytical reduction. These are not the only genres of social analysis of computing. Works are written using other conventions, such as expert surveys and personal reminiscences. But some of our five genres are common, and others are ideal types important for developing systematic analyses. We are concerned with the strengths and limits of inquiries conceived and reported within these two utopian and three empirical genres. We hope that our analysis of these genres will make readers aware that any genre of social analysis has important strengths and limitations.

Technological Utopianism

Utopian thinkers portray societies in which people live ideal lives. The first such description appeared in Plato's *Republic* some 2,500 years ago. But the word *Utopia* derives from Thomas More, who published a story in 1516 of an ideal city called society named Utopia, in which people lived harmoniously and free of privation. This fanciful name, which meant "nowhere," has been applied to a tradition of writing and thinking about the forms of society that would make many people happiest. There have been hundreds of utopian blueprints. They differ substantially in their details: some have focused on material abundance as the key to human happiness, whereas others have portrayed visions of happiness based on austere and simple ways of life. Some utopians advocate private property as a central social institution, whereas many place a primacy on shared property.

The most obvious utopian sources are discourses that the authors identify as fictional accounts and that use traditional devices such as made-up characters and fanciful dialogue. Other sources, such as those concerned with discourse about computerization, electronic publishing, and information technologies, are shaped by the conventions of utopianism and antiutopianism. Their authors present them as primarily realistic or factual accounts (and they are cataloged as nonfiction in bookstores and libraries).

British author Tom Stonier (1983) illustrates the utopian tradition in writing about information technology. He ends his book about the way that information technologies can transform societies with this observation:

> To sum up, everyone an aristocrat, everyone a philosopher. A massively expanded education system to provide not only training and information about how to make a living, but also on how to live. In late industrial society, we stopped worrying about food. In late communicative society, we will stop worrying about material resources. And just as the industrial economy eliminated slavery, famine, and pestilence, so will the postindustrial economy eliminate authoritarianism, war, and strife. For the first time in history, the rate at which we will solve problems will exceed the rate at which they will appear. This will leave us to get on with the real business of the next century. To take care of each other. To fathom what it means to be human. To explore intelligence. To move out into space. (p. 214)

Utopian images are common in many books and articles written by technologists and journalists about computerization in society. We are particularly interested in what can be learned, and how we can be misled, by a particular brand of utopian thought: technological utopianism (Dunlop and Kling 1991; Kling 1994). This line of analysis considers the use of some specific technology—such as computers, electronic publishing, or low-energy, low-impact technologies—to be a key enabling element of a utopian vision.[1]

Sometimes people will casually refer to exotic technologies—such as pocket computers that understand spoken language—as "utopian gadgets." Technological utopianism does not refer to the technologies themselves, which have amazing capabilities. It refers to analyses in which the use of specific technologies is crucial in shaping a benign social vision. In contrast, technological antiutopianism examines how certain broad families of technology facilitate a social order that is relentlessly harsh, destructive, and miserable.

Seductive Images and Equations   Technologists who characterize new or future technologies often rely on utopian imagery when they examine their social meanings or implications. In 1948, before electronic computers, Vannevar Bush (1988) set forth a vision of a fast, flexible, remotely accessible desk-sized computer called "memex," which would allow a researcher to search electronically through vast archives of articles, books, and notes. He wrote:

Wholly new forms of encyclopedia will appear, ready-made with a mesh of associative trails running through them, ready to be dropped into the memex, and there amplified. The lawyer has at his touch the associated opinions and decisions of his whole experience. The patent attorney has on call millions of issued patents, with familiar trails to every point of his client's interest. The physician, puzzled by a patient's reaction, strikes the trail established in studying an earlier similar case, and runs rapidly through analogous case histories, with side references to the classics for the pertinent anatomy and histology. The chemist, struggling with the synthesis of an organic compound, has all the chemical literature before him in his laboratory, with trails following the analogies of compounds, the side trails to their physical and chemical behavior.

The historian, with a vast chronological account of people, parallels it with a skip trail which stops only at the salient items, and can follow at any time, contemporary trails which lead him all over civilization at a particular epoch. There is a new profession of trailblazers, those who find delight in the task of establishing useful trails through the enormous mass of the common record. The inheritance from the master becomes not only his additions to the world's record, but for his disciples, the entire scaffolding by which they were erected. Thus science may implement the ways in which man produces, stores, and consults the records of the race. (p. 32)

Bush continued by describing the memex's abilities to associate items, gather the useful clusters of information that show up during a search, and "instantly" project any or all of them onto displays for selective review, fast or slow. He envisioned a flexible, compliant research assistant able to fish artfully through vast archives of textual information and gather the useful material embodied in an uncomplaining and ever ready machine. A seductive image indeed! This vision was even more remarkable because the image of digital computers that dominated scientific writing at the time—and which dominates scientific thinking even in today's talk of supercomputers—was one of high-speed calculation of numerical data only.

Visions of computerization similar to Bush's rely on descriptions of computer-based devices and their information-processing capabilities, but they ignore social conditions under which these technologies would be likely to be used. These visions are also flawed in the way they characterize technologies, people, and social life. They emphasize ways that a technology should work ideally, under conditions where all the participants are highly cooperative. Other kinds of social relationships in work groups—such as those marked by conflict, competition, coercion, and even combativeness—are not considered.

Computing is often a seductive technology or, more accurately, the centerpiece of seductive dreams. The seduction comes from the attractiveness of the belief that vast possibilities for information handling and enhanced intelligence are readily accessible at relatively low cost and with little effort. Some of the technological advances of computer systems are quite obvious: in each decade, the power of digital computing hardware increases about tenfold for any given price and physical size. Advances in the power and quality of software have also been steady, but much less dramatic. The transformation of these technological advances into social advances (such as higher standards of living or education) has not been straightforward (Dunlop and Kling 1991).

Some technologists suggest that new computer technologies will address social problems—such as overburdened health care systems an unresponsive government and educational inequity—and thus that technological progress equals social progress. They believe that falling prices for computer hardware, the next-generation chip, the new UNIX, and a band of smart programmers will solve most social problems. The remainder will be solved by the 80786 chip and super-computers, international networks, better environments for programming languages, higher-performance database languages, and some artificial intelligence.

Although we are caricaturing this position, we are not fundamentally misstating a view that is held by many technologists and futurists, and popularized by some journalists. Few writers make these claims explicitly; rather, they make them implicitly by focusing attention on new (or "revolutionary") technologies while ignoring crucial aspects of the social environments in which they are used. For example, some educators have argued that schools could best improve their educational programs by investing heavily in computer-assisted instruction, without asking what kinds of equipment most schools can afford.

Many scenarios of life in the year 2000 assume that social progress will come primarily through technological progress within an overall framework of industrialization. Our industrial civilization has created the conditions for increasing our general health, physical comfort, and safety. But this civilization has come at the cost of immense environmental pollution in many regions of the world. We have reached a point at which increasing use of energy and industrial products can lead to more smog, more acid rain, more rapid depletion of the ozone layer, more rapid warming of the planet, and so on. It is possible that some of these problems will be solved through computer technologies. For example, telecommuting may be more environmentally sound than packing urban freeways with commuters driving "smart" cars on their daily trek to work. But other ways of achieving social progress—such as the development and enforcement of ecologically sound fuel- and water-conservation policies—do not rely primarily on technological progress. Unfortunately, it is hard to find balanced accounts that carefully examine the character of various social and technological alternatives and the values that they each support.

Computerization is often bound up with the symbolic politics of modernism and rationality. Advanced technologies offer the giddy excitement of adventure with the liberating lure of new possibilities that have few inherent problems. Talk about new technologies offers a new canvas in which to reshape social relationships so they better fit the speaker's imagination. The presence of advanced technologies often serves as a sign that the computer-using person or organization is worthy of admiration and trust. Sophisticated computing systems signal technological competence, which can be conflated with organizational competence and even domain competence when few other clues are discernible. It is usually easier for casual observers to spot the presence of advanced computer equipment than to understand how the equipment actually alters people's abilities to carry out their day-to-day activities.[2] The social revolutions predicted by such utopian authors as those we are about to discuss are based on changes in ways of life, not just changes in equipment.

The Utopian Genre in Electronic Publishing Literature   Examples of utopian discourses can be found across the spectrum of literature about electronic publishing and digital libraries (e.g., Koch 1991; Lanham 1993; Okerson 1992; Silverman, 1989). Authors may portray information technologies as expanding the number of choices societies can make to direct the future, or they may present a view in which the technology drives and determines societal change. As Tom Koch's (1991) vision of twenty-first century journalism illustrates, a work's perspective does not have to be technologically deterministic to be technologically utopian.

In describing how online databases will affect journalism, Koch begins by assessing the technological basis for journalism's current form and identifying the myths that perpetuate the image of objective, unbiased news reporting. He posits that print technologies have provided a means of systematizing the oral tradition. What is currently presented as the news is a series of statements by officials, proponents, and various "experts." According to Koch, the news, to the degree that it is not contextually based in investigated and verified background information, is essentially a replication of the oral system. He thus feels that news reporting serves to perpetuate the cultural biases of the speakers.

Koch (1991) sees the database repositories of electronic publishing as enabling attainment of the myth; these databases can provide an objective context within which the events of news statements can be situated: "The context must come from outside, from elsewhere than the specific, journalistic event. It is this objectifying context, which is critical to the instrumental goal of public information writers, that electronic databases can provide. . . . Online communication technologies will transform the news from a system of oral transmission to one organized around print technologies. The result will empower the writer and change the context of contemporary news" (p. 50).

Koch recognizes the other elements that contribute to the production of news as conforming to a functional social context, rather than to myths and ideals: these elements include professional standards of journalism, the business aspect of publishing, and the immediacies of reporters earning a living. They will not be immediately transformed by online technologies, but Koch feels that reporters will gain the courage to question authority when they are armed with the facts. Time is critical to Koch's argument: even though the facts in the electronic databases have been available in printed form, reporters have not been given the time to do research in libraries and archives.

Koch considers databases to be facilities that are online and located at one's desktop, and sources of information that are easily accessible, searchable, and manipulable. After a brief foray into a newsroom library, however, he acknowledges that search strategies may be problematic to learn. Koch clearly describes how electronic information resources can empower journalists to achieve professional standards of objective reporting. He brings an interpretivist perspective to bear on the current state of affairs and relies on historical models of technological adoption when predicting events. He reassures those worried about the possibility of access only for the few: "Just as books stored in public libraries became part of the communal knowledge system at no direct cost to the user, so, too, electronic databases will eventually enter the public domain" (Koch 1991, p. 287).

What makes Koch's interpretation essentially utopian is his assumption that the electronic news database is a pristine repository of objective knowledge. He maintains this assumption even though he acknowledges that much of the contents of these databases will be those very statements that currently compose the news.

Utopian assumptions about computerization pervade all levels of discourse and are recognizable at the policymaking level. If electronic publishing efforts are to be successful, they require the establishment of digital libraries. What form these libraries will take and which social, educational, and commercial needs they will service are now being defined. The NSF's 1994 Digital Library Initiative seeks to expand on models such as the World Wide Web (WWW), WAIS, FTP, and Gopher and to fund research into selected successful technological issues: "To explore the full benefits of such digital libraries, the problem for research and development is not merely how to connect everyone and everything together in the network. Rather, it is to achieve an economically feasible capability to digitize massive corpora of extant and new information from heterogeneous and distributed sources; then store, search, process and retrieve information from them in a user friendly way. Among other things, this will require both fundamental research and the development of 'intelligent' software" (NSF 1993, p. 3).

The primary research areas selected for funding (data capture, advanced software and algorithms, and utilization of distributed, networked databases) focus on the technological aspects of transmitted-information use. The information models being adapted from the Internet are examples of transmission-mode communications. These tend to shift the burden of information use onto the end user, where "intelligent" software in the form of Knowbots (autonomous intelligent agents) and user-friendly interfaces can be of great assistance. The initiative, however, is not structured to encourage research into more interactive forms of information access or communication and is not providing funding for researching alternatives to digital libraries. When the distribution of research funds is influenced primarily by utopian perspectives of technological progress, there may be unforeseen (and potentially undesirable) consequences of well-intentioned pilot implementations or full-scale projects.

The Role of Electronic Publishing in Informational Utopias   Powerful images that link computerization and large-scale social change have entered ordinary language through newspapers, popular books, and advertisements. Terms such as "computer revolution," "information society," "knowledge worker," "computer-mediated work," "intelligent machine," and "information superhighway"[3] are catch phrases with have strong metaphorical associations.

These new terms are often worked into common usage by journalists and authors who write for popular audiences. We live in a period of tremendous social changes, and sometimes new terms can capture emerging social patterns or new kinds of technologies better than existing language can. But many authors use these terms casually in ways that reflect important unexamined and often questionable social assumptions.

Alvin Toffler helped stimulate enthusiasm for computerization by using popular terms in his best seller *The Third Wave* (1980). He characterized major social transformations in terms of large shifts in the organization of society, driven by technological change. Toffler is masterful in succinctly suggesting major social changes in breathless prose. He also invented some of his own terminology to help characterize key social changes—terms such as second wave, third wave, electronic cottage, infosphere, technosphere, prosumer, intelligent environment, and so on. Many of his new terms did not become commonly accepted. Even so, they help frame a seductive description of social change.

Toffler's enthusiasm can be contagious, but, because his scenarios exclude the possibilities of social and economic constraints, that untempered enthusiasm also stymies critical thought. Myriad changes in the information environment in the United States are not at all exciting to people who would like to see a more thoughtful culture. For example, television has become a major source of information about world events for many children and adults. Television news, the most popular "factual" kind of television programming, slices stories into 30- or 90-second segments and fits them to simple storylines. Moreover, some evidence suggests that functional illiteracy is rising in the United States (Gray 1993; Kozol 1985). This problem is probably not only a byproduct of television's popularity. Toffler's optimistic account, in which "whole new strata of communication are added to the social system" (Toffler 1980, p. 172), is hard to take seriously when a large fraction of the population has trouble understanding crucial portions of the current communication strata, such as instruction manuals for automobiles and for commonplace home appliances, like refrigerators and VCRs.

Toffler raises important questions about how information technologies alter the ways in which people perceive information, the kinds of information they can get easily, and how they handle the information they get. But his account trivializes the questions by using only illustrations that support his generally buoyant theses.

Today, academic authors of paper-based materials reach most of their readers through the mediation of publishers (and their editors and reviewers) and distributors such as libraries and bookstores. Utopian discussions about electronic publishing often concentrate on using "informational bypass surgery" performed by (Knowbots) to cut out the intermediaries and enable direct, unobstructed communication between author and reader.

Richard Lanham (1993) suggests that the digitization of textual, audio and visual communications will encourage reorganizations of knowledge via hypertext. Common storage representations, transmission protocols, and manipulation algorithms will enable a confluence of data not previously achievable with analog paradigms. In Lanham's view, this technological capability makes inevitable a future in which the reader is the author and where copyright law is irrelevant:

> Texts are not fixed in print but projected on a phosphor screen in volatile form. They can be amended, emended, rewritten, reformatted, set in another typeface, all with a few keystrokes. The whole system of cultural authority we inherited from Renaissance Humanism thus evaporates, literally, at a stroke. The "Great Book," the authoritative text, was built on the fixity of print technology. That fixity no longer operates. The reader defined by print—the engrossed admiration of the humanist scholar reading Cicero—now becomes quite another person. He can quarrel with the text, and not marginally, or next year in another book, but right now, integrally. The reader thus becomes an author. Author and authority are both transformed. (Lanham 1994)

In Lanham's future world, authority gracefully steps aside and clears a path for advancing technology to restructure the relations of authority. In other theories of the impact of electronic publishing—those that confront the institutions of knowledge dissemination—the commercial or nonprofit publisher must be eliminated, or at least beaten to the electronic punch.

Ann Okerson (a coeditor of *EJournal* with Richard Lanham) postulates that the electronic medium may allow universities to significantly reduce their dependence on commercial publishing houses. In the process, intellectual property will return to its rightful owner, the university. Unlike Lanham, Okerson predicts impacts that do not rely on a reorganization of knowledge. Her argument is largely economic, with benefits accruing to libraries, scholars, and universities. The utopian elements of her theory are subtle and easily taken for granted in American culture. She notes with concern that publishing houses are also moving into the electronic medium, and she advances economically utopian arguments that might be characterized as advocating "electronic homesteading": if the universities get there first, they can establish a base from which to compete with the commercial ventures. This and her other references to "academic libraries, who are mapping this new terrain" (Okerson 1992, p. 175) evoke what Amiran, Unsworth, and Chaski (1992) describe as "wild west" utopian visions.[4] This frontier view emphasizes ideals of self-reliance and casts technology as the malleable tool of self-determinism: "Technology is not the only real issue here; it is an accelerant of the problems that have been with us for some time— as well as a potential savior. The real issue may well be how to retain for the academy more control over its own intellectual output, to achieve affordability of its work" (Okerson 1992, p. 176).

Toffler, Okerson, and Lanham characterize computer systems as enabling technologies. Their scenarios reserve an important, though vaguely defined, role for electronic publishing. Will the technology spawn new knowledge formats? Can the universities use the electronic medium to regain economic control over their intellectual property? These questions are central for Okerson and Lanham, and contrast sharply with the central questions of antiutopian authors.

Technological Antiutopianism in Electronic Publishing Literature

Technological utopianism is a common genre for exploring the social meaning of new and future technologies in North America, and it is the genre that is most influential in the North American technological communities. But a relatively small segment of North American literature critically examines claims made about the social virtues of various computerization strategies. These technological antiutopian critiques portray computerization—in almost any form—as likely to degrade social life (e.g., Reinecke 1984; Weizenbaum 1976; Winner 1992).

Much of the antiutopian discussion that pertains to scholarship and electronic publishing focuses on the impending demise of libraries, the rising rates of textual illiteracy, and the segregation of the population into informational classes based on their access to electronic knowledge resources. Other discussions involve the difficulties in controlling the quality of knowledge, from an academic perspective. Authors explain the persistence of the existing knowledge production process by asserting that it is the only process that works; they are unwilling to tamper with its mechanism.[5]

Weizenbaum's *Computer Power and Human Reason* (1976) highlights the negative side of computerized systems. He criticizes visions of computerized databases that record historical data (like Vannevar Bush's memex), because they usually eliminate important information that is too complex or costly to include:

The computer has thus begun to be an instrument for the destruction of history. For when society legitimates only those "data" that are in one standard format, then history, memory itself, is annihilated. The *New York Times* has already begun to build a "databank" of current events. Of course, only those data that are easily derivable as by-products of typesetting machines are admissible to the system. As the number of subscribers to this system grows, as they learn to rely more and more upon "all the news that [was once] fit to print, " as the *Times* proudly identifies its editorial policy, how long will it be before what counts as fact is determined by the system, before all other knowledge, all memory, is simply declared illegitimate? Soon a supersystem will be built, based on the *Times'* data bank (or one very much like it), from which "historians" will make inferences about what "really" happened, about who is connected to whom, and about the "real" logic of events. (p. 238)

Weizenbaum's observations gain more force when one realizes that journalists don't simply report "the facts." They often rely on standard sources, voices of publicly legitimate authority, in framing stories. For example, when a university alters a curriculum, deans and professors are more likely to have a voice in the resulting news story than are students. Gaye Tuchman (1978) characterized reporters in search of a story as casting a selective "news-net" around their favorite kinds of sources. Journalists rarely cast their nets to catch all kinds of informed parties. Although reporters are much more likely to go to the grass roots today than they were in the days of Vannevar Bush, each newspaper prints its own mix of stories in a relatively stable style. Even if the mastheads were interchanged, one would not usually confuse the *New York Times* with a small-town weekly newspaper.[6] Without special design, nothing in the database technology would be likely to provide users with a clue about the real limitations of the data. And yet the convenience of such a database might tempt a busy professional to rely on it as a source, without recognizing its flaws. This cautionary note makes Weizenbaum's bitter observations valuable. But his argument is primarily polemical, and he may mislead the less savvy reader when he speaks with authority about future events ("Soon a supersystem will be built . . .") and presents his speculations as factual accounts. In stark contrast to Koch's projection of twenty-first-journalism, Weizenbaum discusses neither possible virtues of news databases nor conditions under which they might not have the problems that he identifies. Such databases, however, can substantially assist in research, as long as they do not become the sole source of information. Professional historians who have developed strong criteria for verifying events may be less likely to become their prisoners than many professionals (and students) who find them efficacious and seductive, despite their limitations.

Bryan Pfaffenberger (1990) uses less apocalyptic, but still largely antiutopian, arguments to target the rhetoric that heralds the coming of the Information Society. This rhetoric assures us that universal information is an inevitable byproduct of technologically enhanced information networks. In contrast, Pfaffenberger's study of online databases reveals that the information resources which are currently available online may be no more accessible, and perhaps even less accessible, than their precursors.

He finds that online search tools have preserved the structure and content of print-based reference works, thereby perpetuating the need for specialized expertise. Only those who possess this expertise and who function in professional roles that require access to information in a timely fashion are likely to use online search tools. Pfaffenberger concludes that online technology, as currently implemented, is unlikely to democratize information significantly. To the extent that they replace other forms of information access, online databases may make information less available to the public.

Pfaffenberger views technological advances that resolve the difficulties of using online systems as conservative because they do not require any changes to the reference works themselves or to their organizational or legislative forms. As an example he cites databases which provide bibliographic abstracts that not only summarize an article but also "rationalize" its substance, making it more comprehensible to the nonspecialist. He suggests that by transforming information into a commodity and privatizing information produced by public investments in university research, online technology may play a significant role in creating an information elite—the precise opposite of democratization, and not at all what Lanham envisions.[7]

Pfaffenberger also documents the reluctance of professional societies to add their sources of expertise to publicly available online services. He notes that "even though it may seem to be a good idea to democratize information, the 'deskilling' of white-collar occupations could have devastating social consequences. It could accelerate, for instance, massive and ominous changes already under way in the class structure of industrialized societies, such as the decline of the middle-class and the 'proletarianization' of the white collar work force" (Pfaffenberger 1990, p. 12).

Utopian and antiutopian analysts share important conventions. Their narratives are usually future-oriented; they universalize experiences with technologies, homogenize experiences into one or two groups, and portray technologies as totalizing elements that dominate important social interactions. They take extreme (but different) positions. They portray computerization with monochromatic brushes: white or black. The technological antiutopians' characterizations of the tragic possibilities of computerization provide an essential counterbalance to the giddy-headed optimism of the technological utopian accounts. The romances and tragedies are not identical, but the two genres share some inherent limitations.

Strengths and Limits of Utopian and Antiutopian Analyses

To what extent are utopian and antiutopian visions helpful in understanding the social possibilities of computerization? Despite their limitations, we see utopian and antiutopian analyses as important and legitimate forms of speculative inquiry. Questions about the social consequences of new technologies are central to choices about paths for development, levels of social investment, and regulatory policies. These choices merit analysis to help us better understand future possibilities. All such analyses rest on theories of the interplay between technological developments and social life. Utopian visions are sometimes characterized as "reality transcending" (Kumar 1987; 1991). They stimulate hope and give people a sense of direction. But they can be misleading when their architects exaggerate the likelihood of easy and desirable social changes. Writing about technological utopianism in the 1930s, Wilson, Pilgrim, and Tasjian (1986) comment, "Belief in the limitless future potential of the machine had both its positive and negative aspects. During the 1930s this almost blind faith in the power of the machine to make the world a better place helped hold a badly shattered nation together. . . . These science fiction fantasies contributed to an almost naive approach to serious problems and a denial of problems that could already be foreseen" (pp. 3–35).

Antiutopian writings counterbalance technological utopianism. But they can encourage a comparably ineffective sense of despair and inaction. The causal simplicity of utopian and antiutopian visions gives them great clarity and makes them easy to grasp—to enjoy or to abhor. They resonate with our dreams or nightmares. Consequently, they have immense influence on the discussions (and directions) of electronic academic publishing. Their causal simplicity is their greatest strength but also leads to some crippling limitations.

Conflict   Technological utopian analysts portray a world free of substantial conflict. Technological antiutopians usually portray certain fundamental conflicts—those between social classes (Winner 1992), for example, or between government agencies and the public (Crawford

1994)—as almost unalterably unbalanced: one side dominates while the other side mounts negligible resistance. Neither extreme characterizes a world in which social conflicts are important but in which coalitions blur divisional boundaries and the intensity of conflict varies in place and time.

Practical attempts to establish utopian social schemes have been fraught with significant and complex conflicts. For example, the United States was founded on premises that were utopian in the 1700s. The U.S. *Declaration of Independence* asserts that "all men are created equal" and that they should be guaranteed the right to "life, liberty, and the pursuit of happiness." This was in significant contrast to the political cultures of the European monarchies of the time, where the rule of the king or queen and the nobles, most of whom were selected by heredity, determined people's fates. Of course, asserting this right as universal didn't immediately make it so.

Utopian ideals are hard to realize. Their advocates often have to fight hard to change social practices to better fit their ideals. Bloody revolutions were fought in the United States and France to overthrow the ruling monarchies in the late eighteenth century. Almost two hundred years later, Martin Luther King and others advanced the cause of civil rights in the United States through aggressive confrontations—marches, rallies, court injunctions, and sit-ins—as well as through more quiet persuasion. These social changes, which altered the balance of privilege and exploitation, did not come quietly and peacefully.

Distribution of Knowledge In utopian visions of computerization, people have whatever skills they need to use systems adequately and to resolve problems as they arise. Antiutopian analyses vary in their accounts of technological skills. Sometimes everyone is adequately skilled but is using technologies in ways that undermine important social values. In other antiutopian accounts, many people are confused about social relations and the use of technologies. In these analyses, either elites control key skills or no one has key knowledge (as in Weizenbaum's [1993] account of "incomprehensible systems"). These accounts rarely portray people's technological skills as being distributed in complex ways, with many people having adequate technical skills for some of their activities, muddling through on others with help from co-workers or consultants, and being confused about a few others.

Problems Caused by Technological Development   Technological utopians sometimes recognize that new technologies cause new problems, but these are to be solved with additional technologies.[8] Buckminster Fuller argued that it was difficult and almost pointless to teach people to drive cautiously and to harass them with rigid laws. He argued for safer cars rather than for changing human behavior. Today's discussions advocating computerized "smart cars" rather than smart drivers are parallel. Technological utopians usually favor the investment of government funds in stimulating the development of new technologies rather than in increasing the scale and scope of regulatory bureaucracies. Technological utopian discussions of computerization in schools emphasize the potentials of new technologies and ignore that they may be unrealized when classes are overcrowded, teachers are not well versed in the new technologies, and schools put substantial efforts into regimenting students (Kling and Iacono 1988). By focusing on new technologies as agents of social change and assuming that social systems will use them effectively, technological utopians ignore the social conditions necessary for technologies to be effective. Consequently, they often overstate the social value of the technologies. In contrast, technological antiutopians often understate the social value of technological innovations and the fact that all technologies pose problems.

Necessity of Technological Effects   Technological utopian and antiutopian analysts suggest that the changes they foresee are virtually certain to happen if a technology is developed and disseminated. Their arguments gain rhetorical force through linear logic and the absence of important contingencies. This causal simplification is a fatal flaw of utopian and antiutopian speculations, which explore the character of possible social changes as if they were the only likely social changes.

   If one doesn't trust the antiutopian or utopian visions, how does one develop a framework for asking questions about what should be done—in what way, and with what associated practices? In our view, the uses and consequences of academic electronic publishing depend on the way the world works. Conversely, electronic formats may slowly, but inexorably, change the way the world works—often with unforeseen consequences. One must thus understand the social opportunities and dilemmas of electronic scholarship without becoming seduced by the social simplifications of utopian romance, or discouraged by antiutopian nightmares.

Alternative Discourses: Beyond the Utopian/Antiutopian Impulse

Empirical analysts, who study socially situated use of electronic information, write about their invertigations in a way that foregrounds the sociotechnological context and communicates their insights as being solidly grounded in the present and the possible. There are several genres of this type, but those most important for developing systematic social analyses of information technologies are social realism, social theory, and analytical reduction.

Not all technological utopian (or antiutopian) analyses are coherent and credible. But other forms of social analysis can also be incoherent or unverifiable. So clarity does not differentiate between utopian analyses and other modes of social analysis. Attractive alternatives to utopian analysis, however, are more credible in characterizing conflict in a social order, the distribution of knowledge, and the ways of solving problems that arise from new technologies. These alternatives use less-deterministic logics of social change. Most important, they identify the social contingencies that make technologies workable or not, and the social changes that are benign or harmful for various social groups. Analyses in the genres that are anchored in empiricism often acknowledge complex patterns of social conflict, yet are more open-ended and contingent than both genres of utopian analysis.

Social Realism

We use the label "social realism" to characterize a genre that uses empirical data to examine computerization as it is practiced and experienced. Social realists write their articles and books with a tacit label: "I have carefully observed and examined computerization in some social settings that can change the way that you think about technology and social life. I will tell what I have seen." The most common mediums for this analysis are journalism (e.g., Forester 1989; Frantz 1991; Salerno 1991; Stoll 1991) and the empirical ethnographically oriented social sciences (e.g., Dutton and Kraemer 1985; Jewett and Kling 1991; Kling 1978; Kling and Iacono 1984; Kraemer et al. 1987; Ladner and Tillman 1992; Laudon 1986; Markus 1994; Orlikowski and Gash 1994). The genre is best characterized by the efforts of authors to communicate their understanding of computerization by reporting fine-grained empirical detail. Social realism is grounded in observations about the social worlds in which new technologies will be used.

One study of a technology-transfer program enhanced by information technology (IT) (Lamb 1994) illustrates how social realism can identify the discrepancies between the expectations raised by utopian genres and the actual use of information. The findings of the study are of particular interest here because the technology-transfer program incorporates several of the social and technological elements of academic electronic publishing.

In the early 1990s, the University of California sought to augment its program for finding business partners for licensable university-developed technologies by providing online databases to "member" firms. The databases contained information relevant to technology transfer, some of which was commercially available (e.g., through "Federal Research in Progress" or "CorpTech") and some of which was available only through this program or its affiliates (e.g., through "University Technologies" or "Faculty Research Capabilities"). The program had approximately thirty organizational members. They had been intentionally solicited to represent a broad range of local business enterprises, in part to demonstrate the presumably wide applicability of this program. The databases were intended to enhance the "matchmaking" activities of the university technology liaison managers, and to stimulate technology transfer among California businesses and between businesses and the university.

By the end of the first year, however, member firms had not been using the databases as much as the program administrators had expected, even after discounting for program setbacks precipitated by California's budget crisis. One firm, which was closely tied to the university and whose trained research scientists and search specialists were already using other online database services, had been expected to use the program technology-transfer services actively. But it was making only light and sporadic use of this resource. Another firm, which was using commercially available information retrieval services, was also expected to be an active user of the database services. But its staff had some problems adapting to the "easier" information retrieval program interface of the database software.[9] The objectives of the study were to characterize the conditions that influenced online database usage within member firms, and to identify their online database use and information search practices.

As the researchers proceeded with their visits to the firms and interviews with the firms' employees and the university's program administrators, they found major discrepancies between the observed behavior of the member firms and the expectations of the program administrators. The administrators were using access counts of the database (even though the program-specific databases were not yet entirely implemented) as a barometer, because it was too soon for them to have accumulated a significant number of instances of technology licensing that could be directly related to use of the IT-enhanced technology-transfer effort. The program administrators used a conceptual model of online information access similar to that espoused by proponents of electronic academic publishing. They assumed that demand for online resources was high among prospective users. They presumed that end users would prefer to access the databases directly. They thought that the databases would be accessed on both regular and irregular bases (i.e., for general and specific informational needs). Although database use might be erratic at first, they expected use to increase over time, as people began to appreciate the advantages of online access to technologically relevant information. The administrators did not recognize that their expectations were guided primarily by technologically utopian models of computerization.

The study identified some commonalities of organizational structure, work processes, and informational approaches that explained the observed database use as consistent with the existing and emerging information resource use practices of the member firms. Furthermore, low levels of database use did not signify failure or impending failure of the program or the IT enhancement. Participants at the member firms considered the databases a tool that would assist primarily the technology liaison managers; they did not view their own low levels of use as significantly diminishing their chances of finding university-developed technologies. Some were relying on the match-making activities of the technology liaison managers to keep them informed, just as they relied on their own information specialists to keep them up-to-date on other topics. The study did, however, reinforce the value of implementing and evaluating pilot projects before establishing fully funded programs, especially when using new technologies.

Discrepancies between proponents' expectations of a system's use and the actual levels of use have been reported in diverse studies of information technologies in public agencies (Kling 1978) and private firms (Bullen and Bennett 1991; Orlikowski 1991). Academic electronic publishing efforts may experience similar discrepancies, but these discrepancies should not lead to antiutopian predictions. Rather, they could more profitably lead to pilot projects and theoretically informed empirical research into the dependent conditions of information use and information resource usage practices. Such analyses can provide important insights to organizations attempting similar moves toward the use of electronic information formats.

Social realists vary in the extent to which they weave their evidence into tight narratives. Tighter stories can leave us more satisfied. But they may ignore important elements that don't fit the narrative (see Campbell 1991, pp. 22–23). More frequently social realism offers compelling, frank portraits that suffer from particularism. Unlike the preceding example of social realism, many works in this genre do not extract concepts or themes that generalize across technologies and social settings from the rich literature about the social character of new technologies. Nor do their authors often compare their study to many other studies or accounts in the literature of technological studies.

Social Theory

In contrast with social realism, social-theoretical analysts explicitly develop or test concepts and theories that transcend specific situations. Unlike utopian and antiutopian accounts, social-theoretical works are not reality transcending, but they are situation transcending. Some examples are *reinforcement politics* (Danziger, et al. 1982),[10] *web models* (Kling 1987; Kling 1992; Kling and Scacchi 1982), *structuration theory* (Orlikowski 1991; Poole and DeSanctis 1990), *poststructuralist theories* (Poster 1991), Judith Perrolle's (1988) explication of *social control theories* and Terry Winograd's (1988) explication of *language-action theory*.

Web models illustrate this kind of theoretical work.[11] Web analyses are action oriented and examine the political interplay of coalitions in structured—but somewhat fluid—settings (Kling 1987). The main organizing concepts are a focal computing technology that is the center of analysis, the infrastructure that supports its development and operation (including production lattices), its context of development and use, and a history of organizational commitments that structures these arrangements. Researchers have applied web models to a variety of cases, including the development of the Worldwide Military Command and Control System, the conversion of complex inventory control systems in manufacturing firms, the development of software in insurance firms, and the analysis of how desktop computerization changes worklife in offices (Kling 1992).

Social-theoretical studies of computerization offer the traditional virtues of theory: relatively concise general explanations and concepts that help guide inquiry in new situations. But they are much less accessible to a broad audience than technological utopian, antiutopian, and social realist accounts because of their intellectual level, their (necessary) use of specialized terms, and their frequent abstraction from the kinds of concrete situations that readers can readily visualize and perhaps identify with.

The contrast between social realism and social theory is clear, and it is easy to find books and articles that illustrate these types. All social analyses are imbued with theoretical assumptions, however implicit (Kling 1980). Journalists and others who are not trained in the social sciences are much more likely to write as social realists than as social theorists. Social scientists are more capable of developing theoretical inquiries, but they are more likely to publish social realist discourses about computerization, or documents that apply existing theory to realist accounts. There is a shortage of good empirically anchored theoretical explorations of the social aspects of computerization, in general, and of its electronic publishing applications, in particular.

Willard McCarty's discussion of the interconnected dependencies of scholarship and electronic publishing provides an excellent model for examining the issues confronting academic publishing—a model that is founded on social realism and social theory (McCarty 1993). He explores the processes of electronic seminars and a form of "intermediate research product" electronic publication, with which he has some direct experience. Throughout the discussion, he emphasizes the duality of the technology:

No tool is "just a tool," no medium completely colorless or transparent; all, especially tools of thought, are agents or at least filters of perception. . . . I have been speaking about the potential of the new medium; this potential is all too easily trivialized by thinking that electronic tools must do what they can do, or that what they can do will make no essential difference to scholarship or the academy. To embrace either alternative is to surrender, rather than face the challenge of understanding the two central, interrelated terms of electronic scholarship: on the one hand, the characteristics of the medium, and on the other, the kind of world we want to make for ourselves. (p. 94)

By combining the generalizing capabilities of a social-theoretical approach like structuration theory, which informs his discussion of the duality of the nature of tools, with an empirical grounding in his own social realist research, McCarty escapes the particularism that constrains other empiricists.

Analytical Reduction

Some scholars organize their social investigations of computerization by working within a tightly defined conceptual framework. They identify a few key concepts, sometimes derived from theory or abstracted from a group of studies, and examine them in new settings. We label this genre *analytical reduction* because the authors reduce their accounts of the social world and computer technologies to a few elements. If they adopt a strictly quantitative social science approach, they operationalize all their key concepts into variables, measure them, and examine how behaviors are distributed along the variables and via mathematical relations between variables (e.g., correlation). Although completely quantitative studies represent ideal examples of this genre, studies that focus on a few qualitatively described dimensions share enough characteristics to be appropriately grouped with them.

The study by Hesse et al. (1993) on the ways in which networked communications affect the productivity of oceanographers illustrates the quantitative version of the genre. They administered questionnaires to Ph.D. scientists who had access to a network of oceanographic databases and services (SCIENCEnet). They grouped their questions to measure three specific aspects of scientific productivity: scientific publication, professional recognition, and social integration. They also measured many aspects of the scientists' working environments and their use of the network services. Hesse et al. based their conclusions on the magnitude of quantitative relationships between the variables they measured. They found that network use was positively associated with all three aspects of scientific productivity; their results indicated that there was a differential benefit for scientists on the periphery. The relation between SCIENCEnet use and publication was stronger for scientists at inland institutions than for scientists on the coast; the relation between SCIENCEnet use and professional recognition was stronger for younger scientists than for senior scientists.

An adaptation of this study could be directed toward issues concerning digital libraries, especially if scarce educational resources, expensive art collections, or original manuscripts could be made more widely available through digitization. The implications for differential benefits for peripheral networked scientists found by Hesse et al. might be extended to differential benefits for peripheral scholars if quantitative analyses could be extended to measure the effectiveness of remote access to critical resources through digital libraries.

In a similarly analytical approach, Kling and Iacono (1984) examined the extent to which the development of a complex computerized inventory control system could be explained by each one of three kinds of organizational choice processes: rational decision making, organizational drift, and partisan politics.[12] The authors presented a qualitative case study and then systematically examined it for evidence in the form of episodes and social relationships that would support or undermine each of these three models of organizational choice.

Depending on one's view, analytical reduction represents the best or worst of social science inquiry. Those who see it as a valuable genre appreciate how the authors critically examine key concepts and examine the extent to which they shed insight into the social world of computing. They believe that the best hope for systematically understanding the social character of computerization will come from studies in this genre. Those who criticize analytical reduction see it as arcane and inaccessible except to academic specialists. They usually prefer social realist studies because they are more easily accessible and identifiably concrete. Further, the quantitative reductions are less likely to characterize the shifts of understandings that participants have over time, the nature of unusual but important events, or even the occasions when computerization becomes comical or tragic.

Computerization, Electronic Scholarship, and Social Visions

Much of the discussion about scholarship and electronic publishing focuses on the enormous economic incentives for the emancipation of scholarship from commercial publishers, impending demise of libraries, unprecedented potential for the development of new kinds of knowledge, insurmountable difficulties in controlling the quality of information in electronic formats, exponentially rising rates of textual illiteracy, irreversible segregation of the population into information-rich and -poor, and other similarly crisis-laden concerns. Empirically grounded research into these questions can expand the discourse beyond the constraints of utopian and antiutopian genres and can encourage constructive, situationally focused debate and analytically informed experimentation with the technological possibilities of electronic scholarship.

We have indicated the ways in which the conventions of genres amplify some kinds of ideas and mute others. They also make the resulting narratives accessible and attractive to different audiences. Because an authoritative presentation of speculative projection is a prominent device of both utopian and antiutopian authors, this attention to genre conventions blurs the crisp boundaries between fiction and nonfiction.

Writings in each genre have limits (see table 2.1), much in the way that romantic fiction (or any other literary genre) has limits (Cawelti 1976). Cawelti notes that the "moral fantasy of the romance is that of love triumphant and permanent, overcoming all obstacles and difficulties" (pp. 41–42). This does not mean that we can't be entertained or that our appreciation of life can't be enriched by romantic fiction, it is simply a genre with limits. The moral fantasies of technological utopianism and antiutopianism similarly limit the way that they can teach us about the likely social realities of new forms of computerization: one is romantic and the other is tragic. We are not arguing for some simple balance within each account—and certainly not for balance between the utopian and antiutopian genres.

We are much more sympathetic to the empirically oriented genres—social realism, social theory, and analytical reduction. We see the two utopian genres as legitimate, however, because they help to explore the limits of the possible. We don't believe that we can develop "conventionless genres," even though we can benefit from new genres that situate computerization in credible social worlds. It's tempting to explore new genres that combine the richness of social realism with the future orientation of the utopian genres.[13]

One of the dilemmas facing analysts of emerging technologies is how to conduct empirical studies of the use of technologies that do not yet exist, or of new institutional forms that do not yet exist. The most common approach has been to rely on technological utopianism and antiutopianism. We believe that empirically grounded alternatives are worth the effort. But they require a special imagination to conceive and to generalize from. At minimum, social analysts of electronic scholarship and digital libraries can learn about the concepts and theories that have proven useful and valid in studies of computerization in other domains (see, e.g., Kling 1980; Kling and Jewett 1994).

These empirically anchored studies can be criticized superficially as irrelevant because they examine very different technologies or technologies that seem dated. But, most important, provide durable insights about the ways in which people and groups integrate new information technologies into their work. They help reframe key issues concerning electronic scholarship and libraries by helping us see them as work places. Studies of computerization and changing work patterns show that people's fine-grained work incentives influence whether they see technologies as relevant, and the ways in which they appropriate the technologies (Orlikowski and Gash 1994). Organizational change is slow, especially when systems of incentives are not structured. Work is often social, and professionals seem to value the role of technologies that expand their opportunities for interpersonal communication even more than they value those that affect information management (Bullen and Bennett 1991). Even when managers and professionals try to use information technologies to help create closeness, they may find unexpected social distance (Markus 1994). And, in all of this, people's workload and limited resources shape the ways in which they computerize (Kling 1992; Jewett and Kling 1991).

Computerization presents many important social choices, and some of them will restrict our social options in the twenty-first century. An awareness of foregoing debates about efforts toward computerization in other industries and practices may enable the electronic publishing debate to leapfrog past some of the quagmires that have marked computerization controversies. By understanding the dynamics of utopian and antiutopian arguments—their analytical strengths and weaknesses—members of the academic community can recognize when their debates come to terms with the real issues of technological change, rather than merely engage the extremist rhetoric. By punctuating the discussion of technological potential with empirical research and analysis, academics can temper utopian zeal, allay antiutopian fears, and encourage the consideration of sociological scenarios that are informed by perspectives of social theory.

Acknowledgments

Thanks to Howard Besser, Lisa Covi, and Margaret Elliott for comments on this paper and to Paul Evans Peters for stimulating discussions of digital libraries. Our colleagues Mark Ackerman, Jonathan Grudin, Mark Poster, and Steve Franklin contributed thought-provoking discussions about the emerging world of electronic scholarship. Cliff Lynch has been an important but tacit contributor to this research by making the Melvyl System, with several article databases (including Psychinfo and ABI/Inform), available to faculty and students at the University of California.

Notes

1. See Segal 1986 for a description of technological utopianism in the period between 1880 and 1930. The technologies depicted by technological utopians can change from one era to another. But the assumption that a society which adopts the proper technologies will be harmonious and prosperous remains constant.

2. For an interesting case study of the way an organization exploited the image of efficient administration through computerization, see Kling 1978.

3. Also referred to as the "superhypeway."

4. Amiran Unsworth, and Chaski (1992) point out that the discussions about the academic implications of electronic publishing have been overwhelmingly utopian. They characterize the utopian discourse in terms of "movie matinees of yesteryear": the Space Adventure (the electronic medium is viewed as a new kind of space—an internal final frontier), the Western (the medium is a virgin territory to be settled and resourced), and the Return to Eden (the medium returns us to a pretextual state of immediate communication).

5. William Clark (1992) provides one perspective on the roots of academic publishing in his essay about the (late) origination of the Doctor of Philosophy degree.

6. For a very readable and revealing account about the way that newspapers shape the reports that appear as "news," see Manhoff and Schudson 1986.

7. "In the long run, indeed in the short run too, I would argue, digital technology democratizes the arts and letters, rather than the reverse. Simply by opening discourse out from a strictly verbal base, it enfranchises not only the left-handed but the right-brained of all sorts" (Lanham 1993: p. 24).

8. See the analyses of technical problems with, and challenges to, electronic publishing in Silverman 1990 and Crane 1990 for examples of technological utopianism.

9. The program administrators assumed that mouse-driven interfaces would be universally preferred over command-driven interfaces, because it is generally considered easier to click a mouse button than to type a command phrase. They therefore provided only the mouse-driven interface. For a firm that did not own a single mouse, and whose users were unaccustomed to graphic user interfaces (GUIs), the exclusively mouse-driven approach would be useless.

10. Reinforcement politics holds that organizations use technology so that the actors with the most resources gain more influence, while those with fewer resources lose subsequent influence.

11. Walsham, Symons, and Waema (1988) characterize web models in these terms: "The basic tenet of web models . . . is that a computer system is best conceptualized as an ensemble of equipment, applications and techniques with identifiable processing capabilities. Each computing resource has costs and skill requirements which are only partially identifiable; in addition to its functional capabilities as an information processing tool it is a social object which may be highly charged

with meaning. There is no specially separable 'human factor' for information systems: the development and routine operations of computer-based technologies hinge on many human judgements and actions, often influenced by political interests, structural constraints, and participants' definition of their situation.

"The Network of producers and consumers around the focal computing resource is termed the 'production lattice'; the interdependencies in this network form the 'web' from which the model derives its name. The production lattice is a social organization which is itself embedded in a larger matrix of social and economic relations ('macrostructure') and is dependent upon a local infrastructure. According to web models, these macrostructures and local infrastructures direct the kind of computer-based service available at each node of the production lattice, and since they evolve over time, computing developments are shaped by a set of historical commitments. In short, web models view information systems as 'complex social objects constrained by their context, infrastructure, and history' (Kling and Scacchi 1982)."

12. They found that partisan political models of organizational choice best explained the developmental trajectory of computerization in this case.

13. Anthony Giddens has referred to this combination as "utopian realism" (Giddens 1993).

References

Amiran, Eyal, John Unsworth, and Carole Chaski. (1992). "Networked Academic Publishing and the Rhetorics of its Reception." *Centennial Review* 36, no. 1 (Winter): 43–58.

Bullen, C. V., and J. L. Bennett. (1991). "Groupware in Practice: An Interpretation of Work Experiences." In Dunlop and Kling 1991, pp. 257–287.

Bush, Vannevar. (1988) "As We May Think." *Atlantic Monthly,* 1948. Reprinted in *Computer-Supported Cooperative Work: A Book of Readings,* edited by Irene Greif. San Mateo, Calif.: Morgan Kaufmann.

Campbell, Richard. (1991). *Sixty Minutes and the News: A Mythology for Middle America.* Chicago: University of Illinois Press.

Cawelti, John. (1976). *Adventure, Mystery and Romance: Formula Stories as Art and Popular Culture.* Chicago: University of Chicago Press.

Clark, William. (1992) "On the Ironic Specimen of the Doctor of Philosophy." *Science in Context* 5, no. 1: 97–137.

Crane, Gregory. (1990) "'Hypermedia' and Scholarly Publishing." *Scholarly Publishing* (April).

Crawford, Rick. (1994). "Technoprisoners." *Adbusters* 3, no. 2 (Summer): 17–23.

Culnan, M. (1983)."Chauffeured versus End User Access to Commercial Databases: The Effects of Task and Individual Differences." *MIS Quarterly* 7: 55–67.

Danziger, James, William Dutton, Rob Kling, and Kenneth Kraemer. (1982). *Computers and Politics: High Technology in American Local Governments.* New York: Columbia University Press.

Dunlop, Charles, and Rob Kling, eds. (1991). *Computerization and Controversy: Value Conflicts and Social Choices.* Boston: Academic Press.

Dutton, William H., and Kenneth L. Kraemer. (1985). *Modeling as Negotiating: The Political Dynamics of Computer Models in the Policy Process.* Norwood, N.J.: Ablex.

Entlich, Eichard. (1993). "Network Delivery of Full-Text Electronic Journals." Paper delivered at "Emerging Communities: Integrating Networked Information into Library Services." The 30th Annual Clinic on Library Applications of Data Processing, University of Illinois at Urbana/Champaign (April 4–6). URL gopher://gopher.cni.org/cnift/miscdocs/illinois.dpc/text/entlich.txt

Forester, Tom. (1989). "The Myth of the Electronic Cottage." In *Computers in the Human Context: Information Technology, Productivity, and People,* edited by Tom Forester. Cambridge, Mass.: The MIT Press.

Frantz, Douglas. (1991) "B of A's Plans for Computer Don't Add Up." In Dunlop and Kling 1991, pp. 103–110.

Giddens, Anthony (1993). "Modernity, History, Democracy." *Theory and Society* 22: 289–292.

Gray, Paul. (1993). "Adding Up the Under-Skilled: Functionally Illiterate." *Time* 142, no. 12 (September 20): 75.

Greif, Irene, ed. (1988). *Computer-Supported Cooperative Work: A Book of Readings.* San Mateo, Calif.: Morgan Kaufmann.

Hesse, Bradford W., Lee S. Sproull, Sara B. Kiesler, and John P. Walsh. (1993). "Returns to Science: Computer Networks in Oceanography." *Communications of the ACM* 36 (August): 8.

Hillis, W. Daniel. (1992). "What Is Massively Parallel Computing and Why Is It Important?" *Daedalus* 121, no. 1 (Winter): 1–16.

IITF (Information Infrastructure Task Force) (1994). "Libraries and the NII." In *Putting the Information Infrastructure to Work.* U.S. Department of Commerce. May.

Jewett, Tom, and Rob Kling. (1991)."The Dynamics of Computerization Social Science Research Team: A Case Study of Infrastructure, Strategies, and Skills." *Social Science Computer Review* 9, no. 2: 246–275.

Kling, Rob. (1978). "Automated Welfare Client-Tracking and Service Integration: The Political Economy of Computing." *Communications of the ACM* 21, no. 6 (June): 484–493.

Kling, Rob. (1980). "Social Analyses of Computing: Theoretical Orientations in Recent Empirical Research." *Computing Surveys* 12, no. 1 (March): 61–110.

Kling, Rob. (1987). "Defining the Boundaries of Computing across Complex Organizations." In *Critical Issues in Information Systems Research,* edited by R. Boland and R. Hirschheim. London: John Wiley.

Kling, Rob. (1992)."Behind the Terminal: The Critical Role of Computing Infrastructure in Effective Information Systems' Development and Use." In *Challenges and Strategies for Search in Systems Development,* edited by William Cotterman and James Senn. New York: John Wiley, 153–201.

Kling, Rob. (1994). "Reading 'All About' Computerization: How Genre Conventions Shape Social Analyses." *Information Society* 10: 147–172.

Kling, Rob. (1995). *Computerization and Controversy: Value Conflicts and Social Choices.* 2d ed. San Diego: Academic Press.

Kling, Rob, and Suzanne Iacono. (1984). "The Control of Information Systems Development after Implementation." *Communications of the ACM* 27, no. 12 (December): 1218–1226.

Kling, Rob, and Suzanne Iacono. (1988). "The Mobilization of Support for Computerization: The Role of Computerization Movements." *Social Problems* 35, no. 3 (June): 226–243.

Kling, Rob, and Suzanne Iacono. (1991). "Making the Computer Revolution." In Dunlop and Kling 1991, pp. 63–75.

Kling, Rob, and Tom Jewett (1994). "The Social Design of Worklife with Computers and Networks: An Open Natural Systems Perspective." In *Advances in Computers,* edited by Marshall Yovits, vol. 39. Boston: Academic Press.

Kling, Rob, and W. Scacchi. (1982). "The Web of Computing: Computer Technology as Social Organization." *Advances in Computers* 21: 1–90.

Koch, Tom. (1991) *Journalism for the 21st Century: Online Information, Electronic Databases, and the News.* Westport, Conn.: Greenwood Press.

Kraemer, Kenneth L., Sigfried Dickhoven, Susan Fallows Tierney, and John Leslie King. (1987). *Datawars: The Politics of Modeling in Federal Policymaking.* New York: Columbia University Press.

Kumar, Krishan. (1987). *Utopia and Anti-Utopia in Modern Times.* New York: Basil Blackwell.

Kumar, Krishan. (1991). *Utopianism.* Minneapolis: University of Minnesota Press.

Kurzweil, Raymond. (1990). *The Age of Intelligent Machines.* Cambridge, Mass.: The MIT Press.

Ladner, Sharyn, and Hope Tillman. (1992). "How Special Librarians Really Use the Internet: Summary of Findings and Implications for the Library of the Future." *Canadian Library Journal* 49, no. 3: 211–216.

Lamb, Roberta. (1994). "Information Technology Support for Technology Transfer: UC-ACCESS: A Usability Field Study." University of California, Irvine, Technical Report 94-38.

Lanham, Richard. (1993). *The Electronic Word: Democracy, Technology, and the Arts.* Chicago: University of Chicago Press.

Lanham, Richard. (1994). "The Implications of Electronic Information for the Sociology of Knowledge." *Leonardo* 27, no. 2: 155–164.

Laudon, Kenneth. (1986). *Dossier Society: Value Choices in the Design of National Information Systems*. New York: Columbia University Press.

Lougee, Carolyn C. (1994). "The Professional Implications of Electronic Information." *Leonardo* 27, no. 2: 143–154.

Manhoff, Robert Karl, and Michael Schudson, eds. (1986). *Reading the News*. New York: Pantheon Books.

Markus, M. Lynne. (1994). "Finding a Happy Medium: Explaining the Negative Effects of Electronic Communication on Social Life at Work." *ACM Transactions on Information Systems* 12, no. 2 (April): 119–149.

Mauss, Armand L. (1975). *Social Problems as Social Movements*. Philadelphia: Lippincott.

McCarty, Willard. (1993). "A Potency of Life: Scholarship in an Electronic Age." *Serials Librarian* 23, nos. 3–4: 79–97.

McCloskey, Donald N. (1990). *If You're So Smart: The Narrative of Economic Expertise*. Chicago: University of Chicago Press.

National Science Foundation (NSF). (1993). "Research on Digital Libraries: A Joint Initiative of the National Science Foundation, Computer and Information Science and Engineering Directorate, Advanced Research Projects Agency Computing Systems Technology Office national Aeronautics and Space Administration." NSF 93-141 (September). Washington, D.C.: NSF.

Okerson, Ann. (1992). "Publishing through the Network: The 1990s Debutante." *Scholarly Publishing* (April).

Orlikowski, Wanda. (1991)."Integrated Information Environment or Matrix of Control? The Contradictory Implications of Information Technology. "*Accounting, Management and Information Technology* 1, no. 1: 9–42.

Orlikowski, Wanda J. (1993). "Learning from Notes: Organizational Issues in Groupware Implementation." *Information Society* 9, no. 3 (July–September): 237–250. Reprinted in Kling 1995.

Orlikowski, Wanda, and Debra Gash. (1994). "Technological Frames: Making Sense of Information Technology in Organizations." *ACM Transactions on Information Systems* 12, no. 2 (April): 174–207.

Perrolle, Judith. (1988)."The Social Impact of Computing: Ideological Themes and Research Issues." *Social Science Computer Review* 6, no. 4 (Winter): 469–480.

Pfaffenberger, Bryan. (1990). *Democratizing Information: Online Databases and the Rise of End-User Searching*. Boston: G. K. Hall.

Poole, M. Scott, and Gerry DeSanctis. (1990). "Understanding the Use of Group Decision Support Systems: The Theory of Adaptive Structuration." In *Organizations and Communications Technology*, ed. Janet Fulk and Charles Steinfeld, pp. 173–193. Newbury Park, Calif.: Sage Publications.

Poster, Mark. (1991). *The Mode of Information*. Chicago: University of Chicago Press.

Reinecke, Ian. (1984). *Electronic Illusions: A Skeptic's View of Our High Tech Future.* New York: Penguin.

Salerno, Lynne. (1991). "What Happened to the Computer Revolution?" In Dunlop and Kling 1991.

Segal, Howard P. (1986). "The Technological Utopians." In *Imagining Tomorrow: History, Technology, and the American Future,* edited by Joseph J. Corn. Cambridge, Mass.: The MIT Press.

Silverman, Robert A. (1989). "Desktop Publishing: Its Impact on the Academic Community." *Scholarly Publishing* (October).

Stoll, Clifford. (1991). "Stalking the Wiley Hacker." In Dunlop and Kling 1991.

Stonier, Tom. (1983). *The Wealth of Information: A Profile of the Post-Industrial Economy.* London: Methuen.

Toffler, Alvin. (1980). *The Third Wave.* New York: Bantam Books.

Tuchman, Gaye. (1978). *Making News: A Study in the Construction of Reality.* New York: Free Press.

Van Maanen, John. (1988). *Tales from the Field: On Writing Ethnography.* Chicago: University of Chicago Press.

Walsham, Geoff, Veronica Symons, and Tim Waema. (1988). "Information Systems as Social Systems: Implications for Developing Countries." *Information Technology for Development* 3, no. 3.

Webster, Robins (1986). *Information Technology: A Luddite Analysis.* Norwood, N.J.: Ablex.

Weizenbaum, Joseph. (1976). *Computer Power and Human Reason.* San Francisco: Freeman.

White House. (1993). "The National Information Infrastructure: Agenda for Action." Washington, D.C.

Wilson, Richard Guy, Dianne H. Pilgrim, and Dickran Tasjian. (1986). *The Machine Age in America: 1918–1941.* New York: Harry Abrams.

Winner, Langdon. (1992). "Silicon Mystery House." In *Variations on a Theme Park: The New American City and the End of Public Space.* New York: Noonday Press.

Winograd, Terry. (1988). "A Language/Action Perspective on the Design of Cooperative Work." *Human-Computer Interaction* 3, no. 1 (1987–88): 3–30. Reprinted in *Computer-Supported Cooperative Work: A Book of Readings,* edited by Irene Greif. San Mateo, Calif.: Morgan Kaufmann, pp. 623–653.

3

The Impact of Electronic Publishing on the Academic Community

Robert J. Silverman

"The book has now ceased to be the root-metaphor of the age; the screen has taken its place," claims Illich (1993, p. 3) in *In the Vineyard of the Text*, where he takes us to the relationship between the "axioms of conceptual space and social reality . . . [as] mediated and shaped by techniques that employ letters" (p. 4). This paean to the text is the prelude for this chapter, which explores the significance of electronic publishing within the various academic communities. Although examinations of the likely impact of electronic publishing (Burstyn 1991; Cummings et al. 1992; Okerson 1993) forecast, understandably with limited experience, the consequences of electronic publishing on peer interaction and the constitution of knowledge, these treatments consider the academic community as undifferentiated. That is, there is "a community" of scholars who will work and know differently with the advent of electronic journals than they currently do, the only differences among these scholars being in the subject matter embraced and the choices and impacts of emerging technology in relation to this subject matter.

In this chapter I problematize the concept of "academic community" and explore the possible consequences of electronic publishing in communities that have differential dynamics. The communal alternatives that I explore are not known by terms associated with subject matter, such as the natural sciences and humanities, or with concepts made popular and employed ubiquitously, such as "paradigmatic" and associated terms. I first outline a scheme that suggests four generic types of academic community and to suggest a confluence of work coming from different academic disciplines that are complementary in support of this scheme. Then I consider the relation between electronic publishing and the academic contexts presented. It seems self-evident that publication practices of any kind will reflect the way in which colleagues define knowledge and their relation to it and to each other. What are the possibilities?

Communities of Scholarship

In *We Have Never Been Modern*, Bruno Latour (1993) focuses on nature, society, discourse, and being as the four modern repertoires:

The first deals with the external reality of a nature of which we are not masters, which exists outside ourselves and has neither our passions nor our desires, even though we are capable of mobilizing and constructing it. The second deals with the social bond, with what attaches human beings to one another, with the passions and desires that move us, and with the personified forces that structure society—a society that surpasses us all, even though it is of our making. The third deals with signification and meaning, with the actants that make up the stories we tell ourselves, with the ordeals they undergo, with the adventures they live through, with the tropes and genres that organize them. . . . The fourth . . . speaks of Being and deconstructs what we invariably forget when we concern ourselves with being alone, though the presence of Being is distributed among beings, is coextensive with their very existence, their very historicity. (p. 88)

Latour calls for the mediation of these repertoires, noting that they need to connect with each other. And Sassower (1993), in *Knowledge without Expertise: On the Status of Scientists*, independently identifies four critiques relevant to these domains, as reflected by Popperians, Marxists, postmodernists, and feminists.

Anderson (1993) recognizes that our curriculum should be organized in relation to these repertoires, though he is unaware of Latour's (1993) work. In *Prescribing the Life of the Mind*, Anderson first dismisses many of the presumed goals of the university, such as the cultivation of character. He then discusses the university's responsibility to "enhance the powers of mind" (p. 59). His four-part solution is composed of the teaching of (1) reliable knowledge, that is, "fundamental agreed-upon knowledge . . . and the methods by which this knowledge was won; (2) what he calls "radical relativism" or the "systems of ideas that succeed one another"; (3) perspectivism, in which the "crucial point is that it is only when we are *faced* with diverse perspectives that we have to ask which idea is better . . . or the essential purpose we seek"; and (4) "open-mindedness," which he identifies with intellectual anarchism (pp. 63–78).

These contemporary treatments of scholarship all reflect four repertoires, or academic contexts, but differ in their focus and their depth. Silverman (1993), however, developed a fundamental treatment through his attention to the foundational work of Lorraine Code in her book *What Can She Know?* (1991) where she distinguishes constitutive and regulative knowledge from academic communities. The interaction between these binaries suggest four academic contexts that are complementary to the work of Latour, Sassower, and Anderson, among others.

In a *constitutive community,* "every cognitive act takes place at a point of intersection of innumerable relations, events, circumstances, and histories that make the knower and known what they are, at that time. [It focuses on] the complex network or relations within which an organism realizes, or fails to realize, its potential" (Code 1991, pp. 269–270). The community allows for interrogation, renegotiation; it evidences trust, which "involves making oneself vulnerable" (p. 184).

In a *regulative community,* in contrast, authoritarian knowers "claim credibility on the basis of privilege alone or ideological orthodoxy" (p. 85). Code suggests that in this community there is an obsession with autonomy and an overemphasis on the self (pp. 275–276). Much of academic life assumes a regulative model, because of research prizes, citation studies, and other outcome work.

Continuing the distinctions, Code argues that *constitutive knowledge* takes account of testimony and cognitive interdependence (p. 132), "letting 'objects' of study speak for themselves, . . . understand[ing] difference to accord it respect" (p. 151). Further, it grows by accretion without pre-existing patterns. In contrast, *regulative knowledge* "has more standard forms, is more hierarchical, is informed by such principles as objectivity and value-neutrality, [and] at the same time it is adversarial and territorial" (p. 120).

The interaction of these options suggests the following scholarly contexts that are reflected in the distinctions made by the scholars noted previously:

1. Regulative knowledge that is developed in regulative communities as reflected in much of the work of the academy. The study of computer models of space by analytical geographers would be a case in point.

2. Regulative knowledge that is developed by a constitutive community. Foundational or evocative ideas become the focus of a group of scholars who are usually not in contact with each other but who use a common knowledge product and develop it for their purposes. The work of Foucault, Kuhn, Piaget, or Rawls would be so characterized. Scholars analyze their issues within the frame of existing ideas that are unlikely to be changed through such attention.

3. Constitutive knowledge that is developed in regulative communities. Here scholars selectively use the work of various fields to focus on a "problematic." In the social study of science, one could examine a specific science policy through the selective use of work in political science, economics, history, or organizational sociology.

4. Constitutive knowledge that is developed in constitutive communities. Scholars interested in fresh problems attempt to craft new ways of engaging their concerns in order to cast them appropriately. Feminist scholars developing new language symbols to better represent and understand the teaching activities in which they are engaged would be an example of this pattern.

A Differentiated Academic Community

Voices such as Fuchs (1992), in addition to those noted here, confirm the four foci. These academic communities exist among scholars in individual fields, departments, and institutions. Communication practices, processes, and mechanisms, including the use of electronic journals, both reflect and are needed to service the four contexts. It is time for the assumptions of the fully regulative model to be displaced by what we know and experience.

These four contexts are the following:

1. A fully regulative context that is oriented to rational goals and reliable knowledge, that is outside us, that has to do with nature, that one knows calculatively and through mastery, that is mechanical, that requires "we find out," and in which certain tasks are conjoined by patterned relations among the knowers.

2. A context composed of multiple impermeable orientations, each complete and for which change does not challenge fundamental premises but enhances movement within central parameters, where discourse is stylized in terms of the theory or theorists' approach or school of thought.

3. A context in which all depends on context, where persons in circumscribed communities study uncertainties and develop significance and meaning in relation to a problem, where their rhetoric—their narratives—assume primary importance as they present their constructions and perspectives, where their inquiry evokes searching with both tools at hand and those being shaped, as these tools not only confront the uncertainties but are themselves part of the uncertainty.

4. A fully constitutive context in which community and substantive evolutionary growth lead to learning, a deeper appreciation of being that spans time horizons as fusions are created in the movement toward wholeness and as the life of the mind becomes the source of the development of new futures.

What is the meaning of electronic journals for groups of scholars who organize themselves in terms of these academic contexts? Individual scholars may belong to more than one academic community, and these communities may be of the same type or of different types. One might suggest that academic maturity is related to one's appreciation of, if not engagement in, a variety of the communities as opposed to specialization, which is related to more focused depth. A person engaged in more types of complex professional communities will reflect information involvements that require multiple cognitive orientations (Silverman 1994).

Electronic Journals and the Academic Communities

Context 1

The linearity of the geometric world will find its counterpart in the linear literacy of the book, where line by line, sentence by sentence, the chronological structure of the book will mirror the sequential, ordered, linear structure of time in the sciences. . . . The increasing standardization of grammar will also mirror the increasing homogenization of a world quantifiably defined. In these and in other respects too, linear vision will create an ego consciousness not only separate from the world and distant from the body, but also literate, private, and silent, an ego paradoxically standardized in its individuality. (Romanyshyn 1993, p. 351)

The existing literature on the electronic journal (e.g., Burstyn 1991; Cummings et al. 1992; Okerson 1993) assumes that this academic context represents the universal academic community. Each subject-matter community develops and disseminates its truths (e.g., Fleck 1935), which are highly stylized, with their own language and rewards for the enhancement of the community's direction. Many of the commentaries located in the sources just noted are reflections of the likely impacts of the electronic journal in this highly regulative context.

Given the commonplace understanding of this dominant communal pattern, the likely consequences of electronic publishing for this academic community, and the various decision points, are not difficult to discern. As in all prognostications, however, the actual outcomes are likely to diverge from the predicted ones, given, at least, variation within the dominant context. For example, assuming that submitted manuscripts are first reviewed by persons designated by the editor and, upon acceptance, are made available to the community and commented on by the readers on screen, so to speak, we will: (1) alter the influence of persons in the academic subject community depending on the value of their reactions, as opposed to the prestige of their institutional locations or even the presumed influence of gender or other demographic features; (2) enable scholars to participate in the creation of their own intellectual foundations regardless of the resource strength of their universities, because the relatively permanent technology needed for engagement in electronic environments is much less expensive than sending emissaries to conferences around the globe; and (3) modify the role of the editor from strict gatekeeper to rigorous traffic cop, given that the value of work will become apparent as reactions develop. As significant as these impacts will be, the challenges resulting from electronic publishing will be much greater.

As suggested by the quotation opening this section, scholars live primarily in a private world and read to participate intelligently in the work of their specialty. Electronic journals, possibly providing papers on demand, will likely focus reading to one's specialization and reduce serendipitous reading. More important, a kind of online commentary will change the orientation of the scholar to a more public environment and to a reading that can engage more with the comments of others than with what might be of value in the scholar's own production. I call this the "CNNing of scholarship," because one person says this, and another reacts and says that, and then another says something else. The talk-show logic comes to academe as it is now reflected in the ubiquitous network forums. The scholar will read to be public and will employ a rhetoric that has to be different from that employed when one talks to oneself.

In my experience, those active in network forums often are not active in the published literature of an area. Enhancing the opportunities for broad involvement also has the possibility of creating another attempted line of influence, one not dependent on being among those who invite the critical reactions of others through their production. Even more, the electronic journal will problematize the identity of the "author." An argument can be made, at this point, that the notion of authorship is more complex than typically appreciated. Because very little work that appears is not revised before publication, one might claim that all work is coauthored by the field. Papers often go through a number of iterations, with substantial modifications reflected as a consequence of the advice and demands of those engaged in the paper.

Electronic journals problematize the notion of authorship even more. If there is no final paper, but an evolving one, if there are uncertainties regarding whether the original authors should accept the challenges or recommendations of their peers, or even whether they have a choice, then the meaning of authorship becomes complicated. What an author needs to know is challenged.

In a paper examining comments and replies (Silverman 1994), I discovered that critics who react to work in the context under discussion here engage in two ways: a focus on the methodological correctness and, to a much lesser extent, on the paradigmatic appropriateness of the paper in question. Critics raise questions about the research procedures used and at times attempt to replace the foundations of the framework of scholarship informing the author whose work is being engaged. It would seem that, in the electronic journal environment, the scholar must be more deeply educated and articulate about the methodological parameters of the work being executed. One simply will not survive by doing, or knowing how to do, research only in a certain way when it is likely that one will be confronted publicly with suggested alternative ways of performing the inquiry, or elements of it. Ph.D. programs thus may have to modify how methods courses are taught, the variety of courses that a doctoral student is required to take, and the qualifications for teaching in such a doctoral program. The publicness of "scholarship in the making" will require that the process of crafting skills and understanding be more finely understood and more easily articulated than at present. Clearly, conflict and defense strategies and the use of critical reasoning, appraisal, and questioning will become more dominant practices in the academic community. Johnson (1992) suggests that a critical thinker:

Reasons her way through to a position by considering the evidence available;

Knows what objections are likely to be raised to a position and knows how to examine positions by probing their assumptions and consequences;

Does not allow vivid information and anecdotal evidence to carry undue weight in his reflections;

Realizes the effect that emotions and feelings and prejudices may have on her thinking;

Is willing to revise his position in light of the reasoning of others and of contrary evidence;

Is sensitized to the demands of clarity and is able to detect objectionable vagueness in her own thinking and the thinking of others;

Remains unimpressed by the sheer force of someone's rhetoric and conviction when these masquerade as substitutes for reasoning;

Stops to think before arriving at a judgment;

Thinks, judges, acts mindful of the limitations of time and information imposed by the situation. (pp. 75–76)

These skills will have to be taught, learned, and rewarded in a community of scholars whose argumentation will become a much more prominent dimension of their lives.

It is likely that scholars will provide the evidence for their inquiry and resulting composition in a more complete way than is currently the practice, given the little- or no-cost use of space in the electronic medium. Readers will be able to take the original data and engage them in a variety of ways, from confirming the author's conclusions to filtering them through different methodological processes. Amann and Knorr-Cetina (1988, p. 148) use the term *optical induction* in discussing a "curious hybrid between visual operations and conversations" as it relates to the reading of graphs. The public trial of portrayed work may require a similar set of skills and practices, as the data that one examines are not "raw" but situated in a way that makes them usable for a particular scholar. In the "documentary organization of talk . . . it is the image which integrates the series [of exchanges], not the continuity of speakers" (Amann and Knorr-Cetina 1988, p. 140). Thus, one might anticipate that critical readings of "published" work will allow the work to be "read" differently when various scholars engage a data set, not just the evidence that authors previously had selected to support the interpretive case that they were making.

A most serious question is whether, and in what ways, the electronic journal will challenge the normative structure perceived to function in regulative communities (Merton 1957), recognizing the controversies regarding the literal application of the traditional norms (e.g., Hull 1988). Where the norms have focused on the individual scholar, one might argue that norms need to be specified for the consensual community. We must consider the meaning of work that is always in revision by the community, for measuring the value of work other than by counting citations, for rewarding individuals who change their work publicly in response to reactions and who do not simply defend a position. The normative structure now supports individual achievement, not evolving achievement, which locates the author in a different place. The electronic journal promises to make it evident when a paper is of utter nonconsequence to the community by spawning no reactions, or hostile and nonconfirming ones. This publicness will be somewhat like the ratings that appear in movie reviews. A person who consistently garners two-star reactions will hardly be able to sustain a four-star reputation over time.

Context 2

In this context scholars focus on the work that reflects a specific theorist, theory, or circumscribed school with a focused group of attenders. This group may have an inner circle, but at the same time a broader constituency finds something of value in the work.

The substantive work in this context can be empirical or theoretical, but it reflects absolute truth, which is in some sense fixed in its foundational form. That is, it may be extended or revised on the surface, but the premises of a Foucault or Kuhn or Myers-Briggs are not challenged but form the glue that allows for firm or more occasional adherence by scholars who may attend to additional foci. There is literature that explores the making of foundational work of this type (Silverman 1992) and the nature of schools of scholarship that have such salience. These schools include a charismatic leader, discipleship, pools of potential recruits, institutionalization, and resources, among other elements (Henson 1993). The continued value of the scholarship is necessary to maintain its regulative legitimacy, which, in turn, allows for the constitutive community of interest.

Because of the investment that individual scholars have in their preestablished solutions or treatments or truths, reactions are likely to be strongly or quietly confirming. According to Silverman's (1994) study of comments and replies that appear in journals publishing work in this context, one typically finds what I have labeled "contention and fortification," where attack and defense are a high art. Critical responses to such work often demonstrate the falseness of an author's claims, to a point that "just about" allows the perspective to exist so that it can be a foil for one's own position. How can one be critical if the source or occasion of one's criticality is absent? For those sympathetic to a school or theorist's work, it is comforting to see the possible ubiquitousness of an audience that spans fields and disciplines and responds to the same solutions as they do.

I expect that electronic journals are going to play a somewhat different role in context 2 than they will in the more traditional context 1. Readers are more or less likely to interact with the material, depending on their investment in the work and the various fields from which they come. That is, they will be either readers whose legitimacy is at stake in the continuing treatments of a substantive core or theorist, or readers whose legitimacy is confirmed through the attention that this core continues to receive from a far-flung colleague. In fact, for the second type of reader, many objects of attention in which the core is played out would not be of any interest. Thus, a scholar with an interest in Myers-Briggs in relation to the psychological identity of students for placement in residence halls would not have a sustained interest in its use for the psychological identity of middle managers. The reader is likely to be pleased, however, that the tool has such value; it confirms its validity in the user's case. For the members of the inner circle, the electronic medium allows for an up-to-date perspective on each other's thinking, where the wrestling with a question or problem, a kind of agonistic trial, is so important. The constitutive value of a regulative perspective, as reflected in the interaction, has confirmatory significance.

It is not clear that the editor's role in the electronic medium would differ from the editor's role in the print medium. It is important to know what the inner circle is saying, and one might question whether the kind of peer review that operates in context 1 has much meaning for those who are the intellective leaders or translators, as opposed to the disciples. One must wonder whether the guru status of some of these leaders will continue when other members of the group challenge them, or is it if they do? I suspect that one of the critical issues here is the openness of the network, and I suspect that it is possible for access to be controlled to avoid "scholarship flaming," which might raise questions about the position of the intellective trustees. The electronic journal would make more evident the identities of the far-flung empire of adherents, the diaspora, which could affect the contest-like nature of alternatives that have similar potential for claiming loyalties ("Are you a Derridean or Lyotardian?").

Such journals are likely to engage much energy, given the deep affective nature of the commitments. Attending to these discussions may also affect the scholar's other pursuits, possibly in taking time from them or enervating the scholar's general condition and enhancing performance in other sectors. In any case, the electronic journal will be an asset in the continuing struggle for substantive hegemony. Electronic journals likely will strengthen the existing ties that bind, and the greater internal openness to sympathetic dialogue will also cause greater external isolation.

Context 3

Many scholars focus on problems or topics to which they bring disciplinary resources from one or more substantive bases. For example, one might study attrition in college and use Simmel's work on suicide to better appreciate the process of dropping out. Or one might examine the same topic from the vantage of multiculturalism, and so on. The work in this context assumes the primacy of issues to which scholars bring inventiveness in framing ways of understanding and possibly intervening. The electronic journal serving this context will likely focus on the topic or on the persons who examine issues in a specific location, such as the university or science. Such journals will display instances of the uses made by authors of different knowledge resources in dealing with concerns in the same social institution. Some print journals, such as the *Journal of Higher Education* and *Social Studies of Science,* have such an orientation now. Thus, one might ask how the electronic versions will differ or, in general, what they will mean.

As suggested for context 1, the electronic journal, which could make papers available after some sort of peer review, could entertain subscriptions that offer articles on demand, given that readers will have rather focused interests within the broad array of concerns within the boundaries of an area. Thus, the electronic journal might not support the serendipitous learning that a print journal allows, because in print journals variety is often built into the meaning of subscription. Another possibility is the spinning off of an electronic journal with a focused orientation, not unlike the discussion forums that are available today on the Internet. Were such a direction to be taken, I would envision a lessening of standards, given a higher commitment to an issue than would be the case in a general journal, which one might expect to reflect a higher standard of scholarship.

In the print medium, there is a "readerly" interest beyond that of topic. Scholars will be attracted to a paper because it touches on some of the substantive literatures of interest to them, and they then engage with a paper to learn of the knowledge bases' potential in extending to other topics. Thus, a reader might not be concerned with the potential for perspectives from political science to shed understanding on the treatment for malaria but would be concerned about the potential of political science to engage a policy issue of his or her own. The published paper essentially becomes a case study that has epistemological but not topical value. More focused reading, relating to subscription of papers on demand, would likely diminish this type of attention, given the cost in time and money that it would take for such awareness. It is currently more difficult to avoid the presentation of a broad array of work than would be the case in an electronic environment. This is all to say that there is likely to be a growing parochialism in context 3 work, associated with more focused attention and fewer instances of what now appears to be discussions of how different frames allow, comparatively, for different insights. Comments and replies that appear in context 3 journals often explore the advantages of various frames of analysis for a topic or issue (Silverman 1994). Readers can thus explore with the writer the attributes of constructing analyses along different lines of reasoning. More focused forums might not be as hospitable to such cosmopolitanism. This might lead to a growing inwardness, with attention to existing substantive solutions, as a retreat from the inventive or creative edges around which current treatments are distilled.

Context 4

This last academic context reflects the coming together of scholars who are attempting to develop an understanding of an area or issue, or to develop a way of engaging it. Some feminist literature is so situated. The association is based on a common interest in an area, an experience that persons jointly want to explore and make more formal, or a concern on how to symbolize a domain of attention. There develops a web of attention and a kind of intermingling, the development of holism or harmony that reflects a flowing energy.

Craige (1992, p. 99) discusses association based on cooperation and not domination, as best noted by the metaphor of *web*, the "whole of which is affected by the health of its parts." Brann (1992, p. 23) calls this a "spirit of letting be [that allows] what there is to emerge." This type of scholarly literature is the rarest of the possibilities suggested in this chapter; electronic journals are likely to enhance the construction of knowledge developed this way, although it will face difficulties in being sanctioned as knowledge by institutional peers, who will see it as too informal for evidence of scholars' productivity.

These discourse communities are more ephemeral than those in the other contexts, and although they can take advantage of existing technology through which individuals can respond to particular comments of others, such interaction will lack the fullness that accompanies face-to-face interaction, where emotive and nonverbal presence is more fully communicated. Discussions of work in this tradition are more attentive to the metaphor of hearing than that of vision (Levin 1988, p. 993), so the question is how traditional linear gaze-like vision directed toward the screen can reflect inner light, intuitions, and the development of substantively related friendships. From the perspective of vision, however, Levin (1988) compares the assertoric gaze—"narrow, dogmatic, intolerant, rigid, fixed, inflexible, and unmoved, . . . [issuing] from . . . an independent and assertive egobody" (p. 440) to an aletheic gaze: "The aletheic gaze is pluralistic, democratic: it tends to be inclusive, but in a way that does not deny or suppress the differences; and it understands the relationship between visibility and power. The gaze that moved aletheically is a gaze that cares" (p. 440). Scholarship developed in context 4 will evidence an aletheic gaze, as scholars react to one another in their explorations.

The editor or editorial collective is likely to be a maintainer of the special value orientation that makes this form of scholarly community different from all the others. For example, it would be anormative for those in such a community not to listen to each other in the development of ideas. Using such a community for the assertion of an independent observation without regard to the others would be tantamount to misconduct. The editor or collective would probably be chosen by peers on the basis of sensitivity to the development of community rather than the maintenance of standards, the repository of a point of view, possession of expertise, or multidisciplinary knowledge.

Context 4 communities will flourish in the electronic era. The ephemeral and flowing nature of their knowledge matches well the ease with which persons can join and leave the discussion forum. The major concern is the depth of engagement relating to visual versus aural interaction; the expanded electronic community likely will not have the intimacy of a community that publishes in traditional form the outcomes of its face-to-face considerations, but it will allow for greater inclusiveness.

Conclusion

Electronic journal publication will create and reflect different impacts depending on the academic communities with which this medium will interact. We need to reconstitute our understanding of the academic community, just as we need to appreciate the potential for a new approach to the dissemination of knowledge from and within these communities. The old identities and patterns will not do.

It is not appropriate to consider the impact of the electronic journal as either positive or negative. It will have more complex consequences in relation to various interests. It will reshape fundamentally how scholars interact with each other, and sustained inquiry will be needed to appreciate how these interactions change.

References

Anderson, Charles W. (1993). *Prescribing the Life of the Mind: An Essay on the Purpose of the University, the Aims of Liberal Education, and Competence of Citizens, and the Cultivation of Practical Reason.* Madison: University of Wisconsin Press.

Amann, K., and K. Knorr-Cetina. (1988). "The Fixation of (Visual) Evidence." *Human Studies* 11, nos. 2–3: 133–169.

Brann, Eva T. H. (1992). "Critical Reasoning and the Second Power of Questions: Towards First Questions and First Philosophy." In *Critical Reasoning in Contemporary Culture,* edited by Richard A. Talaska. Albany: State University of New York Press, pp. 299–331.

Burstyn, Joan N., ed. (1991). *Desktop Publishing in the University.* Syracuse: Syracuse University School of Education.

Craige, Betty Jean. (1992). *Laying the Ladder Down: The Emergence of Cultural Holism.* Amherst: University of Massachusetts Press.

Code, Lorraine. (1991). *What Can She Know? Feminist Theory and the Construction of Knowledge.* Ithaca: Cornell University Press.

Cummings, Anthony M., Marcia L. Witte, William G. Bowen, Laura O. Lazarus, and Richard H. Ekman, eds. (1992). *University Libraries and Scholarly Communication.* Washington, D C: Association of Research Libraries, for the Andrew W. Mellon Foundation.

Fleck, Ludwik. (1935). *Genesis and Development of a Scientific Fact.* Reprint, Chicago: University of Chicago Press, 1979.

Fuchs, Stephan. (1992). *The Professional Quest for Truth: A Social Theory of Science and Knowledge.* Albany: State University of New York Press.

Henson, Pamela M. (1993). "The Comstock Research School in Evolutionary Entomology." In *Research Schools: Historic Reappraisals,* edited by Gerald L. Geison and Frederic L. Holmes. *Osiris,* vol. 8. Chicago: University of Chicago Press, pp. 159–177.

Hull, David L. (1988). *Science as a Process: An Evolutionary Account of the Social and Conceptual Development of Science.* Chicago: University of Chicago Press.

Illich, Ivan. (1993). *In the Vineyard of the Text: A Commentary to Hugh's "Didascalicon."* Chicago: University of Chicago Press.

Johnson, Ralph H. (1992. "Critical Reasoning and Informal Logic." In *Critical Reasoning in Contemporary Culture,* edited by Richard A. Talaska. Albany: State University of New York Press, pp. 69–88.

Latour, Bruno. (1993). *We Have Never Been Modern.* Cambridge: Harvard University Press.

Levin, David Michael. (1988). *The Opening of Vision: Nihilism and the Postmodern Situation.* London: Routledge.

Levin, David Michael. (1993). "Decline and Fall: Ocularcentrism in Heidegger's Reading of the History of Metaphysics." In *Modernity and the Hegemony of Vision,* edited by David Michael Levin. Berkeley and Los Angeles: University of California Press, pp. 186–217.

Merton, Robert K. (1957). *Social Theory and Social Structure.* New York: Free Press.

Okerson, Ann, ed. (1993). *Visions and Opportunities in Electronic Publishing: Proceedings of the Second Symposium.* Washington, D.C.: Association of Research Libraries, Office of Scientific and Academic Publishing.

Romanyshyn, Robert D. (1993). "The Despotic Eye and Its Shadow: Media Image in the Age of Literacy." In *Modernity and the Hegemony of Vision,* edited by David Michael Levin. Berkeley and Los Angeles: University of California Press, pp. 339–360.

Sassower, Raphael. (1993). *Knowledge without Expertise: On the Status of Scientists.* Albany: State University of New York Press.

Silverman, Robert J. (1992). "Canonical Concepts: Origin, Development, Dissemination, Use: Their Construction and Maintenance." Manuscript.

Silverman, Robert J. (1993). "Contexts of Knowing: Their Shape and Substance," *Knowledge: Creation, Diffusion, Utilization* 14, no. 4: 372–385.

Silverman, Robert J. (1994). "Comments and Replies: Academic Conversations." Manuscript.

4

The Seminar, the Encyclopedia, and the Eco-Museum as Possible Future Forms of Electronic Publishing

Jean-Claude Guédon

In considering the advent of the electronic or digitized text, we must avoid two symmetrical pitfalls. On one hand, the belief that publishing texts electronically will simply offer good solutions to present problems without changing anything essential is naive at best. On the other hand, to claim that it is so radically different from all we have known as to be well-nigh unrecognizable is just as untenable. The question we face is both more difficult to solve and more interesting to contemplate: while taking into account the elements of continuity and change that are always present in history, how can we go beyond the simple listing of contrary characteristics and apprehend the unity of the familiar strangeness that electronic publishing is becoming? In other words, how can we hold together the elements of continuity and those of change in such a way that they merge into something both new and recognizable? Such are the stakes of this chapter.

The first pitfall results from the mistaken belief that the future relates to the present in the same way that a stretched rubber band relates to its unstretched past. In the case of print, this would be true only if it bore no relevant relation to the textual meaning that it helps materialize. In other words, it would be true only if print amounted to nothing more than pure function. It would be true only if medium and message were radically separated—an amusing reversal of the provocative thesis made famous by Marshall McLuhan.

In this perspective, a number of points are generally made about electronic publishing that do support its superiority over print: for example, electronic texts are easier to produce, and they are cheaper to obtain. They can be distributed more quickly, in fact almost instantaneously, and they can be reused within other texts with almost miraculous facility. Also, it is possible to include images, sound, and even animated sequences.

Electronic texts can be searched word by word, or even by character strings with wild cards and Boolean operators. All of these arguments seem to point in one direction—that electronic publishing offers great functional improvements to the print world, and nothing else.

In the wake of political sloganeering or commercial hype, advocacy of electronic publishing sometimes takes on more strident tones. According to some, nothing less than a full revolution is taking place among humans, one that may dwarf anything we have seen so far. Cyberspace and global networks, in this perspective, are the signs of profound upheavals that promise to catapult humanity to some unprecedented level. The information highway in this vision is the obvious path to greater everything: happiness, culture, economic activity, and so on.

Somewhat paradoxically perhaps, the far more sober and quieter words used by those ill at ease with electronic publishing may provide better points of entry into the nature of what we face. For example, when people argue that they prefer reading on paper to reading on screen, they implicitly refer to an ergonomic success that will not be displaced easily. The printed type, enhanced as it is by typographic art, allied to good quality, proves to be difficult to beat in terms of ease of use and portability. Likewise, when people express skepticism with regard to electronic publications, they often do a good deal more than merely display a general resistance to all forms of change. They reflect a malaise that, lucidly or not, reacts to what might be termed the second-order effects of electronic publishing. By second-order effects, I mean indirect and somewhat unpredictable consequences that electronic publishing might introduce into the research process. People worry, for example, about integrity and durability of e-texts, about access and usability, about legitimacy, about copyright and authors, and, finally, about the economics of the new medium.

Electronic publishing, while developing its own specificities, will be neither the simple and functional extension of print, nor a completely alien, quasi-incomprehensible, or miraculous entity. Neither "same" nor "other," to use terms that are fashionable in some circles. Rather, electronic publishing will be the seat of rich but largely unpredictable potentialities while retaining nonetheless a strong resemblance to elements of the past. Revolutionary evolutions or evolutionary revolutions are oxymorons that we could play with to approach this problem. In other words, we can trust history to remain gently radical as electronic publishing increasingly makes its presence felt within the research system.

Most people involved with electronic publishing are too preoccupied with countless small practical problems to reflect on the big picture. At this time, electronic publishing experiments are in most cases just trying to survive. As a result, the broad view is often missing. At the same time, the wide perspective must stay close to a many-faceted complex reality that will not budge easily or any which way.

The efforts spent on building a broad view are not wasted. Historical and sociological concepts that are not necessarily close at hand, however, are needed to approach the transition to electronic publishing. In particular, knowledge about the history of printing, publishing, and editing, their sources and their consequences, can help us apprehend the rich combination of direct and indirect factors at work in the present situation. From such an example, a better understanding of what is happening today, one that can give us a better sighting on the targets we hope to reach, is made possible.

This said, we do not have to feel that we are the toys of technological determinism and that its consequences are either marvelous or calamitous; neither do I suggest that we can control our destinies so well that a perfect design of the future is possible. The best we can do is to decide where we wish to go, and then we must do all we can to try and reach that goal, knowing full well that many eddies and whirlpools will unexpectedly deflect our trajectory, sometimes temporarily, sometimes in a more definitive fashion.[1]

Ultimately, electronic publishing touches on processes of human communication at deep levels. As the essence of being human is largely constructed through the modalities of communication available to us, the issues we are facing here are both difficult and crucial.

Some Lessons from History

Let us begin with an example drawn from the development of the printed periodical, its extension out of the political sphere to that of learning, and its hidden links with the rise of disciplines as the basis for the classification of knowledge. As I have already developed this example in another paper (Guédon, forthcoming) I will limit myself here to a summary.
1. The establishment of a reliable mail system across the various courts of Europe led to nondiplomatic correspondence among a number of civil servants who also viewed themselves as men of letters. In effect, this diplomatic service quickly and spontaneously mutated into a communication

device that had expanded well beyond its original design. In so doing, it displayed a trend that often recurred throughout history; namely, the strong tendency for an information system or restricted communication system to evolve into a fuller communication network.[2] (This tendency is constantly ignored, denied, or resisted by designers of new systems, as examples drawn from the history of the telephone, videotext, and now the electronic network amply demonstrate.)[3]

2. The regular increase in intellectual news being transmitted through the limited postal services was gradually accompanied by comments, evaluations, and judgments that evolved into a full critical mode of expression over the course of a century and a half.

3. As the size of the intellectual market, so to speak, increased, a greater division of labor followed, as is the case in the classical economic market. It became easier to distinguish between those producing new ideas, those writing comments and judgments, and those making sure that all these ideas were circulating correctly. Among the third group, a few came to be extremely important elements of a communication infrastructure that had not yet been identified as such. Marin Mersenne immediately comes to mind, but the Minim Father is but one example among many.

4. The Mersennes, Oldenburgs, Peirescs, *et tutti quanti,* were the crucial dispatchers of news across a system that had come to be known as the Republic of Letters, but they gradually had to acknowledge that they could not keep up with the increasing production of materials that their own letter-writing ability had stimulated. In modern parlance, the Republic of Letters was facing a severe bandwidth problem. The dispatchers, despite personal displays of epistolary prowesses that were nothing short of phenomenal, just could not write enough letters to fulfill all the needs. Clearly, new solutions had to be found if the Republic of Letters was not to collapse under its own weight.

5. The solution came in the form of a paradoxical use of printing. Printing had been designed not only to grant wider diffusion to selected documents, such as the Bible, but also to enhance their material permanence. The storing and managing of ever-greater quantities of printed books had transformed libraries and the skills associated with them, but one of their functions was essentially unchanged; namely, preservation. Conversely, librarians knew that a text selected by them would enjoy a durability that it could not hope to achieve otherwise. In this perspective, printing was a preselection process in the task of preserving literate culture.

The paradox is that printing was suddenly used also to diffuse transitory materials—to spread news that was destined to age quickly. The move appears simple now because we live in a society awash with periodicals of all kinds and because we are accustomed to consuming news in a variety of media, starting with print. In the late sixteenth and early seventeenth centuries, however, this was anything but natural. In fact, it required dissociating the act of diffusion from the act of preservation, although the two had come to be closely linked through the early history of printing. It also required moving from the privacy of a letter to the public exposure of print. Finally, it unwittingly extended the privilege of preservation to texts that had not been expected to survive the moment. Even more surprising was the added legitimacy that these kinds of texts gained by being printed. Printing news changed its nature: it became part of an archive instead of being an information tool, and because of that, news grew to function like a kind of intellectual jurisprudence.

From then on, the intellectual life of communities and countries was stalked, so to speak, by their own archives, and again this induced new consequences. In particular, it favored the quest for new forms of newness. Instead of factual *curiosa*, which tended to equate newness with rarity, a whole civilization learned to gauge originality against the backdrop of a growing historical archive. Rules were stated that could help identify genuine invention or discovery. Priority disputes could begin in earnest. Progress could be measured.

The application of print to pieces of news led to the invention of the periodical. In the course of the seventeenth century, it quickly moved beyond political matters to intellectual—in particular, literary and scientific—news. The extension of the periodical's territory to cultural domains corresponds to the growing role of the intellectual jurisprudence.

Learned journals became an important reality in 1665 when the *Journal des sçavans* appeared in France, quickly followed by the *Transactions of the Royal Society of London* in the same year. Germany and Italy, and then the rest of Europe, followed suit.

6. The transition from private, social correspondence to printed, learned journals strongly specified, identified, and promoted the most critical forms of discourse. In effect, this transition amounted to archiving and giving public legitimacy to a parallel discursive universe that turned out to be that of criticism, again with incalculable consequences.

7. Print, in itself, had already raised the question of the "right" text (the one that deserved to be printed and correspondingly deserved the investment in time and money to undergo metamorphosis). The "hardening"

of texts corresponding to their transformation into a commercial object—the printed book—had also given a new importance and urgency to the question of authorship that, until the advent of print, had been treated in a lighter fashion. Piracy and plagiarism had little meaning in a manuscript culture, but they became of primary concern with the growth of a print culture, not only because of the economic benefits that could be reaped from the printed book but also in terms of responsibility. Diderot, after all, did visit Vincennes' prison a little longer than he wished to, on account of his writings, and Voltaire, after his exile in Britain, cultivated an intimate knowledge of border cultures when he bought land at Ferney, ready to slip out of the French kingdom into Switzerland at the first sign of danger. Authorship, wealth, fame, and risks all came together and, to this day, have remained strongly intertwined through print, as Salman Rushdie could easily testify.

8. The trend toward an enhanced, more visible status for authors quickly transferred to the periodicals, so that critical discourses and metadiscourses also became part of a generalized authorial system.

9. The shift in emphasis from object (of a text) to author that was concomitant with the appearance of print and its evolution eventually resulted in a reorganization of knowledge units. Whereas discourses of old, since ancient Greece, had found their principle of unity in categories that had the trappings of universality or objectivity, those authored under the print system tended to organize themselves very strongly around foci of interests or collections of particular concerns. Instead of general, philosophical systems, specific domains and forms of philosophy started to emerge. A few examples illustrate this crucial and yet complex point.

New domains started being specified to the point where they began to challenge the traditional, globalizing schemes. For example, late-eighteenth-century chemistry challenged the mechanistic and, more precisely, the Newtonian, overarching system that dominated much of natural philosophy at the time.

New ways to organize and present knowledge enjoyed an unprecedented importance after 1750. Among those, the encyclopedic and dictionary forms were particularly visible. Chambers's *Cyclopædia* in Britain and Diderot's *Encyclopédie* in France are but two famous examples of the dictionary genre that grew by leaps and bounds in the second half of the eighteenth century. In Diderot's *Encyclopédie* particularly, the dual presentation scheme—relying on the alphabetical order so dear to dictionaries, on the one hand, and on cross-references, allowing jumps from one article to another, on the other hand—led to the design of a kind of hypertextual prototype that essentially remained unsurpassed until its computer-driven counterpart started to emerge a few years ago.

These trends were accompanied by the rise of specialized journals that started fulfilling original roles: instead of acting as a stable repository of fixed knowledge, they gradually became the evolving reference against which one could check any claim to novelty, invention, or discovery. Citing carefully and accurately became decisive skills, both as modes of expression in this new genre and as a way to position oneself with regard to competing authors. Thus emerged a new kind of virtual space that Pierre Bourdieu, much later, would conceptualize as a field (Bourdieu 1975). The structured aggregation of texts through specialties and citations gave material form to a kind of battlefield where all compete against all for recognition. The printed page in effect grew to become the arena where intellectual debates could unfold permanently and forever.

Correlatively, the printed publication of specialized forms of knowledge—and here again, chemistry historically played a crucial role—strongly contributed to challenge the established forms of knowledge ordering. In particular, natural philosophy gradually fragmented into various forms of special domains that ended up evolving into disciplines in the course of the nineteenth century.

10. Disciplines found their original anchor in a variety of sites. The constitution of "classes" within the Royal Academy of Sciences in Paris, as a result of the 1699 reform of that institution, was a portent of things to come. But more important, these classes became the stable loci of discussions that could last for years. The printed publication of the papers read at the academy strongly reinforced the identity of the classes by associating them with public topics of disagreement. Paradoxically, these did not act as dividing forces; instead, they became the defining principles of flexible intellectual territories that were viewed no longer as the stable repository of eternal truths but rather as permanent dueling courts.[4] The history of a class, rather than its objects, became its defining principle, and nothing could materialize that history better than the printed *Histoire* and *Mémoires* of the academy. With the passing of time, classes were reinforced through a memorialized history. Correlatively, they became harder to define as predicates became less effective at capturing the essence of their evolving nature.

This shift from a static, content-oriented, reference-based definition of a specialty to a dynamic debate scrupulously recorded and published can be seen as the condition of possibility, as epistemologists would be wont to say, of the yet-to-be and still undefined discipline. That condition of possibility was strengthened when, at the end of the eighteenth century, Lavoisier founded the *Journal de chymie*. What is interesting in Lavoisier's creation—a creation ultimately as crucial to the chemical revolution as was his conceptualizing of oxygen as a (weighty) substitute for phlogiston[5]—is that the new chemistry could function and develop on the basis of conditionally valid concepts and contentious projects that had little or nothing to do with physics, and in particular nothing to do with Newtonian mechanics.

Lavoisier was neither hostile to Newton nor interested in subsuming chemistry under the overarching Newtonian conception of universal attraction applied to particulate matter. Lavoisier and his chemistry *were,* and the publication of his *Journal de chymie* simply marks this position. In other words, the foundation of knowledge and the principles of its organization had been completely overturned and a kind of discursive space had been created, allowing for the emergence of new configurations of knowledge that could evolve in new ways. Disciplines as such had not yet acquired their name, status, and legitimacy as the basic building blocks of modern knowledge, but, with Lavoisier's chemistry, they were well on their way to full social existence. Knowledge, henceforth, was to be looked on more like disconnected spots of light on an otherwise dark piece of land (a figure Diderot actually used in his own reflections on knowledge[6]) with uneasy passages from one to the next, than as some general, gigantic architectural whole that would be characterized by its harmony, coherence, universality, and deductive potential, as well as by other principles that had variously inhabited many systems of natural philosophy across the centuries.

The important point in this story is that one of the major and, in fact, indispensable moments leading to the creation of chemistry as a discipline (and not as an art, or as a subset of mechanics) was the foundation of a printed periodical, a learned journal. The advent of disciplines would not have been possible without the presence of printed periodicals.[7] In the limited compass of a journal article, one does not attempt to reconstruct the whole universe; rather, one is satisfied with carefully and modestly building on (or tearing down) a previous, similarly limited assertion. Once more, the model of legal jurisprudence comes to mind and clears the way for an intellectual activity where the article-length text, not the book, becomes the valued form of communication.

The second lesson to be drawn from this exceedingly brief sketch of events is that no one at the time of Gutenberg could have imagined that introducing movable types and the printing press would lead to their being used to industrialize a process of communication, thus laying the foundation for a major shift in the organization of knowledge and ultimately in its very meaning.

The third and most troubling lesson is that similar processes are probably at work at present with the introduction of digitized materials and their electronic diffusion throughout the planet.

Probing the Prospects: Where Are We Heading and Where Do We Want to Go?

Although peering into the past does not give us the ability to penetrate the fogs separating the present from the future, it has nevertheless provided some sense of what we should watch for. In particular, history seems to teach us one constant lesson; namely, that people are quite skillful at inventing unexpected ways to take advantage of new technologies. We should thus be on the lookout for uses that may be emerging right now as electronic publishing is starting to be used. At the same time, we must expect that these innovations will often appear under familiar but slightly displaced labels, making the task of identifying them all the more difficult. Finally, we should begin to think about which innovations are desirable.

The greatest paradox of printed scholarly journals is that they act more like archival and legitimizing tools than like communication tools. Print technology implies long publication delays. These are induced by the batch production pattern that characterizes this mode of publication, and they also result from budgetary constraints that limit the number of pages that can be printed each year. The main consequence is that the communication function of journals has essentially broken down. As a result, invisible colleges resort to a matrix of tools responding to the various needs for informal communication.[8] Meanwhile, print acts like a form of official sanction needed after the fact to guarantee the good value of the bits of information exchanged by mail, telephone, face-to-face communication, e-mail, or preprints. For promotional purposes, for prizes, for grant awards, for teaching purposes, the printed record remains crucial, but for the day-to-day workings of the laboratory, once the retrospective bibliographic search has been covered, it is of relatively little importance. Similar circumstances prevail in the social sciences and the humanities. More than anything else, printing a scholarly text amounts to the monumentalized representation of an activity already located in the past.

Electronic publishing is often credited with the ability to reestablish the communicative purposes of scholarly publications without losing their archival or legitimizing roles.[9] But much more than this can be envisioned, and this is where we may begin to search for possible new uses of this medium.

Because the cost of storing electronic documents is minuscule compared to that of printing, a number of factors may combine to favor the publication of far more details than is presently the case. The need to write in an extremely condensed style thus will decrease, and papers may soon display a more leisurely approach to their subject, as they used to do in the nineteenth century, for example.

But let us go one step further. In the case of experimental science, the full set of experimental data as recorded in the laboratory could easily be appended to the published interpretation. Such a practice could strongly reduce the risks of scientific frauds, a not insignificant concern nowadays. But on a more positive note, it would also permit anyone with the right competence to try his or her own interpretive effort. In this manner, scientists that do not have access to costly equipment could find ways to participate usefully in worldwide research at the highest level. This would represent a marked improvement to the present working conditions of many scientists in developing countries. It would also create all sorts of new possibilities for the training of advanced students, even in rich countries.

This change in publishing practice would make feasible a more thorough and varied exploitation of the results produced in any given laboratory, as several heads or teams could pore over the same data and come up with differing hypotheses, questions, and, in some cases, criticisms. In other words, the inventive processes of scientific research would be enhanced. At the same time, the greater ease of developing alternative interpretive tasks applied to common data sets would certainly favor a higher level of discussions and even controversies. In short, slightly changing a few publication parameters might well strengthen the flow of communications within and across various scientific communities.

Other factors can be expected to work in favor of an increased role for communication among researchers. For one thing, the greater efficiency of electronic publishing compared to print means that the pace of publication can keep up much more closely with that of actual research activities (see Harnad 1990, pp. 342–343). As a result, electronic publications can become an integral part of ongoing research to a much greater extent than is presently the case. Much of what presently belongs to the semiconfidential communication flow typical of any given invisible college, in all likelihood, will materialize into a quite visible discussion forum.

If we grant some degree of plausibility to the hypotheses just stated, discussions among peers will probably take on an importance of such proportions that they will begin to take precedence over publishing per se. At the very least, publishing and communicating will begin to converge to an unprecedented extent. The specific publication phase will begin to act as a sort of stepping stone leading to higher plateaus, a kind of intellectual stocktaking periodically needed to advance to new developments (through further discussions) with concepts relatively well cleaned up and data fully verified. But simultaneously, publication may begin to appear as a way to broadcast the news from a particular discussion group to all other research communities. This possibility is intriguing because, in effect, it reverses the functional priorities of the present objectives of scholarly publishing. In other words, electronic publishing might very well favor interdisciplinary or interspecialty communication, which is hardly the case nowadays.

With electronic publishing, the batch production of knowledge will eventually give way to a flow production of results and interpretations inside the discussion groups. Whatever may remain of batch publishing will take the form of periodic syntheses similar in function to scientific treatises or state-of-the-art articles that regularly recur as part of the communication system of research. The role of this form of publishing will be mainly to allow any given community to regain better control over its own intellectual bearings, while granting it a degree of visibility from the standpoint of wider circles of scientists.

In a separate study (Guédon 1994) I have used the word *seminar* as a way to portray these new trends in recognizable terms, and as a metaphor to convey the potential impact of electronic publishing on the workings of the research system. Indeed, a global, constantly active seminar allowing dozens of specialist to tune in constantly to the best peers and the best laboratories of the planet would certainly be appealing, and it would certainly make ideas, concepts, and theories move a good deal faster than the slow, jerky process of putting small, discrete articles inside slightly larger packages called *journal issues*. A greater synergy of minds and resources would certainly ensue.

At the same time, envisioning the seminar as the fundamental form of scholarly communication within electronic media does not mean abandoning the ability of research communities to establish a ranking order and degrees of visibility for the individuals involved in research. Quite the contrary. The present system of peer-review evaluation serves the print world well and amounts to a process of co-optation in the scholarly author category. Similar processes of self-selection could begin to limit the access to a given seminar. As a result, the peer-review process currently at work in print journals would find itself smoothly transposed into the new environment of the electronic virtual seminar (see Harnad, this volume).

Other comparisons can be adduced to help us grasp some of the potential implications of an electronic publishing system for the research community. For example, if we move beyond the level of a particular specialty while paying particular attention to the stocktaking phase of its publishing pattern, it is easy to note that it acts like a node within a gigantic network made of similar, yet equally evolving, specialties. And the very thought of this network quickly connotes a huge, dynamic encyclopedia growing from every corner of the planet to push back the extreme reaches of knowledge.

This vision of seminars addressing each other beyond their own borders evokes the cross-reference device that Diderot had implanted inside his famous *Encyclopédie* in the eighteenth century. Diderot was quite concerned with two objectives that appeared somewhat incompatible at first sight. On one hand, faithful to the original meaning of the word *encyclopedia*, the *Philosophe* wanted to make manifest the overall oneness of all knowledge, its ability to fit within one huge circle of learning. On the other hand, he was far too skeptical of systems and far too aware of the incompleteness of human knowledge to accept the forcing of what knowledge was available at his time into a system. To integrate these contrary requirements without reducing one to the other, he designed the *Encyclopédie* with a dual structure that exhibited their creative tension. First, he relied on alphabetical ordering and, in this fashion, endowed the *Encyclopédie* with a connotation of exhaustive systematicity. But he immediately proceeded to nuance this message by introducing *renvois* (cross-references), allowing the reader to jump efficiently from one entry to another. This double organization made the *Encyclopédie* a clever prototype of modern hypertexts. It allowed Diderot to introduce modes of reading that could never have existed otherwise. Although it enabled readers to broaden and deepen their understanding of a given topic, these modes were also specifically designed to induce *trouble*, that is, a degree of confusion, on occasions. Presumably, Diderot saw in this unorthodox use of cross-references a tool to teach a healthy degree of skepticism.[10] To use a more modern vocabulary borrowed from Bakhtin, Diderot implemented a profoundly dialogic or polyphonic notion of discourse. The total effect could only be more intense discussions.

The possible development of virtual seminars as the primary cells of scholarly research, particularly in the sciences, coupled with the periodic electronic publication of temporary syntheses emerging from research and communication activities, could indeed fit within an overarching, hypertextual network. Its internal links would constantly multiply and crisscross the intellectual landscape in ways that are almost unimaginable nowadays, accustomed as we are to the well-ordered structure of the disciplines and their specialties marching side-by-side as if on parade. A kind of living encyclopedia would progressively come to the fore, one where distinctions between teaching and research, as well as distinctions between domains and disciplines, would probably be deeply redefined. The limits of the encyclopedia would then become the shifting and moving limits of knowledge itself, and all involved with knowledge, be it teaching, learning, or researching, would envision their work as intellectual moves within the abstract, multidimensional space corresponding to a humanity-wide hypertext. Publishing would lose its function of re-presentation to become an integral, immediate dimension of the dynamics of human knowledge at large.

Earlier on, I mentioned that electronic publishing would in effect make the invisible college come to light to the point of acquiring visibility in itself. This suggests another interesting image with which to apprehend some of the potential transformations that could follow the generalized use of electronic publishing. It comes from museum studies and has to do with a particular movement within museum science, called eco-museums.

Eco-museums start from the premise that, on a given territory, any given individual is little more than a kind of Leibnizian monad in the sense that, through particular location, specific activities, social background, and other factors, that individual acquires both a specific and incomplete vision of the territory. *Territory* should be taken here both as a significant tract of land such as a city or a region and as all the human activities and dynamics that are alive on it. With this basic idea in mind, some museum specialists have imagined that a good objective for any such institution would be to broaden the viewpoint of each social monad, in other words, of each individual on the territory. This results in a particular museum strategy that aims at displaying to certain segments of the population elements of their territory that they never or rarely meet in their usual manner of living. The industrial worker may have but a very faint idea of the way a farmer lives, for example, and a farmer may not understand how journalists do their job, and so on. In other words, the territory crisscrosses itself along a multiplicity of perspectives, each of which corresponds to the interrogation of a particular group addressed to another. Everyone simultaneously becomes an ethnologist and an object of ethnological study. The territory thus displays itself to itself, but always according to some particular angle, some viewpoint that is often unknown or neglected by people who are not directly affected by the activity or status founding that particular gaze.

The advent of the virtual seminar may well foster the rise of eco-museums of knowledge. At any rate, the fragmentation and isolation of numerous domains of knowledge would certainly be relieved to some extent if an analogue of the eco-museum structure were to emerge within the virtual space of electronic publishing. And this structure should appear fairly easily, as the hypertextual links of the global encyclopedia could play that role. If, when I read some piece of information, some links invite me to jump to a completely different, perhaps unexpected, domain, I may discover a new perspective that not only enriches my vision of the whole but also deeply influences the way in which I see the local problems of my own specialty. Interdisciplinarity would become the dominant theme in such a context.

The development just sketched could lead to redefining the popularization of knowledge. At present, we are faced by a somewhat Manichean situation: either a text acts as a vehicle for dissemination of research results to other researchers, or it popularizes research results for a wider audience. The point that is rarely considered, however, even though a magazine like *Scientific American* takes full advantage of it, is that specialists reading outside their own domain often need a popularized version to find their way around an unknown field. There is thus no sharp dichotomy between a classical research paper and a piece of popularization, only a difference in degree. What makes the distinction appear so clearly at the present time is that many of these degrees are not exploited. Yet the example of *Scientific American,* given the high level of scientific culture required to read it fruitfully, shows that scientists can address other scientists across domain boundaries. In effect, *Scientific American* is a limited example of what intellectual eco-museums could do across the whole intellectual landscape.

The combination of an encyclopedic structure based on the notion of hypertext and with the notion of intellectual eco-museum as a way to prod people out of a complacency based on limiting themselves to familiar surroundings will probably lead to the demotion of disciplinary structures while reviving the possibility of connecting the particular with the general and the global. At the same time, this possible evolution of our research system will not signal that some unspoken search for global systems is again at large. Instead, it will point to the growing need for easier ways to change the scale in viewpoints if one wants to go beyond routine or repetitive questions.

In the vision that emerges out of the triad constituted by the seminar, the encyclopedia, and the eco-museum, the way in which the production, reproduction, and acquisition of knowledge are currently organized appears clumsy and inefficient. It even appears counterproductive in parts. What is worse, it discriminates against poor countries. If the advent of electronic publishing were to achieve nothing more than to stimulate us to think about these questions, it would already have a point in its favor. But it is quite probable that some of these changes, or similarly profound ones, are actually beginning to take place, so we must think about their implications and desirability.

Conclusion

Further down the road, deeper changes can be envisioned. For example, the notion of a global, extended seminar could also be interpreted as an enlarged symbolic market, so to speak. But if a symbolic market works at all like the market of classical political economy, enlarging it also means increasing its potential for a finer division of labor. In effect, the creation of more intense, more complete means of communication among scientists and scholars may well favor the development of various tasks that would begin to look like what Francis Bacon described in his *New Atlantis* (1969):

For the several employments and offices of our fellows, we have twelve that sail into foreign countries . . . , who bring us the books and abstracts, and patterns of experiments of all other parts. These we call Merchants of Light.

We have three that collect the experiments which are in all books. These we call Depredators.

We have three that collect the experiments of all mechanical arts, and also of liberal sciences, and also of practises which are not brought into arts. These we call Mystery-men.

We have three that try new experiments, such as themselves think good. These we call Pioneers or Miners.

We have three that draw the experiments of the former four into titles and tables, to give the better light for the drawing of observations and axioms out of them. These we call Compilers. (pp. 296–297)

The list continues in similar tone with various other distinctive tasks that, together, work like some kind of production chain slowly elaborating raw materials into more complex and refined products.

It is not that Francis Bacon should, once again, become the model that he was to some in the eighteenth century. Rather, Bacon can act as a reminder that our present scientific and scholarly enterprises, and their social and intellectual forms of organization, are neither necessary nor permanent. With the advent of new communication tools, new modes of organization and new divisions of labor will probably emerge.

Conversely, there is nothing fundamentally deterministic in the possibilities that have been mentioned so far in this chapter. Electronic publishing may induce some of the changes suggested here, but it may not. Indeed, uncertainty remains, if only because the forces set in motion also induce reactions or forms of resistance. Simple technical advantage is certainly not sufficient to ensure change, especially when social choices or cultural patterns are involved. The main factor working against change is that it threatens to modify the dynamics of research in ways that may not look terribly appealing to some. Visibility, prestige, power, and even financial rewards are also of the essence in the research system, however much it may be transposed, disguised, and symbolically sublimated.

As an example of this, let us look briefly at the reward system of scientific research. Presently, it translates into visibility, and it is based on the publications of individuals who appear as authors. By contrast, the seminar system sketched earlier would probably transform the reward system by linking it primarily to groups rather than to individuals. How would the concept of authorship resist a form of production where fame would be tied to a collective subject, rather than an individual one? To be sure, a kind of group authorship has become common in scientific research, as many articles are routinely signed by many people. Such a trend could certainly ease the path to the kind of transformation envisioned here, but the fact remains that, presently, the individual takes priority over the collective for institutional matter. In fact, this is the reason behind the multiplication of authors. No research team has yet come up for tenure (even though individual promotion is certainly affected by the quality of one's research team). The trends set in motion by the advent of electronic publishing can thus raise questions that are difficult to solve because they imply changes in the ethos familiar to scientific communities.

Modifying a culture is far more difficult than innovating with technology. At any rate, the advent of electronic publishing offers a marvelous opportunity to reexamine some of the latent assumptions of the present research system. In particular, it constantly reminds us that a number of discrete entities—such as the author/reader dichotomy, separate journal issues bundling several articles together, disciplinary and specialty structures, the oppositions between communicating, transferring, and popularizing research results, and so on—may well be nothing more than artifacts of print technology. It may also be that electronic publishing will gradually challenge all these assumptions, with incalculable effects on the intellectual life of the future.

Needless to say, such stakes are much too high to treat them with benign neglect and let a new system of research arise any which way. We need to study and debate these issues a great deal more in these formative years of the new system. Only in this way may we hope to have the tools needed to begin identifying possible objectives and to chart a course that stands a chance to respect the common good.

Notes

1. Defining the kind of society we want and doing all we can to steer our present society in that direction is what is at stake in "prospective studies" and what allows us to distinguish them from "future studies." Future studies tend to rely on some kind of determinism, such as technological determinism, and thus

are far more fatalistic in tone (even if it be an optimistic kind of fatalism). They tend to be far more simplistic than prospective studies.

2. From the telephone to Minitel, this trend is easily perceived. It has been systematically traced in Foulger 1990.

3. From my firsthand experience with Bell Canada's attempt to deploy Alex, a videotex system that imitated the French Minitel with a different norm, it became clear that the telephone company, despite its primary role as a communication industry (or perhaps because of it), had a great deal of trouble seriously considering that a videotext system could be a real communication device.

4. A good example of these debates is the long and acrimonious controversy that opposed Louis Lemery (Nicolas's son) and E.-F. Geoffroy in the first half of the eighteenth century.

5. My point is that Lavoisier challenged many theories, introduced quite a few new ones, and turned out to be partially right and partially wrong. His real contribution, however, lies precisely in this quasi-political approach to knowledge—one characterized by the control of the dynamics of the domain, rather than the building from stable fundamentals. His very reworking of the concept of elements is a good example of this shift. By linking elemental existence to the operational limits of the experimentalist (an element is what I cannot decompose in the lab), Lavoisier transformed essence into consensus building through a kind of experimental rhetoric.

6. Diderot writes, "Je me représente la vaste enceinte des sciences comme un grand terrain parsemé de places obscures et de places éclairées. Nos travaux doivent avoir pour but, ou d'étendre les limites des places éclairées, ou de multiplier sur le terrain les centres de lumière. L'un appartient au génie qui crée; l'autre à la sagacité qui perfectionne" (Diderot 1964, p. 189).

7. In related fashion, the well-known Enlightenment opposition between "esprit de système" and "esprit systématique" certainly underscores the growing importance of critical tools, of well-conducted debates, against the older notion of a complete, ambitious, all-encompassing scheme, as exemplified by first Aristotle and then Descartes (or Newton, who, from this perspective, looks Descartes-like).

8. For the concept of invisible colleges in the sociology of science, see Crane 1972.

9. I have broached this point on several occasions, particularly in Guédon 1994.

10. I have discussed this question at greater length in an older article (Guédon 1984).

References

Bacon, Francis. (1969). *New Atlantis*. London: Oxford University Press.

Bourdieu, Pierre. (1975). "La spécificité du champ scientifique et les conditions sociales du progrès de la raison." *Sociologie et société* 7, no. 1 (May): 91–117.

Crane, Diana. (1972). *Invisible Colleges: Diffusion of Knowledge in Scientific Communities.* Chicago: University of Chicago Press.

Diderot, O. (1964). "De l'interprétation de la nature." In *Oeuvres philosphiques,* edited by P. Vernières. Paris: Garnier.

Foulger, Davis A. (1990). "Medium as Process: The Structure, Use and Practice of Computer Conferencing on IBM's IBMPC Computer Conferencing Facility," Ph.D. diss., Temple University.

Guédon, Jean-Claude. (1984). "Lecture encyclopédique de Jacques le fataliste: Pour une épistémologie du trouble." *Stanford French Review* 8, nos. 2–3 (Fall): 335–347.

Guédon, Jean-Claude. (Forthcoming). "Electronic Publishing of Academic Journals and the Structure of Research Results." In *Computer Networking and Scholarship in the 21st Century University,* edited by Teresa Harrison and Tim Stephen. Albany: State University of New York Press.

Guédon, Jean-Claude. (1994). "Irruption des périodiques électroniques savantes" [sic]. *University Affairs/Affaires universitaires* (May): 12–13.

Harnad, Stevan. (1990). "Scholarly Skywriting and the Prepublication Continuum of Scientific Inquiry." *Psychological Science* 1: 342–343.

Harnad, Stevan. (This volume). "Implementing Peer Review on the Net: Scientific Quality Control in Scholarly Electronic Journals."

5

Tragic Loss or Good Riddance? The Impending Demise of Traditional Scholarly Journals

Andrew M. Odlyzko

Traditional printed journals are a comfortable and familiar aspect of scholarly work. They have been the primary means of communicating research results and, as such, have performed an invaluable service. They are, however, an awkward artifact, though a highly developed one, of the only technology available over the last few centuries for large-scale communication. The growth of the scholarly literature, together with the rapidly increasing power and availability of electronic technology, is creating tremendous pressures for change. The purpose of this chapter is to give a broad picture of these pressures and to argue that the coming changes may be abrupt.

It is often thought that changes will be incremental, with perhaps a few electronic journals appearing and further use of e-mail, FTP, and so on. My guess is that change will be far more drastic. Traditional scholarly journals will likely disappear within 10 to 20 years, and the electronic alternatives will be different from current periodicals, even though they may carry the same titles. There are obvious dangers in discontinuous change away from a system that has served the scholarly community well (Quinn 1995). I am convinced, however, that future systems of communication will be much better than traditional journals.

An earlier version of this chapter appeared in *Notices of the American Mathematical Society* 42 (January 1995): 49–53. A longer version, with more data and detailed arguments, appears in the *International Journal of Human-Computer Studies* (formerly *International Journal of Man-Machine Studies*) 42 (1995): 71-122. A preprint can be obtained via e-mail by sending the message "send tragic.loss.txt from att/math/odlyzko" (for the ASCII version) or "send tragic.loss.long.ps from att/math/odlyzko" (for the PostScript version) to netlib@research.att.com. If your mailer cannot handle large files, include in your message the line "mailsize 40k," if you wish the revision to be sent in chunks of at most 40KB, say.

Although the transition may be painful, it promises a substantial increase in the effectiveness of scholarly work. This promise is especially likely to be realized if we are aware of the issues, and plan the evolution away from the present system as early as possible. In any event, we do not have much choice, as drastic change is inevitable no matter what our preferences are.

Predictions and comments in this chapter apply to most scholarly disciplines. I write primarily about mathematics, however, because I am most familiar with that field and the data that I have are clearest for it. Different areas have different needs and cultures, and their communications are likely to evolve somewhat differently.

The Growth of Literature

The impending changes in scholarly publications are caused by the confluence of two trends. One is the growth of scholarly literature, and the other is the growth of electronic technology.

The number of scientific papers published annually has been doubling every 10 to 15 years for the last two centuries (Price 1956). This is also true in mathematics alone. In 1870 only about 840 papers were published in mathematics. Today, about 50,000 papers are published annually. The growth was not even, and a more careful look at the statistics shows that from the end of World War II until 1990 the number of papers published doubled about every 10 years (*Mathematical Reviews,* 1990). Growth has since stopped, but this is likely to be one of the temporary pauses that have occurred before.

The exponential growth in mathematical publishing has interesting implications. By adding up the numbers in *Mathematical Reviews* (1990) or simply by extrapolating from the current figure of about 50,000 papers per year and a doubling every 10 years, we come to the conclusion that about 1,000,000 mathematical papers have been published so far. What is much more surprising to most people (but is a simple arithmetic consequence of the growth rate) is that almost half of these papers have been published in the past 10 years. Even if we manage to limit the rate of publication to 50,000 papers per year, we will double the size of the mathematical literature in another 20 years.

Scholarly publishing has some features that sharply differentiate it from the popular fiction or biography markets and that make rapid growth difficult to cope with. Research papers are written by specialists for specialists. Furthermore, scholars do not receive any direct financial remuneration for their papers and give them to publishers only in order to disseminate the information to other scholars.

Scholarly publishing would be facing a minor inconvenience, not a crisis, if the scale of this enterprise were small enough. If a university department were paying $5,000 per year for journals, it could deal with several decades of doubling in size and cost of the subscriptions before anything drastic had to be done. Good mathematics libraries, however, spend well over $100,000 per year just for journal subscriptions, and the cost of staff and space is usually at least twice that. Budgets that large are bound to be scrutinized for possible reductions.

Technological Advances

A doubling of scholarly papers published each decade corresponds to an exponential growth rate of about 7 percent per year. This is fast, but nowhere near as fast as the rate of growth in information processing and transmission. Microprocessors are currently doubling in speed every 18 months, corresponding to a growth rate of 60 percent per year. Similarly dramatic growth figures are valid for information storage and transmission. For example, the costs of the NSF-supported backbone of the Internet increased by 68 percent during the period from 1988 to 1991, but the traffic went up by a factor of 128 (MacKie-Mason and Varian, forthcoming). The point of citing these figures and those that follow is that advances in technology have made it possible to transform scholarly publishing in ways that were impossible even a couple of years ago.

If all the 50,000 mathematical papers published each year were type-set in TeX, then at a rough average of 50,000 bytes per paper, they would require 2.5 gigabytes (GB) of storage. We can now buy a 9 GB magnetic disk for about $3,000. For archival storage of papers, though, we can use other technologies, such as optical disks. A disk with a 7 GB capacity that can be written once costs $200 to $300. Digital tapes with capacities of 250 GB are expected to become available soon. The electronic storage capacity needed for the dissemination of research results in mathematics is thus trivial, with today's technology.

It is already possible to store all the current mathematical publications at an annual cost much less than that of the subscription to a single journal. What about the papers published over the preceding centuries? Because there are 1,000,000 of them, it would require about 50 GB to store them if they were all in TeX. Conversion of old papers to TeX seems unlikely. Storage of bitmaps of these papers, however, compressed with current fax standards, requires less than 1,000 GB. This is large, but it is still less than 150 of the current large optical disks. For comparison, Wal-Mart, the retailer, has a database of more than 1,000 GB that is stored on magnetic disks and is processed intensively all the time.

Within a decade, we may have systems for personal computers that can store 1,000 GB. Even before that, university departments will be able to afford storage systems that can store all the mathematical literature. This ability will mean a dramatic change in the way we operate. For example, if you can call up any paper on your screen and, after deciding that it looks interesting, print it out on the laser printer on your desktop, will you need a library?

Communication networks are improving rapidly. Most departments have their machines on Ethernet networks, which operate at almost 10 Mbs (millions of bits per second). Further, almost all universities now have access to the Internet, which was not the case even a couple of years ago. The Internet backbone operates at 45 Mbs, and prototypes of much faster systems are already in operation. Movies-on-demand will mean wide availability of networks with speed in the hundreds of megabits per second. If your local supplier can get you the movie of your choice at the time of your choice for under $10 (as it will have to, in order for the system to be economical), then sending the more than 50 MB of research papers in your specialty for the past year will cost pennies. Scientists might not like to depend on systems that owe their existence to the demand for X-rated movies, but they will use them when they become available.

Not only have information storage and transmission capacities grown, but the software has become much easier to use. Computerized typesetting systems have become so common that it is rare to encounter a manuscript typed on an ordinary typewriter. Moreover, scholars are increasingly doing their own typesetting. This trend is partially due to cutbacks in secretarial support but is caused primarily by scholars' preferring the greater control and faster execution that they can obtain by doing the work themselves. With modern technology, doing something is becoming easier than explaining to another person what to do.

Two centuries ago there was a huge gap between what a scholar could produce and what the publishers provided. A printed paper was far superior in legibility to handwritten copies of the preprint, and it was cheaper to produce than hiring scribes to make hundreds of copies. Today the cost advantage of publishers is gone; it is far cheaper to send out electronic versions of a paper than to have it printed in a journal. The quality advantage of journals still exists, but it is rapidly eroding.

Preprints and Electronic Journals

Advances in technology allow for much more convenient dissemination of information. Preprints have already become the main method in mathematics, and many other fields, for experts to communicate their latest results to each other. Electronics is making this process much easier. Two approaches are becoming common. One is for departments to set up publicly accessible directories from which anyone can copy the latest preprints via anonymous FTP; these tend to be geographically specific. The other is for scholars to use preprint servers and send their preprints to a central, often domain-specific, database. Wide use of these methods is a great boon to scholars, but it is extremely subversive of journal publications. If I can get a free preprint of a published paper, why should I (or my library) pay for the journal?

This subversive effect of wide preprint distribution is bound to force the traditional scholarly journals to change. Moreover, the changes could be sudden. For example, the preprint server that Paul Ginsparg set up for high-energy theoretical physics became the standard information dissemination method in that area within one year. It has since been adopted by other fields as well. Such sudden changes are common in high-technology areas (witness the dramatic rise in popularity of fax machines, or the catastrophic decline of the mainframe) and could occur in journal publishing. During a future financial squeeze at a university, a dean might come to a mathematics department and offer a deal: "Either you give up paper journal subscriptions, or you give up one position." Today such an offer would not be considered seriously, because journals are still indispensable. In the first decade of the twenty-first century, however, once preprints are freely available, giving up the journals is likely to be the preferred response.

Preprints have a deservedly different status than refereed journal publications. The new technologies, however, are making possible easy publication of electronic journals by scholars alone. It is just as easy for editors to place manuscripts of refereed papers in a publicly accessible directory or a preprint server as it is for them to do the same with their own preprints. The number of electronic journals is small, but it is rising rapidly.

I expect that scholarly publishing will move to almost exclusively electronic means of information dissemination. This will be caused by the economic push of increasing costs of the present system and the attractive pull of the new features that electronic publishing offers.

The Interactive Potential of Electronic Publications

Because conventional print journals have been an integral part of scholarly life for so long, their inflexibility is often not appreciated. Most mathematical journals are available at about a thousand research libraries around the world. Even for the scholars at those institutions, access to journals requires a physical trip, often to another building, and is restricted to certain hours. Electronic journals will make articles available around the clock from the convenience of the scholar's study. They will also make literature searches much easier. Journals without subscription fees will be available from anywhere in the world.

Frank Quinn (1995) argues that the issue of reliability of mathematical literature justifies extreme caution in moving away from paper journals, lest we be tempted into "blackboard-style" publishing practices that are common in some fields. He advocates a strong distinction between informal preprint distribution and formal refereed publications, even in an electronic format. I agree that mathematicians should strive to preserve and enhance the reliability of mathematical literature. I feel, however, that Quinn's concerns are largely misplaced and might keep mathematicians and other scholars from developing better methods for communicating their results. A better solution is to have an integrated system that combines the informal network news–type postings with preprints and electronic journal publication. Stevan Harnad has been advocating just such a solution and has coined the terms *scholarly skywriting* and *prepublication continuum* to denote the process in which scholars merge their informal communications with formal publications. Where I differ from Harnad is in the form of peer review that is likely to take place. Whereas Harnad advocates a conventional form, I feel that a reviewing continuum that matches the publication continuum is more appropriate.

I will describe the system I envisage as if it were operating on a single centralized database machine. This, however, is for convenience only and any working system would almost certainly involve duplicated systems or different but coordinated systems. I will not deal with the software aspects of this system, which would surely involve hypertext links, so that a click on a reference or comment would instantly bring up a window with that paper or comment in it.

At the bottom level of this system, anyone could submit a preprint. There would have to be some control on submissions, but it could probably be minor. Standards similar to those at the *Abstracts of the AMS* might be appropriate, so that proofs that the Earth is flat, or that special relativity is a Zionist conspiracy, would be kept out. Discussions of whether Bacon wrote Shakespeare's plays might be accepted (because there are interesting statistical approaches to this question). Digital signatures and digital timestamping would provide authentication. The precise rules for how the system would function would have to be decided by experimentation. For example, one feature of the system might be that no submissions could ever be withdrawn. This would help enforce quality, because people submitting poorly prepared papers would risk having their errors exposed and documented.

Once a preprint were accepted, it would be available to anyone. Depending on subject classification or keywords, notification of its arrival would be sent to those subscribing to services alerting them to new research in the appropriate areas. Comments would be solicited from anyone (subject again to some minor limitations) and would be appended to the original paper. There could be provisions for anonymous comments as well as signed ones. The author would have the opportunity to submit revised versions of the paper in response to the comments (or to the author's own further work). All the versions of the papers, and all the comments, would remain part of the record. This process could continue indefinitely, even a hundred years after the initial submission. Author X writing a paper that improves an earlier result $Y(123)$ of author Y would be encouraged to submit a comment to $Y(123)$ to that effect. Even authors who just reference $Y(123)$ would be encouraged to note that in comments on $Y(123)$. (Software would do much of this automatically.) A research paper would be a living document, evolving as new comments and revisions were added. This process by itself would go a long way toward providing trustworthy results. Most important, it would provide immediate feedback to scholars. Although the unsolicited comments would require evaluation to be truly useful, and in general would not compare in trustworthiness with formal referee reports, they would be better than no information at all. Scholars would be free to choose their own filters for this corpus of preprints and commentary. For example, some could decide not to trust any unrefereed preprint that had not attracted positive comments from at least three scholars from the Ivy League schools.

Grafted on top of this almost totally uncoordinated and uncontrolled system would be an editorial and refereeing structure. This would be absolutely necessary to deal with many of the submissions. Although unsolicited comments are likely to be helpful in evaluating the novelty and correctness of many papers, they are unlikely to be sufficient in most cases. There is need to assure that all the literature that scholars might rely on is subject to a uniform standard of refereeing (at least as far as correctness is concerned) and at the same time to control the load of the reviewers by minimizing duplicate work. Both tasks would be hard to achieve with an uncoordinated randomized system of commentary, so a formal review process would be indispensable. Editors would thus arrange for proper peer review. The editors could be appointed by learned societies, or could even be self-appointed. (The self-correcting nature of science would take care of the poor ones, I expect. We do have vanity presses even now, and they have not done appreciable damage.) These editors could then use the comments that have accumulated to help them assess the correctness and importance of the results in a submission and to select official referees. (After all, who is better qualified to referee a paper than somebody who had enough interest to look at it and comment knowledgeably on it? It is usually easy to judge people's knowledge of a subject and thoroughness of reading a manuscript from their comments.) The referee reports and evaluations could be added as comments to the paper but would be marked as official reports. Someone looking for information in homological algebra, say, and who is not familiar with the subject, could set his or her programs to search the database only for papers that have been reviewed by an acknowledged expert or a trusted editorial board. Just as there is today, there would be survey and expository papers, which could be treated just like all the other articles. As new information accumulated with time, additional reviews of old papers might be solicited as needed, to settle disputes.

This proposal is designed to work within the confines of what we can expect both technology and ordinary fallible people to accomplish. It would integrate the roles of authors, casual readers, and official referees. The system would allow peers to contribute more effectively to scholars' work. The main advantage of this proposal is that it would provide a continuum of peer review that more closely matches the publication continuum that is likely to evolve.

The Future of Publishers, Journals, and Libraries

It is impossible to predict the date or speed of transition to systems like this one, because they will be determined primarily by sociological factors. The technology that is necessary for such systems is either already available or will be in a few years. The speed with which scholars will adopt this technology will depend on how quickly we are prepared to abandon traditional methods in favor of a superior but novel system. For example, how quickly will tenure and promotion committees start accepting electronic publications as comparable to those in traditional journals?

What would be the role of publishers in the projected system? Scholars can run electronic journals themselves, with no financial subsidies or subscription fees, using only the spare capacity of the computers and networks that are provided to them as part of their jobs. This is the model under which most of the current electronic journals in mathematics operate. There is more work for authors and editors in such a system than with traditional print journals, but with advances in technology the effort that is required is decreasing. A major advantage of such a system is that a journal can be available freely, any time and every place that data networks reach; however, the likely lack of copyediting may not be acceptable. I expect that what editing assistance might be required will not cost anywhere near what print journals cost, and so might be provided by the authors' institutions. If that happens, electronic journals can also be distributed freely. If such assistance is not provided, then subscription fees will have to be imposed, together with access restrictions to the information. To compete successfully with free preprint distribution and free journals, however, any subscription journals will have to keep their fees low. In any event, I expect that publishers will have to shrink. Paper journals will have to convert to electronic publication or disappear. The role of paper is likely to be limited to temporary uses, and archival storage will be electronic. Review papers are likely to play an increasingly important role, but they are written by scholars and can be published in regular electronic journals. In contrast, short bibliographic reviews, as are common in *Mathematical Reviews* and *Zentralblatt für Mathematik,* might be replaced by computerized searches, because the entire literature will be available on each scholar's workstation. This might mean the demise of *Math. Rev.* and *Zentralblatt.* I suspect, however, that they will do well, although they will have to change. They are inexpensive enough that they do not need to offer much extra service to justify their price. There will always be a need for ways of classifying papers, ensuring that all significant ones are reviewed, and keeping track of all the changes in the databases. Review journals will need to be accessible electronically and will most likely be paid for by a site license fee, giving unlimited access to all scholars affiliated with the licensed institution. The review journals will provide much more current information than they do today, as there will be no publication delays. The formats of reviews might vary from those of today; specifically, hypertext links will connect the reviews to the papers and the commentaries associated to those papers. Combined with easy electronic access to the primary materials, review journals will then provide all the functions of a specialized library.

What about libraries? They will also have to shrink and change. The transition to the new system is likely to be less painful for them than for publishers. There is much more inertia in the library system, because old collections of printed material will need to be preserved and converted to digital formats. Eventually, though, we are likely to need very few reference librarians. If the review journals evolve the way I project, they will provide directly to scholars all the services that libraries do now. With immediate electronic access to all the information in a field, and with navigating tools, reviews, and other aids, a few dozen librarians and scholars at review journals might be able to substitute for a thousand traditional reference librarians.

Acknowledgments

This article provides my own personal view of the future of mathematical journals. Few of the observations and predictions are original, and I have freely drawn on the ideas in the references listed below. I have benefited greatly from extensive e-mail correspondence with Paul Ginsparg and Frank Quinn, and especially with Stevan Harnad. Helpful comments and useful information were also provided by a large number of colleagues and correspondents, who are acknowledged in the full version of this chapter. The full version contains more data, detailed arguments, and additional references.

References

Harnad, S. (1990). "Scholarly Skywriting and the Prepublication Continuum of Scientific Inquiry." *Psychological Science* 1: 342–343, reprinted in *Current Contents* 45 (November 11, 1991): 9–13. ftp://princeton.edu/pub/harnad/Harnad/harnad90. skywriting

MacKie-Mason, K. K., and H. R. Varian. (Forthcoming). "Some Economics of the Internet." In *Networks, Infrastructure and the New Task for Regulation*, edited by W. Sichel. (Available via Gopher or FTP, together with other related papers, from gopher.econ.lsa.umich.edu in /pub/Papers.)

Mathematical Reviews. (1990). Fiftieth Anniversary Celebration, special issue (January).

Price, D. J. (1956). "The Exponential Curve of Science." *Discovery* 17: 240–243.

Quinn, F. (1995). "Roadkill on the Electronic Highway? The Threat to the Mathematical Literature." *Notices of the American Mathematical Society* 42, no. 1: 53–56.

6

Implementing Peer Review on the Net: Scientific Quality Control in Scholarly Electronic Journals

Stevan Harnad

Trade Publishing versus Scholarly Publishing

I was once at a reception with a vice president of NBC, so I took the opportunity you would all no doubt have liked to take in my place, to chastise him roundly for the low quality of his network's programs. He smiled and asked why I thought he was to blame for that. After all, what did I think the "product" of NBC TV was? I replied that it was TV programs, of course. He shook his head and informed me that it was nothing of the sort: "NBC's product is eyeballs, yours and mine, and we sell them to our advertisers. We're perfectly content to put on the screen whatever it is that will make your eyeballs adhere to it. So you get exactly what you pay for—with your eyeballs."

I don't know if this revelation turns things as much on end for you as it did for me, but I'd like to induce an equally radical shakeup in your conception of the real "product" and reward structure of scholarly and scientific publication. First, a disclaimer. What I am about to say does *not* apply to trade publication. Trade publication really works the way I had thought TV did: the product is the author's words. These are sold as print on paper. In order to reach your eyeballs (and pocketbook), the author relies on the mediation of the publisher and his technology for setting word to page and then selling page to reader. The alliance between author and publisher is necessary and mutually beneficial; even in today's era of desktop publishing, most authors prefer not to be masters of all trades in their finite lifetimes; they leave editing, copyediting, typesetting, proofreading, printing, marketing, and distribution to the experts.

In this symbiotic relationship between trade author and trade publisher, it is quite natural that the author should transfer the copyright for his words to the publisher, for copying is precisely what the author wishes the publisher to do, as many times as possible, to reach all those eyeballs with pocketbooks. And author and publisher share exactly the same interest in protecting that copyright from theft. No one else should be able to sell that author's words as his own, and no one should have access to them without paying for it. These shared interests are clear. If the author were not prepared to transfer copyright to the publisher, the publisher would be investing his time, technology, and expertise in a product that was available by alternative means (courtesy of someone else's time, technology, and expertise, presumably), and it would be quite reasonable for a publisher to decline to invest in a product without the protection provided by exclusivity (there are exceptions to this in the case of multiple editions, countries, or languages, but such details are not really relevant here). Paper publication does require a large investment, even in today's era of desktop publishing. The technology of print is not a trivial one, nor is it cheap.

Although I am sure that trade authors would be happy if there were a way to sell their words to readers without the mediation of an expensive technology (one that, among other things, raises the price of their words relative to what they would have cost if they could be marketed directly, like paintings, perhaps, or performances), the sales-deterrent effect of the add-on cost of the print technology is a small price to pay for the advantages of mass production.

It would accordingly *not* be music to a struggling author's ears to hear that his limited print-run work, which was not selling all that well, was widely available in a contraband photocopied edition for free (or rather, for the cost of photocopying). Hearing this, the author would be as indignant as his publisher, and both would try to take whatever steps were possible to protect their product from theft, and themselves from loss of rightful revenue.

Now comes some perspecival perestroika. Suppose this author were not a writer by trade, but a scholar or scientist, someone whose work is likely to be read by at most a few hundred peers (and usually much fewer) in an entire lifetime. Suppose such a one heard about a similar contraband photocopy trade being done in his words and work: What would his reaction be? The first response would surely be one of delight (as long as the work was not being attributed to someone else): Why are we scholars if it is not to make a contribution to knowledge and inquiry? And surely that contribution is made only if we are read by and influence the work of our fellow scholars, present and future. The scholar/scientist, in other words, wants to reach his peers' eyeballs so as to influence the contents of their minds; his interest is not in the contents of their pocketbooks.

Upon reflection, however, our scholar/scientist would have to wince and duly report the infraction to his publisher and allow him to take steps to put an end to the illicit trade in his words, because if such infractions were allowed to proliferate unchecked, the very vehicle that carries his words to his peers would be at risk. If contraband trade undermines publishers' investment and revenues, then there will be no primary publication to base the contraband on in the first place.

So this potential conflict of interest between scholar and publisher (the former wanting to maximize eyeballs and minimize any barriers—such as price tags—between them and his work, the latter wanting to recover real costs and make a fair return on his investment, and for expert services rendered) is resolved along the same lines as in the trade-publishing model: a financial barrier is erected between word and reader, with the reluctant acquiescence of the author and the justified insistence of the publisher.

This was the sole scenario in the Gutenberg age, in which the only means of reaching eyeballs was through the mediation of the expensive (and slow and inefficient and unecological) technology of paper: that was the only vehicle in town. Today this is no longer true, and although the scholarly community is slow to realize it, the implications of the post-Gutenberg technology of electronic networked communication are truly revolutionary (Harnad 1991). I will illustrate with one seemingly innocent new feature, anonymous FTP, and with it I will recreate the contraband scenario above, but with a rather different outcome (see Harnad 1995a, 1995b, 1995c).

The Subversive Potential of Anonymous FTP and WWW

We again have our fabled scholar/scientist, whose motivation in publishing is to reach the eyes and minds of the highest possible proportion of his relatively small community of peers, as quickly and with as few impediments as possible during his fleeting lifetime, while he is still compos mentis and productive and while his work is still able to benefit from the interaction. He is accustomed to having an article appear in a journal that is subscribed to by about a thousand libraries and individuals worldwide, and to receiving (usually) a dozen to (rarely) a few hundred reprint requests after his article appears (generally the week or two after it appears in *Current Contents* or some other bibliographic alerting service). Before publication, an unrefereed draft of his manuscript might have been circulated to a variable number of individuals as a preprint, and an updated final draft may continue to be disseminated in that form after publication (as long as his publisher is willing to turn a blind eye to this limited form of auto-contraband). Then there are the citations (ranging from none, to the median half dozen, to the occasional hundreds, or even higher for those rarities qualifying as *Current Contents* Citation Classics). This is the small, esoteric world of scholarly and scientific communication among the peers of the realm. (There sometimes appears a second and larger incarnation of the rare paper that is reprinted for educational purposes.)

Enter anonymous FTP (file transfer protocol, a means of retrieving electronic files interactively): the paper chase proceeds at its usual tempo while an alternative means of distributing first preprints and then reprints is implemented electronically. An electronic draft is stored in a public electronic archive at the author's institution from which anyone in the world can retrieve it at any time. No more tedious scanning of *Current Contents* and mailing of reprint request cards by would-be readers, and then costly and time-consuming (but willing) mailing of reprints by authors who would be read. The reader can now retrieve the paper for himself, instantly, and without ever needing to bother the author, from anywhere in the world where the Internet stretches—which is to say, in principle, from any institution of research or higher learning where a fellow scholar is likely to be.[1]

Splendid, *n'est-ce pas?* The author-scholar's yearning is fulfilled: open access to his work for the world peer community. The reader-scholar's needs and hopes are well served: free access to the world scholarly literature (or as free as a login on the Internet is to an institutionally affiliated academic or researcher). And the publisher? There's the rub. Unlike the economy of contraband photocopies, which has not had its predicted disastrous effects on scholarly publication (apart from whatever role it might have played in raising the prices of scholarly journals), the economy of contraband FTP is a tail that can quickly outgrow the dog by orders of magnitude. Will there be any buyers left to pay the real costs of publication?

That all depends on what we mean by publication, and what the real costs of that will turn out to be. Paper publishers currently estimate that electronic publication would cost only 20 to 30 percent less than paper publication (e.g., Garson, forthcoming). If that is true, then FTP contraband could cause a loss of the revenues needed to cover the remaining 70 to 80 percent, and the entire scholarly publishing enterprise could go bankrupt even if it went totally electronic. In this case there would be nothing in those anonymous FTP archives to retrieve. Is this possible? I think not.

Not only do I think that the true cost of purely electronic publishing would be more like the arithmetic complement of the paper publishers' estimates (which are based largely on how much electronic processing saves in *paper* publication), that is, savings of 70 to 80 percent, but I also think that this will put us over the threshold for an entirely different model of how to recover those costs and create a viable purely electronic scholarly publication system. That would be a scholarly subsidy model—whereby scholars' universities (especially their presses and libraries), learned societies and research publication grants support electronic publications—in place of a trade revenue model. Such a system would reflect more accurately the true motivational structure of scholarly publishing, in which, unlike in trade publishing, authors are willing to pay to reach their colleagues' eyeballs, rather than the reverse. In physics and mathematics, page charges to the author's institution to offset part of the cost of publication are already a common practice in paper publication. In electronic publication, where these charges would already be so much lower, they seem to be the most natural way to offset all the true expenses of publication that remain. In line with the real motivation of scholarly publishing, scholars and scientists certainly will not accept having their anonymous FTP access blocked by paper publishers invoking copyright. Either a collaborative solution will be reached, with paper publishers retooling themselves to perform those of their services that will still be required in purely electronic publishing, or scholars will simply bolt and create their own purely electronic publishing systems.

What would publishers need to do to survive the transition? There will always be a need for expertise in editing, copyediting, page composition, graphics and layout, and proofreading. Most important, there has to be a mechanism of quality control—quality of content, rather than just quality of form, which is what the expertise mentioned so far is concerned with. Publishers formerly furnished this quality control— or did they? In the case of book publishing, acquisition editors are often scholars who make judgments and recommendations about the content of their authors' manuscripts, though usually in conjunction with other scholars, unaffiliated with the publisher, whom the editors ask to serve as reviewers, to provide criticism and make recommendations about acceptability and revision, if necessary. In scholarly periodical publishing, the journal editor is usually not directly affiliated with the publisher, and the referees he consults certainly are not. They are us: the author's community of peers. This is why this quality control system is called peer review.

So the ones who monitored and guided the quality of the content of scholarly publishing were always the members of the scholarly community itself. They were not paid for their efforts (in periodical publication, which accounts for the lion's share of the scientific literature and a good portion of the rest of scholarly publishing too; in book publishing they were paid a pittance, but hardly enough to make it worth their while if they were not already resigned to rendering this scholarly community service in any case). So the cost of scholarly quality control certainly cannot be written off as part of the cost of paper publishing: Scholars have been subsidizing this with their free efforts all along. For purely electronic publication, they would simply have to be investing these efforts in another medium.

The Anarchic Initial Conditions on the Net

Electronic publishing is indeed another medium, one about which most serious scholars today are still quite wary. Why? I think it is because of the peculiar initial conditions of the making of the new medium, its initial demography, and the style that has become associated with it. Erroneous conclusions about the medium itself have been drawn from these its first messages.

The Internet was created, and is continuing to evolve, as the result of a collective, anarchic process among computer programmers ("hackers") and professional, student, and amateur users—a networked effort, so to speak. Hence it was perfectly natural to imagine that this creative and enterprising anarchic spirit, which has proven so effective in forging these remarkable new tools, should also be the means of deploying them. Indeed, the rapid proliferation of bulletin boards, discussion groups, alerting services, and preprint archives, complemented now by simple and powerful search and retrieval tools, all pointed in the direction of a new "ultrademocratic" approach to information production and distribution in this new medium.

Problems immediately manifested themselves, however, in this informational utopia: discussions would wax verbose and sometimes abusive; misinformation was difficult to distinguish from information; an ethos of egalitarian dilettantism prevailed; and, worst of all, serious scholars and scientists distanced themselves or kept their distance from the Net, concluding, understandably, that it was much too chaotic and undiscriminating a medium to be entrusted with the communication and preservation of their substantive ideas and findings.

And so things stand in the mid-1990s. There are a few brave new electronic journals, but the medium is still widely perceived as unfit for serious scholarship, more like a global graffiti board for trivial pursuit. The remedy is obvious and simple, and as I have suggested, it is not, nor has it ever been, medium-dependent. The filtering of scholarly and scientific work by some form of quality control has been implicit in paper publication from the outset, yet it is not, and never has been, in any way peculiar to paper.

The scholarly communicative potential of electronic networks is revolutionary. There is only one sector in which the Net will have to be traditional, and that is in the validation of scholarly ideas and findings by peer review. Refereeing can be implemented much more rapidly, equitably, and efficiently on the Net, but it cannot be dispensed with, as many naive enthusiasts (who equate it with censorship) seem to think.

Imposing Order through Peer Review

Psycoloquy, an international, interdisciplinary electronic journal of open peer commentary in the biobehavioral and cognitive sciences, supported on an experimental basis by the American Psychological Association, is attempting to provide a model for electronic scholarly periodicals. All contributions are refereed; the journal has an editorial board and draws on experts in the pertinent subspecialties (psychology, neuroscience, behavioral biology, cognitive science, philosophy, linguistics, and computer science) the world over (Garfield 1991; Harnad 1990; Katz 1991).

In addition to refereed "target articles," *Psycoloquy* publishes refereed peer commentary on those articles, as well as authors' responses to those commentaries. This form of interactive publication ("scholarly skywriting") represents the revolutionary dimension of the Net in scholarly communication (Harnad 1992), but it too must be implemented under the constraint of peer review.

There is no special problem of scientific quality control that is peculiar to the electronic medium. Scholars criticize and evaluate the work of their peers before it appears formally in print. The system is called "peer review." Like democracy, it has imperfections, but it has no viable alternative, whether on paper or on the electronic airwaves (Harnad 1982, 1986).

The objective of those of us who have glimpsed this medium's true potential is to establish on the Net an electronic counterpart of the "prestige" hierarchy among learned paper journals in each discipline. Only then will serious scholars and scientists be ready to entrust their work to them, academic institutions ready to accord that work due credit, and readers able to find their way to it amid the anarchic background noise.

How is peer review normally implemented in conventional paper journals? The journal has an editor and an editorial board. Either the editor in chief, the editor in consultation with the board, or action editors select the referees, usually one or two per manuscript. A third referee, or more, is consulted if a deadlock needs to be broken. The referees advise the editor(s) by submitting reports (sometimes anonymous, sometimes not) evaluating the manuscript and making recommendations concerning acceptance or rejection, and revision. The reports are advisory rather than binding on the editor, who makes the actual decision, but a good editor chooses his referees well and then for the most part trusts them; besides, only in the very narrow specialty journal does the editor have the expertise to judge all submissions on his own. Peer review is intended to free publication from the domination of any particular individual's preferences, making it answerable to the peer community as a whole, within the discipline or specialty. (Interdisciplinary journals always have additional problems in achieving peer consensus, and indeed, even with specialty journals, disagreement rates among referees suggest that consensus is more than one can expect from peer review; nor is it clear that consensus would be desirable; see Harnad 1985.)

In the social sciences and humanities, journals pride themselves (and rank their quality) on the magnitude of their rejection rates. It is not unusual for the most prestigious journals in these fields to reject 80 to 90 percent of submissions. Prestige in the physical sciences and mathematics is not associated with such high rejection rates; indeed, their rates tend to be the arithmetic complement of social science rates, and biological, medical, and engineering periodicals' rates fall somewhere in between

(Hargens 1990). In all these fields, however, irrespective of the prevailing rejection rates, there is a prestige hierarchy among journals, with some known to accept only the best work in the field and some not much more selective than the unrefereed vanity press that exists at the bottom of each field's hierarchy. Lower rejection rates in physics may occur because in this field authors exercise more self-selection in submitting their work, saving only the best for the elite journals. Moreover, in all fields virtually everything that is written gets published somewhere; in the social sciences a manuscript may be submitted to a succession of lower and lower standard journals until it finds its niche; in physics authors may head more directly for something within their reach the first time round.

Another pertinent feature of this hierarchical system of quality control is that most published work is rarely if ever cited. Only a small percentage of what is published is ever heard of again in the literature. This may be because too much is being published, but it may also reflect the inevitable wheat-to-chaff ratio in all human endeavor (Harnad 1986). As a consequence, a scholar is protected on both sides: there is not much risk that a truly valuable piece of work will fail to be published, though it may not make it to its rightful level in the hierarchy, at least not right away (peer review is far from infallible). In contrast, it is also safe for a scholar, in this monumental information glut, to let the quality control mechanism calibrate his reading, reserving it for only the best journals. Again, there is some risk of missing a gem that has inadvertently been triaged too low, but given the prevailing odds, that risk is also low.

I have not described a perfect or ideal system here; only the reality of peer review and the reasonably reliable ranking it imposes on scholarly output. There is nothing about this system that could not be implemented electronically, indeed, in several ways peer review can be made more efficient, fairer, and perhaps even more valid in the electronic medium. The *point faible* of the peer-review system is not so much the referee and his human judgment (although that certainly is one of its weaknesses); it is the selection of the referee, a function performed by the editor. The editor is the weak link if he is selecting referees unwisely (or, worse, not heeding their counsel when it is wise). Editors usually have "stables" of referees (an apt if unflattering term describing the workhorse duties this population performs gratis for the sake of the system as a whole) for each specialty; in active areas, however, these populations may be saturated—a given workhorse may be in the service of numerous stables. So editors must turn to less expert or less experienced referees. In practice, the problem is not the saturation of the true population of potentially qualified referees but the saturation of that portion of it that an editor knows of and is in the repeated habit of consulting.

One of the results of this overuse of the workhorses is that the refereeing process is sluggish. One does one's duty, but one does it reluctantly, other duties take priority, manuscripts sit unread for unconscionably long times, referees are delinquent in meeting the deadlines they have agreed to, and sometimes, out of guilt, hasty last-minute reports are composed that do not reflect a careful, conscientious evaluation of the manuscript. There is much muttering about publication delay, a real enough problem especially in paper publication, but peer review is often responsible for as much of the delay as the paper publication and distribution process.

There are no essential differences between paper and electronic media with respect to peer review. And the Net is populated by frail human beings, just as the paper world is. But the Net does offer the possibility of distributing the burdens of peer review more equitably, selecting referees on a broader and more systematic basis (through electronic surveys of the literature, citation analysis, and even posting calls for reviewers to pertinent professional experts' bulletin boards and allowing those who happen to have the time to volunteer). The speed with which a manuscript can be circulated electronically is also an advantage, as is the convenience that many are discovering in reading and commenting on manuscripts exclusively on-screen. All in all, implementing the traditional peer-review system purely electronically is not only eminently possible but is likely to turn out to be optimal, with even paper journal editors preferring to conduct refereeing in the electronic medium (I am certainly doing this more and more with the paper journal I edit).

Once peer review is in place on the Net, once the quality hierarchy has been established, serious scholars will no longer have reason to hesitate to entrust their best work to the electronic-only medium. Yet my prediction is that this state of affairs will not prove to be the critical factor in drawing the scholarly community onto the Net with their serious work. Much has been said about what the critical "value-added" feature of the Net will be that succeeds in winning everyone over. We have spoken of decreased costs, but I think that even if my estimate is correct and the true expenses of electronic publication will be only 20 to 30 percent of paper publication, that will not do the trick. Decreased publication lags and more equitable refereeing on the Net will also be welcome but still not, I think, the decisive factors. Not even the global access to eye-balls unrestrained by the barriers of subscription cost, photocopying, mailing, or postage, nor the possibility of a (virtually) free worldwide electronic periodical library sitting on every scholar's desk thanks to network links, nor the powerful electronic search and retrieval tools (built on anonymous FTP, Archie, WAIS, Gopher, Veronica, the World Wide Web, and their progeny) that will be within everyone's reach—none of these, remarkable as they are, will be the critical value-added feature that tilts the papyrocentric status quo irreversibly toward the electronic airways.

Interactive Publication: "Scholarly Skywriting"

The critical factor will be a spin-off of that very anarchy that I said had given the new medium such a bad image in the eyes of serious scholars. Once it is safely constrained by peer review, this anarchy will turn into a radically new form of interactive publication that I have dubbed "scholarly skywriting," and this is what I predict will prove to be the invaluable new communicative possibility the Net offers to scholars, the one that paper could never hope to implement or compete with.

I may be peculiarly well placed to make this prognostication. For more than fifteen years I have edited a paper journal specializing in "open peer commentary." *Behavioral and Brain Sciences* (*BBS*, published by Cambridge University Press) accepts only articles that report especially significant and controversial work. Once refereed and accepted, these target articles are circulated (formerly only as paper preprints, but these days in electronic form as well) to as many as one hundred potential commentators across specialties and around the world, who are invited to submit critical commentary, to which the author will respond (Harnad 1979, 1984b). Among the criteria that referees are asked to use in reviewing manuscripts submitted to *BBS* is whether open peer discussion and response on that paper would be useful to the scholars in the fields involved (the material must impinge on at least three specialties). Each target article is then copublished with the 20 to 30 (accepted) peer commentaries it elicits, plus the author's response to the commentaries. These *BBS* "treatments" have apparently been found useful by the biobehavioral and cognitive science community, because already in its sixth year BBS had the third-highest "impact" factor (adjusted citation ratio: see Drake 1986; Harnad 1984a) among the

1,200 journals indexed in the *Social Science Citation Index*. *BBS*'s pages are in such demand by readers and authors alike that it has (according to an informal survey of authors) one of the highest reprint request rates among scholarly periodicals and, of course, the characteristically high rejection rate for submissions—attesting as much to the fact that there is more demand for open peer commentary than *BBS* can fill as to the fact that *BBS*'s quality control standards are high.

Yet *BBS* has some inescapable limitations, because its tempo is far too slow. Peer review (using five to eight referees, from three or more specialties) is, as usual, a retardant, but even if one starts the clock at the moment a target article is accepted, and even if one allows for the fact that preprints are in the hands of one hundred peers within two weeks of that moment, their commentaries received six weeks after that, the author's response four weeks after that, and then the entire treatment appears in print four to six months later, these turnaround times, though perhaps respectable compared to conventional forms of paper publication, are in fact hopelessly slow when compared to the potential speed of thought.

I have discussed the chronobiology of human communication in more detail elsewhere (Harnad 1991; Harnad, Steklis, and Lancaster 1976). Suffice it to say here that the tempo of a spoken conversation is in the same neighborhood as the speed of thought, whereas weeks, months, or years of lag between messages are not. Whatever ideas could have been generated by minds interacting at biological tempos are forever lost at paper-production tempos. Scholarly skywriting promises life for more of those potential brain children, those ideas born out of scholarly intercourse at skyborne speeds, progeny that would be doomed to stillbirth at the earthbound speeds of paper communication.

I hasten to add—so as to dispel misunderstandings that have already been voiced in the literature (e.g., Garfield 1991)—that I am not advocating oral speeds for all scientific publication. First of all, the time it takes to pass through the filter of peer review already puts some brakes on the speed of interaction. Second, even unmoderated electronic mail correspondence is not as fast as a conversation (nor would it be comfortable if it were—as anyone who has engaged in real-time e-writing "conversations" can attest). Nor is the goal the undisciplined babbling that we all recognize from "live" symposium transcripts. The goal is something in between: much faster than paper-mediated interaction, but not as fast or unconstrained as oral dialogue. Moreover, the virtue of scholarly skywriting is as an available *option*. Just as not every article is suitable for *BBS*, not every idea or finding is a candidate for interactive publication. But at last the option is here.

And once you have tasted it (as I have—see Hayes et al. 1992), I think you too will be convinced that it adds a revolutionary dimension to scholarly publication and, even more important, will increase individual scholars' productivity by an order of magnitude (all those stillborn ideas that now have a lease on life!).

Creative Chaos

Let me close by returning to the question of quality control. I have argued that peer review can and should be implemented on the Net, and hierarchically, much as it was in paper, generating a pyramid of periodicals, with the highest-quality ones at the top and the unrefereed vanity press at the bottom. This, I have suggested, should allay the apprehensions of scholars who had wrongly inferred that the Net was intrinsically anarchic. But now let me say a few words in praise of the chaotic regions of such a partially constrained system. Sometimes the brakes applied by referees are "unbiological" too: if all our ideas and findings had to pass through narrow peer scrutiny before they could elicit wider peer feedback, perhaps certain of them would remain stillborn. Within the many possible structures and nonstructures one can implement on a network, unrefereed discussion, perhaps among a closed group of specialists with read/write privileges (while others have read-only privileges), would be a useful complement to conventional peer review or even to electronic adaptations of *BBS*-style peer commentary in the form of editor-filtered skywriting of the kind *BBS*'s electronic counterpart, *Psycoloquy*, specializes in.

Peer commentary, after all, whether refereed or not, is itself a form of peer review, and hence of quality control (Mahoney 1985). Let us be imaginative in exploring the remarkable possibilities of this brave new medium. My argument here has been on behalf of conventional peer review as the principal means of controlling quality, whether on paper or on the Net, and whether for target articles or commentaries. But once such rigorous, conventional constraints are in place, the Net still has plenty of room for exploring freer possibilities, and the collective, interactive ones are especially exciting.

Summary

Electronic networks have made it possible for scholarly periodical publishing to shift from a trade model, in which the author sells his words through the mediation of the expensive and inefficient technology of paper, to a collaborative model, in which the much lower real costs and much broader reach of purely electronic publication are subsidized in advance, by universities, libraries, research publication grants, and the scholarly societies in each specialty. To take advantage of this, paper publishing's traditional quality control mechanism, peer review, will have to be implemented on the Net, thereby re-creating the hierarchies of journals that allow authors, readers, and promotion committees to calibrate their judgments rationally—or as rationally as traditional peer review ever allowed them to do it. The Net also offers the possibility of implementing peer review more efficiently and equitably, and of supplementing it with what is the Net's real revolutionary dimension: interactive publication in the form of open peer commentary on published and ongoing work. Most of this "scholarly skywriting" likewise needs to be constrained by peer review, but there is room on the Net for unrefereed discussion too, both in high-level peer discussion forums to which only qualified specialists in a given field have read/write access, and in the general electronic vanity press.

Notes

1. This utopian transformation has already taken place in at least one area, high-energy physics, in which, thanks to Paul Ginsparg at Los Alamos, there is already a global preprint archive, HEP. Members of the world high-energy physics community rely on this archive both to deposit their own papers and to browse and retrieve everyone else's, to the tune of 35,000 "hits" a day! The project began in August 1991 as an informal electronic preprint distribution list among a hundred of Paul's colleagues, and it scaled up to encompass virtually the entire high-energy physics field (and increasing portions of other areas of physics) within a stunningly short time. The HEP archive can be accessed through World Wide Web at http://xxx.lanl.gov/ (see also Ginsparg 1994 and Odlyzko 1995). Note that since this paper was written FTP has been subsumed by the Web, so my proposal is really to create a Web archive.

References

Drake, R. A. (1986). "Citations to Articles and Commentaries: A Reassessment." *American Psychologist* 41: 324–325.

Garfield, E. (1991). "Electronic Journals and Skywriting: A Complementary Medium for Scientific Communication?" *Current Contents* 45 (November 11): 9–11.

Garson, L. R. (Forthcoming). "Investigations in Electronic Delivery of Chemical Information." *Proceedings of the International Conference on Refereed Electronic Journals: Toward a Consortium for Networked Publications, Winnipeg, Manitoba, Canada, October 1–2, 1993.*

Ginsparg, P. (1994). "First Steps towards Electronic Research Communication." *Computers in Physics* 8, no. 4 (August, American Institute of Physics): 390–396. http://xxx.lanl.gov/blurb/

Hargens, L. L. (1990). "Variation in Journal Peer Review Systems: Possible Causes and Consequences." *Journal of the American Medical Association* 263: 1348–1352.

Harnad, S. (1979). "Creative Disagreement." *The Sciences* 19: 18–20.

Harnad, S., ed. (1982). *Peer Commentary on Peer Review: A Case Study in Scientific Quality Control.* New York: Cambridge University Press.

Harnad, S. (1984a). "Commentary on Garfield: Anthropology Journals: What They Cite and What Cites Them." *Current Anthropology* 25: 521–522.

Harnad, S. (1984b). "Commentaries, Opinions and the Growth of Scientific Knowledge." *American Psychologist* 39: 1497–1498.

Harnad, S. (1985). "Rational Disagreement in Peer Review." *Science, Technology and Human Values* 10: 55–62.

Harnad, S. (1986). "Policing the Paper Chase." (Review of *A Difficult Balance: Peer Review in Biomedical Publication,* by S. Lock.) *Nature* 322: 24–25.

Harnad, S. (1990). "Scholarly Skywriting and the Prepublication Continuum of Scientific Inquiry." *Psychological Science* 1: 342–343; reprinted in *Current Contents* 45 (November 11, 1991): 9–13. ftp://princeton.edu/pub/harnad/Harnad/harnad90.skywriting

Harnad, S. (1991). "Post-Gutenberg Galaxy: The Fourth Revolution in the Means of Production of Knowledge." *Public-Access Computer Systems Review* 2, no. 1: 39–53; reprinted in *PACS Annual Review* 2 (1992), in *Computer Conferencing: The Last Word,* edited by R. D. Mason (East Haven, Conn.: Beach Holme Publishers, 1992); and in M. Strangelove and D. Kovacs, *Directory of Electronic Journals, Newsletters, and Academic Discussion Lists,* edited by A. Okerson, 2d edition (Washington, D C: Association of Research Libraries, Office of Scientific and Academic Publishing, 1992). ftp://princeton.edu/pub/harnad/Harnad/harnad91.postgutenberg

Harnad, S. (1992). "Interactive Publication: Extending the American Physical Society's Discipline-Specific Model for Electronic Publishing." *Serials Review,* Special Issue on Economics Models for Electronic Publishing, pp. 58–61. ftp://princeton.edu/pub/harnad/Harnad/harnad92.interactivpub

Harnad, S. (1995a). "Electronic Scholarly Publication: Quo Vadis?" *Serials Review* 21, no. 1: 70–72; reprinted in *Managing Information* 2, no. 3 (1995). ftp://princeton.edu/pub/harnad/Harnad/harnad95.quo.vadis

Harnad, S. (1995b). "PostGutenberg Galaxy Wars." *Times Higher Education Supplement,* Multimedia, p. vi, May 12.
ftp://princeton.edu/pub/harnad/Harnad/harnad95.postgutenberg

Harnad, S. (1995c). "Universal FTP Archives for Esoteric Science and Scholarship: A Subversive Proposal." In *Scholarly Journals at the Crossroads: A Subversive Proposal for Electronic Publishing,* ed. Ann Okerson and James O'Donnell. Washington, D C: Association of Research Libraries.
ftp://princeton.edu/pub/harnad/Harnad/harnad/Psycoloquy/Subversive.Proposal

Harnad, S., H. D. Steklis, and J. B. Lancaster, eds. (1976). *Origins and Evolution of Language and Speech.* Annals of the New York Academy of Sciences 280.

Hayes, P., S. Harnad, D. Perlis, and N. Block. (1992). "Virtual Symposium on Virtual Mind." *Minds and Machines 2:* 217–238.
ftp://princeton.edu/pub/harnad/Harnad/harnad92.virtualmind

Katz, W. (1991). "The Ten Best Magazines of 1990." *Library Journal* 116: 48–51.

Mahoney, M. J. (1985). "Open Exchange and Epistemic Progress." *American Psychologist* 40: 29–39.

Odlyzko, A. M. (1995). "Tragic Loss or Good Riddance? The Impending Demise of Traditional Scholarly Journals." *International Journal of Human-Computer Studies* 42: 71–122. Condensed version appears in this volume.
ftp://netlib.att.com/netlib/att/math/odlyzko/tragic.loss.Z

II

The New Challenges

7

The Economic Quandary of the Network Publisher

Brian Hayes

Printed journals and magazines have some three centuries of tradition behind them as a medium of communication in the sciences and the world of scholarship. They have been the favored place for reporting research results ever since the *Journal des savants* and the *Philosophical Transactions of the Royal Society of London* began appearing in 1665. But printed periodicals will surely not remain the scientist's and the scholar's medium of choice for another three centuries, or even another three decades. Their future beyond the next three years is somewhat cloudy. Already, much of the day-to-day discourse of science flows over computer networks, and publication in a printed journal is sometimes no more than a formality. Hundreds of electronically distributed journals have sprung up, and there are even more newsletters, discussion groups, and "e-print" archives. Sooner or later, ink on paper will be superfluous.

The new schemes of electronic publication have an irresistible appeal. Information is delivered in minutes instead of days or weeks. It comes right to your desk, day or night, whether the library is open or not. Computer-based methods of searching and indexing make it easier to find what you want. Revised and corrected manuscripts can be distributed instantly, and so can the responses of readers. Perhaps most important in the long run, electronic documents can include more than just text and static images; they can be enriched with large data sets, sounds, video sequences, animations, or simulations. In the right computing environment they could become *active* documents, which invite the reader to participate as well as to peruse. For example, a reader might select an equation and immediately see it solved or graphed.

An earlier version of this chapter appeared under the title "The Network Newsstand" in *American Scientist* 82, no. 1: 108–112.

Electronic publications also have some notable disadvantages. People who do their reading in bed or at the beach find it awkward to drag a network connection along with them. And computer displays cannot yet match the resolution of high-quality printing, so that typographical niceties are lost. There are subtler losses, too, including even olfactory and tactile aspects of the experience of reading. (A day spent in front of the glowing phosphors of the cathode-ray tube is a very different sensory experience from a day spent wandering the stacks of the library.) Furthermore, the promise of active documents has until very recently been forestalled by incompatibilities among computer systems, with the result that many electronic publications stick to the lowest common denominator: plain text encoded in the ASCII character set.

It seems certain that most of the impediments to electronic publication will be swept away by the advance of technology. Computers will eventually be interoperable, portable, and lighter than an average book, with wireless links to a universal network. They will be sufficiently inexpensive that inequities of access will be no worse than they are at present with paper publications. But the most interesting questions about the coming of electronic journals and magazines are not technological questions. They are economic and institutional questions. Who will pay? Who will own? These are the issues that will determine whether the new medium brings an improvement in scholarly communication or just a new set of problems.

Capturing Keystrokes

Publishing has already been transformed by the computer. Manuscripts are no longer typed and retyped by author, editor, and compositor. The author's keystrokes are captured in a computer file, which is transformed in various ways but never wholly loses its identity on the way to the printing press. The handling of illustrations has changed in a similar way. Graphs and diagrams were once drawn on paper and sent to a photoengraver, who made a metal impression of the image. Photographs required even more complex processing, especially those being reproduced in color. Now most diagrammatic artwork is drawn on the computer in the first place, and photographs are scanned and digitized so that they can be manipulated on the computer screen. The pages of many journals and magazines are assembled entirely as computer files, which are output onto photographic film ready for the manufacture of printing plates.

It is easy to imagine one further step in the evolution of ink-and-paper publishing. The time may come when the printing press will be a computer peripheral device not much different from what the laser printer is today. When an issue of a journal or magazine is ready for the press, the editor will select a "Print . . ." item from a menu, then fill out a form specifying the number of copies, the grade of paper, the type of binding, and so on. The content of the issue will then be sent over the network and enter the queue of jobs awaiting time on the presses.

But why stop there? If you can print a journal with the click of a mouse, you can just as easily send it directly to its readers over the network. Think of the trees saved, and the postage, and the delivery time! But if the aim is to get rid of the middleman, there is one more candidate for elimination. Having dispensed with typesetters and photoengravers, and now with printers and postal delivery, the obvious next step is to have done with publishers too. Let authors and readers communicate directly.

In the publishing industry as constituted today, a large and complex infrastructure stands between the writer and the reader. There are editors and subeditors, proofreaders, illustrators, designers, prepress service bureaus, color separators, strippers and platemakers, printers and binders, circulation directors, truckers, mailers, jobbers, customs expediters, catalog agents, and many others. In principle the new technology could sweep all this structure away. Information would flow from the author's computer directly to the reader's computer. Technically, nothing prevents such do-it-yourself publishing ventures from operating right now. If you are connected to the Internet and you have something to say, you can publish your own periodical today, at a distribution cost near nothing.

Electronic Titles Available Today

Not only is network publishing possible today; it is happening today. Following are a few of the publications available to anyone with Internet access. *Psycoloquy* is a refereed journal that publishes "brief reports of ideas and findings on which the author wishes to solicit rapid peer feedback . . . in all areas of psychology and its related fields." *Flora Online* is a "peer-reviewed electronic journal for systematic botany." *Solstice: An Electronic Journal of Geography and Mathematics* is an "online, refereed journal published by the Institute of Mathematical Geography (IMaGe). It is transmitted, free of charge, to a distribution list of subscribers twice yearly, on the astronomical solstices." The *Ulam Quarterly* defines its scope as all areas of science and mathematics that were of interest to Stanislaw Ulam. *Postmodern Culture,* an "electronic journal of interdisciplinary studies," aims to "encourage reconsideration of the forms and practices of academic writing, and to experiment with departures from the traditional idea of published texts as immutable and monologic."

Several electronic publications focus on issues connected with electronic publication itself. Perhaps the best known is *EJournal,* a "peer-reviewed, academic periodical interested in theory and praxis surrounding the creation, transmission, storage, interpretation, alteration and replication of electronic text." *The Electronic Journal of Communication/La révue électronique de communication* is a bilingual quarterly "devoted to the study of communication theory, research, practice and policy." There is also the *Public-Access Computer Systems Review,* a "refereed electronic journal about end-user computer systems in libraries." The quotations in the preceding descriptions are from the "Directory of Electronic Journals and Newsletters," compiled by Michael Strangelove (1992). The 1994 version of this directory, compiled by Lisabeth King (King and Okerson 1994), lists 440 journals, magazines, newsletters, and other periodicals, as well as 1,800 academic discussion lists. Many network periodicals have all the trappings of "real" publications: they have been assigned ISSN numbers, the titles appear in library catalogs, and the contents are included in standard indexes and abstracting services.

Most electronic journals have been launched by individuals or small groups, but some of the learned societies are also experimenting with making their publications and other services available over the network. The American Chemical Society has been a pioneer in this respect: 20 ACS journals have been available on-line since 1984, albeit only through paid-access databases. The American Psychological Association sponsors *Psycoloquy.* The American Mathematical Society has made its monthly *Bulletin* available through an Internet service called e-math. In Britain the Institute of Electrical and Electronics Engineers is publishing a network version of *Electronics Letters.*

Commercial publishers are also testing the waters. Oxford University Press is the publisher of *Postmodern Culture.* Gordon and Breach offers a printed edition of the *Ulam Quarterly,* and Morgan Kaufmann will be selling a print version of the proposed *Journal of Artificial Intelligence Research,* which will be available via the Internet without charge. The

Scientist, a newspaper published by Eugene Garfield, now has a free Internet version, and so does the magazine *Mother Jones*. A large number of other publications, from *DC Comics* to *Scientific American*, have some form of online presence, although most of them are available only through commercial networks such as CompuServe and America Online, and some of them publish only selections electronically, not the entire content of the paper edition.

One of the most ambitious experiments now getting under way is the *Chicago Journal of Theoretical Computer Science,* an online journal planned for 1995. The journal will be edited by Janos Simon of the University of Chicago, but the publisher will be the MIT Press, which will handle marketing and distribution. Subscriptions will be sold to libraries for $125 per year and to individuals for $30.

A development that may well accelerate the acceptance of electronic publications is the rapid growth of the World Wide Web, the distributed hypermedia system developed at CERN, the European Laboratory for Particle Physics in Geneva (Hayes 1994; Rugier 1994). The Web allows electronic publications to escape the bounds of plain text; illustrations, and even sounds and video sequences, can be incorporated into a document and viewed with equal facility with a variety of computer systems. Even a brief exposure to the Web leads to the surmise that publications will not only become electronic but will also be transformed by the new medium.

Free Words!

The economic argument in favor of electronic publishing has been articulated most clearly in the case of scholarly journals, particularly the specialized ones with a small circulation. Authors of papers in such journals are not paid for their contributions. On the contrary, they (or their granting agencies) may be asked to remit page charges to the publisher. The editors and referees who evaluate and select the articles are also usually volunteers from the academic world. In recent years the volunteer community has even been doing the typographic coding of most papers, providing the publisher with computer files ready for automatic typesetting. Then the same authors, editors, and referees pay hundreds of dollars per volume to buy back the fruit of their labor from the publisher. The final irony (Odlyzko 1995) is that few of the insiders actually read the printed journal. By the time the printed version of a paper appears—often years after it was written—workers within the discipline have long since read it in preprint form. (Sometimes even people on the periphery of the field do not read the journal. They send postcards to the authors, requesting reprints.)

Those who see an injustice in this situation urge scholars and their universities to reclaim ownership of their work. Through the technology of the network, they could produce their own journals, bypassing the publishers who, according to this view, live as parasites on the scholarly enterprise. In the new system, the volunteer authors, editors, and referees would continue to work much as they always have. The main difference would be that when an article was ready for publication, it would not have to wait months or years to see print; it would be distributed immediately by electronic mail or some other network protocol. Instead of charging libraries and other subscribers hundreds or thousands of dollars for the journal, the editors would send it free to all who have an interest.

This vision of freely flowing scholarly discourse may seem dreamy and utopian, but quite a number of electronic journals are already operating on just such a basis. In fact, among the few hundred network publications now appearing, only a handful impose a charge on readers. Of course, a few hundred network journals amount to only a minuscule fraction of the publishing industry, and as yet no traditional periodicals seem to be threatened by the no-cost competition. But when most journals and magazines are distributed electronically, the economics of publishing will surely be transformed.

One possible endpoint of the evolution toward network distribution of scholarly writing is that publishing may simply cease to be an economic activity. Information will no longer be bought and sold—at least in the academic world—but will flow without barriers from creator to consumer. Any costs of publication will be paid indirectly, as other costs of doing research are already paid in universities and government laboratories. After all, the Internet itself has long been supported this way, as a part of the infrastructure. Why not devise a publishing economy that works the same way?

It is worth noting that giving away a publication is quite different from selling it cheaply: there is discontinuity when the price falls to nothing. With free distribution, there is no need to collect fees (which in itself saves much cost) and, more important, there is no need to defend property rights. A publisher can encourage readers to share, rather than prosecuting them for copyright infringement. The Internet community has a particularly strong tradition of sharing. For example, when several people from the same university subscribe to a network mailing list, the recommended practice is to enter a single subscription and make multiple copies locally. The copying can be done automatically by the network software. This arrangement is a convenience to the publisher of a free journal, but it is a horrifying prospect to anyone trying to make a living from subscription fees.

Making It Pay

Free distribution may well be the answer for some network periodicals, but much publishing simply will not happen without monetary incentives. Volunteer labor and indirect financial support might well suffice to put small quarterly journals on the network, but something more will be needed to create electronic editions of *Nature* and *Science*. At this point I must confess a personal interest. For two decades I have made my living as a writer and editor for scientific periodicals, and I cannot imagine how my work would ever have been supported if those periodicals did not earn revenue for their publishers. It is not only profit-making enterprises that rely on such income; many nonprofit societies derive important revenue from publishing activities.

The most obvious economic model for network publishing is the one that now dominates print publishing: the familiar practice of selling annual subscriptions. You send the publisher a check, and in return you receive a year's worth of issues by electronic mail. Several variations on this scheme could be considered. Issues might be sold individually, as they are on a newsstand. Or perhaps the fundamental unit of exchange should be even smaller: the individual article rather than the entire issue. Still another economic model is based on the practices of computer information systems such as DIALOG and STN, which bill their customers by the minute or the byte.

All such pay-as-you-go, fee-for-service arrangements have a worrisome feature in common: they conflict with that generous spirit of sharing that is so much a part of network culture. Twenty years ago, the proliferation of photocopying machines led to occasional skirmishes over the "fair use" of copyrighted material. In a world of densely connected computer networks, the problem will be far worse. Digital information can be copied instantly, effortlessly, and perfectly, at near-zero cost. The copying can be made automatic, so that when one subscriber receives a journal, his or her colleagues get it seconds later. Furthermore, in a fully networked environment, copying isn't even necessary. Over a high-bandwidth network link, you can read your colleague's journals as easily as your own, without making a permanent copy. Thus publishers would need not only to regulate the copying of their works, as they currently do, but also to prevent people from reading over their neighbor's shoulder. Magazines might have to be marked "for your eyes only."

The problem of sharing is made worse by an unfavorable feedback relation. As more readers share a subscription rather than buy their own, the publisher must charge more per subscription in order to maintain the same revenue stream. Rising prices, however, increase the incentive for sharing. In the limiting case, the entire cost of publication is paid by one subscriber, who then shares with all other readers.

Of course publishers can impose legal strictures to discourage those forms of sharing that infringe on the publishers' property rights, but the experience of the software industry suggests that such a strategy is unlikely to be highly effective and very likely to be unpopular. The real problem in this situation is not that some people will violate rules forbidding the sharing of network publications. The real problem is that some people will abide by such rules. Sharing, after all, is supposed to be a good thing. It is one of those fine kindergarten virtues that ought to be cultivated rather than suppressed. In the worlds of science and scholarship, in particular, the free exchange of ideas is much celebrated. It seems a shame to adopt an economic system that requires people to act contrary not only to their own selfish interests but also to the public good.

In 1991 the economic consequences of electronic publishing were considered in depth at a meeting convened in Monterey, California, by the Coalition for Networked Information. Many of the ideas discussed at the meeting were subsequently presented in a special issue of the journal *Serials Review* (Grycz 1992), along with other views on the same topic. Here are some of the alternatives considered in the special issue.

The music industry offers one model. Broadcasters pay royalties to songwriters, but without attempting to keep track of each time a song is played. Instead, radio stations contribute to a fund that is allocated according to the estimated air time received by each composer's works. In the case of network publications, fees collected from all readers could be distributed among publishers based on estimates of each periodical's total circulation or readership. Plans of this kind have the important advantage that the reader pays the same fee no matter what he or she chooses to read and whether copies are obtained from the publisher, from a library or from a colleague. On the other hand, the publisher's compensation is based entirely on quantity, not quality. In effect, all magazines and journals are sold at the same price, which makes it much more attractive to be publishing the widely circulating *People* than *Physical Review.*

The world of broadcasting is also the source of another economic model. Peter Young of the National Commission on Libraries and Information Science has proposed forming a Corporation for Scholarly Publishing, analogous to the Corporation for Public Broadcasting. It would be federally chartered and funded but would also seek contributions from the private sector. Just as the CPB fosters television programming that might not be commercially viable, the CSP would subsidize publishing ventures judged to be in the public interest.

Serials Review is a journal of library science, and several of the papers in the special issue focus on the role of the library in the distribution of electronic information. In one proposal (Lesk 1992) a library would buy a site license, allowing it to make published materials available to a community of scholars. In effect, the libraries would become regional distributors or wholesalers for the publishers. Presumably, their licensing fees would be adjusted according to the size of their patronage. It is not clear whether libraries would be eager to take on this role.

Another mechanism for financing electronic publications is not mentioned by the *Serials Review* authors, nor have I seen it discussed elsewhere. Many print publications are supported partly or wholly by the sale of advertising space. Perhaps the same idea could be made to work in the networked world. Internet veterans cringe at the very thought of ads on the network, which remains one of the last refuges in modern life still relatively free of commercial speech. But as a means of sustenance, advertising has a key advantage: it gives publishers an incentive to encourage the widest possible dissemination of their work. And advertising itself has a legitimate economic function: just as scientists need a forum in which to announce their new results, companies need a place to announce and sell their products. Still, advertising is a curious institution that has taken more than a century to evolve to its present state in printed media. Over the years readers have learned how to discount or disregard it; they distinguish advertising from editorial content in an instant, and they apply different standards of veracity to the two kinds of reading matter. Such sophistication may take a long time to develop in a new medium.

Competing for Readers

Many discussions of network publishing seem to start with the premise that the dominant cost in conventional publishing is the cost of manufacturing and shipping the physical artifact: paper, ink, printing, postage (Quinn 1994; Rawlins 1992). It follows that if you eliminate all these things at a stroke, the true cost of publication must become very small. I am skeptical of this assumption. To explain why, I find it most convenient to look at publishing from the point of view of the author.

If you have a scholarly paper ready for publication, why submit it to a journal? Why not just photocopy the manuscript and send it around? The journal may well offer better and cheaper reproduction, but I think that few publishing decisions are made on that basis. Authors seldom choose journals because of the quality of their presswork. Malcolm Getz (1992) of Vanderbilt University points out three benefits that a journal offers an author: the author's work is disseminated to a wide audience; it is archived (mainly by libraries) so that it will be available to future readers; and its selection by editors or peer reviewers certifies its quality. These are really three facets of a single benefit: what the journal is offering to an author is readers, now and in the future. You publish in a journal because people subscribe to it, because they save it, and because they read it. And thus the critical task for a journal is not to deliver paper and ink to its readers but to deliver readers to its authors. To a surprising extent, this imperative dominates the economics of periodical publishing.

For mass-market magazines—where readers must be delivered to advertisers as well as to authors—the competition for readers is plainly visible to anyone who has gone through a supermarket checkout line. Consider that American publishers find the need for readers sufficiently urgent that they are willing to pay out $10 million sweepstakes prizes in order to get them, and to pay the much larger costs of mailing sweepstakes entry forms to almost every household in the United States. Other means of enlarging a magazine's audience—direct-mail solicitation and advertising—are also expensive. For many magazines the cost of acquiring a subscriber exceeds the price of an initial subscription; the publisher begins to make money from the subscription revenue only in the second or third year, assuming that the subscription is renewed.

In another branch of periodical publishing, the "trade press" that caters to various specialized businesses and industries, the imperative to find readers is just as powerful but manifests itself in a different way. Readers are considered valuable enough that publishers are willing to distribute their products without charge to anyone who can produce suitable credentials. The publications are supported entirely by advertising revenue.

In the world of scholarly publishing, competition for readers is more subdued, but it nonetheless has had profound effects on the nature of the journals appearing today. Economies of scale in printing would seem to favor the consolidation of journals into fewer titles, each with a broader editorial scope and a larger circulation. In fact the trend is in the opposite direction: publishers have been introducing ever more specialized and narrowly defined journals, each with a smaller audience. There are multiple reasons for this development, but one important factor is that such an audience is easier to identify and reach, making a marketing effort more efficient. Librarians complain bitterly about the proliferation of titles and the fragmentation of interest. No doubt publishers would also prefer to have fewer titles with more readers per title, but they cannot afford to pay the cost of finding those readers.

How will the shift to electronic distribution change the economics of reader acquisition? No one knows, because no one has any extensive experience with circulation promotion over the network. Electronic junk mail may turn out to be even less welcome than the paper kind, in which case publishers may have to find some new way to solicit subscriptions. Or the search for readers may be more efficient on the network, because the cost of sending mail is so much less. When your $10 million sweepstakes offer arrives by electronic mail, will you be more or less likely to respond? Lower costs of publication should lead to lower journal prices, which in turn should make the job of persuading buyers somewhat easier. On the other hand, as Michael O'Donnell (1993) has pointed out, the attention of readers is a finite resource. If all magazines and journals were free and instantly available, how many more would you read than you read now?

Answers to questions like these will be of interest even outside the publishing industry. In decades to come, a significant share of the world's business is going to be transacted over computer networks. There will be not only a network newsstand but an entire networked economy. It's time to learn how to do business there.

References

Getz, Malcolm. (1992). "Electronic Publishing: An Economic View." In Grycz 1992, pp. 25–31.

Grycz, Czeslaw Jan, ed. (1992). "Economic Models for Networked Information." *Serials Review* 18, nos. 1–2.

Hayes, Brian. (1994). "The World Wide Web." *American Scientist* 82, no. 5: 416–420.

King, Lisabeth, and Ann Okerson. (1994). "Directory of Electronic Journals, Newsletters and Academic Discussion Lists." Washington, D.C.: Coalition for Networked Information. gopher://arl.cni.org/11/scomm/edir

Lesk, Michael. (1992). "Pricing Electronic Information." In Grycz 1992, pp. 38–40.

Odlyzko, Andrew M. (1995). "Tragic Loss or Good Riddance? The Impending Demise of Traditional Scholarly Journals." This volume. A longer version appears in *International Journal of Human-Computer Studies* 42: 71–122. ftp://netlib.att.com/netlib/att/math/odlyzko/tragic.loss.z

O'Donnell, Michael J. (1993). "Electronic Journals: Scholarly Invariants in a Changing Medium." University of Chicago Department of Computer Science Technical Report 92-07. Available from librarian@cs.uchicago.edu.

Quinn, Frank. (1994). "A Role for Libraries in Electronic Publication." *Ejournal* 4, no. 2.

Rawlins, Gregory J. E. (1992). "The New Publishing: Technology's Impact on the Publishing Industry over the Next Decade." *Public-Access Computer Systems Review* 3, no. 8: 5–63.

Rugier, Mario (compiler). (1994). *Preliminary Proceedings of the First International Conference on the World Wide Web, Geneva.* http://www1.cern.ch/WWW94/PrelimProcs.html

Strangelove, Michael. (1992). "Directory of Electronic Journals and Newsletters." Edition 2.1. ftp://ftp.cni.org/pub/net-guides/strangelove (superseded by King and Okerson 1994).

8

Integrity Issues in Electronic Publishing

Clifford A. Lynch

One potential difficulty in the transition of the scholarly publishing system to the networked information environment is that of maintaining the integrity of electronic publications. Several concerns, gathered together under the general issue of integrity, are most clearly defined by contrasting the perceptions of the evolving channels for network-based distribution of information to the established system of print-based scholarly publication. Experience and expectations based on custom determine our view of the print publication system. To some extent, we perceive the current print system as having a degree of robustness and integrity that is hard to justify objectively, given current publishing technologies and practices, particularly if we consider mass-market publishing as well as scholarly publishing.

This chapter contains two major sections. The first looks critically at the perceived strengths—in areas related to integrity—of the print publication system as opposed to electronic information distribution. The second specifically examines and evaluates electronic publication and information distribution in each of these areas where the print system is viewed as being strong, and discusses the extent to which integrity concerns are real. Both available and developing approaches to addressing the relevant concerns are discussed.

The Perceived Strengths of the Print Publication System

The print publishing system has four great perceived strengths with regard to integrity, described in the following sections.

Resistance to Unpublicized and Unidentified Version Changes
Publication in print is assumed to create a permanent record of a distinct version of a work. All the published copies of a given version of a work

are expected to be identical. Publication is an irrevocable act that causes the distribution, beyond recall, of a number of identical copies of a work. A single canonical version of the work is typically made available through an act of publication (or a small number of clearly different canonical versions are issued in paperback and hardback editions). Print publication relies on the characteristics of mass production technologies such as the printing press, which produces large numbers of identical objects on the assumption that publication represents the distribution and ceding of access control for a work. Publishers are expected not to distribute different versions of a work without identifying that one differs from another. Availability of a revised version of a work represents a new act of publication or republication, and the revised version is assumed to be marked as such and readily distinguishable from earlier versions of the same work.

Electronic distribution of information, particularly when not supported by the repeated act of physical distribution of some information-bearing artifact such as a CD-ROM, is perceived as an environment in which versions of digital works can be infinitely revised and updated without warning or notification. Indeed, visionaries such as Ithiel De Sola Pool have argued that this is a strength of electronic information dissemination, and some projects have built on this capability by translating scholarly works that are traditionally issued in periodically revised editions into continually updated databases of the current "best knowledge" in a given area. This constantly evolving view of a work not only can produce valuable, high-quality, and timely reference works in the electronic environment (following a database model) but defines the developing work as a locus and reference for ongoing discourse on a topic as it grows and combines contributions from many scholars. Yet a work of this nature is culturally opposed to the view of the scholarly record as comprising a series of discrete, permanently fixed contributions of readily attributable authorship.

In fact, the distinction between the fluid electronic work and the permanent, fixed, printed contribution is arbitrary and is a distinction more of perception than of reality. The difference is far more a case of business policy and editorial practice and discipline than an artifact of technology. Book publishers often make corrections from one print run to another. Newspapers and magazines are often published in a large number of "targeted" editions for specific geographical or demographically characterized readerships, and they often carry little or no indication to allow the casual reader to recognize that one edition will differ from another, both in advertising and editorial content. Most national newspapers such as the *New York Times* or the *Wall Street Journal* are routinely published as a series of regional editions. And newspapers frequently change the content of stories from one press run to the next as new information becomes available. Continually updated loose-leaf reference works are common in areas such as law and finance where timeliness of content is considered essential. Although content revision is still rare in scholarly publishing, this is more a tradition than a limitation on technology or editorial capabilities, and can even be considered as evidence that timeliness is not important in most archival scholarly publication.

Electronic distribution of information is no less reliable than print distribution in controlling and identifying revisions, and in ensuring that a complete record of all the revised versions are available for review by the reading public. True, it is easier to update repeatedly a file that is available for retrieval on the network if one gives little or no warning to users of that file, but this is really more a matter of policy in file maintenance than an inherent weakness of technology. Policies concerning updates have often been less formal in the electronic environment than in print. Some aspects of electronic documents, however, have not received enough credit for their contribution toward identifying version changes. Given two printed works, it's quite difficult to tell whether one differs from another without obvious differences in, for example, the number of pages or the pagination breaks, and even these may not be meaningful if the works have been typeset in different fonts. It is simple, in contrast, to apply utility programs to see if two versions of an electronic work are identical and to produce a summary of differences between the versions.

Perhaps the greatest difference between print and electronic distribution is the guarantee of an available audit trail. When a version of a work is published in print, one may assume that print copies are distributed and leave the publisher's control permanently, and thus they will continue to exist as a historical record of that version. Publication is assumed to pass control of a copy to institutions like libraries, which will permanently maintain that copy and keep it accessible, beyond the control of the publisher. When a file on the network is updated, however, it is anyone's guess whether a copy of the file prior to the update has been replicated elsewhere, along with enough bibliographic information to identify it as a copy of a given version of the base file at a particular point in time. Such a copy, if it does exist, can be found only by accident. It is unclear which instants in time demarcate versions, and thus it is unclear which copies may be significant in trying to reconstruct a record of changes.

Further, publication in the electronic environment represents much less of a release of control over a copy. Legal restrictions may accompany the use of a file, effectively permitting the publisher to "recall" all but the most current version of the information. But there is no analogue of the doctrine of first sale in the electronic environment. Once an individual or organization has legally obtained a copy of a work that has been printed, it owns it and has authority over its disposition (subject to limitations on its ability to make copies of the work as defined by copyright law). This legal principle supports the integrity of the print publication system as a means of ensuring a historical record of discourse.

A Well-Established System of Citation

The system of citation for print literature is based primarily on content, not on where that content is stored or on what institution holds a copy of it. For example, one cites an article by title and page numbers in a specific issue of a journal. This content designator is known to the overall system of libraries, publishers, and readers who create, manage, preserve, offer access to, and use the print publication base. Part of the validity of this system of citation is predicated on the assumptions outlined in the previous point. That is, one assumes that publishers will not distribute multiple, variant versions of a work without clear indication that permits libraries and readers to distinguish one version from another.

Citation systems in the electronic world are still immature. Typically, one cites content stored at a specific location (file x in directory y on host z, accessible through anonymous FTP, for example). This is like citing a printed work by referring to the holdings of a specific library, stored on a specific shelf in a specific place in the stacks of that library. This type of citation is no longer used for printed matter, except for unique physical artifacts such as incunabula.

Trust in Distribution Channels

This trust is so obvious in the print world that it is difficult to explain without sounding preposterous, yet the perception of the Internet as an "environment of pervasive deceit" (to use Gustavus Simmon's memorable phrase) prompts questioning of everything about electronic versions of works.

In print, we typically assume that things are what they appear to be. The validity of a printed journal received through the mail is rarely questioned. The author and publication attributions on a printed book's title page are usually assumed to be accurate. Laws, such as postal fraud statutes, help justify these assumptions. But this credibility of printed matter is based on our belief that such information would be extremely difficult to falsify. In fact, current technology allows high-quality micropublishing, digital capture, editing, and duplication of almost anything, from currency to video clips. Yet, in the networked environment, we question where files really come from and whether they are true copies of what the publisher distributed. In the networked environment we feel compelled to verify complex evidential chains to validate the provenance of a given document. Although I am not aware of any case of distribution of a fraudulent simulacrum of a printed journal through the mail, this is a straightforward (though not inexpensive) possibility, given today's printing technologies.

Distributed Control

In the print world, the act of publication implies giving up control of copies to individuals and to libraries. Under the doctrine of first sale, recipients of these copies own them and can retain them indefinitely. They can share them with others who wish to view them (though they cannot, by and large, duplicate these copies further, except under some constrained circumstances defined by the copyright laws). Once a work is published in print, there is no turning back; distributing revised and updated editions is the only possibility. There is a strong link between integrity and access to the historical record as maintained by libraries and other institutions. Readers can audit this record by requesting published materials through libraries. To be sure, this system is stronger in theory than in practice. It may be exceedingly difficult to locate a specific version of a work that has had only limited distribution through publication, particularly if the publisher has not been scrupulous about identifying the various published versions. But the system seems to be one of highly distributed control, and the record defined by acts of publication thereby seems strongly and permanently auditable.

The implications of distributed control as a guarantee of access to the print record goes beyond simply knowing that copies of a work exist and cannot be withdrawn. The library system essentially ensures anonymous access to this history. One can inspect published works without any need for the publisher or author of these works to know that one is reading them. This is an important feature outside the scholarly domain, particularly in areas such as government records.

None of these perceived strengths of print publication have clear parallels for electronic works. In the networked information environment, the act of publication is ill defined, as is the responsibility for retaining and providing long-term access to various "published" versions of a work. Because of the legal framework under which electronic information is typically distributed, matters are much worse than they are generally perceived to be. Even if the act of publication is defined and the responsibility for the retention of materials is clarified, the integrity of the record of published works is critically compromised by the legal constraints that typically accompany the dissemination of information in electronic formats.

Ensuring Integrity in Electronic Information Distribution

In the networked information environment, new issues emerge in each of the areas just discussed. In some cases, conceptually straightforward (though not necessarily widely deployed) technological mechanisms permit the electronic environment to mimic the print world closely, if this is considered desirable. (Sometimes, however, as is the case with validating distribution channels, the electronic world is being held to a much higher standard because people seem to be more comfortable with the print world than the electronic one.) New considerations in the networked information environment, however, often make these concerns more valid and increasingly difficult to address.

Versions and Editions
Good technologies are available that track bit-level equivalence of digital objects (e.g., MD-5 checksums) and that identify when objects differ at this level. With appropriate management policies, discipline of editors and publishers, and protocol and citation structures, it is feasible to retain and manage a record of publication of even frequently changing versions of works, where versions are defined as files that contain different sets of bit sequences. Some practical problems arise, however, in tracking large, frequently updated databases. The question is whether to maintain a series of large snapshots of the database or to build the maintenance of changes into the database itself.

But we increasingly view documents at a level higher than simple collections of bits. We seek a definition of content that transcends particular representations of an object. We sense that a document should be considered the "same version" whether it is encoded in ASCII or EBCDIC or UNICODE—at least sometimes, in those cases where any of the character codes in question can fully represent the contents of the document and the different versions can be viewed as isomorphic to each other. Unfortunately, matters become confused as we look at the variety of document representations available today.

Consider textual documents. These can be represented in a wide range of word-processing formats and in some platform and software representations, such as SGML. Although software is readily available to perform transformations from one such format to another, these transformations are imperfect. Information (such as formatting, table layouts, perhaps character sets) is lost. The transformations are not fully invertable. We are beginning to develop concepts that define a canonical representation of a document as being the format in which the author or publisher cast the work, and that then define a series of surrogate alternative representations that can be algorithmically generated. In a client-server environment, these transformations can be accomplished either by the client or as a service provided by the server as part of preparing a document for intersystem transfer. We are trying to develop vocabulary to describe such canonical formats and to allow servers to indicate to their clients how much information is likely to be lost in transferring a document in a given format.

Debates also rage over what constitutes meaningful characteristics of a document. For example, many documents are typeset in specific fonts. To what extent is a document corrupted from the original version when it is re-rendered in a new font, or rendered in a computed font (such as Adobe's multiple master font system)? Many of these issues may seem somewhat artificial and inflated; one may argue that words are words—as long as the words are accurately retained, the essence of the work is transmitted—and that concerns with layout and typography are cosmetic. Although fonts and formats are often not critical in simple English-language textual documents, they take on considerably greater importance in works involving complex tables and equations, multiple languages and character sets, and other types of scholarly material (consider, for example, works on the history of typesetting).

Images represent another useful case in point. They occupy a special place in our historical and cultural record because of the expectations and assumptions that surround them. Historically, people have assumed that it is inappropriate to edit images without some indication that such editing has occurred, except for special cases such as trick photography and art images. Images that are presented as representations of events are presumed, rightly or wrongly, to be accurate representations, that is, evidence (Mitchell 1992). As images are increasingly created, edited, and transferred in digital form, a wide range of integrity issues arise that go far beyond the simple ability to create strikingly realistic images of events that never happened or to alter records of events that did occur in virtually undetectable ways. As images of photographs, paintings, and other materials are captured digitally to enhance access to these materials, subtle distortions and inaccuracies are introduced, often as a consequence of editorial and technical choices involved in the image-capturing process and with the best intentions of those involved in capturing the images. Issues of resolution and compression algorithms are central, as are questions such as the accuracy of color representation. Perhaps most troubling is that the viewer of a digital image often is unaware of the choices being made in capturing and delivering an image and the inaccuracies being introduced (see Lynch 1994b for a more detailed exploration of these issues).

All the questions raised thus far relate to the nature of representations of content in digital format and are intrinsic to the digital medium. As such, they have a certain intellectual legitimacy. But another, more subtle series of challenges to the integrity of digital works is emerging.

The ability to duplicate digital information easily and indefinitely, with each copy being identical to the original (and thus of identical quality as the original) is threatening to some rights holders. One response to this threat is to make each copy that is legally distributed to a licensee or purchaser unique by adding information that is difficult to identify, alter, or remove. Any unauthorized copies of the work that are discovered can thus be traced by extracting this unique information from the unauthorized copy and matching it to an audit trail of information that has been added to the legitimate distributed copies of the work. This added information is analogous to a watermark on paper that includes a unique number for each copy of a work that is distributed.

A wide range of techniques for watermarking various types of digital materials have been proposed. For textually oriented material, these include deliberately introduced typographic and layout variations such as line spacing, word spacing, and character spacing (Brassil et al. 1994). More elaborate watermarking techniques, which make use of the ability of computers to alter not just presentation but content, have also been suggested. For example, Tom Clancy, in his novel *Patriot Games,* describes a technique called the canary trap, in which classified documents are prepared with variant summary sections (which are expected to be particularly quotable if a copy of the document is leaked to the press, for example), and each time a copy of the document is distributed, a computer selects a specific set of variant versions of these summary sections, thus permitting the source of an unauthorized copy to be traced. Such techniques may come into use (if they have not already) to try to protect high-value, limited-distribution intellectual property such as specialized newsletters, as they are distributed on the network. For digital files that represent images or sounds, various schemes have been proposed that introduce minor perturbations in the data that will be nearly imperceptible to the viewer or listener.

In essence, all these techniques involve hiding secret messages within literate, aural, or visual communications. They thus strike at the core of concerns about integrity of works. What does integrity of digital information mean in an environment when authors, publishers, or others can introduce hidden messages or subtexts into works in arbitrarily complex ways? This type of concealed communications has a rich history, not just in a cryptologic context but in the history of the occult, dating back to at least Johannes Trithemius in the late fifteenth and early sixteenth century. The term used to describe this type of message is *steganography* (covert writing). Steganography is enjoying a resurgence in the digital environment, with a number of programs in the public domain that can encode secret messages within various types of files available on the network (for example, *Stego* for the Macintosh, by Romana Machado). In all these approaches to protecting intellectual property rights, we can see a direct conflict with expectations about the integrity of electronic information as publishers move away from their traditional role as mass replicators of works.

Finally, all questions of versions and editions still assume that identifiable acts of releasing works (publication, distribution, or whatever the appropriate term is in the networked environment) take place. In fact, an increasing number of networked information resources are better modeled as continuously updated databases. Other examples, such as the continually updated half-hour CNN Headline news broadcasts, however, illustrate that this problem is not unique to networked information resources but is commonplace outside the print world. It is impractical and possibly impossible for an external agency like a library to maintain a complete record of changes to such a resource. At best, such an agency can capture a series of snapshots of the state of the resource at specific points in time. If it is necessary to maintain a complete record of the changes to such an information resource, this record needs to be built into the design of the resource itself (for example, it could retain timestamped copies of each object that is part of the resource as objects are added, deleted, or updated). Such features may add substantial cost to the construction and operation of an information resource. The user community (and the broader library community) must be prepared to make a case for such investments when necessary. And we must trust the operator of the resource to maintain and preserve this audit trail of changes accurately. This calls for a somewhat higher level of trust than is typical in the highly distributed, explicitly versioned print environment.

Citation in the Networked Information Environment

A reliable system of bibliographic citation is a requirement for any system of scholarly publication. The lack of such a system today is, I believe, more a reflection of the immaturity of the networked information environment than of any intrinsic problem in citing electronic information. Various proposals have been offered that basically extend current models for print citation to cover nonprint materials, including electronic information, and there do not seem to be major problems in doing this other than the problems of versions and editions discussed earlier. Standards and standard practices are still evolving for such citations.

In the networked information environment, a higher standard is being demanded than has been typical in the print world. Simply having a citation to a printed work does not necessarily mean that one can obtain easily a copy of that work. Indeed, document delivery based on citations is an exceedingly complex and costly process. There is often considerable uncertainty about the exact printed work to which a citation refers. But in the electronic environment one expects that it should be possible to click on a citation and immediately obtain access to the work (if one is willing to pay for it). Some people would like (perhaps indicating the general distrust of the electronic information environment) to be able to verify that the digital object retrieved by following a citation is in fact the same object that the creator of the citation intended to identify. Citation models are thus being extended to include the ability to determine where an electronic work is held or stored and how to obtain access to it, and the ability to verify that one has retrieved the correct work. Proposals such as the Internet Engineering Task Force's work on Uniform Resource Locators (URLs), Uniform Resource Names (URNs), and Uniform Resource Characteristics (URCs) are an attempt to combine citation, access, and verification mechanisms (Lynch 1994a) and to address some of the issues involved in having variant representations of a work available.

Trusted Channels of Distribution

Concerning the need to verify the integrity of a distribution channel for an electronic work (that is, to verify that a copy of a work was obtained from an authoritative source), the electronic environment is again being held to a much more rigorous standard than the print environment. Although attempts to define precise standards and implement them widely in the networked environment create substantial problems (which include issues related to intellectual property rights of various cryptographic algorithms and export restrictions that inhibit the widespread implementation of these algorithms in an increasingly global network), the basic techniques for establishing chains of provenance for digital objects are well understood and can be found in any good current textbook on cryptography.

The more difficult issues here are at a higher level. What are the trusted sources for obtaining a work? How does one identify these sources for a given work, or the sources with which one may verify that a copy that one has obtained from a third party is a true copy? Are publishers, libraries, third-party brokers such as bookstores, or authors among these trusted sources? By and large, we have not addressed these questions specifically in the print environment, where we tend to assume that any source that has one of the mass-produced copies of a printed work will be sufficiently authoritative. These are ultimately questions about the roles and responsibilities of the various participants in an electronic publishing system.

Access to the Published Literature

In the print world the act of publication typically implies the irrevocable release of control over at least some copies of a work. These copies are acquired and retained by organizations such as libraries, which ensure that the copies are accessible to the community of readers and preserve the copies for the future use of society. Underpinning this guarantee of access and preservation is the current copyright law and the doctrine of first sale, as well as an economic framework that includes the sale of physical artifacts that are then controlled by the copyright law.

In the electronic environment, the economic model is one of license (contract) that is typically for a limited period of time and a specific user community, thus weakening the assumptions about both preservation and access to electronic content that is part of the published literature. The legal structures of copyright law do not come into play, as they are superseded by the specifics of contracts (Lynch 1993). Resolution of these problems is not a technical issue; it is rather an issue of economics, law, and public policy. The issue of preservation is readily addressed by an insistence on perpetual licenses by the library community, though it is not clear that the library community has sufficient economic strength to negotiate such licenses successfully. In addition, the community of authors and readers is not sufficiently sensitized to the problem to bring the necessary pressure to bear on publishers and rights holders.

Ensuring access is more problematic. Although it seems likely that access guarantees at some level can be negotiated, they may be more restrictive than those offered by today's interlibrary loan system for printed works. Increased restrictions on access to electronic information will be difficult to accept for a community of readers focused on the technical potential of computer communications networks to increase information access.

I believe that in order to create a viable system of electronic scholarly publication that meets the needs for integrity of the published record, it will be necessary for the publisher and rights-holding community to address explicitly the questions of guaranteeing access and preservation in their agreements with libraries. This problem can be solved if the parties involved are willing to make the concessions needed to solve it. But in an environment of severe economic pressures and revenue ambitions, the solution will be difficult to negotiate.

Conclusion

The integrity of a future electronic system of publication is essential if such a system is to supplant or even substantially supplement the print-based system of scholarly publication. Ensuring the integrity of such a system involves a complex mix of questions: deep intellectual issues about the nature of versions and editions of works, which have been pondered by the community of scholars for centuries but which take on new and problematic (but fascinating) proportions in the electronic environment; relatively routine engineering problems involving standards and algorithms; and public policy questions about how to ensure the continued preservation of, and access to, the published literature.

What is striking to me is the level of distrust with which some people view the electronic information environment, and the stringent demands that are being placed on a system of publication in this environment, which go far beyond what the current print-based system can deliver. As we begin to migrate to a networked information environment and become more comfortable with this new world, it seems likely that some of these expectations will become tempered with realism. Even in cases where we can meet the requirements being proposed for electronic publishing, we may find that most authors, readers, and publishers are unwilling to pay the costs to do so.

The print-based system is in many ways a good model; it has served us well in many respects. A transition to an electronic environment offers us two challenges as we consider the central issues of integrity of the publication system: it challenges us to ensure that we maintain the strengths of the print system and do not discard them in the name of economic convenience; and it challenges us to be realistic about what new guarantees of integrity we truly need.

References

Brassil, J., S. Low, N. Maxemchuk, and L. O'Gorman. (1994). "Electronic Marking and Identification Techniques to Discourage Document Copying." In *Networking for Global Communications Source: Proceedings of INFOCOM '94 Conference on Computer Communications, Toronto, Ontario, Canada, June 12-16*, vol. 3. Los Alamos, Calif.: IEEE Computing Society Press, pp. 1278–1287.

Lynch, Clifford A. (1993). "Accessibility and Integrity of Networked Information Collections," Background Paper BP-TCT-109. Office of Technology Assessment. Washington, D.C.: Government Printing Office.

Lynch, Clifford A. (1994a). "Uniform Resource Naming: From Standards to Operational Systems." *Serials Review* 20, no. 4: 9–14.

Lynch, Clifford A. (1994b). "The Integrity of Digital Information Mechanics and Definitional Issues." *JASIS* 43, no. 10: 737–744..

Mitchell, William J. (1992). *The Reconfigured Eye: Visual Truth in the Post-Photographic Era.* Cambridge: The MIT Press.

9

The University Press in the Electronic Future

Lisa Freeman

The world of scholarly publishing has changed a great deal since the first book was published by a university press (Oxford) in 1478, but few if any of those changes will likely prove to have been as significant as the introduction of high-speed networked communications technology (Hawes 1967). The fact that university presses have been around for more than five centuries suggests that they play an important, perhaps even essential, role in the dissemination of research, scholarship, and knowledge. Such endurance also suggests that university presses, and not libraries, faculty consortia, or scholarly societies, are uniquely well suited to performing this crucial task. In this chapter, I argue that a successful transition to electronic publishing in academia will depend in part on the degree to which university presses are incorporated into the process. Likewise, I suggest that university presses offer a great deal of expertise that can help to ensure that such a transition is successful.

Current Trends in University Press Publishing

In order to understand how university presses can contribute to the expansion of networked scholarly communication, it is necessary to begin with a brief overview of the state of university press publishing. University press book sales were collectively estimated to be $400 million in 1993, roughly 2 percent of sales revenue from book publishing in the United States. Conversely, unit sales of university press titles exceeded eight thousand in that same year, or nearly 17 percent of the total number of books sold.[1] It is this gap between revenue and units that is at the heart of the university press publishing enterprise: university presses were created in order to ensure that the best research and scholarship would be made available to the widest possible audience, independent (in theory) of commercial considerations, a lofty but increasingly unattainable goal. No other type of publishing places such singular emphasis on editorial quality. As a result, university press profits are nonexistent, and financial crises frequent: university presses are not, nor have they ever been, in the business of making money. This observation is obvious but often overlooked.

In this context, it is important to point out that the rapid growth of the Internet (and the realization that reasonably affordable networked communication is possible) is only the latest in a series of changes in the political economy of higher education that have rocked the scholarly publishing community in recent years. Among these changes are the following:

• A general leveling off of support for university presses from their parent institutions, as well as reductions in the amount of money available to support specific publications.[2] The highly dispersed nature of any given university press's constituency (i.e., academic readers and authors, university and some public libraries, and, to a lesser extent, the more general book-buying public) makes it difficult to organize effective on-campus support, thus making the press an easy target for provosts and presidents under pressure to trim university budgets.

• A significant downward trend in the purchase of scholarly monographs by academic research libraries, which for decades formed the core of the market for scholarly books. As the prices for scientific, technical, and medical journals have risen, larger portions of university library budgets have been devoted to serials buying. This has in turn reduced the amount of money available for the purchase of books, particularly in the humanities and social sciences, disciplines that have traditionally been at the heart of most university presses' editorial programs.[3] When I began to work in scholarly publishing in 1980, we assumed that a typical peer-reviewed social science monograph, bound in hardcover and priced below $35.00, would sell a minimum of 1,500 copies. That number is now closer to 400 or 500, and anecdotal evidence suggests that it may be declining further.

• The introduction of the photocopier, and with it, the enormous increase in the widespread use of course packets and interlibrary loans, which in turn has further reduced sales to the classroom and library markets.

• Continued pressure to offer deeper discounts to wholesalers and bookstore chains in an increasingly centralized national book distribution system. University presses are heavily dependent on book wholesalers to enable them to reach thousands of bookstores around the country, but discounts to wholesalers now frequently exceed 50 percent of list price. The more recent spread of "superstores" (Barnes and Noble, Borders, and so on) has generated further pressure, as large chains squeeze out small independent stores and demand higher discounts as well. For book publishers, this means fewer dollars are taken in for each unit sold, and in a market in which unit sales have declined precipitously, there is little option but to raise prices even further, a strategy that can backfire if prices move out of the individual book buyer's reach. Price increases also reduce the effective purchasing power of libraries operating with fixed collection development budgets.

University presses have adopted a number of strategies to cope with these changes. They have turned increasingly to publishing regional books and other general-interest trade books in order to generate revenue, and they have increased the number of titles they publish with the classroom market in mind, books that ten years ago might have been deemed inappropriate for a university press. They have adopted much more aggressive marketing and sales policies—employing commissioned sales representatives and hiring publicists—generally behaving more like commercial publishers and less like university departments. They have embraced technological innovations (such as desktop publishing and disk-to-film printing), which have in turn reduced production costs. And most have chosen to focus their editorial programs on particular subject niches, developing depth of expertise in lieu of breadth of subject matter.

In many respects, these are positive changes for a segment of the publishing industry that has not always been the most efficient. But these moves have also had the unfortunate effect of further distancing university presses from their home institutions. Trade books can be lucrative, but not all of them can be justified in terms of a press's academic mission. Aggressive sales and marketing policies inevitably require that presses decline to publish books of intrinsic quality for which the markets are too small. And more focused editorial policies tend to alienate those portions of the faculty whose interests are not represented by a press's program.

As the various participants in the system of scholarly research and education scramble for increasingly scarce dollars, the pressure on university presses to achieve self-sufficiency grows. The more financially successful a press is, the less support it is likely to receive from its parent institution. (Even more perverse is that financial success largely depends on reducing the number of specialized books on a press's list, the very books that the press was created to publish in the first place.)

As subsidies are withdrawn, costs formerly covered by such funding must be passed along to the customer. The "hidden" costs of publishing research and scholarship—that is, the cost of producing materials that are not commercially viable—are thus being shifted from universities (in the form of subsidies to university presses) to university libraries, faculty, and students (in the form of higher prices).

Largely in response to rising costs, some scholars and librarians have suggested that the fact that anyone can now "publish"—that is, mount a text on a network—eliminates the need for scholarly publishers altogether. Advocates of this approach argue that universities are being forced to "buy back" research for which they have already paid (in the form of salaries, support, and grants). The advent of electronic networks makes it possible for universities to become their own publishers. Online publishing will be cheaper than print because it will no longer be necessary to print and bind books in advance of actual demand (thus reducing the amount of money spent on, and tied up in, physical inventory), and as an added benefit, the publishing process will be accelerated by eliminating or at least reducing the amount of time that it takes to produce the book. Access to scholarly work will be increased because distribution will no longer be tied to the physical object of the book or journal.[4]

I would like to argue precisely the opposite: that at least in the short term, and certainly through the 1990s, online publishing will be more expensive, more time consuming, and a less effective means of distributing scholarship than the present print-based system. Moreover, if higher education as a whole is to realize the potential benefits of networked publishing, we must begin now to develop a viable long-term plan for the shift from a print-based mode to an electronic mode of distributing scholarly research and information, and that plan needs to take into account the roles and contributions of the various participants in the present system, especially university presses. What is needed is a *publisher's* perspective on what has largely been viewed as a technical problem. It is therefore helpful to begin with some discussion of what it is that publishers generally, and university presses in particular, actually *do*, in order to determine which functions can and should be retained in the electronic environment, and who should perform the ones that are retained.

The Unique Contributions of University Presses

Publishers and librarians generally agree that in the print-based publishing environment, university presses perform three basic functions that are essential to the successful operation of the current system of scholarly communication and which much be preserved in the electronic environment. These are the selection, refinement, and marketing and promotion of the best scholarship presently being produced.

Selection

Gatekeeping is the term usually used to refer to a process that culminates in the management of peer review. Gatekeeping also includes the much less obvious process of encouraging, commissioning, and influencing what is actually written. Peer review as practiced by university presses not only ensures adherence to certain standards of scientific practice; it also helps to assess the likely usefulness of research and its relevance to, and potential long-term impact on, a particular field or fields of study. More important, perhaps, is the active role that university press editors play in identifying new fields of inquiry and in nurturing authors and their ideas. It is this editorial expertise that ultimately lies at the heart of a press's imprint. The importance accorded a university press book by promotion and tenure committees is only the most visible acknowledgment of the value of this process.

Refinement

University presses help to make scholars' ideas more accessible through general editing, copyediting, proofreading, and design. The process of turning a good book idea into a good book requires not only a unique combination of knowledge about subject matter, previously published materials, and intellectual trends in other fields but also an eye for good writing and clear thinking. Painful and time consuming as copyediting can be, most authors will admit that this process is ultimately of inestimable value. Proofreading ensures accuracy and the effective transmission of ideas from writer to reader. Typography has evolved into an art form precisely because the type's appearance on a page substantially affects the ease with which one can read it. The contributions are best understood when reading a poorly edited, poorly proofread, or poorly designed book.

Marketing and Promotion

University presses also market, promote, and distribute scholarly books and journals. Physically making a book is only part of the process; making the right readers aware of its existence is a complex, time consuming, and costly part of a system that currently handles over 40,000 new books annually.

Selection, Refinement, Marketing, and Promotion in the Electronic Environment: Do We Need Them?

The power of the networks to enable the creation and distribution of so-called fugitive documents (or gray literature)—working papers, conference presentations, and so on—is enormous, and scholars will (and already do) make good use of network technology to facilitate the exchange of ideas and information, particularly that which is not in "final" or "publishable" form. That the technology exists to enable such exchanges in no way diminishes the need for peer-reviewed, well-edited versions of an author's work, however. To the contrary: the need for fully peer-reviewed work will increase as more scholars are technically able to distribute their work without the assistance of intermediaries. Distinguishing between that which is peer reviewed and that which is not will be increasingly important as the volume of material increases.

Word processing has not significantly improved the quality of scholars' writing. Editorial development, copyediting, and proofreading are just as important online as they are in the print world. Authors are notoriously bad at editing and proofreading their own work, and typographical errors and improper grammar seriously detract from any text. More important, errors in language use, accidental or otherwise, can severely hinder the effective transmission of ideas. Ineffective communication not only limits the usefulness of a document but also undermines a scholar's credibility.

Finally, simply creating a document is insufficient. The textual proliferation that has resulted from the fact that anyone can "author" an electronic text makes it more difficult to find the specific article or text that one wants, a situation exacerbated by the still rudimentary nature of most Internet searching tools. Effective electronic equivalents to advertising and direct mail will be necessary if the people who want and need to know about a particular kind of research are to find it.[5] Indeed, adequate marketing and promotion will probably be more important in the early stages of development of online scholarly publishing than they are in the print world because of the massive growth in the numbers of texts available and the relative inexperience of the community of users.

Why University Presses?

There is much to be gained by retaining one of the key features of the present system of scholarly communication: the existence of independent not-for-profit publishers supported by the scholarly community whose primary purpose is to manage the functions previously described. University presses are not by and large beholden to their institution's faculties, although the work of faculty editorial committees is essential to the system. Rather, university presses are able to select, evaluate, and develop work independently of the political pressures to which many scholars, and junior scholars in particular, are often subjected within their own institutions. For example, a scholar who works in a newly emerging field, one that is perhaps not entirely accepted by the faculty of her or his department, still has the opportunity to see that work published by a university press that functions independently of her or his own institution.

It has been suggested that the peer-review process can and should be performed either elsewhere within the university or by scholarly societies. Neither alternative appears to offer any advantages over the present system, and several disadvantages come immediately to mind. Would scholarly communication truly be improved by having department chairs or university administrators assume responsibility for deciding what is to be published? Do scholarly societies, which are membership organizations with elected rather than professional officers, really offer a better alternative? Would university departments or scholarly societies foster the kind of interdisciplinary work that is so characteristic of innovative scholarship in the humanities and social sciences? Would the selection process remain relatively independent if the site of selection were to shift to one of these venues?

Finally, it is worth stating the obvious: publishing is a complex process that requires a delicate balance among the often competing concerns of content, economics, readability, market, and packaging. Although the necessity of making certain specific decisions—whether to publish in hardback or paperback, for example—may ultimately disappear in the electronic world, other similar questions will remain: Should the work be illustrated? Is it badly written? Would an introduction by a scholar from another discipline help to make it accessible to a wider audience? What price is appropriate? The final form of scholarly work may be different, but the process by which it is created, refined, and produced will remain essentially the same, and these questions will still need to be answered.

Some Unexamined Assumptions: Distribution, Speed, Cost

A great deal could be gained from a move to electronic publishing of scholarly materials. Such features as hypertext, interactivity, and multimedia will greatly enhance scholars' ability to express and circulate their ideas. It is in part the availability of such technologies that has fueled the expansion into CD-ROM publishing, and which makes networked communication so exciting. These are the unique aspects of electronic publishing: technologies that enable an author to do things that simply are not possible in the print world.

In discussions concerning the future of scholarly publishing, the most attention has been paid to those features of electronic communication that are not unique but that instead appear to be better versions of what is already done in the print environment. The argument, stated simply, is that networked distribution of scholarly materials will be more effective (that is, such distribution will reach a wider audience, presumably at lower cost), more rapid, and less expensive than under the present system. These largely unexamined assumptions deserve further attention.

Distribution

Virtually all arguments about the benefits to be realized from a shift to networked distribution of scholarly materials proceed from the assumption that everyone will have a computer that is hardwired to the Internet (or some other network) and fully capable of downloading text and graphics at high speed. It is also assumed that each individual will either personally possess substantial technical expertise or will have ready access to highly trained technical support staff. Of the three benefits being discussed here, none depends more heavily on the realization of such an environment than does the argument concerning improved distribution of materials, yet inadequate access to hardware, software, training, and support is still the norm in most institutions of higher education.[6]

Given the financial stresses under which most universities operate, it seems unlikely that this situation will change any time soon. For many scholars—particularly those in nontechnical fields, those with especially limited financial resources (such as those who teach part time or at junior colleges and technical institutions), and those located outside of

North America and Europe—the effort, expense, and time required to achieve integration into the networked world will be even greater. Although the Internet has enabled individuals in remote locations to communicate more effectively with others, the number of people who have access to this technology remains extremely limited.

One of the primary functions of university presses, and, by extension, of the present system of scholarly publishing, is to ensure that the best research and scholarship are made available to the widest possible audience. Given the difficulties enumerated here, it seems clear that online distribution will remain far less effective than the present system of print-based publishing for some period of time.

Speed

Speed of publication varies significantly depending on the type of publication. To the extent that the printing process takes longer than distribution over a network, publication time will be reduced, although the amount of time that will be saved is fairly insignificant (an average of six to eight weeks for a monograph, somewhat less for a journal). Likewise, an electronic text can be delivered more quickly to a potential reader than a printed book can, although most publishers and suppliers are now capable of supplying books overnight (whether they deliver on such promises is another question). Again, for the typical book, the time savings would be minimal.[7]

The time that is required at the front end—to select, review, develop, edit, and revise—is not likely to be reduced substantially by electronic publishing, however. Although it may appear that networked communications can make certain tasks easier or less time consuming, this has not generally proven to be the case. Most university presses already employ electronic technology in varying degrees in the production of their books and journals: on-screen copyediting, coding and correcting author-supplied disks, desktop publishing, and disk-to-film printing are widespread. In most cases, the time savings realized by the implementation of one of these technologies is time lost at another stage. Although the time required to typeset a book, for example, can be reduced by providing coded and corrected disks, additional time is required to prepare the disks for use by the typesetter. And that time would still have to be invested if the text were to be made available online. The time required to perform the essential value-added functions discussed earlier—selection, refinement, and marketing and promotion—will not be reduced by the introduction of electronic technology.

Cost

It has been suggested that the cost of publishing on the networks will be substantially lower than the cost of traditional print publication, but, as with time savings, many apparent cost savings are in fact cost shifts. For example, the use of author-supplied disks reduces typesetting costs only if editorial changes are keyboarded by someone other than the typesetter. The cost of paying in-house staff or using freelancers to input changes on disk is no lower than the cost of traditional typesetting, as keyboarding is a time-consuming, labor-intensive process. Thus many publishers have shifted responsibility for entering changes to authors. If publishers rely on authors to enter changes, the costs have been effectively shifted out of the cost-of-goods calculation for the final product (perhaps reducing the final price to the consumer), but costs still exist. Moreover, relying on an author to enter changes increases the likelihood of errors, incurring a cost that may not be as easily measured in dollars but which is a cost nevertheless. At the same time, technical support for computer users (whether provided by libraries, computer centers, departments, or others), as well as hardware, software, and training, is a cost in addition to, not instead of, those for printing and binding. And many of these expenses are ongoing (e.g., for software upgrades), whereas printing and binding expenses are not.

In the immediate future, publishers will have to expend substantial amounts of time and money to learn how to publish in the networked world. It is one thing to suggest that university presses should begin publishing on the networks. It is another entirely to suggest that we—as publishers, or anyone else for that matter—have a clear idea of what an electronic book or journal looks like, or what our readers want in an electronic book, or how they would use such a book if it existed and they had ready access to it. The codex book has survived for so long precisely because it is so well designed for its purpose; the design of an equally successful—that is, readable, usable, and enduring—electronic text is not obvious.

Under these circumstances, it seems inevitable that university presses will be required to produce parallel print and electronic products for some time. Although access to network technology is spreading rapidly, large segments of the academic community are still not served by the Internet. Questions about media longevity and preservation are still being investigated, and until they are resolved, most archives and libraries will prefer to acquire print (or perhaps print and electronic) versions of most scholarly works. And the generation of scholars for whom books hold special meaning beyond the ideas and information they contain will, in the immediate future at least, prefer a printed book to an electronic text.

The effect of these trends will inevitably be to increase, rather than decrease, the cost of scholarly publishing in the short to medium term. In the long term, it is less clear that production costs will decrease substantially, although the combination of reduced manufacturing, physical handling, and storage (i.e., library facilities) costs may reduce the overall expense to the system. From the manufacturing side, physical book production—printing and binding—rarely accounts for more than 20 percent of the overall unit cost of a book. The added expense of investment in computer hardware and software, and the ongoing costs of training and maintenance, may well exceed the amount saved by not having to print and bind.

Facilitating the Transition to the Electronic University Press

Realistically, then, networked communication is not a panacea for the troubles of higher education, nor should it be a death knell for university presses. The potential long-term benefits, especially in the areas of technology that are unique to online communication, are significant, but so will be the costs of implementing such a system. University presses are in many respects uniquely well qualified to manage online publishing in ways that could ease the transition. If we are to manage the shift to online publishing successfully, however, without losing the very features of the present system that have made it so important, we must begin to confront a number of issues that continue to prohibit the rapid entry of all publishers, and university presses in particular, into the networked world.

Intellectual Property

Arguably the most vexing problem confronting university presses with regard to online publishing is the question of copyright and intellectual property protection. For university presses just as for any publisher, adequate intellectual property protection is the sine qua non of publishing online, despite the persistent and pervasive tendency of some people to conflate the notion of nonprofit publishing with the nonsensical idea of "publishing without costs." Without sufficient intellectual property protections, university presses have no (or no adequate) means of recouping their expenses, costs which are likely to be no lower, and perhaps even somewhat higher, than they are in the print world. Even university presses have to pay their bills—out of budgets that are increasingly less subsidized.

At one extreme end of the spectrum of the copyright debate are those who have argued that in order for everyone to benefit fully from the potential of networked information, the application of copyright law to electronic documents should be heavily modified, if not eliminated. This technologically deterministic view proceeds from the assumption that the technology that enables the virtually instantaneous exchange of ideas should not be monitored or controlled in any way. Less extreme but no less potentially damaging is the "use it or lose it" approach to fair use, a point of view that has become increasingly widespread within the library community. Even a modest expansion of fair use in the electronic environment, however, would likely have the reverse of its intended effect by substantially reducing both the amount of information available and the level of access to that information: too broad an interpretation of fair use would undermine university presses' ability to recoup their costs, and thus they would lose the incentive (and the ability) to provide the added values described earlier.

At the other end of the spectrum are those who would completely eliminate the notion of fair use and require that all uses be metered and charged. Much of this debate stems from a belief that because abuse is easier in the electronic world, it will become more widespread. The obvious cynicism inherent in such an assumption aside, there are strong arguments against so limited an approach. Scholars need to have access to one another's work, and they need to be able to browse and search without having to have one eye on the meter if they are to do their best work. Moreover, publishers simply will not be able to control what happens to an electronic document once it has been downloaded or printed. The way to reduce abuse is not to restrict access but to develop fee structures that encourage users to obey the law. Eliminating fair use will not, in and of itself, prevent abuse.

What Does It Look Like and How Much Does It Cost?
Achieving the goals of a user-friendly, ubiquitous, content-rich networked environment will take time and money, not only because of the need for ongoing technological research and development but also because there are no precedents, no models, to help guide the development of these new texts or of the tools that will be necessary to use them.

As a publisher, my first inclination when trying to decide whether or not to publish something is to ask a potential reader. It seems logical, then, when we begin to discuss electronic publishing, to think about what our authors and readers want before trying to decide how to do it or how much to charge.

In the case of electronic publishing, most of our primary audience is poorly informed about such matters. Many have little or no idea about the potential benefits to be gained from electronic publishing, and a smaller subset of that group actively opposes it. Although one can explain the concept of hypertext relatively easily, it is nearly impossible to convey the potential inherent in, for example, a hypertext-linked database or an interactive CD-ROM to someone who has not actually used one. Nevertheless, without the involvement of our authors and readers, we run the risk of devising a system of scholarly communication on the networks that no one wants to use.

We must undertake serious studies of online text usage if we are to reach sensible decisions about how to publish, and how much to charge for those services, on the networks. Will users want to browse, or are they more likely to search for specific information? Will they search and download? Search and print? Search and read on screen? The answers to these questions should drive decisions about which kinds of scholarly materials are most suited for networked publishing. Similarly, decisions about how much and how to charge for electronic documents depend heavily on how they will be used. University presses and librarians continue to disagree about the most efficacious ways to bill for access to networked resources—by the byte, by the number of users, by the document, by the year—and their arguments contain almost no reference to users' preferences or actual patterns of usage.

A number of questions still to be resolved relate to the transferal of qualities specific to the printed book into electronic text, problems for which technical solutions may and probably do exist, but about which users have yet to express an opinion, let alone a preference. For example, we are accustomed to a citation system based on "pages," an artifact of the print world that has no relevance in the electronic world. How easily will scholars move to paragraph-citation style (the likely candidate to replace the page)? Might another citation method might be more effective? What happens to indexes (and who will prepare them)? How will version control (that is, the identification of original, modified, or other versions of electronic texts) be implemented? And finally, there is the question of how to deal with the new kinds of added value. Does the author or the publisher provide the hypertext link—and is the link itself copyrightable? Technology alone will not provide the answers: good, workable solutions to these problems will be found only over time.

The Special Needs of the Arts and Humanities

The bulk of most university presses' publication lists are composed of monographs in humanities and social sciences, a state of affairs that is directly linked to the mission of university presses to publish research without regard for commercial merit. University presses do not publish much in the hard sciences because science publishing is generally very profitable, which has contributed greatly to the present serials-pricing crisis. Humanities publishing is far less profitable. Without university presses, a great deal of work in the humanities and social sciences would probably never have appeared in print.

Much of the discussion about electronic publishing has focused on the production and dissemination of technical information, whether it be the conversion of technical journals from print to electronic formats or the increasing opportunities for database publishing. We talk about facilitating the exchange of data or facts or information among researchers whose highly specialized interests often make them a small, cohesive, and easily identifiable group of both producers and consumers. From a publishing standpoint, this is an ideal situation, as consensus about what works and what doesn't work is easier to achieve among a group whose interests are similar.

The specific needs of artists, humanists, and social scientists in the electronic environment have not been so well documented. The research interests of such scholars are typically much more diffuse and thus much less easily categorized; it is, in other words, much more difficult to reach agreement about what constitutes a useful e-text or e-visual in these fields. Humanists and many social scientists are more dependent on text than they are on numbers, and their work relies heavily on having access to authentic, well-documented versions of prior texts. The issue of authenticity is especially important for scholars who do textual analysis or who work in the visual arts. The artifacts of intellectual work that we know as books are not the same as a data set, for it is the actual expression of ideas—the specific choice of words—rather than the physical transmission of facts per se that is at the core of their value. The technologies, policies, and modes of access developed to produce, distribute, access, and make use of such texts will likely be different from those designed to deal with large data sets (see American Council of Learned Societies 1994).

Academic Freedom

Good scholarship is heavily dependent on an assurance of academic freedom, that is, the ability to pursue one's own ideas within certain ethical constraints yet free of intellectual restriction. The inevitable commercialization of the networks, the centralization of the service-provider function, and the information storage and retrieval capabilities of the network all point to an enormous increase in both the likelihood and the extent of surveillance. These issues are particularly salient for scholars who work in controversial areas—from AIDS research to bioengineering—but they should be of general concern to everyone engaged in the generation and dissemination of ideas.

As with so many other emerging policy areas, technical solutions already exist, or can readily be developed, to ensure privacy. But as the furor over the Clinton administration's endorsement of the Clipper Chip showed in 1994, there is little consensus about how to enact such protections. For example, the headers that a publisher may require to ensure copyright protection (that is, technical information permanently imbedded in, or attached to, an electronic text) could easily be used to infringe on a reader's privacy (if information identifying what an individual was reading were systematically collected and analyzed).[8] The point here is that technology alone will be inadequate to ensure privacy or to guarantee the protection of First Amendment rights. Both university presses as institutions and the people they employ have historically been staunch First Amendment supporters and advocates. Any possibility that such guarantees are lacking on the networks will likely discourage their use.

Conclusion

In order for any change to electronic publishing to work, universities must make substantial commitments to their presses, both financial and otherwise. A major infusion of capital will be required if university presses are to gear up successfully to publish on the networks: hardware, software, and technical training are only the first steps. In an environment in which the lack of funding has contributed to the decline in the number of scholarly books and journals being published, money will also be required to encourage demonstration projects designed to answer questions about readers' preferences and actual uses of electronic materials. This will be especially true for publishing efforts that move to take advantage of the networks' unique offerings (such as multimedia publishing, which will require presses to learn new technical skills).

Finally, universities will need to take seriously their own commitment to the electronic delivery of scholarly materials by publicly acknowledging their value. This will mean a significant cultural shift from an environment in which the physical artifact of the book is considered to have inherent value. Promotion and tenure committees in particular will have to adjust their thinking, for the distinction between a book and a journal article is nearly nonexistent when discussing electronic documents. (This represents one of the more interesting areas of growth in academic publishing, because scholars may now be able to publish research without being subject to length constraints dictated by the economics of print publishing.) Whatever other anxieties scholars may feel about electronic publishing, their concern about the legitimacy accorded their electronic work is certain to be great.

University presses perform a number of unique functions in the present print-based system of scholarly communication, and these functions can and must be incorporated into the networked world if the transition to electronic scholarly publishing is to be successful. It is this process—the process of publishing—and not the form of the final product (printed book or electronic file) that is at the heart of the present system of scholarly communication, a system that has endured for more than five hundred years with only minor modification. Preserving those contributions and facilitating the emergence of the electronic university press will be essential to ensuring that researchers, scholars, librarians, and students will continue to have access to the best work five hundred years from now.

Notes

1. University presses publish both books and journals, but for the most part this chapter will concentrate on book publishing.

2. According to Annual University Press Statistics, Association of American University Presses, April 1994. Support that all 56 presses surveyed received from their parent institutions was a mere 7.0 percent of net sales in 1993 (compared with 7.3 percent in 1990). Other subsidies, grants, and endowments represented 4.0 percent of net sales in 1993, compared with 4.1 percent in 1990. The drop is most significant for presses with sales below $1 million annually, where parent-institution support fell from 41.8 percent in 1990 to 34.9 percent in 1993, and external funding dropped from 21.0 percent in 1990 to 13.5 percent in 1993.

3. According to the so-called Mellon Report (Cummings et al. 1992), the rate of increase in books acquired by university research libraries virtually halted in the 1970s and 1980s, whereas the number of books published annually increased at a rate of at least 2 percent per year. The report also found that serials prices had increased steadily from 1963 to 1990 at an average rate of 11.3 percent per year, compared with 7.2 percent per year for book prices.

4. One of the earliest statements of this view is Okerson 1991. Although Okerson has since modified her view, this argument continues to appear in discussions about the future of scholarly publishing, most recently in Association of American Universities 1994.

5. Standards for advertising and promotion on the Internet are still evolving, but it seems clear that the Internet's former acceptable use policy is destined for substantial revision. For a fuller discussion of issues related to marketing and advertising on the Internet, see the Coalition for Networked Information archives for cni-advertise and cni-modernize (@cni.org).

6. My favorite example of the problems to be overcome on this score are the rotary phones in humanities departments at both the University of Wisconsin and the University of Minnesota.

7. In the case of journal publishing, the potential for time savings is much greater, as individual articles would not need to be held for a particular issue.

8. This is not mindless paranoia. I know of a Korean graduate student whose reading patterns were carefully monitored during his time at a major U.S. university by the systematic collection of information regarding which books he had checked out of his university's library. These were used as evidence that his research interests were "inappropriate."

References

American Council of Learned Societies and the Council for Networked Information. (1994). *Humanities and Arts on the Information Highways: A Profile*. Washington, D.C.: Coalition for Networked Information.

Association of American Universities. (1994). "Report of the Task Force on Intellectual Property Rights in an Electronic Environment." AAU Research Libraries Project. Washington, DC: Association of American Universities, April 4.

Cummings, Anthony M., Marcia L. Witte, William G. Bowen, Laura O. Lazarus, and Richard H. Ekman. (1992). *University Libraries and Scholarly Communication: A Study Prepared for the Andrew W. Mellon Foundation*. Washington, D.C.: Association of Research Libraries.

Hawes, Gene R. (1967). *To Advance Knowledge: A Handbook on American University Press Publishing*. New York: American University Press Services.

Okerson, Ann. (1991). "Back to Academia? The Case for American Universities to Publish Their Own Research." *Logos* 2, no. 2: 106–112.

10

Networked Information Is Not Free

Ira H. Fuchs

Laying Out the Myth

Many scholars who rely on computer networks and networked information have come to the conclusion that such access and information are free, or at least nearly free. For their Internet access, universities pay a flat fee for bandwidth that is completely independent of use. In turn, the universities have tended not to charge individual network users in proportion to the amount of traffic they generate, regardless of the amount. In addition to their network access, researchers have often received a number of other related benefits. Universities, often in conjunction with federal and state grants, have purchased and outfitted scholars' workstations, provided and sustained local area network access, and worked hard to augment the online collections of relevant data that are now becoming an essential element of scholarship. Our effort at Princeton University may not be typical, but in recognition of the growing importance of such activities, we have created a large support organization for computing and information technology. The responsibility of our staff is to provide support for the full range of the needs of the campus's faculty, students, and staff concerning computing and information technology, but the magnitude of the effort related to network support continues to grow.

As a result of the creation of the networking infrastructure as well as such support efforts, scholars have grown accustomed to using e-mail (electronic mail) to communicate with colleagues around the world. They are using FTP (file transfer protocol) to share thoughts, drafts, and completed manuscripts. They are exploring library catalogs and data collections around the world. Many have discovered the convenience of tools such as Gopher and Mosaic to find information when they need it.

With network service, unlike with telephone service, scholars or their departments see no personal bills for the data they receive or the traffic they initiate. At Princeton, the only bill we distribute is a fixed monthly fee for Ethernet service that is based on the amortization of the fixed costs associated with the creation and maintenance of the campus telecommunications infrastructure, not with the amount of ongoing traffic generated by individuals.

As an economist would be quick to note, a valued good that has no cost or even the perception of a low cost will tend to be consumed in substantial quantities. So has it been on the Internet. Over the past decade, every indicator of network use, including the number of users, the number of network services and applications, and the amount of traffic, has grown exponentially. The quarterly measure of Internet size showed that in mid-1994 there were 3.2 million reachable machines (more than 2 million in the United States alone), an increase of 81 percent in a year with an even steeper increase during the second half of that year.[1]

There is substantial good news here. In an environment ungoverned by individual charges, scholars have been highly motivated to integrate networked resources into their research methodologies, to augment online data holdings at a wonderful rate, and to explore research collaborations with others throughout the world. But there are also concerns: Can we sustain such growth indefinitely without charging users or in some way regulating their access? In the absence of usage-based charges, will we be able to extend such capabilities throughout K–12 institutions and to the population at large when we know that there will be fewer economies of scale to exploit? Can we continue to stimulate use and avoid inequitable access in a networked environment governed, at least in part, by usage-based pricing? In the absence of usage-based or site-license pricing, will we be able to gain access to the most useful and important sources of information?

History and Philosophy Play a Part

The philosophical and economic underpinnings of the first academic networking efforts encouraged users to employ and explore the network without regard to the costs of their actions. Subsidizing access promoted use, encouraged the development of exciting network tools, and helped us to understand the usefulness of access. Users have built up a valuable and cooperative networked community that serves as an integral research tool in most disciplines.

The Internet began in the late 1960s as the ARPAnet, a Defense Department network designed to support research into sustaining communication during times of sporadic power and communication outages. If a link between two computers were severed, the network was capable of rerouting the traffic. In this peer-to-peer scheme, the computers, rather than the network, were responsible for enclosing messages in properly addressed Internet Protocol (IP) packets. For all intents and purposes, all the users of the ARPAnet received their connections as an integral part of their government work and related grants.

BITNET and CSnet were broader-based networking efforts, connecting more than just those with Defense Department affiliations. BITNET began in 1981 when Grey Freeman and I installed a leased line between Yale University and the City University of New York. We felt that it was time that universities and colleges had a communications network that was simple to use and which could be accessed by scholars in any discipline for research and instruction. BITNET was set up as a store-and-forward network, with files and messages sent from computer to computer across the network. It provided electronic mail, remote job entry, and file transfer facilities, and it supported an interactive message facility.

To connect to BITNET, academic institutions only had to sustain their connection to another, usually nearby BITNET institution. Here too, individual BITNET users saw no charges. BITNET soon became an indispensable tool, an appropriate technology, for research, education, administration, and scholarship. Users continue to use BITNET to transmit papers and manuscripts, access databases of proposals and journal articles, obtain remote consulting on research or programming problems, and participate in a wide variety of newsgroups and online conferences. Users have come to understand that they are free to explore the network and consider new ways of integrating its capabilities into their work.

During the 1980s, in order to connect researchers to five new regional supercomputer centers, the U.S. National Science Foundation (NSF) created its own network, the NSFNET, based on the ARPAnet's IP technology. The original 56 kbps connections were slow by today's standards, but researchers were nonetheless quick to discover that their connections were useful for much more than sending and receiving data to and from the supercomputer centers. Most universities and research institutions are connected by leased lines to one of eighteen regional Internet providers. Many of these providers receive subsidies from federal and state governments and derive funds from the connection fees they charge to the universities and others. Owing to its government support, the NSFNET has operated under an acceptable use policy that limits network use to activities in support of education and research.

Amid the continuing surge in activity from the 1980s to the present, the Internet relied on self-policing to govern Net conduct. From the earliest days, users came to promote a distinctive Net culture, governed by two overriding principles: avoid wasteful use of bandwidth, and do not do anything to threaten the network. In an atmosphere devoid of apparent charges to the individual, users created their own information utopia, sharing information, providing access to massive data collections, and working hard to maintain the Net's inherent esprit de corps.

By 1994, the NSFNET had been joined by many other public, for-profit backbones, and the market for Internet connectivity had become quite competitive. Traffic from the NSFNET and the commercial backbones now interconnects, lessening the meaningfulness of the NSFNET's acceptable use policy and opening the door for a range of interesting for-pay services. Extremely intense skirmishes related to the emergence of commercial activity on the Net underlie the ingrained feeling, particularly on the part of many long-time NSFNET users, that the Net is a place for camaraderie and cooperation, not commercialism. Continuing arguments that commerce has no place on the Net will do little to prevent it from opening for business. Nonetheless, existing passions reflect the noneconomic view of the network as a place for collaboration, not an environment in which every machine, every logged-on hour, and every message carries an explicit price tag.

The Costs

Most of the costs that are directly related to the national networking infrastructure are unaffected by the number of users or the extent of use. Key infrastructural components include the transmission lines, routers (computer-based switches), and access circuits that complete the "last mile" of the connection. Using the estimate of $45 a mile a month, the NSFNET's 16,000 miles of long-haul T-3 backbone circuit costs approximately $720,000 a month.[2] In 1993, the NSF paid Merit Network, Inc. (Michigan Educational Research Information Triad), approximately

$11.5 million to run the NSFNET backbone. Merit reports that 80 percent of this amount covers lease payments for the backbone circuits and routers. Another 7 percent supports their Network Operations Center (NOC), which is responsible for monitoring traffic and troubleshooting. In addition, during 1993, the NSF provided $7 million in subsidies to the regional Internet providers.[3] The regional Internet suppliers charge institutions a fixed fee that usually depends on the speed of the access line. Institutions of higher education have clearly preferred such flat-fee pricing, as opposed to usage-based schemes that might inhibit use and complicate network planning.

Potentially, the access circuits required to provide the final connection to the home or desktop form the highest cost component, especially if we are to commit to access at speeds that can accommodate compressed video, multimedia, and interactive graphics. New fiber-optic and digital transport facilities such as ATM and reconstructed cable TV networks with reverse channel capabilities may help to decrease the last-mile costs.

Universities have had an advantage in being able to employ economies of scale in providing such connections. Routers, wires, and support are more easily shared among users on a single compact campus. Despite these economies, building and sustaining a university's local network infrastructure carries enormous costs; I believe that universities are currently spending at least an order of magnitude more than the government in maintaining their local infrastructure and in sustaining connectivity. Studies suggest that the true institutional cost of a workstation over five years, after factoring in support, maintenance, and the chronic need to augment and upgrade the local infrastructure, is close to $40 thousand (Fisher 1994). Although much of this cost has more to do with traditional office functions than with networking or network access, the high figure underscores the effort required to sustain the infrastructure.

As vice president for computing and information technology at Princeton University, I understand very well indeed the substantial costs associated with our local communications infrastructure. Since my arrival at Princeton in 1985, the university has spent more than $12 million to bring the network infrastructure to every academic and administrative site and to install wiring within buildings that were not designed with such infrastructural tinkering in mind. At Princeton, more than seven thousand network connections now reach every administrative and academic office, including the dormitories. The main expenses, for which we charge a fixed fee of approximately $20 per month per user, include the amortization of the network electronics, installation and maintenance of the backbone and local area networks, monitoring of the network, Internet expenses, and research and testing of network technologies.

Year by year, as the community's dependence on network services accelerates, we have had to upgrade our mail servers and mass storage devices. Increased reliance on electronic data requires data archives that, in turn, need maintenance and support. Even data collections in the public domain have had to be scanned or manually entered into machine-readable form. In disciplines less well served by data archives, universities are often stepping in, again at substantial cost, by converting existing data collections into formats that are more efficient for researchers. As data formats change over time, universities have to take on an archival function in order to perpetuate the usability of the data.

The Cost of Data

Much of the information on the Internet is available at no additional charge. Individuals, government agencies, universities, and commercial agencies are freely distributing a wealth of information available to anyone who can find it. Research results, scientific data, and software archives consisting of shareware and freeware are all online. The presence of all this free information undoubtedly reinforces the notion that networked information is free, but there are costs.

To begin, the growing use of networks is beginning to reveal two somewhat intangible costs. The first is the increasing congestion on our networks, as users compete for access to finite bandwidth resources. When electronic mail and file transfers were the predominant uses of the network, access via Ethernet or a T-1 link might have seemed extravagant. Today, as the use of services such as "Internet talk radio" grows and as new network applications such Mosaic and Gopher ease access to audio and visual stores of information, the competition for access to resource has perceptibly slowed performance. During the 1994 week of Comet Shoemaker-Levy's impact with Jupiter, for example, more than 930,000 users gained access to telescope images maintained by NASA. Many more were frustrated by their inability to connect or by the impact of so many users transferring such large image files.[4] In an environment governed by flat fees or the perception of no fees (and given the fact that even novice users are able to employ Mosaic and other tools to tie up the network without even realizing the implications of the information requests), congestion will only worsen, frequently obstructing scholars and others from access to information that they sorely need and standing in the way of services. Videoconferencing, for example, cannot tolerate any significant delays. In the long run, it might be possible to assign different administrative priorities to different types of traffic, and to rely on peer pressure to punish bandwidth abusers, but such rationing schemes are nearly impossible to sustain and enforce and would require significant modifications to the existing Internet protocols.

Second, just as scholars are coming to realize the inherent usefulness of having access to electronic serials and free data stores, they are also coming to find that much of the information they most need is either unavailable or otherwise beyond their financial reach. During the mid-1980s, scholars in the classics were first exposed to the Ibycus, a creation of David Packard's that provided access to all ancient Greek and Latin literature. They were instantly amazed. A lifetime's investigation into the derivation of words could now be done instantly and flawlessly. Needless to say, one cannot today be a classics scholar without such access. In most fields, unfortunately, we have nothing comparable to the Ibycus. The materials required in research are usually much less well bounded and, especially in the humanities, much less likely to be available in machine readable form. The wonderful pictures of Jupiter notwithstanding, the data that are freely available on the Net tend not to provide a complete enough corpus to entice many researchers, and the data required to compel a significant methodological shift are either unavailable or available only at a high price. Expensive electronic resources of vital interest to scholars are beginning to proliferate, and some universities are attempting to acquire such materials as a normal part of, or supplement to, their normal acquisitions. But the relatively high costs of databases, information collections, bibliographical aids, and the like make it clear that libraries will not be able to afford indefinitely what amounts to a site license for every networked data collection.

Although the costs for subscriptions to electronic indexes, collections of abstracts, and serials archives are high, we have become unfortunately accustomed to alarming increases in the charges for information. The cost and number of printed serials (especially scientific, technical, and medical serials, but also serials in the social sciences) have been rising at a far greater pace than the university's acquisitions budget for more than 20 years.[5] Such increases altered the balance between the acquisition of serials and monographs. Universities have been canceling serials to keep an appropriate balance. In the short term, it may be possible to counteract the effects of cancellations by experimenting with document delivery services. In 1994, for example, Princeton has examined several services such as CARL UnCover, UMI, and ISI. In the long run, however, publishers, who generally fear that the ease of electronic copying will lessen the number of subscribers, may raise the copyright fees on these services to the point that they will not be cost-effective alternatives. Alarming copyright increases are already beginning to occur. Firestone Library at Princeton observed a 100 percent increase in copyright fees in 1993–1994. Moreover, some science publishers have refused to permit their materials to be distributed through document delivery services. Increasing charges in an electronic environment may therefore diminish the usefulness for scholars and students of the emerging online materials.

The trend in the rising cost of printed serial subscriptions and the emergence of the new electronic capabilities lead many to believe that the journal, as we know it, will not long endure. Faculty in the sciences and engineering already note that, in many instances, printed periodicals are no longer the mechanism by which researchers are sharing information at the cutting edge. Rather than depend on print publications whose cycles often involve months or more, researchers are relying instead on electronic mail, file transfers, telephone conversations, and conference videotapes.

This somewhat less formal collaboration is now beginning to result in the production of "accepted" refereed electronic journals (the University of Chicago Press, Johns Hopkins University Press, and the MIT Press have begun to publish refereed electronic journals). In order to succeed, these efforts will need to establish standards for storage formats, protocols for search and retrieval (such as ANSI's Z39.50 standard), network management, and procedures for authentication and accounting. And although many of the first electronic journals published all comers, there is no reason why materials in an electronic format could not still be reviewed and refereed with standards comparable to print.

Such electronic journals hold the promise for a variety of solutions. Publishers will be able to save production and distribution costs that amount to perhaps 20 to 25 percent of their total outlays. Efforts in using the Internet for targeted marketing suggest that publishers may be able to accrue additional savings in marketing, perhaps another 10 to 20 percent of their outlays. Libraries may no longer have to pay an up-front subscription for serials. Rather, libraries and users might obtain access based on usage charges or print-on-demand.[6] With an incentive to disseminate only materials that generate some demand, publishers may become more likely to distribute only the most important contributions. Electronic dissemination may also facilitate new services, including research disclosure through abstracts and summaries, and flash publishing of important works. Many of these possibilities, however, will involve usage-based fees. Universities or the users in their communities will have to confront the need to pay for electronic subscriptions, connect time, and page charges. Scholars who have until now received a free ride may be surprised by the cost of their information access.

Currently, many academics and publishers are sidestepping the copyright issues. In higher education, rather than test the impact of various pricing mechanisms and the extent to which fair use permits access to copyrighted texts and other media, many researchers experimenting with scholar's environments and digital libraries either use materials in the public domain or write their own texts. Their projects have been extremely useful in demonstrating the technical feasibility of creating such environments. By avoiding copyrighted material, however, they may not teach us enough about the benefits of having easy electronic access to a full range of sources and about the elasticity of demand for scholarly material.

A Changing Environment

Researchers might remain relatively unconcerned about the cost of information were it not for a number of factors that are changing the ways in which many of us will gain access to the data we need.

Perhaps the most obvious change is that institutions of higher education are being asked to absorb some of the government's networking subsidy. In 1993, the National Science Foundation stated that the NSFNET will undergo a "transition to a networking infrastructure that is increasingly provided by interconnected network services providers operating in a competitive environment," and the federal government's support for the Internet has recently begun to diminish (NSF 1993). Universities have been asked to provide support for a share of the backbone and to help sustain the regional networks. Clearly, the emergence of an information superhighway that relies on unsubsidized connectivity and which involves access to commercial data augurs at least the prospect of higher prices, and quite likely charges that will reflect the data preferences and the extent of use among individual users.

I should note that the government, by itself and in partnership with others (notably IBM and MCI), has played a key role in developing the Internet by supporting research and development of network technologies (such as protocols and routers) and for the construction and maintenance of the NSFNET backbone. Although this support has amounted to significantly less than the private dollars invested in the telephone and cable infrastructure, the transition to commercial Internet service may lead to higher charges to sustain technological investigation and upgrades.

Charges may be higher still to support a new class of users. It was one thing to support academics. But the successful delivery of Internet service to academic groups tells us very little about the future economic behavior of the much larger number of nonacademic network users. We generally assume, for example, that home users will generate pressure for ever higher bandwidth to support high-speed information exchanges, but we base that conclusion in part on the behavior of academic groups, whose use is predicated by their assumption that there are no usage-based fees.

The explosive growth of the Internet is already bringing it users who are different in their network use from the original academic audience: users with a demand for much more than the customary academic collections. Nearly every news report mentions some information consolidation, some new or ongoing plan to bring information and entertainment over data lines to our offices and homes. There is no question that the holders of assorted copyrights in the various media are encouraged by the economic promise of charging users directly for access. It is a powerful notion, and undoubtedly a potentially lucrative one. But, from our experiences with the Internet, we understand very little about user behavior in a for-pay environment.

Delivering Internet service to a mass market will require that Internet suppliers connect users in locations that, by and large, are not yet networked. The institutional approach is the most affordable, but scholars and others will want access from other locations. As more and more individuals seek network access from their homes and other disparate locales, the nature of the networking infrastructure will change. In our universities and corporations, we have been able to capture economies of scale by providing network access to large numbers of users within a relatively fixed area. As we disperse such access, users will face the prospect of supporting a much higher cost for gateways, other local electronics, maintenance, and support.

In a competitive environment, Internet service providers will have to cover their capital and operating costs, which for most users will depend on their distance to the nearest network node. The U.S. National Information Infrastructure (NII) hopes to sustain relatively low charges by building on the existing data communications infrastructure, but without additional government subsidies the result may be the disenfranchisement of whole groups. Classes of users may become unable to afford access. Educational institutions in rural areas, particularly rural K–12 districts, may face disproportionately higher bills than their peers in larger urban districts because there will be fewer opportunities to share facilities and support services and because the costs of their connections will be substantially higher. In many cases, these rural districts have traditionally had to fight for adequate electrical and telephone service, let alone computing and networking hardware and support. Here, fortunately, the federal role in support of developing a national infrastructure is well established, and the government, in its NII planning, appears to be well aware of the need to support equitable access in our schools and communities.

In just the past year, the World Wide Web has emerged as the key mechanism through which Internet users are gaining access to information. Many new information resources are being added to the Web every day; most of today's three million sites were unavailable just a year ago. For the moment, access to most of these sites is available at no additional charge, but it is already clear that the sites with the most valued information tend rapidly to become overloaded. The providers of such resources are, in some cases at least, contemplating the burdens associated with maintaining and sustaining their information servers. It is not hard to imagine that such providers will begin to charge for use. Organizations such as America OnLine, CompuServe, and Prodigy may compete to acquire the highest-quality resources. AOL's Internet Services Company, for example, has just acquired Webmaster and the popular Global Network Navigator (GNN [http://nearnet.gnn.com/gnn/GNNhome.html]).

The resulting charges for access to important information sources may have serious implications for higher education. When commercial users need to decide whether to access for-pay services, they can base their decision on the value of the information. A consultant or lawyer can pass the fee to a client, while information producers can attempt to recover the fee from revenues generated from their own efforts. By contrast, scholars' use will rarely generate direct income, and universities may find it difficult to compute the value of scholars' access. As a result, universities may have to make difficult choices about which Web resources they will make available to their respective communities. Princeton has already decided to acquire a site license to the *Encyclopedia Britannica*, a resource that the university community finds extremely useful. But many smaller universities, already reeling from the costs associated with developing and maintaining their telecommunications infrastructure, may become quickly exasperated with the additional burden. Universities should seek favorable pricing from information providers because the marginal cost of their information is close to zero (putting aside some additional load on their servers) and their potential lost revenue is not great because most universities would not otherwise be able to afford commercial rates. Barring such agreements, the Web and its resources may soon contribute to the further polarization of information haves and have-nots.

New Charging Schemes

During the early years, relatively few users complained when they faced occasional congestion. With the recent introduction of highly interactive services, however, we have had to face the reengineering of the network's capacity.

The current flat-fee model, which involves the sharing of high bandwidth for aggregate use, certainly encourages consumption and assists institutions whose planning involves fixed annual budgets. But there is no other inherent reason why network use, as opposed to use of the telephone, fax, and postal services, ought to be free. Unless we can miraculously continue to find ways to maintain sufficient network capacity to support ever increasing demands at peak hours, movement toward at least some usage-based fees may be inevitable. Disappearing federal subsidies will require that Internet suppliers recover additional costs from users. Nascent commercial providers will expect a clear return on their investments. Unless we introduce some usage-based fees, the continuing emergence of powerful software tools for the network and the integration of audio and video capabilities in our workstations will only worsen the congestion caused by unbridled use. Many of our individual academic users are beginning to express the need for high bandwidth dedicated for their own work. Such demand may only be a precursor to the needs of home users who can, by taking advantage of today's interactive services, demand a significant proportion of network bandwidth. Existing schemes such as ISDN seem unlikely to provide the necessary speed to support interactive video, animation, and video conferencing. The result may be an awakening among scholars and others of the real costs associated with networking and vastly more concern for planning and supporting these important infrastructural resources.

All these factors point to the need for a pricing scheme that can recover costs from those who most tax the facilities. Many users in higher education would prefer access schemes analogous to the library model. There, users are not charged by the visit, by the hour, or even by the access of individual resources. Libraries have budgets for acquisition, for their support staffs, and for related equipment. Such an approach, however, does not address the two main concerns, congestion and the unusually high cost of access to the most important information sources. The approach also has publishers fearful, principally because electronic copying is so easy that users would be less likely to pay for access from their homes and offices if they can gain free access in a library.

Telephone charging schemes may offer a more useful analogy. We are accustomed to paying a flat fee for local calls and usage-based fees for long-distance traffic with variations that depend in part on peak and off-peak use. By regulating its traffic in this way, the telephone system has been able to balance the quality of its service. By contrast, the flat-fee networking approaches are now resulting in an unpredictable quality of service.

It is easy to imagine the introduction of a similar model for networking, with low, fixed prices for use of electronic mail and access to data in the public domain, and higher usage fees to help balance the demand for video and multimedia data as well as access to commercial services. Peak and off-peak charging schemes would help to shape user behavior in order to alleviate Internet congestion and to assign fees more equitably and directly to usage. Users interested in obtaining video and interactive graphics at lower rates would have an incentive to gain access to the information at slower speeds or to schedule access during off-peak times.

Variants are certainly possible. Some Internet providers now offer a "committed information rate" that charges users a two-part fee. The first is a fixed rate that depends on the speed of the connection; the second is based on the maximum guaranteed speed available to the user. In effect, the Internet supplier will use flow regulators to guarantee network transport at this committed rate, with excess capacity available on a first-come, first-served basis.

Jeffrie MacKie-Mason and Hal Varian at the University of Michigan suggest the imposition of a "congestion price" (MacKie-Mason and Varian 1994). In their "smart-market," there would be no charge for use so long as the network remained uncongested. In congested situations, packets would be placed in queue to await delivery. Users would be able to place a priority on the packets, in essence paying a premium for immediate or quick delivery. Like some auctions, users would be charged not at the rate of their bid but at the rate of the lowest-priority packet admitted to the network. The scheme has the merit of continuous efficiency but would upset planners, especially at not-for-profit institutions, who like or need to know in advance what costs they are likely to incur.

Introducing usage-based pricing or any of its variants would require efforts to measure, account for, and bill for the various types of usage. The inherent reliance on packets and packet switching, however, will make such accounting and billing difficult because, unlike in the telephone model, a complete transmission might consist of thousands of independent packets, each of which would require separate and, as a result, expensive accounting. For the moment, also, the packets we receive do not include information that would permit us to charge specific user accounts. Additional information related to authorization and user accounting would be required.

Usage-sensitive charging may appear first in small home markets where the relation between users and associated costs may appear to be more tangible and where users of interactive commercial services may be less likely to expect a flat-fee approach. Such fees are also likely to govern services, such as videoconferencing, that cannot tolerate congestion. Traditional scholarly activities, including electronic mail, file transfers, and access to textual information, are likely to remain tariffed at low rates so long as users are willing to tolerate sporadic delays.

Without question, however, many not-for-profit institutions, especially K–12 schools and smaller institutions of higher education, are constrained financially. They will undoubtedly want access to multimedia, video images, and the like. But they also tend to perceive usage-based fees as too expensive and as a drag on use. In its planning of the so-called information superhighway, the federal government has expressed concern with regard to equitable access and the need for full integration into the curriculum. Such a commitment will undoubtedly require subsidies for the creation and maintenance of educational connections.

Continuous increases in network capacity (which would drive down the incremental cost of sending packets through the network) and increasingly tolerant applications that can work around network congestion can help to delay a change to new charging schemes. As it has throughout higher education, flat-fee pricing would also help to stimulate use into commercial and home markets. But a change to a usage-based fee structure, at least for the most sophisticated network applications, would appear to be inevitable.

Notes

1. Lewis (1994) cast doubts about the usefulness of the Internet's growth, but it is certain that use is well up and that the number of useful Internet services continues to rise.

2. Chapter 5 of NRENAISSANCE Committee 1994, "Financial Issues," examines the costs of the network infrastructure and the likelihood of usage-based charging. The authors recommend continuing federal assistance in order to guarantee equitable access to networking and neworked information.

3. Hal Varian maintains a collection numerous articles and items related to the economics of the Internet (MacKie-Mason and Varian 1994).

4. At Princeton, we have connected our undergraduate dormitories to the campus network at Ethernet speed. Undergraduates have already created their own Mosaic home pages, and others are experimenting with video over the Net. Without question, even limited transmission of live video would visibly congest the network.

5. For further reading on the serials crisis, I recommend Carrigan 1992.

6. Also see a series of articles in "Economic Models for Networked Information," *Serials Review* 18, nos. 1–2 (1992).

References

Carrigan, Dennis. (1992). "Research Libraries' Evolving Response to the 'Serials Crisis.'" *Scholarly Publishing* (April).

Fisher, Lawrence. (1994). "Reining in the Rising Hidden Costs of PC Ownership." *New York Times*, March 27, F10.

Lewis, Peter. (1994). "Doubts Are Raised on Actual Numbers of Internet's Users." *New York Times,* August 10, A1.

MacKie-Mason, Jeffrey K., and Hal Varian. (1994). "Economic FAQs about the Internet." University of Michigan and NBER, May 13.

http://gopher.econ.lsa.umich.edu/EconInternet.html

NRENAISSANCE Committee. (1994). *Realizing the Information Future: The Internet and Beyond.* Washington, D.C.: National Academy Press.

NSF. (1993). "NSF Program Solicitation." NSF 93-52, Washington, D.C.: National Science Foundation, May 6.

11

University Libraries and Scholarly Communication

Ann Okerson

Introduction

Libraries are and will remain central to the management of scholarly communication for the foreseeable future. Out of concern for the well-being of institutions vital to scholarship and science, the Andrew W. Mellon Foundation set out to address two main issues in a study completed in 1994. This chapter is based on the introduction to the study report.

• The explosion in the quantity of desirable published material and a rapid escalation of unit prices for those items jeopardize the traditional mission of research libraries to create and maintain large self-sufficient collections for their users. Issues of pricing, acquisition, and collection are the focus of the study's sustained statistical analysis, which brings together kinds of information that have not often, sometimes not ever, been gathered in one place before.

• The rapid emergence and development of electronic information technologies make it possible to *envision radically different ways of organizing collections and services* that the library has traditionally provided. Insofar as the finances of collection development approach a crisis, the new technologies offer possible mitigation and perhaps a revolution in ways of knowing.

This chapter is the synopsis of a study prepared for the Andrew W. Mellon Foundation: Cummings, Anthony M., Marcia L. Witte, William G. Bowen, Laura O. Lazarus, and Richard Ekman. (1992). *University Libraries and Scholarly Communication*. Washington, D.C.: The Association of Research Libraries (for the Andrew W. Mellon Foundation). Available as http://www.lib.virginia.edu/mellon/mellon.html

This study is distinctive in taking the long view. Moreover, its purpose is not to project the near future but to consider the issues raised by a better understanding of the past and present. It relates current concerns to the fundamental principles of scholarly communication and to the role of the research library in facilitating that communication.

We have lived for many generations with a world in which the technology of publication meant that access *required* ownership; in other words, that scholarly information was usable only if it were gathered in a large, site-specific, self-sufficient collection. The pressures that libraries now feel have already driven them to various forms of resource sharing, notably interlibrary loan, that begin to provide alternative models. New electronic technologies allow the possibility of uncoupling ownership from access, the material object from its intellectual content. This possibility is revolutionary, perhaps dramatically so.

In the study some related issues remain unresolved: Is access to scholarly information narrowing as libraries respond less comprehensively to general trends in book production (that is, as they purchase less printed output)? Does contraction in acquisitions expectations mean that libraries sacrifice some of their individual aims in favor of pursuing goals that they share with other libraries? Is distinctiveness and worse, overall national richness of collections lost, as libraries are chastened to more modest collecting ambitions? Can we say with confidence what rate of acquisition is optimal? In any event, might the restraint of the larger institutions in the 1970s have reflected a sense that they could afford the contraction without damage to their mission, while the smaller institutions may have felt they simply had no alternative but to keep up their buying levels? What is the viability of the traditional model of the library as a single-site comprehensive collection of printed materials?

Methodology

The study concentrates on research libraries. It uses as its database the experience of 24 major U.S. research libraries, chosen for their range of size and mission and for the availability of high-quality information over a substantial period of years. The database of library statistics of the Association of Research Libraries (ARL) is the main source, from which this study selects libraries for closer examination. In some cases, data are reported for all 24 or for the 12 grouped below as Private 1 and Public 1 (especially for the period before 1963, when data tend to be thinner), but in most they are described under four subgroupings based on institutional character (public versus private, on one hand, and size and age, on the other). The groupings follow: Private 1–large private institutions (Chicago, Columbia, Cornell, Princeton, Stanford, Yale); Public 1–large public institutions (Berkeley, Iowa, Michigan, North Carolina, Virginia, Wisconsin); Private 2–small private institutions (Boston University, Georgetown, NYU, Northwestern, USC, and Washington University in St. Louis); and Public 2–small public institutions (Florida, Iowa State, Maryland, Michigan State, Rutgers, and Washington State). In general, the same trends tend to be found within all four composites.

Data on overall university expenditures were obtained from the Higher Education General Information Survey, which was administered annually by the National Center for Education Statistics and is available up to 1985-1986. Data for expenditures after that academic year come from the Integrated Postsecondary Education Data System.

Data on domestic book production come from the R. R. Bowker Company (compiler of, for example, such reports as *Books in Print* and the *Bowker Annual of Library and Book Trade Information*) and the Association of American University Presses; international production is tracked through data from UNESCO. Data on periodical production in selected fields come from the Modern Language Association and the Institute for Scientific Information, and data on prices of books and periodicals come from R. R. Bowker and various issues of the *Library Journal* and *Publishers Weekly.* Note, finally, that for more recent years, chronological datasets were constructed for the periods 1963–1970, 1970–1982, and 1982–1991.

Part 1 of the Study: The State of Research Libraries Today

The broad patterns of development that this study reveals are unsurprisingly congruent with the recent history of higher education in this country. The 1960s saw an unprecedented boom in library acquisitions; then the 1970s and early to mid-1980s saw a sharp slowdown in the rates of increase of acquisitions expenditures in the face of rapidly inflated costs, thus a drop in the purchasing power of the acquisitions dollar. As a result, the rate of increase in number of volumes added to collections slowed considerably and at many institutions was actually negative—that is, in a given year fewer books were be purchased than in the year before.

From 1912 to 1991, the major libraries grew steadily and rapidly. Annual growth rates peaked in the mid to late 1960s and then fell slowly throughout the 1970s. One of the closest correlations with other academic trends is with the number of doctorates conferred, for research libraries and doctoral programs tend to grow hand-in-hand. But when the number of doctoral degrees conferred contracted in the 1970s, library acquisitions were reined in less sharply. Acquisitions decisions are, after all, investment decisions affecting the long term, while degrees conferred reflect year-to-year production decisions taken with an eye on many variables. Furthermore, during the 1970s caution seems to have set in, so a modest recovery in the number of doctorates granted was matched by an even more modest recovery in the annual number of "volumes added gross."

The boom of the 1960s affected the private universities, on the whole, more than the public ones; and the recovery since the mid-1980s has also been more pronounced in the private institutions, while there is little if any evidence of persistent recovery in acquisitions at the Public 1 institutions. But the most vigorous performers in the 1960s boom were the Public 2 institutions: for the most part, these smaller institutions had more rapid expansion plans, especially in their graduate programs, than more senior public institutions.

The patterns of growth, contraction, and modest recovery are nationwide and do not reflect specific stages in growth or maturity of institutions. Indeed, although smaller libraries might attempt to catch up in boom times, larger libraries proved in the 1960s that they could still stay well ahead of smaller ones: all parties showed enthusiastic growth. It was in the contraction of the 1970s that the gap between larger and smaller libraries narrowed most, as the largest libraries showed the sharpest contraction.

It is difficult to select the most accurate measure of library expenditures over time, but however they are expressed, the increases are substantial and do not show signs of being closely tied to the GNP deflator (a form of general price index). The study's analyses further confirm that the boom years of the 1960s were anomalous and that a longer-term view shows a more consistent pattern. In fact, analysis of the years after the 1960s shows that increases in library expenditures have been much more modest than might have been expected.

The principal findings of the Mellon study are numbered and italicized:

1. Libraries have not taken a larger percentage of the university budget; their percentage has shrunk.   Contrary to conventional wisdom, library budgets have tended to increase less rapidly than other university expenditures. The library's percentage of total expenditures has tended to decline. It may well be that as old ambitions became impossible to realize, newer, more modest aims gave ground for a more restrained growth in expenditures. The developments affecting library budgets in the past 20 years have, in fact, led to institutional adjustments in fundamental assumptions as to what was both desirable and sustainable.

When measured against Department of Education figures for educational and general expenditures by universities, budgets (of the libraries studied) took an increasingly large share of the pie through the 1960s, leveled out through the 1970s, and actually declined through the 1980s to the point where they have lost almost all the ground gained in the previous 30 years. These institutions' library budgets may now have stopped dropping, as some evidence suggests a plateau over the past few years. When measured against instructional and departmental research expenditures, the decline in library share of university expenditures over the past 20 years is slightly less pronounced than by some other measures, but the pattern is still clear.

Analogously, limited assessment of the comparative situation in college libraries shows that in these smaller institutions the library characteristically looms significantly larger as a percentage of overall expenditures. The same broad trends just described appear in small college library budgets over the past decades, although the growth in library budgets from 1983 to 1993 has been much less pronounced in the colleges than in the universities.

Having considered overall expenditures (termed "total library expenditures" or TLE by the ARL), the study then analyzes the TLE's chief components. In the ARL's statistical reports, these are: "materials and binding" (combined until 1963; two separate categories thereafter); "salaries and wages"; and "other operating expenditures." Materials and binding is subdivided into "nonserials" (largely though not entirely books and monographs, and hereinafter so called) and "serials" (heavily but not entirely journals).

2. Materials and binding: these acquisitions-related expenditures have remained a remarkably constant percentage of TLE as a whole, but the figures mask a significant reallocation between books and serials. In the 24 libraries studied, the total materials-and-binding component of TLE ranges between 33 and 35 percent of the whole—in other words, a similar percentage of the budget has bought books and serials over the years. Nonetheless, though that share has increased in dollar value, fewer book and serial titles can be bought for that money.

An essential comparison matches "volumes added gross" (a rough surrogate for acquisitions) with expenditures. The curves first began to diverge in the late 1950s and then diverged sharply beginning about 1970. From about that time, measured in real terms, expenditures on materials and binding continued to rise at the same time that the rate of volumes purchased actually declined.

Furthermore, the overall stability in the share of the TLE that has been devoted to expenditures on materials and binding conceals a pronounced internal shift in allocations: a far higher proportion of the materials and binding budget is now being spent on serials. Serials hold an important place in the budget: Research 2 institutions, smaller and working harder to maintain their standing, spent through the 1970s and 1980s approximately 10 percent more of their materials budgets on serials than did Research 1 institutions.

3. *Books (nonserials): in the 1970s and 1980s, the rate of increase in volumes added at university research libraries virtually halted, while domestic and international publishing continued to produce greater numbers of new titles each year.* The growth of collections is measured against the trends in the numbers of books and periodicals published. In its broadest terms, book publication can be said to reflect general economic conditions. The boom in publication that began moderately in the 1950s and took off in the 1960s has slowed only slightly. Library acquisitions in the 1960s showed a growth that ran ahead of the increase in book publishing, but in the years since 1970 volumes added gross have remained roughly flat, while the figures for all domestic titles published have continued to rise steadily. Comparison of publishing output to library collecting is difficult, and the questions must be asked in several different ways in order to reach comparable approximations of the truth. Subjective issues arise easily, such as whether abundant production of scholarly information reflects a decline in its quality or is merely a function of the growth in the community producing such material, with the per capita output remaining close to what it was in the past. One probable influence is that the decline in the academic job market in the 1970s and 1980s increased competitiveness, one measure of which has become quantity of publication. All other things being equal, per capita scholarly production might be more likely to increase in bad times than in good.

Changes in the relative popularity of specific subjects of publishing have an important influence as well. Literature/poetry/drama as a category, for example, fell from a 17.2 percent share of the total national output in 1970 to a 9.1 percent share in 1988. In contrast, the fields with some of the greatest increases in their share of the total output have been those with the highest average per-volume hardcover prices: business, law, medicine, and technology. (Science has the highest average prices and remained at a more or less constant and significant market share of about 9.5 percent.) Library acquisitions reflect shifts in curriculum and research interests, and so may be presumed to reflect heavy purchasing in precisely the fields with the greatest price increases and the greatest increases in share of total titles published.

Among book prices, scientific and technical titles have diverged significantly from the other categories since the mid-1980s and are now being joined at the leading edge by medical books, while titles in the arts and humanities, social sciences, and business have stayed with rates of increase close to the GNP deflator. As the most expensive fields have been the ones with the highest percentage increases in recent years, book prices are now showing some of the price-increasing tendencies characteristic of serials—not an encouraging sign for those who must be concerned about library budgets.

Examination of U.S. university press output also provides a measure of the adequacy of library acquisitions. Since 1974, it is clear that university press output has far outstripped the increase rate of library acquisitions. International publishing production has also increased, ahead of the rates of increase of libraries' acquisitions for the period 1950–1988. From 1950 to 1970, U.S. libraries actually increased their buying faster than the European publishers increased their production, but the two curves began to converge after 1970 and crossed around 1980, with the publishers' output now advancing at a rate steadily ahead of that of U.S. libraries' acquisitions. European book publishing indeed has grown at a rate substantially ahead of U.S. publishing, so that the six most productive European countries (Switzerland, Italy, France, Germany, the United Kingdom, and the Netherlands), which in 1971 produced about 1.5 times as many titles as American publishers did, now produce almost twice as many titles as the American industry.

To add to the difficulties, the sovereign position of the dollar through the boom years for libraries was lost when the dollar was allowed to float in 1971, and at various times during the period of study the dollar's low value has exacerbated the consequences for library buying of all materials. In one hapless interval from 1985 to 1988, the dollar fell against Western European currencies by about 60 percent. (West) Germany has been the most productive publishing country in Europe and the least favorable exchange-rate partner since the early 1970s.

In sum, the number of volumes added yearly (books and serials) within the group of 24 libraries decreased between 1970 and 1982 at an annual rate of -1.4 percent, while the number of titles published, domestically and internationally, was increasing at a rate greater than 2 percent per year. Over this period, libraries have been able to purchase less comprehensively in response to output in the publishing industry than at any time in the twentieth century.

4. Serials: many speak of a "serials crisis" at the heart of library difficulties today, and it is serial prices, and in particular science journal prices, that drive the crisis.   Because of the high rates of serials price increases, the forces creating the gap between volumes added and publishing title output have been principally external rather than internal to universities, and individual institutions have been unable to respond proportionately. It would not be an exaggeration to say that of the various factors in the constellation affecting university libraries in recent years, the rapidly rising prices of periodicals have in many respects been the most important. Subscriptions encumber the materials budget, and serials prices help explain the widening gap between volumes added gross and book titles published. Library budgets have been steadily redeployed toward serials as the primary way of dealing with the pressure of rising serials prices.

In particular, the study makes the following findings:

• Serials prices have run consistently ahead of the GNP deflator, even in the years 1963–1970, with scientific and technical journals consistently leading the rises.

• Within similar groups of fields (e.g., among humanities fields as disparate as history, philosophy, and literature, or among the sciences in chemistry/physics, mathematics, and engineering) remarkable consistency is noted: subject area is a powerful determining force.

• The most expensive serials show the largest *relative* price increases. The highest rates of increase are sustained by the journals whose prices are largest in absolute terms.

Serials expenditures have increased rapidly for the entire period since 1976, but 1981–1986 saw moderate increases, while 1986 to 1991 showed the most rapid increase (an overall annual rate from 1986 to

1990 of more than 11 percent). Some institutional data suggest that science journals account for approximately 29 percent of the total number of serials but 65 percent of the serials budget.

Comparing book and serial prices, the study shows that average prices increased at comparable rates between 1963 and 1970, but about 1970 the pattern changed profoundly. Book prices remained close to the GNP deflator in their rate of increase until about 1978, when the periodicals index began to rise sharply. The proliferation of journal titles presumably created more specialized journals with shorter subscription lists and higher unit prices. For the whole period from 1963 to 1990, serial prices have increased at 11.3 percent per year, against 7.2 percent per year for book prices, and the GNP deflator lagged at an increase of about 6.1 percent per year (average).

Serial prices for scientific and technical journals from 1970 to 1990 have increased at an average rate of 13.5 percent per year. In so doing, they lead a serials price surge in which virtually all science- and technology-related fields run well ahead of the GNP deflator. In 1970, the typical U.S. journal in chemistry or physics cost $33, and in 1982 it cost $178; in history, the average journal cost $7 in 1970 and $20 in 1982. To reduce such increases too quickly to measurement by constant dollars would be a mistake; it is useful to remember that many of the factors driving the national inflationary spiral (e.g., energy prices) have little effect on serials pricing, and thus the nominal numbers are important in their own right.

Several factors correlate with high serials prices:

• Scientific and technical journals can be more expensive to produce than others, and journals with specific higher costs of production for pages per issue, issues per year, and the presence of artwork are more expensive.

• Journals published by commercial publishers are more expensive (not least because a fuller range of their costs are passed on to subscribers, unlike those managed by nonprofit publishers, with hidden and not-so-hidden subsidies contributed against the costs of production).

• Journals with smaller subscription bases are more expensive.

• Specialization plays an important role. New journals tend to be more specialized than older ones, and hence have a smaller subscription base and higher prices.

• Demand for periodicals is less elastic than that for monographs: journals are perceived to be important vehicles for scholarly communication, and continuity of series is a powerful factor in discouraging cutbacks.

• Discriminatory pricing has been a factor. It would appear that in the early 1980s foreign publishers began charging differential rates to compensate for a relatively strong dollar but made no compensatory decreases when the dollar later weakened.

• Concentration of scientific journals within a few publishing houses has had some impact. Three European commercial publishers (Elsevier, Pergamon, and Springer—the first two of which merged in 1991, further concentrating control of pricing decisions) accounted for 43 percent of the increase in serials expenditures at one university between 1986 and 1987.

• Additionally, journals that accept advertising can have lower prices.

Measuring production of serial titles is fraught with difficulties. What constitutes a serial, and what within that group constitutes a scholarly journal, is not easily measured. How many journals are published? Estimates range from less than 5,000 per year to upward of 100,000. One standard guide is *Ulrich's International Periodicals Directory,* and, on that measure, libraries have lagged. From 1972 to 1988, total serials listed in *Ulrich's* have grown by more than 50 percent, while serials acquired by the 24 libraries under study have increased by only about 25 percent. Measures that look the at date of founding of journals show a corresponding proliferation in the 1960s and especially through the 1970s, with some tapering off in the 1980s, but those numbers are hard to assess because there is no count of numbers of journals ceasing to do business during the same period. Some say that in recent years cessations may in fact be running ahead of inceptions. One study of language and literature journals finds that more than half the titles currently available were first published after 1970.

In sum, in view of the increasing size of the periodicals universe (and increasing specialization of journals), the relatively fixed materials-and-binding budgets at libraries have resulted in decreasing numbers of subscriptions per title. Prices per title increase further, and the vicious cycle continues. A similar dynamic is beginning to affect monograph publishing: one academic press confessed to a decline in average print runs between 1976 and 1986, from 1,200–1,500 to fewer than 1,000. Of course, university libraries constitute a significant part of the market for university press titles, and the pressures on library budgets, for example, as they shift resources from monographs to serials, are an important contributing factor to this cycle.

In the face of this pricing crisis, libraries have responded essentially by redistributing their resources, a mode of response that cannot go on

indefinitely. Instead there is a growing realization that no research institution can hope to sustain a self-sufficient collection into the indefinite
future. Even before the crisis, libraries were actively collaborating and
sharing resources. Under the circumstances described in the study, even
without new technologies, libraries would have been led to pursue
"without walls" philosophies energetically. With technological hopes
rising, possible contributions to mitigation of the crisis can come from a
combination of the following tactics:

• modification of the academic reward system that drives proliferation of
publication;

• possible reduction of first-copy costs by publishers' application of technological advances;

• savings through use of electronic technologies in distributing and storing
information;

• accelerated resource sharing; and

• perhaps even alterations in the law of intellectual property governing
"published" material.

*5. Salaries as a percentage of total library expenditures have declined over
the past two decades, while "other operating expenditures" (heavily
reflecting computerization) have risen markedly.* Salaries in the compos-
ite libraries consistently constitute more than 50 percent of the average
library budget. Staffing has increased since 1912, but at a rate somewhat
less than that of collection size, so the number of books held per employ-
ee has risen to the highest level ever. The number of volumes added gross
per staff member has declined, however, reflecting not staffing so much as
the even greater effect of negative forces on acquisitions.

Between 1960 and 1970, average staff size in the Research 1 libraries
nearly doubled. In the next fifteen years, the *total* increase in staff size
was a little less than 7 percent; and from 1985 to 1991, a total increase
of almost 6 percent showed a modest recovery. There can be no doubt,
however, that drastic constraints were placed on staffing size around
1970 and that the subsequent easing has been modest in comparison.

Other operating expenditures have taken a larger share of the library
budget over the past 20 years, apparently largely to reflect computerization of such internal operations as circulation, cataloging, and acquisitions. The share of library budgets taken by salaries, meanwhile,
declined from around 62 percent in 1963 to 52 percent in 1991. That
decline was offset by increases in other operating expenditures, up from

6 percent in 1963 to 14 percent in 1991. That the decline in the staff share began in the 1960s probably reflects the shift in the age distribution toward younger employees as the staff size increased—rapid increases in staffing are often accompanied by less rapid increases in payroll costs because of the growing fraction of staff earning entry-level salaries. After 1970, the decline in share taken by salaries reflects the sharp curtailment in recruitment, while other operating expenditures grew across the four sample groups of libraries.

Part 2 of the Study: Electronic Possibilities

6. *The pressures described in the first part of this chapter will need to be addressed in many ways, but the possibilities of a significant increase in the role of electronic text distribution, maintenance, and use have the potential for being the most dramatic.* The technology of print turned information into a material commodity. Recorded usually in linear form on sheets of paper and distributed in multiple identical (or almost identical) copies, printed works have a relatively high cost for production of the first copy and relatively low cost for subsequent copies. The physical objects—the books—contain a fixed, immutable text with which the reader is permitted to interact only in limited ways. Aids to nonlinear access (e.g., tables of contents and indexes) are relatively limited and are supplied largely at the author's discretion. The study examined a few trends that closely affect traditional arrangements. Large changes in conceptions of property and association may well accompany adoption of new electronic information technologies on a wide scale. Consider that few are likely to have guessed in 1470 what changes would result from the printing press, or to have anticipated in 1910 what the automobile would bring.

Currently, both publishers and libraries inhabit a world in which their standard practices require them to anticipate demand: the publisher must predict the market and the library must know its users, in order for all the economic transactions to be carried out with the greatest efficiency. Backups are in place (e.g., interlibrary loan) to compensate for unexpected demand, but so far those makeshifts have been considerably less satisfactory than successful anticipation of demand and providential provision of suitable materials. This "just-in-case," local-ownership model has familiar costs and benefits—including such bonuses as the creation of large, intricate collections of information that lend themselves to serendipitous discoveries made by searchers on another trail or merely by browsers.

Technological advances, however, support suggestions that management of scholarly communication can now begin to separate access from ownership and concentrate on assuring access to scholarship and research, with questions of physical location of materials becoming secondary.

7. *Until recently, automation in libraries had addressed itself to existing internal functions (circulation, cataloging, and acquisitions), but the range of uses is becoming much broader.*   Now electronic technologies have been conceptualized to provide secondary bibliographical resources (catalogs, information about information, access to other institutions' holdings, periodical indexes, etc.). And increasingly the technologies are beginning to be applied to problems of assembling and ordering the primary information. The virtual library, with all the world's published riches at one's fingertips, is largely a vision at this point, but a potent one.

Large-scale projects that provide computerized bibliographical information are under way. The two most notable national organizations in this area are the OCLC (the Online Computer Library Center) and the RLG (the Research Libraries Group). Both these organizations are experimenting with ways to make their very large databases, reporting the holdings of member libraries, more accessible and useful to scholars. Of particular interest are the RLG's efforts in improving the quality and availability of bibliographic information for what might be called nontraditional materials, from musical compositions to unpublished archival sources. In addition to the national services, many individual libraries make their catalogs available on the Internet. The utility of such online catalogs is limited when retrospective conversion of the card catalog is not yet substantially complete, but more than half of ARL member libraries report that they have already converted 90 percent or more of their card catalogs to machine-readable form.

Unlike books, serial literature is regularly indexed not by libraries but by independent, often commercial, services. Because many of these services are provided outside the not-for-profit institutional environment, however, costs of access have been and can be substantial to individual users. When institutions purchase or use such indexing and abstracting services online, they try to contain costs by having their own trained personnel conduct the search. Yet allowing individual access would be ideal.

The next step beyond obtaining information about information is to share the texts themselves, as has been done traditionally by interlibrary loan (ILL). As emphasis shifts from ownership to access, models of information provision and electronic text availability permit, in principle, a degree of resource sharing among institutions that is far greater than that allowed by traditional ILL. As transmission improves, availability of resources outside the home institution will increasingly affect local collection development. Already the RLG Conspectus project attempts to help libraries make better-informed choices about their acquisitions.

A newer model of resource sharing is document delivery. Document delivery services include the Colorado Alliance of Research Libraries' (CARL) UnCover service, which supplies abundant bibliographical data on articles, and UnCover2, which provides rapid delivery service for full texts, via mail or fax with Internet delivery planned. A copyright royalty fee is collected and paid through the Copyright Clearance Center for each transaction. RLG's Ariel system allows any printed material to be scanned directly as a page image, then stored, transmitted over the Internet, and received for printing at the target site. Among commercial for-profit services, Faxon Research Services, in a program called Faxon Finder (for bibliographic information) and Faxon Xpress (for document delivery), looks promising. Only fuller experience with such experiments will enable institutions to make the necessary careful analyses of contrasting cost implications, balancing collection development with resource sharing.

8. Electronic publishing now comprises many different kinds of information discrimination.   This chapter's discussion to this point assumes that the primary text is printed and that the electronic technologies are used to facilitate access and delivery. But when the primary artifact is electronic, the real revolution will begin. The changes that such electronic publishing will bring, for example in the relation between interpretive works and the underlying data or primary texts on which they are based, are the subject of much thoughtful speculation. Over time, for example, printing costs have worked against the thorough presentation of data: in electronic media, the possibility re-emerges of substantially complete publication of all the data on which research is based, and better still, publication in a form that others can continue to manipulate and enhance. It may soon be possible to think of producing shorter, less expensive print products that contain little or no supporting documentation, as the documentation will be available in electronic form elsewhere.

What remains to be seen is how new forms of publication will emerge, ones that that can only be displayed in an electronic environment, for example, using sophisticated hypertext functions or offering three-dimensional, graphic, moving simulations. Electronic texts can remove the limitations of print on paper. They can be dynamic, mutable, and are potentially eminently interactive. They may allow the producer and the user to uncouple the material object from the intellectual content.

Electronic texts have one signal advantage over print: they are far easier to transmit for purposes of resource sharing. Experiments are under way in which, for instance, textbooks are created on demand out of available online materials and distributed for a fee.

The transition to alternative forms of scholarly communication will not be easy. A particular technology, of whatever type, is joined to a set of economic and legal arrangements appropriate to it. So one must not underestimate the difficulties involved in anticipating a reconfiguration, nor the important role that traditional print media are likely to retain far into the future. For many applications, print products retain considerable advantages over electronic ones. There will be no near-term, wholesale replacement of print with electronic media (the way the vinyl platter was overwhelmed by the CD for music reproduction). The electronic media add a dimension to what we already have, but for the foreseeable future the old media will be with us as well.

It is impossible to be sure how far the technological changes will go. A wide range of predicted futures has been arrayed by thoughtful observers, and at some future point the changes may be considerably more far-reaching, affecting every aspect of our institutions and the communications on which they thrive. The library, the publisher, the printed book, the monograph, the learned journal, the process of peer review, copyright practices: all these and other familiar elements of the current system are at least somewhat at risk in the face of the new technologies. The continuation of the list of the study's findings suggests some areas in which difficult issues will have to be faced.

9. *Scholarly publishing is closely tied to academic prestige, a link that exercises a conservative force on new arrangements.* The reward system for scholars and scientists now depends on traditional publication for defining rank and status, with the real compensation for publication coming not from sales of the material but from the advancement in rank, salary, and prestige that publication makes possible. Any new system will have to satisfy scholarly and institutional leaders that it is adequately peer reviewed and reliable before new types of publications can

be rewarded. Until assurances of such rewards are in place, faculty will be reluctant to put their best work in new forms.

10. Options for distribution of electronic texts are numerous and their costs at the present time uncertain.   Options for electronic text distribution are many, and no one can predict which system will prevail where, or how. Individual institutions might choose to maintain local electronic repositories of frequently used titles; some publishers, in contrast, might choose to retain their texts at central sites and distribute them on a fee-for-use basis; collaborative arrangements between repositories of various kinds in various places may emerge in which a consortium of libraries, say, may hold a full set of resources together, without each institution having to pay the full cost of housing such a set.

Cost-related factors may well force choices on institutions irrespective of technological possibilities. Some say that electronic scholarly communication will be more affordable than print on paper. To determine with any precision what cost savings, if any, might emerge from any new methods of distribution is difficult, and costs will undoubtedly be reallocated within the university system. Who will pay and how much are vital, but still unanswerable, questions. Consider the development of the serial or journal in a new environment. The very concept of an "issue" of a journal is challenged: individual items can be distributed separately, as they are in many existing experimental e-journals. This calls for different subscription and pricing policies for both individuals and institutions.

11. Campus computing and telecommunications infrastructures will need to be upgraded to make the new technologies possible.   Some of these upgrades are necessary in any event, but they carry real costs. Proponents of the new National Research and Education Network (NREN) in 1984 estimated that for every dollar appropriated for this system by the federal government, five to ten dollars would need to come from state and local governments and private institutions. The full realization of the potential model of electronic scholarly communication described here depends, finally, on the development of an adequate national telecommunications infrastructure, capable of moving vast quantities of text and data at very high speeds. The final part of the study provides a brief history of the emergence of the national scientific and academic networks now in existence and describes the upgraded, harmonized network that is, or will be, the NREN. The three-tier structure (a national backbone, then regional networks, then campus or local networks) puts heavy responsibility on individual institutions to maintain a significant share of the national network. But the improvements to service will be astonishing: a roughly 600-fold increase in speed of transmission, up to a billion bits a second, will almost make speeds acceptable for transmitting the more data-intensive forms of information, such as high-resolution graphics, moving pictures, and multimedia formats.

12. Traditional roles in the publishing process will undergo transformation.   Libraries and publishers as we now know them are institutions created in and for the technology of the printed, or at least the written, word, depending on information to be produced, distributed, and possessed as a collection of material objects. But both libraries and publishers have additional functions. Publishers, for example, are gatekeepers to the world of scholarly communication in their management of scholars' and researchers' peer review, which determines what is printed. Libraries, in turn, engage in collection development and management, but they also serve as indexers and pathfinders for information they do not own. Already such a model departs from the "just-in-case" approach to acquisition and approaches a "just-in-time" model, where material is acquired as it is needed. Some blurring may occur in the distinctions among the historical roles of publishers as producers, vendors as intermediaries, and librarians as archivists. The electronic revolution may provide the potential for developing university publishing enterprises through scholarly networks supported either by individual institutions or consortia. Peer review, editing, and composition will remain important parts of the preparation of scholarly material for distribution. How much of them will remain the role of publishers and how much will be taken on by other participants in the process remains to be seen.

13. Consistency of standards and of protocols has not yet been found.   Existing heterogeneity of access and retrieval protocols poses a problem in the short to medium term; this problem is and various interest groups will have to negotiate a suitable solution. So-called expert systems should further ease translation among computer formats.

14. Adaptation of current copyright practices to the new electronic environments poses numerous difficulties.   The ease with which electronic material can be duplicated and retransmitted means that any controls that the publisher places and seeks to enforce on users, whether by copyright or licensing agreements, can be circumvented with ease. If revenue depends on "sales" of the retail product, the retransmission represents a potentially threatening black market that could undermine publishers' ability to recoup their costs. The need to control will compete with the demand for wide and easy access to material. Implications also exist for accuracy and integrity of information.

The most critical issues arise from the challenges to the law of copyright implicitly posed by the new technologies. Copyright in the United States is based on the Constitution and confirmed by statute. The original intent of the constitutional protection was to encourage intellectual productivity by securing rights for the authors. In scholarly practice today, rights are commonly assigned to publishers, in return for the substantial contribution they make to scholarly communication, while the rewards expected by the scholars are those of prestige, rank, and institutional compensation.

The U.S. copyright law's doctrine of fair use defines the way reproduction of copyrighted materials may be carried out. Some copyright scholars maintain that a key factor affecting determination of fair use appears increasingly to be the effect of that use on the potential market for the work, and it is on economic grounds that publishers scrutinize practices carefully for possible violation. Litigation continues to define more precisely the scope of this doctrine.

The point at which resource sharing runs the risk of violating copyright can be a delicate matter to determine. Eventual development of fee structures and payment mechanisms is one way to respect current copyright privileges. Licensing agreements freely entered into by purchasers of information are already used somewhat and offer another resolution for some of these issues.

Alternatives to current copyright management can be imagined. For example, universities could claim joint ownership of scholarly writings with the faculty they pay to produce them, then prohibit unconditional assignment to third parties, thus becoming important players in the publishing business. Or universities could request that faculty members first submit manuscripts to publishers whose pricing policies are more consonant with larger educational objectives. Another possibility is that university-negotiated licenses could grant unlimited copying to libraries and individual scholars and specify such permission in the copyright statement. All these proposals are extensions of the broader idea under discussion, that universities should reclaim some responsibility for disseminating the results of faculty scholarship.

15. In the end, larger social issues will need to be addressed. Many concerns about management of the networks that distribute this material are already being articulated. Who has access, who pays, who worries about integrity of texts and privacy, who monitors ownership and legitimate use? Academic institutions, individual scholars, and their commercial partners in the transactions to come will all have their own agendas, and they must learn to work in an atmosphere of mutual respect and cooperation.

Conclusion

The heart of the scholarly enterprise is the exchange of ideas. University campuses offer myriad informal loci for dialogue, but the formal locus par excellence is in the dialogue between scholarly writer and scholarly reader that has been mediated for half a millennium by the printed page. One scholar is quoted in the study and summarizes well the sense of responsibility that accompanies that dialogue: "In *Notes on Virginia*, Jefferson described the process: 'A patient pursuit of facts, and cautious combination and comparison of them, is the drudgery to which man is subjected. . . if he wishes to attain sure knowledge.' Jefferson is still right about the patient pursuit of facts. . . . We have, however, taken much of the drudgery out of the process and made it easier to find sources, but we still have to read carefully—probably more carefully than ever—and we still have to think. The difference is that searching no longer takes much time and energy from the scholarship of thought" (Woolpy 1991). The optimism of this passage is specific to the dawn of the computer age, but similar optimism has been expressed at each historical moment in which the advance of technology brought new riches closer to readers.

The indispensable mediator in the dialogue between writer and reader has been, for more centuries than the printed book has existed, the institutional library. The study addresses the present and future of scholarly communication with particular reference to the research libraries that bear so much of the responsibility for making that communication possible, with particular focus on the research university library, whose special purpose is to support advanced scholarship and scholarly communication.

Reference

Woolpy, Sarah J. (1991). "World in a Keystroke." *Earlhamite* 111 (Fall): 5–6.

12

A Consortium for Refereed Electronic Journals

Larry W. Hurtado

Of the various ways in which electronic publishing can affect and enhance scholarly work, I am particularly interested in the development of network-published journals.[1] The International Conference on Refereed Electronic Journals (Winnipeg, October 1–2, 1993), hosted by the University of Manitoba, was organized to consider some of the important questions about whether and how the Internet can function as a medium for the publication of refereed-journal-quality research.[2] During this conference two things became apparent. First, there are good reasons at present, and will be even more compelling reasons in the near future, to plan for proper use of the Internet (and any successor network) for publication of serious research of the sort we most commonly associate with refereed paper journals. Second, the issues involved in developing electronic journals properly and in integrating them fully into the academic world should probably best be addressed by academia collectively, even institutionally.

One of the major objectives of the conference's organizing committee was to promote the idea of some sort of consortium of universities and academic societies to be a vehicle for the cooperative and programmatic development of electronic research journals. In the final session of the conference, participants responded to a direct proposal along these lines, and the clear sentiment of the discussion was to affirm the proposal with enthusiasm. But if a cooperative and planned development of electronic scholarly journals is to be carried out, a wider discussion of the idea is necessary, involving influential scholars, university administrators, and, very important, the leadership structures of a wide variety of academic societies. In the interests of promoting such further discussion, in this chapter I sketch the need for a consortium, its objectives, and its basic makeup.

The idea of some sort of cooperative academic effort for network publication has been suggested by others already, and some steps along these lines have been initiated (especially the Association of Research Libraries in cooperation with a few academic societies).[3] But, to the best of my knowledge, the idea has not received the serious and focused attention it deserves in the academic community as a whole. Until this point, the discussion of a consortium approach to developing the Internet for research publication has been carried on mainly among university librarians and a few far-sighted individual scholars in various fields. As yet, the major academic policymakers, particularly university administrators and executives of academic societies, have not shown awareness of the problems and the need for collective solutions. In the hopes of helping to change this situation, I offer the following remarks.

Options

It was clear from the material presented in the sessions of the Winnipeg conference that it is desirable and increasingly feasible for the Internet to become a major medium for the publication of research of the quality we associate with respected refereed journals. Given this, it is practically certain that the network will be used increasingly for this purpose, and that respected refereed journals published on the network will become an accepted and important feature of scholarship sooner or later. The key question, however, with which academia should be urgently concerned, is how the Internet will and should be developed for the publication of refereed research. Specifically, what role will academia play? Will academics participate in a major way in shaping the research use of this new medium, or will we allow this essentially to be done for us by others? I see several possible ways in which the network could be cultivated for research publication.

First, the present voluntary use and development led by academics with a certain pioneering mindset may well continue, especially in the foreseeable future. Nearly all the serious use of the Internet for scholarly purposes thus far has been initiated by such people, producing many academic discussion lists and a small (but growing) number of experiments in publishing journals on the network, including some refereed journals (e.g., King, Kovacs, and Okerson 1994). At the Winnipeg conference we heard from some of those who have been at the forefront in these experiments (e.g., Stevan Harnad, Jean-Claude Guédon, and other contributors to this volume). Given the practical benefits of the network (e.g., no arbitrary limits on article length, greater dissemination speed, lower costs, and much in the way of value-added developments in coming years that will involve the ability to present data in ways not possible in traditional paper form), individual academics with a particular vision for networked publication will likely continue to play an important role in its development.

But, as those who have led these experiments will attest, I think, the potential value of networked publication extends to all scholars, not only to those advanced in computer usage who get themselves networked on an individual basis. That is, networked publication is potentially valuable for much more than satisfying the curiosity and increasing the convenience of circles of electronically oriented scholars, and it is in the interests of scholarship generally to see the Internet developed properly and fully for research publication.

Moreover, so long as network-based publications are seen as the experimental efforts of individuals and voluntarist groups of scholars, some degree of uncertainty will remain about the academic legitimacy and acceptance of material published on the network. Let us face facts. The academic community is a conservative lot (perhaps quite appropriately so) when it comes to changes in matters as important as conferring academic respectability. We are often surprisingly slow in accepting developments in the way we transact our academic business. Consequently we are, and will remain, concerned about academic credibility and legitimacy of any new form of academic publication, which should be recognized and addressed by the academic establishment collectively, not merely by self-selecting groups of scholars. Unfortunately, the significantly different format of electronic publication will require programmatic effort to provide appropriate assurances of the academic quality of networked publications, if they are to be widely and seriously respected. This programmatic effort requires far more than the labor of individual scholars or of a particular group of scholars.

Second, alongside the experimentation and pioneering by scholars, commercial publishing firms are seriously examining the development of the Internet as a medium for research journals, with the intention of producing profits as well as disseminating research. Especially in those disciplines where commercial publishing firms have already found it economically attractive to publish scholarly journals (medical, natural, and applied sciences), it is most likely that we will see networked journals published for profit.

But if commercial firms are allowed to dominate the development and use of the network for publication of research, we will be in a situation similar to the present state of paper-journal publishing, with a rich supply of (often expensive) journals in some commercially attractive fields, priced for profit and not to recover costs, and other fields neglected as unattractive commercially with significantly fewer outlets for refereed research publication. Important facts about commercial publication of research journals are not well known among academics (at least outside the fields of medicine, science, and technology): in some fields, commercial publishing dominates; the prices of commercially produced journals in these fields are incredible; commercial publishing firms co-opt scholars into the promotion of their for-profit journals; and massive financial problems are caused for university libraries. I find that scholars are often stunned when given these facts. Perhaps university librarians should take a much more active role in acquainting faculty members with them. Certainly, in my judgment, colleagues in the fields concerned should promote a more academically responsible attitude toward the blandishments of commercial publishers of scholarly journals.

Commercial firms are of course free to pursue their legitimate quest for profits. But I do think that academia in general, and perhaps especially in the sciences and technology, needs to consider seriously whether it is desirable to leave the development of the Internet for research publication as fully in the hands of commercial firms as traditional paper journals are in some fields. In other words, I suggest that academia should take the emergence of this new medium of publication as an opportunity to reaffirm the historic role of scholars as both producers and disseminators of research. If this is to be done, however, it will probably have to be done collectively, with universities and academic societies being the key players.

Perhaps not since the invention of the printing press has a technological development so profoundly altered the way things can be published, and so fully reopened the opportunities for scholars to become directly involved in the publication process. It is difficult and costly for scholars to acquire the means to produce a traditional paper journal. But the electronic network is in place and will continue to become more fully a part of the academic environment, as familiar as the postal system, telephone, or card catalog became for academic work in previous generations. Scholars attached to universities and colleges normally have ready access to this powerful means of communication through institutional participation in the Internet, and usually comparatively little is required in the way of additional special equipment to use the network for publication purposes. But we still lack a widely enough shared recognition that academia can and should take the impressive opportunity offered through the network to significantly change the way research is published for the better.

A third way in which the network is likely to be used for academic purposes is the development of networked publications by institutional academia, which is to some degree already emerging. Some academic societies are studying the possibility of sponsoring network-published journals. University presses, especially those already involved in publishing scholarly paper journals, are considering network possibilities too. Some university libraries have also begun to experiment with ways of providing institutional access to networked journals.

With no wish to constrain such initiatives by individual scholars or institutions, I urge nevertheless that there be some sort of cooperative structure for sharing relevant experience and information, lest mistakes be repeated and needless duplications of effort take place. Furthermore, as commendable as it is for individual academic bodies to be taking initiatives in light of their own perceived needs, it is desirable to promote the proper development and acceptance of the Internet as a publication medium for all disciplines and throughout the academic establishment. At these initial stages of Internet usage, it is important to acquaint scholars in various disciplines with the advantages of networked publication and to legitimize this medium in academia generally. Also, in view of the potential for powerful commercial firms to dominate research publication on the Internet, individual academic societies and universities should work *together* for maximum effect, to make sure that genuine academic concerns, and not the profit motive, shape the development of the Internet for research publication.

A Consortium for Network Publication

I suggest, therefore, a fourth option: a consortium of universities, colleges, and academic societies to promote and develop the Internet for research publication. That is, there should be a collective commitment to pursue the development of the Internet, a commitment expressed through the involvement of the major modern academic institutions through which scholars today conduct their academic work.

Through their libraries, universities have historically been the major repository and access point for research publication. Through university presses, scholars have had a historic role in not-for-profit academic publication, and it is generally conceded that university presses set the standard of quality in academic publications.

Modern academic societies have come to play an increasingly important role in the dissemination of research through society-sponsored journals, and, more generally, academic societies are a means for scholars to consider disciplinary needs and to act collectively in matters directly connected with their profession. Indeed, I suggest that it is crucial to bring the executives of learned societies fully up-to-speed on electronic publication in general and the advantages of networked publication in particular, and on the possibilities for being key agents in helping to reshape research publication in coming years. Others have stressed the importance of universities' working together on developing the network, and I agree. I also think that academic societies should be involved as major partners.

Universities and academic societies have been settings in which scholars have developed standards and policies in research publication. These two types of academic bodies are today primary structures through which modern scholars collectively conduct academic work, and are perhaps the main institutions in which scholars have the controlling voice in matters of protocols and academic standards. It seems obvious that a consortium of universities and societies is the best way for scholars collectively to take a major role in developing the Internet for research publication, to see that academic needs are addressed, and, in an appropriate manner and on a sound basis, to promote acceptance and legitimacy of networked publication.

Ideally, I think, such a consortium should extend across disciplinary lines and, if possible, across national frontiers as well. It may well be desirable for those working in the same discipline or related disciplines to caucus about their special needs. Granted, given that the networks tend to be funded and physically managed nationally, it may be that national groups of academic institutions will need to have structures for planning and development. But, for the purposes of devising practical policies and standards and for the task of promoting acceptance and assuring quality of networked publication, a cooperative effort across disciplinary and national boundaries would be best.

Some groups are already working to promote the Internet, such as the Coalition for Networked Information and Educom in the United States. But I believe that the particular concerns of academics, especially concerns connected with the publication of research journals, justify a consortium dedicated specifically to high-quality, not-for-profit publication of refereed research on the network, and to the acceptance and use of such publication within the academic community generally. The Winnipeg conference exhibited the value of ongoing, focused discussion of the kind featured there, and the value of wider and more formal cooperation in academia on electronic journals. A consortium seems a logical next step, to continue to deal with the questions addressed in the Winnipeg conference: questions about quality and need; about how the electronic medium demands or allows changes in the form and format of research journals; about technological developments needed to permit networked publication of special types of data such as images and languages not using the Latin alphabet; about proper distribution, access, and archiving of networked journals; about how to promote the use of the network and the acceptance of networked publication; and about other matters that may yet arise. The modern academic world is full of structures, and I have no wish to complicate our lives further. But the sort of consortium I propose seems a clear desideratum.

A Sketch of the Operation of the Consortium

It may be helpful for stimulating the imagination of others (who will no doubt be able to suggest improvements to what follows) to sketch a bit more precisely how such a consortium might operate. In the discussion that I hope will ensue, other models may well be proposed. The model I have in mind is inspired somewhat by the operation of Scholars Press, a not-for-profit publishing cooperative of academic societies and universities, now located on the campus of Emory University in Atlanta, Georgia.[4] In founding purposes and commitments, and in its general structure and operation, Scholars Press is thus far a paper-medium consortium that shows how, in principle, academic societies and universities collectively can take responsibility for being not only producers and consumers of research information but also quite successful disseminators. Through a consortium, expertise and expenses can be shared, making it possible for individual bodies, even smaller societies and universities, to take part in the publication process. I mention Scholars Press not to propose slavish imitation but to offer a successful example of scholarly cooperation across disciplinary and institutional lines. Based in part on my acquaintance with Scholars Press, I offer now an initial sketch of how a consortium for networked publication might operate.[5] I invite and expect others to be ready to make improvements, supplements, and corrections.

1. To ensure that academic concerns control decisions, I propose that only universities, colleges, and academic societies should be voting members of the consortium. The main justification for the consortium is to provide a means whereby the collective weight of academic opinion and needs could be brought to bear on the development of the computer network for the purposes of research publication. Consequently, the consortium should be composed mainly of the major institutions through which academia transacts its business.

In the discussion that followed the presentation of the consortium proposal at the Winnipeg conference, a few suggested that groups such as national research granting councils and government research councils should be full members. My opinion is that such groups should probably be associate members and that the decision making should be in the hands of the working academics through their universities and academic societies. I am convinced that academics are the best judges of the best standards, practices, and policies to follow in aiming for scholarly quality and effectiveness in research publication.

Because I think that academic societies as well as universities should be key players, I also think that federations of societies such as the American Council of Learned Societies in the United States and in the Canadian Federation for the Humanities and Social Science in Canada should become promoters of consortial commitment in academia toward proper cultivation of networked publication of research.

2. Unlike the traditional medium of paper publication, the network still has to be developed as a practical medium for research publication, and the traditional academic structures have to be equipped and informed as to how to take advantage of this new medium. As the Winnipeg conference showed, many questions involved will concern us for some time to come. Consequently, any consortium will have to address much of a foundational nature. For example, it will be essential for universities and colleges to collaborate on how they are to play their traditional role as repositories of research publication with respect to network-published material, a question that will require collective wisdom from university library administrators.

Such a consortium could also develop coordinated practices and standards for the indexing of network-published research journals. Scholars will need means of finding publications, and contributors will want to know that their work can readily be found, at least as readily as articles in respected paper journals are found through familiar indexing and abstracting services. It will be best if existing index services are extended to cover electronic journals, and this will happen more easily if it is clear that academia collectively wishes to have access to them.

It will also be vital for academics collectively to establish policies and protocols for producing and identifying those network publications that should be considered fully credible and respectable. Scholars will be reluctant to publish first-rate research on the network unless they know that their publications will appear in vehicles that are appropriate to such work and that these vehicles will be received as fully respectable by their colleagues. Those involved in tenure and promotion processes will need to know how to regard networked publications in evaluating the research and publication accomplishments of candidates for career-advancement processes. Scholars in most fields can readily identify the journals that count, in which publication means highly respectable research work. Networked publications are (and will continue to be for a number of years to come) relatively new and unfamiliar, not only individually but also, and more seriously, as a type of research publication. Much work will need to be done to create proper standards and procedures for them and to identify those journals that meet the standards and follow the procedures. And this work has to be done for networked journals as a class or type, so the task requires a committed and collective effort.

A consortium of respected universities, colleges, and academic societies could quickly develop appropriate standards and policies for high-quality networked journals and could provide the means for identifying those networked publications that should be treated with the same respect given to peer-refereed paper journals. The good name of the participating universities and societies would provide strong assurance of quality. The involvement of these important academic institutions would help ensure quick familiarity and acceptance of a potentially valuable medium of scholarly publication.

Because all this is vital, and because it will take some serious thought and collective consideration, a consortium-type effort seems the logical step. Universities could contribute their long tradition of commitment and high standards of publishing, their tradition of library standards, and their investment and participation in computer technology. Academic societies could bring the expertise and needs of their membership, and their growing commitment to playing active roles in the dissemination of research. Together, they would provide a powerful store of resources for the responsible and expeditious development and acceptance of network-published research.

3. Once standards for promoting and ensuring quality control are developed, the consortium could recognize or sponsor networked journals that meet its standards. That is, the consortium could provide a kind of Good Housekeeping Seal that would assure potential contributors and readers of the quality of networked publications that meet the consortium's criteria. To cite the Scholars Press operation, each journal or monograph series has to be sponsored by a university, college, academic society, or other bona fide academic body. The board of the press must approve each new journal or monograph series and requires the sponsor to specify the editorial structure and policies, the refereeing protocols to be followed, and the need for the project. Something similar could be required in order for a network-published journal to receive the approval or endorsement of the sort of consortium I have in mind.

4. A consortium would also need to establish policies and obligations with respect to the permanent archiving of approved networked publications and their ongoing viability. Technological developments over the next few decades might make today's form of computer records obsolete. We need to guarantee that research material published on the network will be maintained and will continue to be available in a form accessible to future researchers. Some designated body or institution should be responsible for each networked journal, making a commitment to store and update as may be needed the format of electronically published research material.

A consortium could require that each approved journal be the responsibility of an academic society or a university. The body responsible for the journal would vouch for those chosen as editors and referees, for the refereeing practices and policies, and the stability and continuity of the journal, and would also be required to guarantee the preservation of the material appearing in the journal. We can be grateful for those pioneering individuals who have given birth to today's experimental journals. But, as is true of paper journals, for networked journals to receive the highest confidence of contributors and readers, their quality should be vouched for through recognizable channels, and their survival should be the responsibility of an ongoing institution, not of a few mortal individuals.

A First Step

The planning committee of the Winnipeg conference hoped that the conference would result in a growing commitment of the academic community to participate directly and institutionally in the development of the network for research publication. Specifically, we hoped that universities and academic societies would seriously consider joining interests and efforts in some sort of consortium. The conference committee wished not to try to control this process but to stimulate it. Consequently, we hoped that the Winnipeg conference would itself be a springboard for further developments. In the months since the conference, it has become clear that it will in fact take a good deal more than a conference and the presentation of a good idea to bring together the academic community for responsible collective action toward proper use of the network for research publication. It has also become clear, as represented by the publication of this volume and by other developments, that there is a significant, growing interest in making academia more widely aware of what needs to be done and what can be done.

It will take time for universities and academic societies to become sufficiently aware at the decision-making levels to take the collective action needed. A good first step would be for concerned scholars to bring this idea to the attention of university administrators and academic society executive committees, urging them to engage in some serious discussion of this proposal now, in the long-range hope that at least far-sighted academic bodies will take the lead in setting up some such collaborative structure, a cooperative for scholarly publishing on the network. The idea of a consortium should be presented to existing associations of learned societies, university administrators, research libraries, university presses, and other relevant organizations with sufficient information to permit those unfamiliar with electronic journals to respond intelligently. Those of us involved in organizing the Winnipeg conference hope that our labors will see fruit in further steps toward organized, well-considered, and timely development of what can become a most useful new medium for publication and evaluation of high-quality research.

Notes

1. The interest in, and discussion of, "electronic" journals (usually meaning refereed-journal-type material published on the network) is already considerable and is growing. This is not my professional research area, so I cannot claim control of the literature available. Among publications influential in shaping my thinking are the following: Okerson 1991, especially pp. 432–436; King 1991; Bailey 1992; and notably Metz and Gherman 1991, especially pp. 323–327. The problems that need to be addressed if we are to develop networked journals are presented in Piternick 1991. In my acquaintance, perhaps the person who has been most vigorously and persistently insistent about the advantages of network journals is Stevan Harnad, whose publications on the subject are simply too numerous to list.

2. This conference was organized and run by a committee drawn from a wide range of disciplines within the University of Manitoba. Although many on the committee gave generously of their time in making the conference the successful event it was judged to have been by participants, I wish to cite especially Paul Fortier, who took direct and efficient charge of the arrangements. I also gratefully acknowledge the subsidizing funds from all three Canadian federal research granting councils: the Medical Research Council, the Natural Sciences and Engineering Research Council, and the Social Sciences and Humanities Research Council. The conference was the first of international scope focused specifically on electronic journals. Abstracts of the conference presentations are available via anonymous FTP from the University of Manitoba (ftp.cc.umanitoba.ca). Printed conference papers are available from Carolynne Presser, Director of Libraries, Dafoe Library, University of Manitoba, Winnipeg, Manitoba, R3T 2N2, Canada.

3. See especially Okerson (1991, pp. 432–436), who urges universities to work together to develop university-based network publishing; and Metz and Gherman (1991, pp. 323–327), who more specifically favor consortia-type efforts of universities to develop network-based journals. I think that there are good reasons for advocating that professional academic societies and universities work together toward this goal.

4. Scholars Press was founded in 1974 initially to serve the publishing needs of two large academic societies, the American Academy of Religion and the Society of Biblical Literature. The press now includes as sponsors other academic societies and a number of universities and colleges. A board sets policies regarding such things as refereeing practices for monograph series and journals published by the press. The sponsors of press publications must be nonprofit educational and research institutions or groups.

5. The University of Manitoba became a sponsor of Scholars Press in 1990, launching in that same year a new monograph series published through the press: University of Manitoba Studies in Religion. As executive editor of the series, I have been able to learn a good deal about the operation of Scholars Press.

References

Bailey, Charles W., Jr. (1992). "Network-Based Electronic Serials." *Information Technology and Libraries* (March): 29–35.

King, L. A., D. Kovacs, and A. L. Okerson. (1994). *Directory of Electronic Journals, Newsletters and Academic Discussion Lists.* Washington, D.C.: Association of Research Libraries.

King, Timothy B. (1991). "The Impact of Electronic and Networking Technologies on the Delivery of Scholarly Information." *Serials Librarian* 21: 5–13.

Metz, Paul, and Paul M. Gherman. (1991). "Serials Pricing and the Role of the Electronic Journal." *College and Research Libraries* (July): 315–327.

Okerson, Ann. (1991). "With Feathers: Effects of Copyright and Ownership on Scholarly Publishing." *College and Research Libraries* (September): 425–438.

Piternick, Anne B. (1991). "Electronic Serials: Realistic or Unrealistic Solution to the Journal 'Crisis.'" *Serials Librarian* 21: 15–31.

13

Revolutionary or Regressive? The Politics of Electronic Collection Development

Marlene Manoff

Given that we are in a transitional period between print and electronic literacy, it is inevitable that research and scholarship will be pursued in new and different ways in the future. Libraries and the tools and resources they offer are currently participating in this process of transformation, even as libraries themselves are being transformed. In this chapter I will attempt to provoke consideration of the implications that libraries' decisions to offer electronic access and resources will have on scholarship.

In adopting new electronic technologies, libraries are, in effect, making themselves over so as to accommodate the demands of these technologies, whether through reallocation of funds or staff, training, space changes, or complete rethinking of the organization. In the rush to integrate these new tools, libraries have been turning to business and management theory for blueprints and even a language to deal with change. But we are, I think, too ready to be seduced into thinking that corporate models alone can provide solutions to the dilemmas raised by technical innovation.

What seems to be lacking in discussions of how to "manage" our electronic transformation is serious consideration of what difference it makes politically or socially that library collections and services are becoming more computer dependent. It seems impossible that our increasingly machine-driven library environments and the fantastic array of electronic text and databases we offer could not have serious social and political implications. Why aren't we thinking more about the ways new technology and new tools may improve, constrain, or simply alter the ways in which scholarship can and will be conducted? Perhaps the problem is that we are so close to these changes, and struggling so hard to keep up, that we lack the energy and inclination to sit back and consider not only what computerization means for libraries but also what it means for the disciplines we support.

There has been a considerable amount of conjecture about the effects of electronic communications technology, much of it outside the library literature. Some of the more interesting and compelling analyses of the political implications of technology for the library profession as a whole are collected in a recent volume edited by John Buschman (1993b). One focus of such work is a form of speculation about whether the Internet and related technologies, having evolved out of DARPA originally to meet the needs of the defense and military research community, might themselves bear that imprint. This "contamination thesis," if you will, grows out of the recognition that technology is embedded in culture; it is shaped by individuals who bring to their work values and assumptions that are reflected in those technologies, as are the values and goals of the organizations that support their work. Or, to put it another way, because there can be no value-free scientific research, there can be no technology without some kind of ideological baggage.

This contamination thesis is loosely tied to a second slightly more concrete form of speculation about how, given that computers are essentially computing or counting machines, we need to think about what we lose if computers become our basic research tools. Computers privilege the quantifiable because that is what they can measure. We can see the implications of this fact as they are being played out in current debates in the field of humanities computing. Mark Olsen and others argue that humanists must learn to ask different kinds of questions if they are to benefit from the use of high-speed computers. Olsen (1993), himself a historian, claims that computers are not suitable tools for traditional literary scholarship because such work tends to focus quite narrowly on particular authors and particular works. In a special issue of *Computers and the Humanities* called "A New Direction for Literary Studies?" (Fortier 1993), Olsen and several others maintain that humanists should redirect their energies and formulate new questions involving large corpora because this is where computation can be most helpful. This special issue also includes comments from a number of humanists who rebut Olsen's claim, but only to argue that computers can be useful in studying single texts or authors. No one really addresses what I take to be the more important question of whether Olsen's claim, if true, constitutes sufficient reason to rethink and redesign the field of literary study so as to accommodate the abilities of computers.

To me it seems crucial that we think of the development of electronic scholarship as involving, at the very least, a two-way process. If we are expected to identify needs that can be met by computers, we must also find ways to shape the technology to conform to our evolving needs. I think that this is as much an issue for libraries as it is for literary study.

This debate about humanities scholarship demonstrates the ways computers can actually alter the process of doing research. Computers promote certain kinds of scholarship, as well as certain ways of thinking, certain kinds of language, and even certain kinds of metaphor (Buschman 1993a). And in other ways as well, the "language" of computers is one of the factors affecting their utility for research. Disciplines with softer vocabularies, fields that are less hierarchically organized than scientific and technical fields, may be less amenable to digitization (Saule 1992, p. 804). This may simply mean that some humanities and social science disciplines will be slower to harness the computer. But it will also mean that, as they do, they will be more radically changed in the process. Our role should be to see that equivalent emphasis is placed on adapting the technology to conform to the needs of scholarship.

In the field of literature, for example, work is under way to develop electronic analytic tools that can help to perform the kinds of readings that have always interested literary researchers. Susan Hockey (1994) of the Center for Electronic Texts in the Humanities (CETH) claims that software programs will be developed that will be able to recognize metaphor, word play, irony, and various other phenomena central to literary analysis.

Although many of the questions about the possibilities and limits of computer technology are presently unanswerable, some changes are already quite clear. We are witnessing a kind of exaltation of scientific and technical knowledge at the expense of philosophical or more contextual or aesthetic knowledge. We often behave as if we believed that technological innovation were a form of enlightenment. Cutting-edge technologies are assumed to be progressive: conducive to the greater good. We need to remember that new technologies can be harnessed for a variety of ends and may function in ways that are not easily classifiable as positive or negative.

An interesting example of the complexity of this issue is the case of the ARTFL (American and French Research on the Treasury of the French Language) database. This is a collection of about two thousand authoritative French texts from the sixteenth century to the twentieth. The database includes mostly literary texts but also philosophical ones as well as a selection of scientific and technical works. It is searchable through sophisticated but relatively easy-to-use software that is even now being made easier to access, through the World Wide Web. It is clearly an amazing and wonderful product for French scholars. But as Robert Morrissey (1993) has pointed out in an issue of *Profession*, the ARTFL database contains few popular works, not much political writing or private material such as diaries or correspondence, and, most notably, women are conspicuously underrepresented. In an early survey of the database, only 30 of 588 authors, or approximately 5 percent, were women. As Morrissey puts it, "There is little doubt . . . that the collection reflects a rather traditional notion of the canon: the written language of a male elite" (p. 30).

The two thousand texts represent only a very small percentage of the works written in French in the five centuries spanned by the database. Work is under way to augment the holdings of women writers. But currently, the exclusionary policy of this database serves to reproduce a conservative view of the culture; it ensures that fancy new computer studies can be performed only on the very works that have always gotten the most attention. Is this what we expect cutting-edge technology to do for us?

But just as this new electronic medium may work to further exclude the marginal, it may also provide a kind of access to the marginal that was previously unthinkable. The perfect counterexample to the ARTFL database is the Women Writers Project at Brown University. In this instance, the support available for work with electronic text has made possible the preparation of editions of works by women authors long out of print, which otherwise had no prospect of ever being printed. As Kathryn Sutherland, an eighteenth-century scholar affiliated with the Brown project, puts it, "If computers do not substitute for books they may substitute for the absence of books" (1993, p. 53).

The original goal of the Brown Women Writers Project was to make available everything written in English by women prior to 1830, including works of literature, diaries, letters, sermons, conduct books, polemic writing, and so on. That ambitious goal is still a long way off; the database now includes about 350 texts, but about 4,000 or 5,000 more exist. Nevertheless, the work already done on the Brown project will be invaluable to scholars concerned with the pre-1830 period in a variety of disciplines. The technology has made the difference by providing sophisticated means of reconstructing and authenticating some material previously almost indecipherable. Much of early women's writing exists only in manuscript or in editions with typefaces that are extremely difficult to read. Many are housed in obscure archives and are effectively inaccessible to those who might be interested in them. Now a growing body of this material is available in electronic form; the Brown database allows for the creation of customized texts of individual authors, or of anthologies organized by period or subject, and provides the option to produce more popular editions as well as editions with full scholarly apparatus (Sutherland 1993).

Not long ago, many of these works were completely unavailable and could not even be taught; support for the electronic medium has meant that now any titles in this database could, without great additional expense, be turned into print editions. Several have already been published by Oxford University Press. This capability is less of an issue for the ARTFL database, which consists of major editions of canonical works that are not at particular risk of disappearing. In one case technology provides us with improved access and searchability for mainstream work, and in the other it provides easy access and searchability for work that would otherwise be lost. Databases of electronic text may serve progressive ends, or they may simply reproduce the privileged center. As Neil Postman puts it, "Every technology is both a burden and a blessing; not either-or, but this-and-that" (1992, pp. 4–5).

Therefore, one of the crucial questions we need to ask when providing our patrons with particular electronic indexes and searchable databases is, precisely what is it we are giving them with this new technology and, perhaps more important, what aren't we giving them access to? I think that we are more used to asking this type of essentially political question when considering our collections of print materials. In an earlier essay I attempted to elaborate some of the implications of traditional patterns of book and journal selection and the ways in which collection development policy tends to ratify mainstream culture (Manoff 1992). But over the past few years there has been a growing awareness of the library's role in both constructing and transmitting a cultural legacy and therefore a recognition of what it means to not collect particular kinds of materials, be they alternative, minority, or merely popular works. Most of our thinking on this subject has focused on print materials; it is important that we begin to consider the slightly more complicated way these issues play out in the electronic environment.

Most of us are aware that in the past 20 years or so, libraries' commitment to serials has meant a significant erosion of the percentage of collections budgets devoted to monographs. According to statistics of the Association of Research Libraries (1994), by 1993 research libraries were acquiring 5 percent fewer serials but 23 percent fewer monographs than in 1986. Moreover they increased their expenditures for serials by 92 percent while increasing the amount spent on monographs by only 16 percent. This translates into a pretty clear loss for certain disciplines. It is primarily scientific periodicals that have exploded in price and eaten away money for monographs. And it is humanities disciplines and to a lesser extent social science disciplines that are intensely monograph dependent and which have suffered by libraries' commitment to maintaining scientific and technical journal holdings (Perrault 1994).

The growth of electronic technologies may simply exacerbate this trend of undermining support for humanities and social science material. Having taken money from monographs to support serials, libraries are now taking money from collection budgets for print material to fund electronic products. One of the questions we need to ask is whether this is providing an equivalent level of benefit across the disciplines.

One of the more telling early examples of the differential benefits of electronic access is Dialog searching.[1] Of these several hundred Dialog databases, the vast majority are in scientific, technical, and especially business fields. If libraries decide to fund Dialog searching by skimming off some small or not-so-small percentage of the collections budget across all disciplines, then the real gain is to people in sci-tech and business fields who are much better served by Dialog databases.

With the growth of CD-ROM technology and the glut of products in the sci-tech and business fields, there has been a mini-boom in the number of general reference, humanities, and social science CD-ROM databases. Although this represents an improvement over Dialog, the CD-ROM situation is not without problems.

Ironically, one of my major concerns is how much easier it is to search electronic indexes. Patrons are becoming accustomed to the convenience of not having to go through many volumes of an index and being able to search it all at once with a much greater variety of access points than most print indexes provide. And they can print out their searches or download their citation lists to disk and turn them into a bibliography without ever having to lift a pen or pencil. With products like this, many people are increasingly loathe to consult paper indexes, and it's hard to blame them.

But this means that if, as in many humanities and social science fields, there is only one CD-ROM index for a field, it really matters which titles are not indexed in that source. Scores of alternative, minority, or perhaps only insufficiently mainstream titles are not covered by any CD-ROM index. We thus need to think of CD-ROM indexes as nifty new (or not so new anymore) technology that may cut off access to the noncanonical or nontraditional periodical literature. Many users believe that if they have searched an electronic index they have searched the entire world of information. If it's not in the computer, they assume that it must not exist.

So there are essentially two different problems here. One is the question whether we are devoting a considerable amount of our limited resources to providing electronic access to some fields rather than others. The other question is whether electronic products in particular fields are providing access only to mainstream, centrist, or socially sanctioned views. How much oppositional material, either of the Left or Right, is covered by CD-ROM indexes? I haven't seen any work done on this question, but it is precisely the kind of question that librarians should be addressing.

One field that has clearly suffered as a result of inadequate coverage by electronic abstracting and indexing services is women's studies. Students, faculty, and researchers working in women's studies have not been well served by print indexes; still, the dearth of computerized indexing is even more noteworthy. Researchers in this area quite simply cannot get anywhere near the level of benefit that electronic indexing provides to some other fields.

But women's studies is also an example of a discipline in which librarians have been successful in lobbying for greater coverage by indexing services; it is largely because of the encouragement of women's studies librarians that G. K. Hall's *Women's Studies Index* will be available on CD-ROM in mid-1995. Even now, librarians are working with the publisher to expand the number of journal titles covered by the electronic version. This is an important way in which librarians can play a role in shaping the products that are crucial to research.

We need to think about what kinds of scholarship we are supporting with our expensive new tools. Are areas that rely more heavily on monographs or print indexes being less well supported in order to pay for the technology? We also need to ask whether, because these new tools provide so much better and easier search capability for the serial and journal literature, we are in effect discouraging the use of monographs and therefore monograph-dependent fields.

Slightly different issues come into play when libraries decide to mount their own Gopher or World Wide Web servers, as they are increasingly doing. Both of these types of servers may provide library patrons with a selection of the most relevant and useful of the thousands of resources now available on the Internet, as well as access to local electronic resources. Gathering and organizing these resources have become a new and important function in many libraries. At MIT we have involved reference, collections, and technical services staff in assembling material for the library's Gopher and Web servers. Given the considerable investment of time, especially if staff are to be trained to create and use these new resources, one cannot help but ask what kind of contribution they are making to scholarly research.

When I first started looking for Gopher resources and found recipes, weather information, song lyrics, innumerable copies of the CIA *World Fact Book*, lists of classes at various institutions, and a smorgasbord of articles on this and that, I thought that it was merely a matter of time before really useful things would become the norm. Unfortunately, even now, much of the material on the Internet is of only marginal interest for scholarly purposes.

Locating the more valuable resources continues to be a problem. WAIS, Archie, Veronica, and Jughead are the standard tools for searching gopherspace, and they are all extremely crude. They respond to most queries with vast quantities of junk that requires slow and tedious sorting. Web searching tools such as Lycos and WebCrawler have similar limitations. Under development right now are Web searching tools that can be used on Z39.50 compliant databases. These should offer the most refined Internet searching available, but they cannot be used on all Web material.

Gopher was, at least conceptually, a very promising tool. It allows one to pull together electronic resources from all over the world, or just local resources. With a simple menu system that provides easy access, all these resources can be assembled and offered to users through a single simple interface. Nevertheless, it appears that the technology is maturing faster than we can shape it to our purposes.

Before we managed to figure out what made the most sense to put on our Gophers—what our students and faculty might actually use to do their research and write their papers, and before we even figured out how to organize Gopher resources in the most efficient way, along came the much snazzier World Wide Web. Many institutions, MIT included, are now replacing their Gophers with Webs.

Although it is easy to see why anyone might find Webs much more impressive and fun to play with than Gophers, they present even more severe organizational difficulties. Lacking Gopher's hierarchical menus and offering rather more text and graphics on each screen or home page than most users can quickly assimilate, Webs are harder to navigate. And because the graphics demand so much bandwidth, they can be incredibly slow, which makes the navigation process even more frustrating. Inevitably, as soon as we all master the Web authoring tool, HTML, and figure out the kinds of resources best suited to diffusion on World Wide Web, a new technology will come along that moves faster and looks better. And once again we will be clueless about what resources are most appropriate to mount on it and how best to organize them.

When tools are developed to serve particular needs of particular communities, they may require considerable modification if they are to be made useful for general research purposes. The World Wide Web, for example, was developed to provide access to material on high-energy physics to a small homogeneous group of researchers in one academic specialty. It has not, however, despite the considerable hype surrounding its introduction, proved to be easily adaptable as a reference tool. Nevertheless, librarians are trying to use it as a means of finding quick answers to questions not easily answered through print sources and they have begun to voice their frustration with the process on a number of library-related electronic discussion lists. Librarians and others are slowly realizing that the Internet is much too chaotic an accumulation of resources to treat as if it were one vast database; and they are also realizing that Webs do not function very well as searching tools. On first discovering World Wide Web, many of us assumed that it would provide us easy access to a vast array of resources. But Webs are configured in such a way that they function mostly as browsing tools. They can be notoriously frustrating if one is attempting to find specific material and doesn't know precisely where that material is. Webs do not allow one to locate documents or information in the manner of indexes or other structured reference tools, merely by figuring out the most logical path to it. This isn't to say that some future version might not combine improved searchability with the graphic capabilities of World Wide Web. But the point is that unless librarians actually participate in its development, this future version is unlikely to meet their needs or the needs of their users. This is precisely why it is crucial for librarians to be involved in Web development and the development of other electronic products.

Also, Webs or Gophers may function as better tools for some fields than others. In my view, Gophers are of limited use to many humanities disciplines. I have put a great deal of material in the literature section of the MIT library Gopher, and I have spent a considerable amount of time working with an MIT cataloger to organize it, and yet I don't feel that there was anything in it compelling enough to convince electronically challenged literature faculty that this is a tool they must begin to use. I am more optimistic about the collection of literature resources that I was able to assemble for the MIT Libraries' Web (http://nimrod.mit.edu), but it's a little too soon to know precisely how useful these will prove to be. One positive sign is the tremendous growth in the number of Web resources being mounted by faculty and graduate students in English departments across the United States.

I also worry that a collection of subject-related resources in a library Gopher creates the expectation that it will contain some degree of comprehensiveness, or at least some degree of representativeness of the field as a whole. But this is not possible in most disciplines, as most materials are not yet available electronically and those that are often constitute a seemingly haphazard assortment.

What kinds of literary resources does one typically find included in Gophers? Plain-text versions of many out-of-copyright literary works, lists of electronic discussion groups relating to literature, lists of courses, occasional papers, science fiction book reviews, lists of the holdings of electronic text centers, electronic versions of thesauri and dictionaries, an occasional connection to a full-text database, and back issues of several electronic journals related to literature—hardly the sort of things that students or faculty are likely to consult on a regular basis. Webs are beginning to provide more diverse and interesting humanities resources, but they have only just begun to be noticed by the majority of humanities scholars.

Because of problems with content and organization, most Gophers and Webs are crying out for librarians' expertise and will never function effectively as research tools without it. We need subject specialists to evaluate the material we make available on our Webs and Gophers, and we need experts in classification to organize them. There is growing recognition of the importance of such work. In anticipation of a presentation he was making at the June 1994 American Library Association conference, J. E. Kosokoff, a library science student at the University of Indiana, sent out an announcement to various electronic lists. He offered to provide, to anyone who requested it, an outline of his project. He had solicited input and then assembled a summary of the anatomical and structural features that constitute a well-constructed Gopher. Kosokoff (1993) claims that within 24 hours of his postings, more than two hundred people requested copies. The outline he sent in response covers such Gopher issues as menu language, maintenance and monitoring, menu structure, and formatting of text. This list begins to suggest the issues that remain problematic for Gopher implementors.

The usefulness of Gopher resources to various disciplines remains in question. If one searches Gopherspace for servers devoted to specific disciplines, one finds numerous Gophers devoted entirely to scientific, technical, and some social science fields. Many Gophers are devoted solely to agriculture, biosciences, geology, and medical and legal resources. There are even whole Gophers devoted to soybean data or forest tree genome mapping, or microbial germplasm. New Gophers are being announced all the time. But there are few history, philosophy, linguistics, or literature Gophers. There is the English Server at Carnegie Mellon and the Literature Gopher at the University of Montreal; the American Philosophical Association hosts a server, and Johns Hopkins has a history of science server. But such sources are few and far between. Most Gopher resources in the humanities are contained in sections of college and university Gophers that are devoted to a wide range of subject areas. Most appear to have been casually assembled by either systems people or librarians looking for as many humanities sources as they could find to put in their Gopher. And again, they do not provide materials likely to be heavily used by most humanities students and scholars.

It looks as if the World Wide Web is potentially a more promising technology for nontechnical fields than Gopher. There has been a flowering of decidedly varied offerings on the Web. The Institute for Advanced Technology in the Humanities at the University of Virginia has mounted a number of interesting projects, including a Civil War Web, a Web of Dante Gabriel Rossetti images and text, and one called the Pompeii Forum project. Scholars at the institute are also creating a Web of scholarly material and artifacts from the sixties. But exciting as many of these Web concepts are, even many existing Webs are incomplete, much closer to being good ideas than fully implemented projects.

Nevertheless the advantages of the Web environment to humanistic study are considerable. Particularly valuable is the ability to combine text and image so one can move easily from one to the other or consult both simultaneously. Also important is the ability to provide access to many variants of a particular text and to a huge body of ancillary scholarly material, giving the user the option to choose the desired version, graphics, and supporting material to be consulted. In the case of an author like Rossetti, the Web enables the easy juxtaposition of the paintings done to illustrate a poem or the sonnets written to accompany a painting.

Jerome McGann (1994), the creator of the Rossetti project, points out how limiting book technology has been for scholarly editions. He claims that technical, commercial, and institutional constraints have resulted in impoverished versions of many literary texts. A scholar, primarily of nineteenth-century British literature, McGann shows how the works of major figures beginning with William Blake and including William Morris, Dante Gabriel Rossetti, Emily Dickinson, William Wordsworth, and Charles Dickens have not been adequately represented by scholarly print editions.

McGann argues that the evolution of book design and production was both crucial to and inseparable from the development of modernism. He maintains that features such as text design, typography, and illustrations are utterly central to the texts produced by many nineteenth- and twentieth-century authors. But the only print editions to include all the visually significant features of these works are facsimile editions, which have rarely been able to incorporate a full scholarly apparatus. Hypermedia archives such as those being developed on the World Wide Web hold out the possibility of much fuller treatments of these works.

McGann asserts that he has been able to create something much more inclusive than a scholarly edition with the portion of his Rossetti project that he has mounted on the Web. A computer archive can include vast numbers of documentary materials, certainly, more than any print edition. And unlike print editions, such archives can remain permanently open, expanding as new material becomes available. The Rossetti archive will hold digitized images of the author's works, including manuscripts, proofs, and first editions, as well as color images of the drawings and paintings. It will also contain scholarly notes and other secondary sources.

But Web technology has its own limitations. As McGann acknowledges, plenty of technical problems are yet to be solved. One of the most thorough discussions of these limitations for the construction of literary or historical archives is an article by John Price-Wilkin (1994), who, like McGann, has been working at the University of Virginia, home of the Institute for Advanced Technology in the Humanities, where he is a systems librarian.

Price-Wilkin explains the difficulties imposed by HTML, the authoring tool used to compose Web documents. He demonstrates why even expanded versions of HTML will not accommodate complex documents and why it is impractical for large-scale information delivery. HTML is limited for representations of literary and historical documents, in part because it does not allow for differentiation of all the important elements of a text. Or, to put it in the author's slightly more technical terms, HTML is an "impoverished tag" set with little ability to reflect textual complexity. But Price-Wilkin does suggest that because Webs can communicate with more sophisticated programs, solutions may be devised. He goes on to describe some of his own work in this area.

Again, new tools are being developed faster than we can adopt them and harness them. Products like Webs and Gophers, no matter how slick, how fast, how much fun to play with, will not be especially useful to scholarship or research until they deliver material that researchers can use in their daily work, and I'm not talking about answers to "Internet Hunt" questions or occasional reference queries, or even stunning graphics.

Librarians, as much as anyone, are in a position to help in the process of converting new tools into useful tools. As the volume of material on the Nets has grown, so has the need for librarians' evaluation of resources, as providers of quality control. Authenticity, reliability, and currency are all problems that need to be addressed. Equally crucial is the need for librarians to help organize Gopher, Web and other Internet resources so people can actually find things instead of just stumbling on or splashing against them as they surf the Net. We need to develop tools and structures for systematic organization and searchability.

From a library perspective, the instability of Net resources may be our greatest challenge. The fluidity of the electronic environment is one of the primary obstacles to organizing and providing reliable access to material on the Internet. Resources appear and disappear or reappear in slightly different form. What are the implications for our institutional Webs or Gophers when we can't count on the resources we point to being kept current or even staying put?

In order for libraries to provide better access, new electronic standards for resource identification will have to be established, although they may look a little different from those of a print environment.

Absolute bibliographic control is unlikely and perhaps even undesirable in certain electronic environments. But, for researchers in humanities fields, in particular, there is tremendous concern about developing standards for uniform identification of primary materials and ways to distinguish new electronic editions. CETH has been working to develop such standards (The Text Encoding Initiative—TEI) and ways to link bibliographic records for electronic files to actual locations on the Internet.

It is also crucial for librarians to develop the ability to look dispassionately at new tools and technology. We must work to ensure that new tools provide access to something more than mainstream material. We must learn to consider the long-term impact on users and the implications for future research of new products and services. But it is not sufficient merely to make wise decisions about what to acquire. Libraries should create and encourage the creation of a broad range of Internet resources. Librarians must collaborate with scholars in shaping the next generation of research tools. If librarians do not want to be continually adapting to externally imposed forms of technological development, then they must make whatever efforts they can to participate in that process. If we leave the development of the technology to the technologists, we will get the tools that they want to develop or that they think we need. But if we are willing to learn more about the technology and participate in its development, then perhaps we will end up with products that we want and not just the products we might otherwise deserve.

Note

1. Dialog is a company that supplies access to more than 300 databases via its own computers. Established in 1972, it is a leading provider of online searching and data retrieval.

References

Association of Research Libraries. (1994). ARL Statistics 1992–93. Washington, D.C.: Association of Research Libraries.

Buschman, John. (1993a). "Issues in Censorship and Information Technology." In *Critical Approaches to Information Technology in Librarianship: Foundations and Applications*, edited by John Buschman. Westport, Connecticut and London: Greenwood Press.

Buschman, John, ed. (1993b). *Critical Approaches to Information Technology in Librarianship: Foundations and Applications.* Westport, Conn., and London: Greenwood Press.

Fortier, Paul A., ed. (1993). *A New Direction for Literary Studies?* Special issue of *Computers and the Humanities* 27, nos. 5–6.

Hockey, Susan. (1994). "Electronic Texts in the Humanities: A Coming of Age." Paper presented at Literary Texts in an Electronic Age: Scholarly Implications and Library Services, 31st Annual Clinic on Library Applications of Data Processing, University of Illinois at Urbana-Champaign. April.

Kosokoff, J. E. (1994). "Well-Constructed Gopher Summary." Personal communication via email.

Manoff, Marlene. (1992). "Academic Libraries and the Culture Wars: The Politics of Collection Development." *Collection Management* 16, no. 4: 1–17.

McGann, Jerome. (1994), "The Rationale of HyperText." Electronic document available via Gopher; URL: gopher://jefferson.village.virginia.edu/00/pubs/publications/rationale.txt

Morrissey, Robert. (1993). "Texts and Contexts: The ARTFL Database in French Studies." Profession 93: 27–33.

Olsen, Mark. (1993). "Signs, Symbols and Discourses: A New Direction for Computer-Aided Literature Studies." *Computers and the Humanities* 27: 309–314.

Perrault, Anna H. (1994). "The Shrinking National Collection: A Study of the Effects of the Diversion of Funds from Monographs to Serials on the Monograph Collections of Research Libraries." *Library Acquisition: Practice & Theory* 18, no. 1: 3–21.

Postman, Neil. (1992). *Technopoly: The Surrender of Culture to Technology.* New York: Alfred A. Knopf.

Price-Wilkin, John. (1994). "Using the World-Wide Web to Deliver Complex Electronic Documents: Implications for Libraries." *Public-Access Computer Systems Review* 5, no. 3: 5–21.

Saule, Mara K. (1992). "User Instruction Issues for Databases in the Humanities." *Library Trends* 4: 596–613.

Sutherland, Kathryn. (1993). "Challenging Assumptions: Women Writers and New Technology." In *The Politics of Electronic Text*, edited by Warren Chernaik, Caroline Davis, and Marilyn Deegan, pp. 53–67. London: Office for Humanities Communication Publications and The Centre for English Studies, University of London.

14

Traditional Publishers and Electronic Journals

Janet Fisher

From 1989 to 1995 there has been a growing demand for electronic journals, first from librarians and then from researchers. Journals in this new form are expected to improve the speed of communication of research, enhance informal discussion and comment between scholars particularly in interdisciplinary fields, reduce costs of published material, and reduce backlogs of accepted manuscripts waiting for publication. The first electronic journals were more like newsletters than scholarly journals, but *Bryn Mawr Classical Review*, *Postmodern Culture*, and *Psycholoquy* were three that began the recent wave of interest in electronic journals. In the period from 1993 to 1995, the number of e-journals has increased, but they are still almost entirely free and created almost entirely by dedicated groups of individuals without production subsidy from institutions or scholarly associations.

Where does the traditional journal publisher fit in this movement toward electronic journals? Is there a place for traditional publishers, or will academicians or librarians take on all the functions that publishers have previously handled for these types of publications? What functions must be retained in the transition from print to electronic publication, and what organizations are prepared to take on those functions? What models for electronic journals can provide the enhancements that scholars and librarians are looking for, retain the positive aspects of the current journal publishing system, and fit into the traditional publisher's structure and processes?

What Do Publishers Do for Journals?

The processes that publishers are involved in for scholarly journals fall into the following categories: editorial, production, marketing, fulfillment, subsidiary rights, and financial oversight. Regardless of the discipline, publishers are usually involved in most, if not all, of these functions for the journals they publish. It is important to outline these functions in detail in order to look at what should and can be retained in electronic journals.

Editorial

Publishers support, and are supported by, arrangements with academic journal editors who agree to oversee the peer-review process, assemble an editorial board, and be responsible for the quality of material in the journal. To do this, the editors are supported by staff in the form of editorial assistants, equipment, office space, postage and supplies, and phone and fax. The editor typically reviews manuscript submissions; nominates potential reviewers; analyzes reviews; makes the decision to accept, accept with revisions, or reject the submissions; and communicates with the authors. The editorial assistant backs up the editor in these tasks by acknowledging receipt of manuscripts; contacting potential reviewers; sending manuscripts out to reviewers; reminding them that their reviews are due; and handling form letters and record keeping. The vetting of manuscripts may be handled under the supervision of the editor in his or her office, or under the supervision of the publisher in its office.

Editorial offices may also handle some production tasks (depending on the arrangements with the specific publisher), including copyediting, checking proofs (galleys, page proofs, or blueline proofs), and occasionally dealing with the typesetter and printer. These tasks, however, are generally the responsibility of the publisher.

Production

The publisher is usually responsible for the design, copyediting, typesetting and layout, proofreading, and printing and binding for the journal. It establishes and monitors the production schedule, the number of pages, and the production costs, and controls the production quality of the publication by making decisions about paper, cover stock, level of editing and proofreading, and whether authors' changes should be allowed after typesetting is completed. In addition, production staff may produce offprints of individual articles or materials bundled with the print journal, such as CDs, videotapes, or CD-ROMs.

Marketing

The journal publisher handles promotion and marketing of the journal in a number of ways: mailing flyers and catalogs to individuals and institutions; displaying the journal through exhibits at appropriate scholarly meetings; sending out press releases to appropriate news media; placing advertisements in relevant publications; contacting journals, magazines, and newspapers soliciting review attention; exchanging advertisements with other scholarly journals; and promoting the sale of back issues or single issues of journals. Editors may be asked to review the text of promotional materials and may also be involved in the design of such materials (depending on the editor's particular interests and the journal's audience). The marketing staff may also be responsible for producing materials for sales representatives who call on bookstores or librarians. In addition, the marketing staff may be heavily involved in the sales of advertising in the journal as well as marketing of the journal's mailing list.

Fulfillment

The publisher processes all orders for the journal—including subscriptions, single copies, back issues, and claims for unreceived copies of the journal—and orders for any ancillary publications it may have, such as special supplemental issues, videotapes, CDs, and so on. Usually from three to six rounds of renewal notices are mailed to customers as their subscriptions expire. The fulfillment staff is also responsible for handling the paperwork required by the post office to mail the journal in the most cost-effective and timely way, and for communicating with subscription agencies who handle most orders from libraries and other institutions. The journal may also be sold through distributors to individual bookstores, or directly to bookstores. These orders are usually at bulk discounts, and revenues must be collected from 60 to 120 days after delivery of the issues. Distributors and bookstores typically sell 50 percent of the issues they receive and expect full credit for unsold issues (which are usually not returned to the publisher).

Subsidiary Rights

The publisher makes arrangements with other publishers for additional forms of distribution of the journal such as reprints, translations, microfilm or microfiche, CD-ROM, document delivery, online database distribution, and inclusion of articles in course packs for classroom use. The publisher must thus keep copious records of copyright arrangements with authors and of payments from secondary publishers and copy shops. The publisher registers the copyright of each journal issue with the Copyright Office of the Library of Congress and assumes responsibility for fighting unauthorized and illegal use of the journal articles. The publisher also contacts the appropriate abstracting and indexing services for the discipline and urges inclusion of the journal in the service's products.

Financial Oversight

The publisher is responsible for recording revenues and expenses following standard accounting procedures, which usually means matching revenues with expenses. Publishers must monitor the financial performance of each publication, and of the whole group of publications, and set prices according to the market and the financial requirements of the publisher and, frequently, of the sponsor of the journal. This includes monitoring production costs, page counts, and subscription levels, and collecting and processing revenues expeditiously and carefully. The publisher is usually financially responsible for the journal and assumes the entire financial risk of publication. It must therefore balance the risks with the financial requirements of the publisher's sponsoring society, university, or shareholders.

What Do Electronic Journals Need?

If scholarly electronic journals are to disseminate the highest-quality research, they must have many of the same qualities required of print journals in order to be accepted for tenure consideration by other faculty and administrators: wide dissemination, citation by other researchers, good organization and presentation of content, peer review, inclusion in indexing and abstracting sources consulted by researchers in the field, and a reputable editor and editorial board. Without these, e-journals will remain out of the mainstream of scholarly research and will not attract the high-quality material that researchers are looking for. In some fields, fast publication of accepted material would also be a requirement.

Because of their method of dissemination, electronic journals distributed online have some additional requirements that do not exist for print journals. They must be able to ensure the authenticity of the article's text and the long-term availability and accessibility of the material (archiving), which has traditionally been the responsibility of librarians.

Virtually all the requirements for credible electronic journals are managed now for print products by publishers or societies acting as publishers. Although some print journals are managed by entrepreneurial editors who enjoy the details of the publication process, most journal editors prefer to focus on the review process and to use their specialized knowledge to influence the choice of material and improve the journal's content. Is this likely to be different for electronic journals? Probably not, although the initial flush of newness and excitement concerning the technology has made some scholars interested in starting electronic journals when they would not consider starting a print journal. Startup funds that are usually not available to publishers of print products may be more readily available for individuals from universities, departments, and granting agencies. These funds, however, are not likely to last forever, and a model will eventually have to exist in order for these journals to survive.

Can Traditional Publishers Handle Electronic Journals?

Significant hurdles await both commercial and not-for-profit traditional journal publishers who are interested in publishing electronic journals. There is widespread concern about attracting enough high-quality material, given the uncertainty about acceptance of electronic journals for tenure consideration and for inclusion in traditional indexing and abstracting services. The experience of the American Association for the Advancement of Science (AAAS) and On-Line Computer Library Center (OCLC) in publishing *Online Journal of Current Clinical Trials* (Wilson 1994) has reinforced these fears.

Publishers are uncertain about how to guard published materials from malicious tampering and how to ensure that customers can place orders safely by credit card. Products such as the Digital Notary timestamping service from Surety Technologies, Inc. (Bellcore 1994), are becoming available and provide hope that the first problem will be solved. A product to ensure the security of financial interactions over the Internet was announced in the August 15, 1994, issue of *Publisher's Weekly* (Reid 1994), and others are on the way.

The lack of an established economic model showing the financial viability of electronic journals is a more intractable problem. Experiments such as Red Sage (Taylor 1993; DeLoughry 1993), Tulip, Project Muse (DeLoughry 1994), and ELVYN (Rowland 1994) are under way to determine pricing models for ancillary electronic distribution of existing print journals. However, few purely electronic journals depend on fees from users to recover their costs. The 1993 *Directory of Electronic*

Journals Newsletters and Academic Discussion Lists (King, Kovacs, and Okerson 1993) listed 240 electronic journals and electronic newsletters, of which 45 (19 percent) were labeled as electronic journals and 195 (81 percent) were labeled as electronic newsletters. Of the 45 electronic journals, only two (4 percent) were fee charging: *Journal of the International Academy of Hospitality Research*, begun in 1990 and published by the Scholarly Communications Project of Virginia Polytechnic Institute; and *Online Journal of Current Clinical Trials*, begun in 1992 and published by AAAS. Of the 30 or so new electronic journals announced on the *VPIEJ* electronic discussion list called "Publishing EJournals: Publishing, Archiving, and Access" in 1994, only 3 have been fee charging (*Chicago Journal of Theoretical Computer Science*, beginning in 1994 and published by the MIT Press; *Electronics Letters*, beginning in October 1993 and published by the Institute of Electronic Engineers and distributed by OCLC; and *Online Journal of Knowledge Synthesis for Nursing*, beginning in November 1993 and published by Sigma Theta Tau, International Honor Society of Nursing, and OCLC). The continuing dominance of free e-journals makes it difficult to convince the market that a charge is necessary to cover the costs of producing an electronic publication.

Another troubling problem for publishers is the lack of uniformity in electronic publishing platforms. The electronic journals that exist today are predominately in ASCII form, but some are in PostScript, T_EX, RTF, HTML, or SGML. The ability of readers to access information varies widely with the equipment they own. Researchers in most disciplines need to be able to include charts, tables, line drawings, halftones, micrographs, color photographs, moving video, and audio files, which are difficult to include in electronic journals that aim for a wide audience of readers with the lowest common denominator of equipment.

Finally, there is the culture of traditional print publishers. For electronic journals, the publisher faces losing ultimate control of aspects of the publication that they have always believed were their responsibility. Design, or presentation of the material, becomes increasingly up to the end user, unless the publisher uses a fixed-page form of publication such as PostScript. Control of access to the material—which has never fully been under the control of the publisher but which has seemed under its control—is largely lost. Production processes face upheaval as journals become increasingly unbundled and move to article-by-article publication. Computer fulfillment systems must be modified to incorporate room for e-mail addresses and alternative forms of distribution other than traditional mailing labels.

These problems will exist for the foreseeable future, but established publishers must begin to experiment by offering purely electronic journals. If such experiments do not begin to happen, the forces that espouse the opinions that publishers are not needed in the electronic environment, that researchers can take back publishing of their own material, that copyediting does nothing to enhance the quality of material and that authors can handle all of what used to be called typesetting through macros and existing word processing programs (as exemplified in the ongoing discussions on the *VPIEJ* electronic bulletin board under the heading "Subversive Proposal") will gain credibility and publishers will be relegated to print products with a shrinking market.

Authors as Publishers

What would be different if authors handled publication of their own material through either electronic distribution of preprints or self-publication of e-journals by their editors?

First, the management of subsidiary uses of material would disintegrate. Without the publisher's coordination of the licensing of materials between authors and secondary publishers (such as University Microfilms, Information Access, Lexis/Nexis, and National Association of College Stores), products that are compilations from many sources that are gathered together and issued in another form (i.e., microfilm/fiche, CD-ROM, online databases, course packs) would not be possible. Secondary publishers would have to approach authors directly for permission to reprint articles, which would be an impossible task given the scale of these publications.

Second, the way that an individual, library, or tenure committee views a research article under the current system is significantly influenced by the name and reputation of the journal, the journal's editor and editorial board, and the publisher. Without those signs, the judging of quality will be a much more time-consuming process for all participants in the scholarly communication chain. Most would agree that, with the amount of published research growing all the time, a more difficult system of judging quality is the opposite of what the scholarly communication system needs.

Third, standards of reference, citation, and style that currently exist and vary by discipline would be difficult to enforce and uphold.

Copyeditors and publishers work to standardize contributions to a journal to a particular style in order to enhance the usefulness of the material to the reader. Scholarly associations in some disciplines may be able to enforce such style standards in their particular disciplines, but many disciplines are not served by such overreaching societies.

Fourth, the marketing that publishers do to increase awareness of the journal among the varied segments of the market is unlikely to be done as professionally by an author or editor. The specialized knowledge of lists and marketing techniques greatly enhances the journal's distribution and will be increasingly necessary as the volume of material competing for the reader's attention continues to grow.

Libraries as Publishers

Sessions at a number of conferences in the past few years have broached the subject of whether the university library can and should take on the role of publisher. Questions have been raised regarding the value that publishers add and whether the library's role can be expanded so that there is no need for publishers. This possibility is behind the movement urging authors to retain copyright of scholarly journal articles, which is embodied most clearly in the TRLN Copyright Policy Task Force's report published in 1993 (see "Model University Policy Regarding Faculty Publication in Scientific and Technical Scholarly Journals"). Frank Quinn's paper entitled "A Role for Libraries in Electronic Publication," which was distributed on the *VPIEJ* list on January 19, 1994, outlined how libraries could proceed to become the publishers of electronic publications and why they should. The expected outcome of all these proposals is lower cost to the libraries than would be necessary if electronic publications were purchased from traditional publishers.

There are three basic problems with libraries as publishers: their lack of marketing expertise, their lack of editorial management expertise, and the question of whether this would ultimately reduce the library's costs. The lack of marketing expertise is similar to that outlined in the previous section of this chapter. The lack of experience with editorial standards in terms of both the peer-review process and the copyediting process is a significant problem for libraries if they intend to create publications of high quality comparable to products of traditional publishers. Ensuring such quality would require libraries to invest in staff and training and would therefore increase the library's costs substantially. If the burden of such publications were evenly distributed among libraries and all such publications were available free, there could conceivably be savings over the long term for each individual library. But getting there would take a long and costly period of transition in a time when universities are cutting budgets wherever possible.

Potential Models for Electronic Publications

Experimental models are only now beginning to be proposed for electronic journals, and experience will show us what the market responds to and is willing to pay. Such models are significantly influenced by the academic discipline of the journal, and a number of models will likely exist simultaneously.

Some experiments follow:

• Birkhauser Boston announced an experiment in which the *Journal of Mathematical Systems Estimation and Control* would move to a partially electronic format in 1994, beginning with volume 4 (Beschler 1994). The paper edition of the journal is to contain four-page extended summaries of papers, with the full text available electronically in PostScript form via anonymous FTP.

• Duke University Press's publication *International Mathematics Research Notices* (IMRN) is another example. Designed for fast notification of short research results in mathematics, IMRN separated from *Duke Mathematical Journal* in 1994 and can be received as either an e-mail file in TeX or a paper version printed using DocuTech. A broad site license is available to libraries that wish to subscribe.

• Oxford University Press has entered into an arrangement with the free electronic journal *Postmodern Culture* to distribute floppy disk and paper versions of the journal. In addition, the ASCII version of *PMC* is now available via the World Wide Web and Gopher. A graphically enhanced WWW version is expected shortly and will be available for a fee, while the ASCII version remains free.

• The MIT Press is launching a peer-reviewed electronic journal entitled *Chicago Journal of Theoretical Computer Science*. Available article by article, the journal is being sold for a subscription fee that covers a broad license for libraries to use the material at their local campuses. The journal was started in the fall of 1994.

• Other existing models for electronic journals come from OCLC (Online Computer Library Center) using the delivery platform developed for

Online Journal of Current Clinical Trials. This platform is being used for several journals, and OCLC hopes to use it for more.

Other experiments are in the works, particularly at large scientific societies such as the Astrophysical Society (in conjunction with NASA and the University of Chicago Press), ACM (Association for Computing Machinery), and AMS (American Mathematical Society).

Conclusion

The expertise that publishers contribute to the scholarly communication process is not trivial. They enhance the quality of the material through editorial review and revision, and facilitate the distribution of material to the scholarly community by substantial marketing efforts. The publisher's imprint communicates to readers, libraries, and tenure committees the level of quality they can expect of the material. Publishers increase long-term access to research through licensing arrangements with subsidiary distributors and document delivery services. They format material for consistency and improved readability. Removing publishers from the process of scholarly communication would create chaos throughout the system, and no other party is capable of taking on their many roles.

Publishers are showing the community of scholars that they are ready to improve scholarly communication by developing high-quality cost-effective electronic journals that can increase the speed of publication of research and enhance the ability for scholars to get feedback on their efforts. Libraries are supporting such efforts during this transitional phase so that everyone in the process can benefit. Authors and readers need to show publishers that they are willing to pay for material distributed in electronic form and to respect the copyright holder's distribution rights. As these tentative steps taken toward these goals become institutionalized, the scholarly communication chain will be improved rather than destroyed.

References

Bellcore. (1994). "Bellcore Spins Off New Company to Offer Digital Notary (TM) (SM) Service." Bellcore press release, 22 March.

Beschler, Edwin. (1994). "An Electronic Journal Approach." *Newsletter on Serials Pricing Issues*, no. 110 (March 17): section 110.2.

DeLoughry, Thomas J. (1993). "Effort to Provide Scholarly Journals by Computer Tries to Retain the Look and Feel of Printed Publications." *Chronicle of Higher Education* (April 7): A19–A21.

DeLoughry, Thomas J. (1994). "Journals via Computer: Three Scholarly Publications Are Available On Line in a Project at Johns Hopkins." *Chronicle of Higher Education* (March 9): A25–A26.

King, L. A., D. Kovacs, and A. L. Okerson. (1993). *Directory of Electronic Journals, Newsletters and Academic Discussion Lists.* Washington, D.C.: Association of Research Libraries.

"Model University Policy Regarding Faculty Publication in Scientific and Technical Scholarly Journals: A Background Paper and Review of the Issues." (1993). *The Public-Access Computer Systems Review* 4, no. 4: 4-25.

Reid, Calvin. (1994). "BiblioBytes New Encryptor Secures Credit Cards on 'Net." *Publishers Weekly* (August 15): 14.

Rowland, J. F. (1994). "ELVYN: The Delivery of an Electronic Version of a Journal from the Publisher to Libraries." *VPIEJ* (electronic bulletin board). March 31.

Taylor, Sally. (1993). "AT&T, Springer, Wiley in Document Delivery Project." *Publishers Weekly* (October 18): 7.

Wilson, David L. (1994). "A Journal's Big Break: National Library of Medicine Will Index an Electronic Journal on Medline." *Chronicle of Higher Education* (January 26): A23, A25.

15

The Need for Management of Electronic Journals

Fytton Rowland

The place of the scholarly journal in the electronic future is hotly debated. Much of this debate is not new and has little to do with the issue of print versus electronic access. Instead it reflects the cultural differences between academics, publishers, and librarians with, on the whole, the publishers being the people everybody else loves to hate. Stevan Harnad (this volume) in particular has argued that most scholarly publishing is "esoteric"—that is, has a very small potential readership—and should not be part of the commercial publishing trade in the electronic era; the only reason, in his view, why scholarly publishing came into the commercial arena at all was the need for specialized technical skills concerned with printing, which academics did not possess.

In my 25 years of experience in the scholarly publishing business, academics have always wanted to control their own scholarly publishing system. Initially they did so (Meadows 1980): journals were run by their academic editors, learned societies were administered by their honorary officers, university libraries and university presses were controlled by committees of academic staff. Insofar as full-time staff worked in these institutions they were low-status people, mainly clerical, who wielded no power and enjoyed little respect from the academics. The exception, perhaps, was the university librarian, who in earlier times might well have been a scholar from a humanities discipline who did not necessarily have any specialized librarianship training.

When we consider how the electronic scholarly publishing system of the future might be administered and financed, it is instructive to ask ourselves why this golden age of academic self-help in the publishing business passed away, and whether it is likely or practicable that the facilities of the networks, cheap computer power and modern software can lead to its return. Is it the case, as some such as Andrew M. Odlyzko (1995) have argued, that the involvement of skilled professionals as full-time employees in the scholarly publishing chain was due purely to the technological limitations of print on paper? Is it true that, in the near future, all the functions that these professionals performed will be achievable through the use of user-friendly software that any academic, even one not especially interested in information technology, can use? Odlyzko has likened publishing staff to bank tellers rendered redundant by automatic teller machines. Are their functions really as routine as that?

Academic staff perform a variety of tasks: teaching, research, and administration are those usually cited. The writing of research papers for publication is rightly seen as an integral part of their research activity, because there is little point in undertaking research unless you tell others what you have discovered. In both the United Kingdom and the United States, and I suspect in other countries as well, academics have been coming under increased pressure owing to the growth in numbers of students: as a greater proportion of the population is provided with the opportunity for a higher education, the scale of the teaching and administrative duties required of academics increases. Furthermore, they are under great pressure to publish, for the advancement of their careers and of their department's reputation. The "publish or perish" mentality has spread from the sciences into the humanities and from the United States across the Atlantic. Tasks other than those that are essential for academics' careers are unlikely to be undertaken in these circumstances. The one thing that advancing technology cannot alter is the length of the academic's week: it remains stubbornly fixed at 168 hours available for all of life's activities.

Many journals, print as well as electronic ones, are still largely run by their academic editors today. The academic editor (though not, in general, the referees) may receive a financial honorarium from the journal's funds. More commonly, the publisher makes a contribution to the clerical costs of the journal by paying for an editorial assistant. According to Janet H. Fisher (1994) academic editors are increasingly likely to ask the journal publisher to provide them with computer hardware and software for their editorial work as well.

Mostly, though, the journals run directly by their academic editors are relatively small, publishing only tens of papers per year and appearing perhaps quarterly. Large, long-established journals, especially in the sciences, handle thousands of submissions per annum. Any operation on this scale, in any industry, needs an administrative system to monitor and control work flow, and needs people for whom running the system is a full-time job, not just a sideline. Any substantial-sized operation, computerized or not, needs managerial, administrative, and clerical employees. My experience, both work-connected and recreational, with voluntary organizations convinces me that beyond a certain size—measurable in financial turnover, number of people interacting, or number of items being dealt with—the organization will tend toward instability if it does not have full-time employees at a fairly responsible level.

The key issues in the scholarly publishing system of the future do not include the technology that is used to deliver it but the following: The key issues are: What is the scholarly publishing system for? Can these objectives be achieved at little or no cost? If there is a cost, what features does it pay for? (If there is no cost, the implication is that these features are not needed.) And if there is a significant cost, how and by whom will this cost be paid? We can probably agree that one purpose of the system is to deliver reliable, correct, quality-controlled scholarly information from its authors to its users all over the world in such a way that the users can retrieve and assimilate it readily, and to retain that information archivally for the foreseeable future. The second important function—arguably more important—is to award due credit and priority to researchers for their work, in a way that is recognized and accepted as valid by their peers.

Those who have argued that electronic journals on the network are almost cost-free have in general assumed that refereeing is the only form of quality control that is needed. Where any reference is made to copyediting, the presumption is that this is largely an artifact of print, and in any case is not very important. All experienced academic editors, however, including Harnad, know that the version submitted by the author is very rarely published without amendment. The improvements needed are not only the changes in the substantive content that may be requested by academic editors, they are also those of presentation that are attended to by copyeditors.

Few specialists find it easy to write readable prose; spellchecker programs have removed the bulk of spelling errors from typescripts today, but many other errors of grammar and syntax occur. Many authors are writing in a language that is not their native tongue, and copyeditors do a great deal to make the valuable scholarly work of these authors more understandable to their peers of other nationalities. Copyeditors with a background in the subject area of the journal, as are usually employed by learned-society publishers, also detect and correct many minor errors that are not noticed in the necessarily broad-brush approach of academic referees, and thus contribute to the archival correctness of the scholarly record.

Conspicuous by its absence from this debate, generally speaking, is any reference to the ergonomics of reading. But we all know from personal experience that reading material on a screen is not very pleasant and furthermore that, given the choice between reading a typescript and reading the same material in proper print, the latter is pleasanter and less tiring. For this reason vendors of word processing programs have been incorporating many features formerly found only in desktop publishing software, for example, a wide choice of fonts and type sizes. But to produce an attractive, readable document (in any medium) requires more than just technology. It requires skill and flair. This is not a chance phenomenon. Typographical designers have a wealth of craft knowledge going back centuries that helps to provide documents that are comfortable to read.

Furthermore, and very important, in many scholarly fields high-quality graphics, including half-tone photographs and full-color illustrations, represent a significant proportion of the information content of each paper. This is certainly true in the biological sciences, for example. The free journals made available so far on the Internet have tended to be text only. It is true that the information superhighways of the immediate future will have the bandwidth to accommodate high-resolution graphics in real time in a way that current networks cannot; although in passing it must be noted that it is not clear how soon the superhighways will provide a complete international network.

High-quality graphics of high information content are not easy to produce, however, and are often not provided by authors. Trade publications almost invariably require input from professional artists and graphic designers; esoteric publications (Harnad's [this volume] term) perhaps do not need and cannot justify that level of expense, but certainly work usually needs to be done on the crude graphics supplied by authors before they can be regarded as publishable. This is a professional task that academics—however skilled they are with words—probably cannot perform.

Academics are not paid for refereeing, which, like authorship, can be seen as part of their job. The provision of copyediting, typographic and graphic design, and art services cannot. Even though all these professionals, like academics and authors, are likely to be using information technology extensively, they will be using it in specialized ways and with skills that academics do not possess.

Almost all typescripts today are created in machine-readable form, and the few publishable ones that are not—received from developing countries or from self-employed independent scholars, perhaps—could be cheaply rendered into machine-readable form by data-preparation agencies. Progress toward putting a journal together entirely from the author's machine-readable input has, however, been slower and more laborious than had been expected. Some subject areas—notably mathematics and physics, the areas of work of Odlyzko (1995) and Frank Quinn (1994)—are considerably standardized in the use of T_EX, which is helpful. But in most subject areas authors use a variety of software.

This situation is not likely to change; although most academics today are using information technology (IT) to some degree, all academic authors cannot ever be expected to reach precisely the same level of technological sophistication. Although the average level of IT skill will no doubt rise, some scholars will be at the technological leading edge and others will lag, and journal editors will probably pitch their systems somewhere in the middle of the current range in their discipline. Furthermore, as fast as standards committees seek to agree on technical standards for IT, entrepreneurs are developing advanced systems that go beyond current standards. This situation will not alter either, so there will always be software and hardware incompatibilities. Thus an editor accepting submissions from an open-ended set of authors scattered around the world will, I believe, always find that finicky work remains to be done on some of the submitted text and graphics, which software cannot deal with automatically.

The high quality in presentation and scientific content for which I am arguing is important not only for the benefit of readers but also to ensure that electronic journals receive the support of authors. The major obstacle in the way of most innovations in scholarly publication is the conservatism of authors. Even in fields such as high-energy physics or human genome research, where networked preprints are the favored means of communication (Meadows 1980), most material is ultimately published in printed journals, both to give the authors career credit and for archival purposes. At present, some universities and grant-giving institutions will not accept electronic publications for the author's credit. This situation is likely to change, but, for some time to come, researchers whose career is not yet fully established may wish to play safe by putting their best work into the best traditional journals. If that is so, these journals will logically be the last ones to be canceled by libraries—because they contain the best work—and a situation foreseen by Bernard Naylor (1994a, 1994b) may arise, in which printed journals are regarded as first rate and electronic ones as second rate.

If there is to be a system of scholarly publications that is both electronic and high quality—and I believe that this will happen—that system will require staff, both routine clerical staff and skilled professionals. These staff will need salaries; a system as extensive, and as important, as the scholarly information system of the world cannot be run on a wholly voluntary basis. Hence it will require an income. This income can be derived in a number of ways, but given the ideological preferences of the governments of the most industrialized nations, a private-sector element involving competition and the profit motive seem likely to be included. The idealism of the first generation of Internet enthusiasts, though admirable, seems unlikely to prevail as the networks become the major method by which the world and its industrial and commercial activities are administered.

Many have argued that the falling costs of computer hardware, especially mass storage devices, and the fact that the academic networks are free of charge at the point of use, mean that the price of the scholarly communication system can be reduced to a small fraction of its present cost. There has also been debate about where this residual cost should be paid, with suggestions that it might be covered by the authors' making their own papers available on a server (Harnad 1994), for example, or by each university library's mounting a few journals so that collectively the world's higher education system could provide all the journals that the academic world requires, free of charge at the point of use (Quinn 1994). Gail McMillan (1994) has expressed this idea: "Rather than having many journals free to a few users, the library would have a few journals free to many users. However the net effect is that all users get better access to more information."

Quality has to be paid for somehow. University libraries may decide that they would obtain better value for money by using McMillan's (1994) model than by buying journals (in print or electronic form) from publishers. If so, they need to recognize that they, rather than publishers, will need to employ staff with publishing skills as described earlier; they thus will have reinvented the university press!

The initial costs of publication are not the only costs that the scholarly information system has to bear. In a printed publication system, the journals are stored in libraries. In most academic libraries the issues are bound into hardback volumes, and these volumes occupy shelf space, which has a price; efficient librarians can tell you what their annual cost per shelf meter is. In the electronic future, the accumulating archive of published electronic material will need to be stored and maintained. Computer storage, albeit inexpensive, is never going to be free. When hardware and software are replaced by a new generation, it will be necessary to ensure that all the archived journals can be retrieved and read on the new equipment. Unlike printed journals, electronic journals may be archived in only a few places, possibly in only one—perhaps on the publisher's machine. A cost will be attached to the availability in perpetuity of historic materials; instead of shelf-meters, it will be measured in gigabytes, and like the shelf-meters the gigabytes will be accompanied by a staff cost. Libraries bear these costs for the printed journal; how will these be covered if the library no longer holds stock and the sole copy of the electronic journal is held by the publishers? What if a publisher goes out of business?

I predict that the system for the dissemination of research will become increasingly fragmented, presenting an interesting challenge to serials librarians, and that almost all the models that have been described during the recent debates will be tried out in one field or another. Many of the major established journals in many fields already belong to not-for-profit organizations that are themselves part of the academic world, such as learned societies and university presses. If these organizations sometimes seem to behave commercially, it is because of some of the imperatives described previously: to maintain quality they need skilled staff, those staff must eat, and the organizations have to be not-for-loss as well as not-for-profit. Their journals will survive for decades yet, but will be available electronically as well as, and eventually instead of, in print. A subscription will continue to be required.

Other new, free electronic journals will spring up, as indeed they are already doing; many will be relatively small in terms of number of items published per annum, and they will probably replace many of the smaller, weaker printed journals from commercial publishers. Academic library costs will not fall, because numbers of students and publications will continue to rise, but the cost per item published (and the library expenditure per student) will fall. This can be perceived as increased value for money, or as deterioration of quality of library service, according to your political preference. But in the end the scholarly research information system will have a significant price tag; my guess is that, when the transition to an electronic system is complete in perhaps 2025, the cost per published article will be between 25 percent and 50 percent (in real terms) of that of the purely printed system of scholarly journals that we had in 1980.

References

Fisher, J. H. (1994). "Editorial Costs." Message posted on the Publishing E-Journals: Publishing, Archiving and Access discussion list (VPIEJ-L), July 29, 1994.

Harnad, S. (This volume.) "Implementing Peer Review on the Net: Scientific Quality Control in Scholarly Electronic Journals."

Meadows, A. J., ed. (1980). *Development of Scientific Publication in Europe.* Amsterdam: Elsevier.

McMillan, G. (1994). "VT (Virginia Tech) Model." Message posted on the Publishing E-Journals: Publishing, Archiving and Access discussion list (VPIEJ-L), July 27, 1994.

Naylor, B. (1994a). "The Future of the Scholarly Journal." Paper delivered at the general meeting of LIBER, July 7, 1994.

Naylor, B. (1994b). "A Small Contribution to the Subversive Discussion." Message posted on the Publishing E-Journals: Publishing, Archiving and Access (VPIEJ-L) discussion list, August 4, 1994.

Odlyzko, A. M. (This volume.) "Tragic Loss or Good Riddance? The Impending Demise of Traditional Scholarly Journals." A longer version appears in *International Journal of Human–Computer Studies* 42 (1995): 71–22.

Quinn, F. (1994). "A Role for Libraries in Electronic Publication." *EJournal* 4, no. 2: lines 68–416.

16

The Challenges of Electronic Texts in the Library: Bibliographic Control and Access

Rebecca S. Guenther

As computers have changed the way information is made available, the library and research communities have had to adapt to new ways of describing and locating information. Librarians and other information professionals are working in increasingly networked environments, with electronic resources such as online databases or electronic text centers becoming an integral part of their frame of reference. The "library without walls" is indeed becoming a reality, and cataloging rules and format specifications need to change as well.

Libraries have a great deal invested in machine-readable cataloging records. Large bibliographic utilities and local systems provide services to libraries and other institutions for access to materials through the online catalog. Records for resources that are available only electronically should be included in the same database as traditional library materials so that researchers can tap this type of information as additional source material. Researchers should be able to find bibliographic citations to relevant material regardless of its format or location. Because these electronic resources cannot be accessed in the same way as other materials (i.e., by a location that indicates the library and call number or shelf number housing the material), new methods of access need to be developed.

Standards must be developed and used for these new types of locator devices so that records can be exchanged between institutions. Given the

An earlier version of this chapter was presented as a paper at the 1992 Data Processing Clinic at the Graduate School of Library and Information Science at the University of Illinois at Urbana-Champaign and was published in the proceedings of that conference: Sutton, J. Brett, ed. (1994). *Literary Texts in an Electronic Age: Scholarly Implications and Library Services.* Urbana: Graduate School of Library and Information Science at the University of Illinois at Urbana-Champaign.

growth of availability of electronic texts, sharing bibliographic records will be a necessity, so that institutions do not expend valuable resources on redundant cataloging. The Library of Congress, the Online Computer Library Center (OCLC), and various committees of the American Library Association have made progress in developing cataloging and machine-readable (MARC) standards for describing and providing location information for electronic resources, particularly those available on the Internet, the global network of networks.

Cataloging Challenges

The *Anglo-American Cataloging Rules, 2nd edition, (AACR2)* has generally been adopted as the standard cataloging code in most English-speaking countries (Joint Steering Committee 1988, p. ix). The rules are revised according to changing needs of the library community by the Joint Steering Committee for Revision of AACR. The Committee on Cataloging: Description and Access, a committee of the Association for Library Collections and Technical Services of the American Library Association, initiates proposals for revisions to the cataloging code and advises the official ALA representative to the Joint Steering Committee (American Library Association 1992, p. 32). In some cases specific guidelines are issued to supplement *AACR2*, such as the *Library of Congress Rule Interpretations* (Hiatt 1990) or various guidelines for cataloging specific types of material (e.g., *Guidelines for Bibliographic Description of Reproductions*).

Electronic texts pose special problems in using the cataloging rules, partly because the rules often assume that the cataloger is physically examining an item "in hand," which is not true for those electronic texts available by remote access. In addition, electronic texts often contain minimal information from which to create a catalog record. Chapter 9 of the *AACR2* provides the standard for cataloging computer files and is intended for the bibliographic description of "files that are encoded for manipulation by computer," including both computer data and programs, either stored on local media available for direct access or available by remote networked access (Joint Steering Committee 1988, rule 9.0A1, p. 221).

Sources of Information

Electronic texts, particularly those available remotely, often do not contain adequate information for the cataloger to be able to completely describe the item bibliographically. Applying the concept of "chief source of information," which is used to determine the title and authorship statement in *AACR2,* requires flexibility because of the difficulty in determining the chief source. The cataloging rules direct the cataloger to the title screen or screens; in the absence of a title screen, information may be taken from "other formally presented internal evidence," such as menus or program statements. Additionally, the cataloger may use the physical carrier or its labels, documentation or accompanying material, or the container (Olson 1992, p. 1). If the item cannot be physically examined (i.e., it is accessible remotely, as is the case with electronic texts available in online databases), the rules do not give much guidance.

Another problem arises when the electronic text is in a format that is not "eye readable," so that the cataloger cannot examine the item at all (for instance, in a compressed or PostScript format). In these cases, often only the filename and size of file may be available for descriptive cataloging. The rules discourage the use of filename or dataset name as the title proper, but in some instances it is the only possible title (Joint Steering Committee 1988, rule 9.1B3, p. 224).

Identification

Ascertaining whether an electronic text is a new edition of a previously issued item is difficult at best. This decision determines whether a new bibliographic record is created, and *AACR2,* supplemented by the *Library of Congress Rule Interpretations (LCRI)* guides the cataloger in making this determination. An edition in terms of computer files is defined in *AACR2* as "all copies embodying essentially the same content and issued by the same entity" (Joint Steering Committee 1988, p. 617). Does one consider a computer file that has been compressed the same edition as one that is uncompressed? In other words, does one catalog the item as it is intended to be used, or as it is encoded? In addition, it is not often clear who issued an electronic text because of a lack of sufficient information, so that issuing body cannot determine the item's identification.

The *LCRI* for rule 1.0 provides general guidance for determining whether a new manifestation of an item constitutes a new edition, thus requiring a new bibliographic record. After consulting the definition of edition (as specified previously for computer files), the cataloger is instructed to consider the item a new edition if it meets the specified criteria. Among these are an explicit indication of changes of content, a difference in certain portions of the bibliographic record (e.g., title, edition, physical description), or variations in the publication area (unless they are only minor variations, as defined). For electronic texts, this section does not always assist the cataloger because of the scarcity of information about the item, the difficulty in determining the chief source, and the focus in the rules on an item that the cataloger physically holds. In addition, the publication area takes on a new meaning for electronic texts, because many of them are not published in the traditional sense. Further, the criterion that a different physical description requires a separate record is irrelevant for those electronic texts that are available remotely, because the rules specify that a physical description is not given when there is no physical item (Joint Steering Committee 1988, rule 9.5, p. 231). Even the title cannot be relied on to determine whether the item is a new edition, because in the electronic world it is very easy to change a filename or even data in a file, and the filename could be the only information to use in constructing a title for the item.

Other characteristics of electronic texts compound the difficulty in deciding whether to consider the item a new edition. Is an ASCII text of a work a different edition from the PostScript version? Or, for that matter, is the scanned version different from the text itself? Will it serve library catalogs to create separate records for each manifestation, or should a hybrid record be created, containing information on all the available versions? When stored on a network, the same electronic text may move from one host to another as computers are in and out of service, and files are also copied to different sites. The content of the electronic text may not change, but its location or its filename may. Identifying that two items are actually the same in content becomes problematic in the electronic world.

As catalogers gain more experience in cataloging electronic texts, some of these questions might be answered. How catalogers handle editions may depend on the use of the data or the system constraints. Some of the questions concerning cataloging of electronic texts may be compared to the issues concerning the cataloging of reproductions. The handling of reproductions in online bibliographic systems has been problematic. Some institutions favor the use of holdings records linked to the bibliographic record for the original, and others favor separate bibliographic records with certain fields added for aspects of the reproduction. It may take time and experimentation for institutions to decide which approach works best for electronic texts.

USMARC Standards for Electronic Texts

Although many navigational tools exist for accessing electronic texts over the Internet, librarians are interested in describing and providing access to electronic information resources within the USMARC record structure, so that records for these resources can reside in the same database as other library materials. In addition to the description (identifying what the information is, whether it might suit the researcher's needs), the user requires location information (where can I obtain a copy of it?) and access information (how do I get a copy?). If records for electronic information resources are accessible in the same format as other library materials, the systems can process them in the same way. In addition, these records can then be shared between systems in the same way that other USMARC records are.

In the USMARC environment, systems exchange records, so that duplication of effort is minimized. Because of the difficulty of identifying and describing electronic information resources, it would be of great benefit for institutions to exchange information about this type of material. If the institution providing the service or data contributed records about that data for exchange between libraries (as now many types of bibliographic records are exchanged), users might more easily be able to locate information they need. For instance, an institution making a library catalog, mailing list, or database accessible could provide the record that describes and gives location and access information for the service. Using the USMARC format would be appropriate for the library community because of the format's familiarity and flexibility, as well as the desirability of incorporating these types of records into the existing frameworks.

Background on the USMARC Format

The USMARC formats are standards for the representation and communication of bibliographic and related information in machine-readable form. The *USMARC Format for Bibliographic Data* contains format specifications for encoding data elements needed to describe, retrieve, and control various forms of bibliographic material. Most systems use their own internal formats for storing and displaying bibliographic data, but they use USMARC, a *communications* standard, to exchange data between systems. The USMARC formats are maintained by the Library of Congress's Network Development and MARC

Standards Office in consultation with various user communities (Library of Congress 1989, p. 2). The USMARC Advisory Group and the Machine-Readable Bibliographic Information Committee (MARBI) of the American Library Association consider proposals for additions and changes to the formats, and discuss USMARC issues.

USMARC formats other than the bibliographic format were developed to satisfy additional needs of libraries. The USMARC Holdings Format is a carrier for holdings and location information. It includes copy-specific information for an item; information peculiar to the holding organization; information needed for local processing, maintenance, or preservation of items; and information required to locate an item, including holdings organization and sublocation. The USMARC Community Information Format, recently approved as a provisional format, is a carrier for descriptions of nonbibliographic resources to which people in a particular community might want access. These include programs, services, organizations, agencies, events, and individuals. The USMARC Classification Format contains authoritative records for library classification schemes, and the USMARC Authority Format is a carrier for authoritative information on standard forms of names and subjects.

USMARC Specification for Computer Files

In the early 1980s, a MARC specification was developed for communicating information about machine-readable data files within the USMARC Bibliographic Format, describing both the data stored in machine-readable form and the programs used to process that data. The data elements were intended to be used to describe both data files and computer software. Data elements needed for the description of these files were integrated into the USMARC Bibliographic Format under the broader term "computer file"; many of the data elements were defined in *AACR2, c*hapter 9. The computer files record specifications were developed before the widespread use of the personal computer, particularly for data files, such as census tapes and raw data maintained by large computer centers. Later, data elements were added to accommodate software, after microcomputers began to gain attention, and more attention was given to physical form, particularly physical and technical details about the software (Crawford 1989, p. 124). The specifications are generally adequate for description of machine-readable files and software but, before several changes in 1993, were limited in providing information on access. Because information in electronic form requires special description, location, and retrieval information, the Network Development and MARC Standards Office has been considering how to enhance the USMARC formats to accommodate online information resources. These enhancements should improve the ability to locate and access electronic texts.

Enhancing Descriptive and Access Information to Electronic Texts

The USMARC Advisory Group recognized the need for accommodating electronic information resources by considering two discussion papers about the topic, "Discussion Paper No. 49: Dictionary of Data Elements for Online Information Resources," discussed in June 1991 (Library of Congress 1991a), and "Discussion Paper No. 54: Providing Access to Online Information Resources," discussed in January 1992 (Library of Congress 1991b). Participants attending the meetings agreed that USMARC should be expanded to accommodate description and access of machines as resources on the network as well as data files on the machines, and that further work needed to be done. They decided that electronic data resources (e.g., electronic texts, software, databases) might be more amenable than online systems and services (e.g., FTP sites, online public access catalogs, bulletin boards) to bibliographic description using current AACR2 cataloging rules for computer files and the USMARC Bibliographic Format with minimal format changes.

As part of its Internet Resources Project—funded by the U.S. Department of Education, Library Programs—OCLC investigated the nature of electronic textual information accessible via the Internet (Dillon et al. 1993, p. 2). A group of representatives from OCLC, Online Audiovisual Catalogers (OLAC), Library of Congress, and MARBI reviewed work on the project, examined sample documents, and planned a cataloging experiment of Internet resources. The experiment was intended to test and verify the applicability of the cataloging rules and the USMARC Bibliographic Format's computer files specifications, and to provide sufficient data to determine what changes needed to be made to AACR2 and USMARC to accommodate these materials.

The cataloging experiment was held during May and June 1992 and involved the cataloging of three hundred computer files collected from Internet sites, half of which were types of electronic texts, and the other half of which were randomly selected text, software, and data. After a call for participation was issued and distributed electronically via the Internet, a group of catalogers was selected to participate and was given instructions for cataloging. Each file was cataloged by three different catalogers.

Results of the experiment indicated that *ACCR2* and the USMARC format generally accommodate the description of Internet resources, but that clear guidelines needed to be developed to assist catalogers. The format needed to be modified to include, among other things, more choices in identifying the type of file in the USMARC fixed field (coded) area; guidelines for the appropriate and consistent use of note fields, and standards for including location and access information to find and retrieve the item.

Two initiatives resulted from the analysis of the OCLC Internet Resources Cataloging Experiment: the drafting of guidelines for the use of *AACR2* cataloging rules for Internet resources, presented to the American Library Association's on Cataloging: Description and Access (CC: DA) Committee; and a proposal for changes in the USMARC bibliographic format to address the deficiencies.

Cataloging Guidelines

Draft cataloging guidelines were formulated by the cataloging experiment planning committee and submitted to the ALA CC: DA. The guidelines were intended for OCLC users preparing bibliographic descriptions of items from the Internet but are also applicable to anyone performing cataloging of electronic resources. They review special provisions in *AACR2* for materials available by remote access and attempt to give guidance for preparing bibliographic description of difficult parts of the catalog record. The "Guidelines for Bibliographic Description of Internet Resources" (1992) have been reviewed by a task force of CC: DA, and some changes have been requested. The following list summarizes some of the more problematic areas of the cataloging rules, which the guidelines address:

Published versus nonpublished. The guidelines suggest that electronic journals be considered published, because they are distributed electronically by a formal mailing list, even if they do not carry formal publication information. Many other electronic texts are similar to manuscript material and are to be considered unpublished. If the item carries a formal statement of publication similar to that on a title page, however, it may be considered published. In case of doubt the cataloger is to consider the work unpublished.

Chief source. For remotely accessible electronic texts the guidelines suggest that the chief source is the title screen or other information displayed on the terminal or on a printout. This section was later revised to include any first display of information, the subject line, or the header to a file. In addition, it was changed to address the situation where a file is unreadable without processing (e.g., a compressed file) and suggests taking the information from the file after it has been processed. The title is to be taken from the chief source if possible and must always be present; it is supplied by the cataloger if necessary.

File characteristics. Although a section in the guidelines addressed the portion of chapter 9 of *AACR2* dealing with file characteristics, the changes suggested to the cataloging rules have been withdrawn. The guidelines suggest that "number of records" not be used for Internet resources in the file characteristics area of the cataloging record, because the information may vary greatly from the form in which it is received to the form in which it is used and stored. Because the number of records is related to the way a file is stored at a particular location, the guidelines recommend including this data in the area indicating location and access information.

Notes. The guidelines instruct the cataloger in the use of notes and give examples of the types of notes that might be included.

Location and access. The guidelines instruct the cataloger to use the new USMARC field 856 electronic location and access for all information necessary for accessing the electronic resource.

Accommodating Online Information Resources in USMARC Formats

As a result of the earlier discussion papers on accommodating online information resources in USMARC and the OCLC Internet Resources Cataloging Experiment (Library of Congress 1991a, 1991b), the Network Development and MARC Standards Office submitted a proposal to the ALA USMARC Advisory Group for changes to computer files specifications of the Bibliographic Format. The paper was intended to address those deficiencies found in the cataloging experiment for describing and locating electronic resources. Proposal 93-4 ("Changes to the USMARC Bibliographic Format [Computer Files] to Accommodate Online Information Resources") included three recommendations. First, it proposed the addition of new codes in the fixed field area for "type of computer file" to include bibliographic data, font, game, and sounds. In addition it called for changing a few definitions. Among them was the use of the word *text*, which it considered confusing, because many electronic files include text (instructions for software, etc.). The term *document* was suggested, to limit the use of this code to textual material that is intended to constitute a document, whether represented as ASCII or image data. The intent of the file (as document, rather than graphic) would then be expressed in the code. The second recommendation was to broaden the descriptors in the file characteristics area (USMARC field 256) to allow for more specific terms. Finally, the third portion of the proposal was to add a new field to the USMARC bibliographic and holdings formats for electronic location and access, to allow for the encoding within the record of all information needed to locate and make accessible an electronic resource. Proposal 93–4 dealt only with the subset of online information resources called "electronic data resources" (e.g., electronic texts, databases, software), not with online systems and services, because only a few modifications to current format specifications would be necessary in order to accommodate these resources.

Proposal 93–4 was discussed at the American Library Association midwinter meeting in January 1993, and the USMARC Advisory Group made modifications to the fixed field "type of computer file" changes. The second recommendation, concerning broadening the descriptors, was deferred pending its consideration by the CC: DA, because it affected area 3 of *AACR2*, chapter 9. (After consideration by a CC: DA task force, this portion of the cataloging guidelines was withdrawn, so it will not be reconsidered by the USMARC Advisory Group.) Field 856 (electronic location and access) was approved as a provisional field with several modifications; after institutions use the field in catalog records, its status as provisional will be reconsidered.

Field 856 is intended to give the user the information required to locate and access the electronic item. It has been noted that the MARC record is deficient in providing nonbibliographic information except in 5XX note fields, which may or may not be searchable by systems, and that it is thus unsuitable to aid in the direct retrieval of electronic texts (*CETH Newsletter* 1993, p. 13). The proposal attempts to allow for the retrieval of the electronic text (as well as any other electronic resource), perhaps directly if systems are programmed to use it for automatic transfer. Of particular interest in the development of the proposal was the electronic journal or newsletter, because of the phenomenal increase in the number being issued and the need for better bibliographic control of them.

During the initial planning of the OCLC cataloging experiment, participants felt that the capability of machine access to the item should be provided for those items that are self-identifying (i.e., do not require interactive searching). All data elements that a user needs to know to make the connection, locate the document, and retrieve it should be included in the catalog record. In the case of library catalogs or other databases, the information needed to connect should be given, although only site-specific information about the server to which a user is connecting (information that everyone would need to know) is included. Information that might be needed about the client (i.e., the system from which the connection is made) is not given and must be dealt with locally. Data elements are parsed and transportable between systems and formats. Although the content of this field was developed with Internet resources specifically in mind, as an outgrowth of the OCLC Internet Resources Project cataloging experiment, it is expected that the field can be extended to non-Internet resources.

An electronic data resource can reside in many directories at any number of hosts in several formats. It might be stored as both a compressed file and an uncompressed file with different filenames, yet the end result is the same item. These characteristics were considered in the planning of the new "electronic location and access" field. Location data in the USMARC format properly belongs in a field for holdings and locations (85X block), which, according to the USMARC standard, can be embedded in a bibliographic record. The electronic location and access information could be considered comparable to the "library location and holdings" field for a book, which gives the institution, shelving information, and specific information about the item at that particular location (e.g., copy number, piece designation, notes). Thus, information applicable to the particular "copy" of the electronic item would be recorded in the electronic location field, rather than at the record level in a bibliographic field. Consequently a separate bibliographic record need not be created if the only difference between electronic items is, for example, the host name making them accessible, the compression used, the filenames, and so on. This type of information can be considered copy-specific and recorded in a separate field of the bibliographic record for electronic holdings and locations. A separate record is made only if the intellectual content of the item is different.

Field 856 functions as a locator for an item and includes various data elements in separate subfields that are sufficient for the user to locate and access the electronic resource. The indicator after the tag value shows the access method (e.g., telnet, FTP, e-mail, or other) for locating the resource and determines how the rest of the field is used. Data elements that are descriptive are included in the other bibliographic fields in the record. The separate subfields allow for parsing of elements so that they can be separately maintained, accessed, or, searched. They also permit special displays to be generated by the system, if it is programmed to do so. The field is repeated for different locations, filenames, or access methods. Figure 16.1 shows the subfields defined in field 856; figure 16.2 shows how the field might be displayed in an online public access catalog.

The Network Development and MARC Standards Office prepared two proposals for adding data elements to field 856, for discussion at the meeting of the USMARC Advisory Group in February 1994. Because of a desire to be able to communicate information that links a bibliographic record with an electronic object, whether an image, text file, or any other type, the American Memory Project at the Library of Congress suggested the addition of two subfields that are currently recorded in a local field (Library of Congress 1993a). Other projects are also considering the use of the electronic location field to link bibliographic records with other electronic resources. VTLS, a library system vendor, has developed a multimedia product called InfoStation, which uses a local field in bibliographic records to link sound and image files, and plans to use the standard field 856 to do this in the future. The system uses the information in this field to find the file and display the image associated with the bibliographic record. The Research Libraries Group (RLG) has launched the Digital Image Access Project, a collaborative project to explore the capabilities of digital image technology for managing access to photographic collections. Eight RLG institutions are attempting to improve access to collections for shared access across networks. A project at Cornell University Engineering Library is attempting to build a multimedia network to enhance the undergraduate engineering curriculum. Using Cornell's NOTIS system, a telnet session is initiated to the Iowa State University catalog through another server. The computer uses a unique number contained in a MARC field, which is matched in the database on the remote server, and the file transfer protocol (FTP) enables the transfer of the necessary image files.

In addition, the second proposal concerning field 856 considered in February suggested the addition of a subfield for recording the Uniform Resource Locator (URL), a standard under development (Library of Congress 1993b). MARBI, a subgroup of the USMARC Advisory Group that votes on proposed changes to the USMARC formats, approved the new subfields.

(R) means repeatable; (NR) means nonrepeatable
856   Electronic Location and Access (R)

(Contains the information required to locate an electronic item. The information identifies the electronic location containing the item, or the location from which it is available. Field 856 is repeated when the location data elements vary (subfields ≠a, ≠b, ≠d) and when more than one access method may be used. It is also repeated whenever the electronic filename varies (subfield ≠f), except for the situation when a single intellectual item is divided into different parts for online storage or retrieval.)

Indicators

First   Access method
(Contains a value that defines how the rest of the data in the field will be used. If the resource is available by more than one method, the field is repeated with data appropriate to each method. The methods defined are the main TCP/IP protocols. Subfield ≠2 may be used to specify others not defined in the indicator.)

0   E-mail
1   FTP
2   Remote login (Telnet)
7   Source specified in subfield ≠2

Second   Undefined
ƀ   Undefined

Subfield Codes

≠a Host name (R)	≠n Name of location of host in subfield ≠a (NR)
≠b IP address (NR)	≠o Operating system (NR)
≠c Compression information (R)	≠p Port (NR)
≠d Path (R)	≠q File transfer mode (NR)
≠f Electronic name (R)	≠s File size (R)
≠g Electronic name–End of range (R)	≠t Terminal emulation (R)
≠h Processor of request (NR)	≠u Uniform Resource Locator (R)
≠i Instruction (R)	≠x Nonpublic note (R)
≠k Password (NR)	≠z Public note (R)
≠l Logon/login (NR)	≠2 Source of access (NR)
≠m Contact for access assistance (R)	≠3 Materials specified (NR)

EXAMPLES OF FIELD 856 (for files that can be transferred using FTP):

856 1b≠awuarchive.wustl.edu≠cdecompress with PKUNZIP.exe≠d/mirrors2/ win3/games≠ffatmoids. zip≠xcannot verify because of transfer difficulty

856 1b≠aseql.loc.gov≠d/pub/soviet.archive≠fk1famine.bkg≠nLibrary of Congress, Washington, D C ≠oUNIX

856 1K≠uURL: ftp://path.net/pub/docs/um2urc.ps

Figure 16.1

OPAC BRIEF DISPLAY:

TITLE: North American Free Trade Agreement
PUBLISHED: 1992

PRODUCER: United States. Office of the U.S. Trade Representative.

SUBJECTS: Free trade—United States.
Mexico-Commercial treaties.
Free trade—Mexico.
Free trade—Canada.
United States—Commercial treaties.
Canada—Commercial treaties.

ELECTRONIC ACCESS:
Access via GOPHER or telnet. For assistance contact Law Library Reference,
607 255-7236.
DOMAIN NAME: fatty.law.cornell.edu
FILE TRANSFER MODE:
ASCII
FILE SIZE: 2020 bytes

CODED MARC FIELD:

856 12≠afatty.1aw.cornell.edu≠m Tom Bruce≠n Cornell University Law
School≠q ASCII≠s 2020 bytes≠z Access via GOPHER or telnet. For assistance
contact Law Library Reference, 607 255-7236

Figure 16.2

Those involved in developing field 856 have questioned whether it is
desirable to store in a USMARC record such information as an electronic location, given the volatility of electronic objects on a network.
This information, however, could be used in a variety of ways.
Institutions may wish to store only the unique part of the locator and to
then use a lookup table on a remote server to determine where and in
what form the electronic object is located. If a system were programmed
this way, it then could generate the other pieces of the 856 field (e.g.,
host name, path, etc.) for display in an online public access system. Only
the unchangeable piece would be stored in the USMARC record, and if
other pieces of information changed, they could be generated on the fly.

Uniform Resource Identification
The Uniform Resource Locator (URL), newly defined in field 856 of
USMARC, is one of a family of standards being developed by the

Internet Engineering Task Force (IETF) called Uniform Resource Identification (URI). The following is a list of specific standards under development to identify, describe, locate, and control networked information objects on the Internet:

Uniform Resource Locator (URL): address of an object, containing enough information to identify a protocol to retrieve the object.

Uniform Resource Name (URN): a persistent, location-independent identifier for an object; similar to an International Standard Book Number (ISBN) or International Standard Serial Number (ISSN) in the library world, providing a unique element to identify the object (anonymous personal communication 1992).

Uniform Resource Citation (URC): a set of metainformation about an electronic resource, which may include owner, encoding, access restrictions, location, and so on. Similar in library terms to a bibliographic record. (The group developing this is currently considering renaming it "uniform resource characteristic.")

The URL is the most fully developed of the standards but is still a draft Internet standard, although it is already in widespread use. It allows systems to "achieve global search and readership of documents across differing computing platforms, and despite a plethora of protocols and data formats" and is a "universal syntax which can be used to refer to objects available using existing protocols, and may be extended with technology" (Berners-Lee 1993). Elements of the draft URL standard are contained in separate subfields of field 856 in USMARC; in the URL the elements are strung together with separators between them. If an institution wishes to use the URL as it has been established, the new URL subfield could accommodate it. An institution may wish to record only the URL rather than use the separate subfields, record both parsed elements and the URL, or record only the parsed subfields. Recording the elements in separate subfields may be useful to create a display or to verify the separate data elements even if the URL is also used.

The Uniform Resource Name (URN) will "provide a globally unique, persistent identifier used both for recognition and often for access to characteristics of or access to the resource." It may identify "intellectual content or a particular presentation of intellectual content," depending upon how the assignment agency uses it. A resource identified by a URN may reside at many locations under any number of filenames and may move any number of times during its lifetime. The URL identifies the location for an instance of a resource identified by the URN (Sollins and Masinter 1994). The URN is still under development. When it is finalized, it will provide bibliographic control similar to that of the ISBN or ISSN, to uniquely identify a resource. It will have an impact on the decision to consider a resource a new edition and thus create a separate record.

The Uniform Resource Citation (URC) is under discussion, and a draft standard has not been fully developed. Participants in the IETF-URI group have begun to develop requirements and functional specifications.

Other Developments in USMARC Computer Files Specification

Also approved in February 1994 by the ALA-MARBI Committee was a proposal to add a fixed field (i.e., one that has a fixed length and is used for coded data) to record physical characteristics of computer files. Often this type of field gives a coded form of information that is expressed in textual form in a note or other field in the record. The field thus facilitates indexing and retrieval. It was particularly needed for serials, because of the increased numbers of serials being published in different media, particularly CD-ROM and electronic journals, and the ability to retrieve serials on the basis of their physical form has been an important goal. This new fixed field for computer files will include coded data concerning the following: category of material (i.e., computer file); specific material designation (e.g., tape cartridge, magnetic disk, CD-ROM laser optical disc, remote file); original versus reproduction aspect (not clear how this will be used, but valid in other fixed fields for physical description); color (e.g., monochrome or color), sound (sound or no sound). Because bibliographic records for electronic texts would be encoded using the specifications for computer files, this new data element could be useful for their identification.

Interactive Multimedia Guidelines

Another development in the use of the USMARC formats is the attempt to provide cataloging and USMARC coding for interactive multimedia. Because of the very specific definition of "interactive multimedia," this coding may be of only limited use in the bibliographic control of electronic texts. Interactive multimedia is defined as follows: "Media residing in one or more physical carriers (videodiscs, computer disks, computer laseroptical discs, compact discs, etc.) or on computer networks. Interactive multimedia must exhibit both of these characteristics:

1) user controlled, non-linear navigation using computer technology; and, 2) the combination of two or more media (audio, text, graphics, images, animation, and video) that the user manipulates to control the order and/or nature of the presentation" (CC: DA 1994). It has been reported, however, that the number of these types of materials is quickly growing. After conducting a cataloging experiment, the Interactive Multimedia Guidelines Review Task Force recommended the use of the USMARC Bibliographic Format, computer files specifications, until format and cataloging rule changes might be made to accommodate this type of material. The ability to record coded descriptive elements about more than one aspect of an item (e.g., sound recording and computer file) will be available under format integration, which integrates the tag sets for bibliographic records for materials in different physical formats; this development is of benefit to the description of interactive multimedia.

Accommodating Online Systems and Services in USMARC

The Library of Congress's Network Development and MARC Standards Office has also explored accommodating online systems and services in the USMARC format. This effort has included the presentation of several papers to the USMARC Advisory Group, including a proposal to add fields to the bibliographic format for those data elements needed for online systems and services that are not currently included. Because these records would be created for nonbibliographic data, some extension of the format is necessary.

With the development of tools, such as Gopher, WAIS, and Archie, to locate online information resources on the Internet, one might question the need for describing these resources in USMARC. A number of directory services are now accessible on the Internet as well. Available Internet tools, however, are not always efficient for pointing to the resource. Many do not give any indication of which servers they actually searched and which were unavailable, and they do not discriminate between various versions of the data in terms of usefulness or completeness. They are poor at locating known items, as opposed to possibly relevant things. In addition, the subject analysis available in USMARC records is lacking in these other tools. Library users are not all familiar with (nor should they be expected to) tools like Gopher. Such tools could complement rather than replace USMARC records as a source for locating electronic texts and other online resources.

Creating records within USMARC for online services would provide not just access but also organization. Librarians' knowledge of online resources can be used to provide, within library catalogs, pointers to Internet services and resources. In addition, librarians can select the online services that are important to include in catalogs, just as they select books. Picking out online resources that might be useful to the library user, rather than forcing the user to select from the overwhelming number of sources available on the Internet, is a service that libraries should provide.

Making this type of directory information for online systems and services accessible in the USMARC environment would allow for such information to be available and integrated within the same systems as other records. Bibliographic citations to electronic texts could point to the USMARC record for the online service that issues the texts, and only that record would need to be kept current in terms of its electronic location. A subject search could give the user records not only for printed items but also for electronic items and the systems that provide them.

Other Projects Involving Access to Electronic Texts

The American Memory Project

The American Memory Project is the "Library of Congress's pioneering effort to share some of its unique collections with the nation via new electronic multimedia technology" (Library of Congress 1993c). American Memory, which makes archival collections available in electronic form, offers original printed texts in machine-readable form, which allows for detailed searching of the contents of a collection and of the bibliographic records describing these items. For manuscript materials, images of the original may be displayed, so that researchers can examine the original item's appearance. For photographs and films, analog videodiscs have been used, although the library expects to convert these materials to digital form. A hierarchical combination of collection-item- and finding-aid-level records describe each collection. The bibliographic record is stored in an internal MARC format, with links to other related records if appropriate, and a link to the reproduction of the item described. The user can thus call up the bibliographic record, which describes the item, and view either the ASCII text (which has been converted from the original) or the image of the printed original.

The project uses an "electronic call number" as its link to the converted text and image. In the past a local MARC field (938) was used.

Because the project wanted to use a standard MARC field, especially to communicate the data on electronic location, it will convert all local 938 fields to 856 fields, particularly after the approval of two new subfields in field 856 to accommodate other data elements needed for the program. Access to the electronic text is possible because of a unique number that resides in the electronic location field. That unique number is also the filename, which is derived from an acronym for the collection and an item number. The additional information—such as the computer where the file resides, directory on the computer, compression information, and so on (data elements that all have defined subfields in field 856)—is not stored in the record. Instead the unique element, in this case the filename, is stored in that field, and a lookup table tells the system the other information. Consequently, if the host name or directory changes, the unique number will provide the link to the information necessary to locate the item.

The program has encoded ASCII text with Standard Generalized Markup Language (SGML) to retain any information that might be lost in conversion from the original published form and to facilitate searching. SGML is also used to link page images to text images. The filename of each page image is in coded form at the head of each page of the electronic text, allowing for a linkage; the filename for the image file is an extension of the filename of the converted electronic text.

The American Memory Project has great potential in enhancing access to archival collections and bringing historical collections to anyone with a computer. Because it has lost congressional funding, however, program planners are soliciting private donations to continue the program.

Electronic Cataloging-in-Publication Project

The Cataloging in Publication (CIP) Division of the Library of Congress embarked on a project in February 1993 to explore the viability and practicality of an online link between the Library of Congress and publishers participating in the CIP program. The CIP program is a cooperative effort between publishers and the Library of Congress to provide cataloging in advance of publication for most mainstream titles published in the United States. The advantages of acquiring CIP data electronically include greater efficiency, time savings in the transmission of CIP applications, greater accuracy in the CIP record, and the establishment of the foundation for an electronic library of books (Celli 1994).

The Electronic CIP Project enables publishers to provide the full text of galleys for forthcoming titles and thus provide catalogers with ample text to perform accurate subject analysis. In addition, portions of the electronic galleys could be used in the bibliographic record; for example, a relatively simple block-and-copy command can move the table of contents into the note portion of the catalog record. A few publishers have participated in the project, and Library of Congress staff expects more to do so. The project is still experimental, and future efforts will involve the use of SGML.

The Electronic CIP Project has the potential to provide the foundation for an electronic library of texts primarily because of the 23-year relationship that has been established between the Library of Congress's Cataloging-in-Publication Program and publishers. More than 3,500 publishers participate in the CIP program, which provides cataloging for more than 48,000 titles a year. Consequently, the Library of Congress is ideally positioned to develop a system for acquiring archival masters of electronic manuscripts representing much of the U.S. publishing industry. Much needs to be accomplished for this to happen, but as more traditional print publishers develop electronic versions of their titles, it would be relatively easy to acquire a significant collection of electronic texts at the Library of Congress. Many questions, however, will need to be answered, including those about copyright and royalty, and about distribution and access. In addition, the concepts of publishing and what constitutes a published work need to change in an electronic world, which may affect the future of the project.

Government Information Locator Service (GILS) to MARC Mapping

The Government Information Locator Service (GILS) has been established to help the public locate and access information from the U.S. government. Although it is a system to locate databases and services that provide information rather than to locate electronic texts themselves, it is important because it extends the MARC format to provide for access to electronic information resources. Federal agencies are organizing GILS as a component of the National Information Infrastructure (NII)(GILS 1994). It is intended to make governmental information available electronically by identifying, describing, and providing access information to locations where information resides. Federal agencies will be responsible for their participation in GILS by providing locator records.

GILS will use the information search and retrieval standard known in the United States as ANSI/NISO Z39.50 (known internationally as ISO 10162/10163). Locator records are to be available in three specified formats, one of which is USMARC. Consequently, an effort is under way to map GILS data elements to the USMARC Format for Bibliographic Data. Data elements have been defined and appropriate fields indicated. In most cases no new fields are needed to accommodate the data, but some USMARC definitions have been expanded.

Because of the work that has been done on accommodating online information resources in USMARC, the GILS project to expand USMARC to nonbibliographic data has not required substantial rethinking or new definitions of fields in the format. The mapping has made extensive use of the new field 856, for electronic location and access.

The Relation between SGML and USMARC

A common misconception is that Standard Generalized Markup Language (SGML) could replace the MARC formats, in which libraries have invested considerable time and money. This misconception is based on the observation that most SGML documents contain information that is bibliographic in nature. The SGML tags used in the header and front matter of a full-text document often have a one-to-one relationship with the MARC tags defined for the same information in bibliographic records. In spite of the similarities between SGML and MARC, those who jump to the conclusion that MARC can be abandoned in favor of SGML are overlooking important differences in the design and intended use of each standard.

SGML and MARC both provide a standard structure for machine-readable information. They are both system independent in that they may have different implementations, and the data is in a format that can be exchanged between systems. Each standard is nonproprietary, which means that they can be implemented without having to pay a royalty to the original developers. The structures for MARC (ISO 2709; also ANSI/NISO Z39.2) and SGML (ISO 8879), as international standards, provide the basic framework for bibliographic and full-text systems that have gained worldwide acceptance and use. Conformity to standards increases the marketability of products and facilitates the exchange of information between a variety of sources.

SGML and MARC are different in the functionality they were designed to support. The structure and syntax associated with SGML-encoded documents were intended to make the processing of full-text data system-independent. SGML uses a Document Type Definition (DTD) to define the tags and the syntax associated with them. Depending on the level of markup, the SGML encoding can support a wide variety of print and display features. SGML markup will also support context-sensitive retrieval, based on indexing of data encoded with specific SGML tags.

SGML is intended to facilitate the processing of large amounts of data, while the MARC record structure was developed for bibliographic data. MARC data is typically concise and dense, packing a great deal of intelligence into a small number of characters. The average MARC record is only 1,500 characters, whereas even the shortest full-text document involves many times that number of characters. The MARC formats, which are implementations of the standard MARC structure (ISO 2709), define data elements designed to make optimum use of small amounts of data in a machine environment. These data elements easily support the print and display needs of bibliographic data, and the complex indexing and sophisticated retrieval needed for bibliographic data.

MARC is highly standardized and accepted worldwide. The precision and consistency needed for cataloging data have promoted the development of standardized cataloging rules for both description and choice of access points and the implementation of the MARC record structure that reflects these rules. In the United States, only one DTD for MARC is used, that is, one tag set and syntax (USMARC). This high level of acceptance of a single tag set and syntax is one of the reasons MARC is so successful and has the support of so many national libraries and computer system vendors. In comparison, there are some 60 DTDs for SGML. Anyone with a MARC system can usually read in and process USMARC data. Export of bibliographic data in either the USMARC or UNIMARC format is also an almost universal capability of bibliographic systems. Full-text systems do not enjoy this level of standardization and will not, even with the advent of SGML, until a small number of implementations of SGML have become well established.

Library catalogs have no need to change the way bibliographic data is encoded or processed. The capability of MARC records to provide links to full-text SGML documents (or other non bibliographic entities, like image or audio data) has prevented libraries from seriously considering any encoding for bibliographic data other than MARC.

MARC and SGML have shown themselves to be compatible, and each has its own use in the computer age. It is important for experts in each structural standard, and system implementors, to be aware of the needs and uses of the other standard, so that library materials in machine-readable format and bibliographic information about them can be easily integrated. Rather than embed text in MARC records, the bibliographic records can be linked to SGML-encoded text. For instance, the American Memory Program uses links between the MARC bibliographic record and other electronic resources to access full text, which contains SGML coding or images in non-ASCII format.

The Text-Encoding Initiative (TEI) guidelines, a specific application of SGML that defines an encoding and interchange format for electronic texts, can assist in cataloging and identification of texts (Gaunt 1994). Electronic texts often lack a usable chief source of information on which to base the description, and the TEI header can provide information not found elsewhere.

Conclusion

With the tremendous growth of the Internet and the wide availability of electronic information resources, libraries must adapt to a changed world and reevaluate what bibliographic control and access really mean. Electronic information resources have become critical to scholarship and research, and librarians need to use their many years of experience in organizing and providing access to information in order to adapt traditional library tools to this new electronic world. "The library community needs to extend traditional descriptive catalog practices to networked resources—in essence, to permit bibliographic description and control of such resources in order to incorporate them integrally into library collections . . . and to improve access to them" (Lynch 1993).

The nation's existing infrastructure of libraries and library systems can continue to provide service in the quest for information. Librarians provide value-added service by selecting the materials to be described and providing access to them; this is particularly important in the electronic world, where anyone can "publish" a text if he or she has access to a network. Not all the items available electronically deserve to be cataloged, and librarians can determine which ones should be, as they have for years with printed and other items (Dillon et al., p. 35).

The *AACR2* cataloging rules and USMARC format have served us well in our quest to identify, describe, and locate library material of all sorts, and can do the same for electronic texts. An enormous amount of time, money, and intellectual effort has been expended on the library infrastructure that serves scholars, students, and the general public in the United States. New tools, such as Gopher, Mosaic, and the World Wide Web, have been developed to facilitate access to networked information resources, but they do not provide the same function as libraries in cataloging these materials. Not only do librarians select materials deemed worthy to be controlled bibliographically, but they also provide detailed subject analysis, generally through controlled subject thesauri, which is not available through those Internet tools. As anyone knows who has used the tools to locate items by subject, the available system of access by keyword is not efficient, given the vast quantities of data. As efforts are being made to create directory services, it will be of great benefit to provide description and access to this material within the familiar USMARC environment using the National Information Standards Organization's Z39.S0 standard for information retrieval.

The library community has made great strides in adapting existing cataloging rules and format standards to accommodate electronic information resources. This work will continue and will remain consistent, if possible, with other efforts to standardize electronic locators and identification. Only by experimenting with new approaches will librarians be able to make informed decisions about the difficult problems concerning the bibliographic control of and access to, electronic texts. Already many library catalogs are available by remote access, and thus bibliographic records for electronic resources will be widely available. As information technology changes rapidly, libraries need to continue to provide improved description and access to electronic information using existing, though modified, formats and cataloging rules.

References

American Library Association. (1992). *ALA Handbook of Organization 1992/1993*. Chicago: American Library Association.

Berners-Lee, Tim. (1993). "Uniform Resource Locators (URL): a Unifying Syntax for the Expression of Names and Addresses of Objects on the Network." October. Available through FTP at ftp.cern.ch

CC: DA Interactive Multimedia Guidelines Review Task Force. (1994). "Guidelines for Bibliographic Description of Interactive Multimedia." Final draft. Chicago: Committee on Cataloging: Description and Access, Cataloging and Classification Section, Association for Library Collections and Technical Services, American Library Association.

Celli, John. (1994). "The Electronic CIP Project." *Collections Services News* 2, no. 6 (March).

CETH Newsletter. (1993). Vol. 1, no. 2 (Fall).

Crawford, Walt. (1989). *MARC for Library Use.* 2d ed. Boston: G. K. Hall.

Dillon, Martin, et al. (1993). *Assessing Information on the Internet: Toward Providing Library Services for Computer-Mediated Communication.* Dublin, Ohio: OCLC.

Gaunt, Marianne I. (1994). "Center for Electronic Texts in the Humanities." *Information Technology and Libraries* 13, no. 1 (March).

GILS. (1994). "Government Information Locator Service (GILS): Draft: Report to the Information Infrastructure Task Force." January 22. Available through FTP.

"Guidelines for Bibliographic Description of Internet Resources: Draft." (1992). In Dillon et al. 1993, pp. Bl–B19.

Hiatt, Robert M., ed. (1990). *Library of Congress Rule Interpretations.* Washington, D.C.: Cataloging Distribution Service, Library of Congress.

Joint Steering Committee for Revision of AACR. (1988). *Anglo-American Cataloging Rules,* edited by Michael Gorman and Paul Winkler. 2d ed. Chicago: American Library Association.

Library of Congress. (1989). "The USMARC Formats: Background and Principles." Washington, D.C.: Library of Congress.

Library of Congress. (1991a). "Discussion Paper No. 49: Dictionary of Data Elements for Online Information Resources." Washington, D.C.: Library of Congress, Network Development and MARC Standards Office.

Library of Congress. (1991b). "Discussion Paper No. 54: Providing Access to Online Information Resources." Washington, D.C.: Library of Congress, Network Development and MARC Standards Office.

Library of Congress. (1993a). "Proposal 94–2: Addition of Subfields $g and $3 to Field 856 (Electronic Location and Access) in the USMARC Holdings/Bibliographic Formats." Washington, D.C.: Library of Congress, Network Development and MARC Standards Office.

Library of Congress. (1993b). "Proposal 94–3: Addition of Subfield $u (Uniform Resource Locator) to Field 856 in the USMARC Bibliographic/ Holdings Formats." Washington, D.C.: Library of Congress.

Library of Congress. (1993c). "American Memory: Multimedia Historical Collections from the Library of Congress." Washington, D.C.: Library of Congress.

Lynch, Clifford A. (1993). "A Framework for Identifying, Locating, and Describing Networked Information Resources: Draft for Discussion at March-April 1993 IETF meeting." Electronic mail message distributed March 24, 1993, on uri@bunyim.com discussion list.

Olson, Nancy B. (1992). *Cataloging Computer Files.* Lake Crystal, Minn.: Soldier Creek Press.

Sollins, K., and L. Masinter. (1994). "Specification of Uniform Resource Names." March 18 (electronic mail message distributed March 20, 1994, on uri@bunyim.com discussion list).

17

Scholarly Communication in the Networked Environment: Issues of Principle, Policy, and Practice

Brian Kahin

The globalization of innovation, industry, and commerce has spurred interest in intellectual property as a set of ground rules that may have profound distributive consequences for nations, industries, firms, or forms of economic activity (e.g., Rushing and Brown 1990; Sherwood 1990). This attention has focused on the scope of underlying rights in scientific research (Nelkin 1984; Weil and Snapper 1989), but the digitization of information and the growth of networking as a research tool raise a distinct set of issues: How should the flow of research information be managed in the interests of scholarship and technological progress?

Although electronic publishing has conventionally meant remote access to large databases on mainframe computers, the advent of distributed computing—in the form of interconnected workstations and powerful microcomputers—has led scholars and researchers to look both to electronic equivalents for the scholarly journal and to faster, less formal means of communicating new knowledge. The result is an increasingly articulated and multifaceted spectrum of scholarly communication, ranging from casual private messaging to complex software environments. At the same time, the greatly expanded scope and connectivity of the networks will enable publishing and resource sharing on a sustainable scale.

In this chapter, I look at some of the critical points where these developments raise important legal and ethical issues. This chapter moves roughly in sequence along the production and distribution cycle, beginning with matters related to authorship and ending with distribution across national boundaries. Accordingly, the issues may be broken down into two principal areas: first, those arising from the greatly expanded opportunities and relations within informal communication, prepublication, and formal publication; second, postpublication issues associated with the network as a distribution environment.

The goal of the chapter is to invite suggestions for policies and practices from the research community that produces and uses scholarly information, on the premise that the shared values within this community may be amenable to consensus. Indeed, the research community is unique in that revenues generated by publications do not flow to academic authors. To the contrary, academic authors are sometimes obliged to pay page charges from their research funds. Rather than monetary reward, the scope of dissemination within the community, including citations and word-of-mouth, motivates the author (Byrd 1990; Merton 1988). Producers are also users, and scholarly communication is seen as a cooperative enterprise in which value is added to original work to the extent that others cite it and build on it. Much primary and secondary information is published by organizations that are politically accountable to interests of authors and readers academic and professional societies and, to a lesser extent, university presses.

Although copyright defines a baseline of rights and responsibilities between owners and users of information,[1] the basic framework it provides is overlaid by institutional policies, practices, and culture, as well as technological and market realities.[2] The 1976 Copyright Act sought to be technology-neutral and in large measure succeeded through careful attention to principles. Although there are a number of technical problems with the act, relating to use of digital information, there are no burning controversies such as those surrounding the scope of protection for computer programs. Where copyright is lacking, it should be possible to develop overlays of practice and expectation that could be adopted by organizations, publications, and individual projects within the academic research community.

Communication, Prepublication, and Publication

Joint Authorship and Ownership

Computer networks greatly facilitate collaboration between distant individuals or teams, including research projects in which multiple principal investigators may be thousands of miles apart.[3] Differences over who has the right to claim authorship in varying versions of research reports and articles are not unique to network-based remote collaboration. Research teams, however, have traditionally worked in close proximity under the direction of a senior figure who reviews all material intended for publication. Remote collaborations are likely to involve two or more individuals of relatively equal stature, each of whom is accustomed to acting independently, thereby increasing opportunities for misunderstanding and conflict.

In addition, use of electronic mail tends to flatten hierarchies within organizations. This increases the risk that research results will be disseminated without explicit clearance from the top, especially because external networks facilitate distribution of material for review among an expanding set of formal and informal advisors. Interdisciplinary work that brings together researchers with different backgrounds and different sets of colleagues is particularly susceptible to leakage.[4]

Except for industry-funded research that contemplates patent filings[5] or the submission of advance information to project sponsors, research projects often lack formal agreements or explicit policies on dissemination and publication.[6] Individual responsibility for reporting research results may be distinct from the conduct of the research or, indeed, the maintenance of project data or the discovery of patentable inventions. One aspect of a project may be owned by one person, and another aspect may be owned by a remote institution; a third may be owned jointly by an individual and a distant institution.

Researchers on contract rather than salary are likely to end up with independent interests in their writings—unless they are contractually obliged to assign copyright.[7] Indeed, because universities allow faculty to retain copyright in their writings, there may be both a faculty interest and an institutional interest deriving from work performed by institutionally employed research assistants.[8]

A jointly authored work, or "joint work," results if a work is "prepared by two or more authors with the intention that their contributions be merged into inseparable or interdependent parts of a unitary whole" (Sec. 101, title 17 U.S.C.). Joint authorship means joint ownership, and a joint owner can legally license the work for publication—or simply distribute it over the network without permission of the other joint owners. The joint owner who distributes the work is liable to the others only for their share of any money received.

Thus, the more co-owners there are, the more parties with different interests are empowered to do what they wish with the work and the more it behaves as if it were in the public domain. As the number of co-owners increases, however, it becomes increasingly difficult to execute an assignment of copyright (which most publishers require) because all owners must agree to the assignment in writing. The publisher can be authorized to print the work by a nonexclusive license[9] from any one of the joint owners, but only by receiving an assignment of copyright can the publisher be assured that the work will not be printed elsewhere.[10]

A related problem is that one co-owner can single-handedly modify the jointly owned work and thereby create a new derivative version to which he or she owns an exclusive copyright. The underlying work remains jointly owned, but the modifications are the exclusive property of the modifier. For example, standards and associated documentation are typically the work of volunteers from different companies and institutions working together as joint authors. Some standards organizations hire reporters to synthesize the conclusions of working groups, so that the organization can claim copyright in the reporter's synthesis, which is published as the official version. It is easy to imagine situations where various jointly authored versions of a paper circulate among the authors, but one version has been modified by one of the authors for a special audience that the others are unaware of. Any reproduction or public performance of that version requires the permission of the person who modified it (Weissman v. Freeman 1989).

Rights in Computer Conferencing
In the conventional print environment, it was relatively easy to distinguish between publishing and person-to-person communication. Publication required a threshold investment in setting type and preparing plates, so it was not undertaken lightly. This threshold was lowered by a series of technologies—mimeograph, offset printing, and photocopying. Even so, paper had to be distributed physically, with costs attributable to each copy and each delivery.

Within the new networked environment, these incremental costs virtually disappear or are borne by the end user in the form of storage and printing costs. There is an infinite spectrum between personal communication and publication; boundaries are defined by individuals and institutions rather than technologies.

Much of the territory between personal communication and conventional publication is covered by the computer conference—in which all participants are potentially authors as well as audience. A distributed computer conference can be used to carry out a collaborative research project involving multiple institutions. Simple distributed computer con-

Table 17.1
Characteristics of computer conferences (mailing lists).

selection	edited	←——→	open
creation	centralized	←——→	distributed
access	private	←——→	public

ferences are known as mailing lists. They may be "moderated," in which case contributions are reviewed by an editor before they are redistributed to the participants. In the case of "digests," contributions are edited and redistributed in batches, rather like printed periodicals. An electronic journal may be peer reviewed like a conventional scholarly journal. At the other extreme are computer conferences based on public mail reflectors or "exploders"—computer addresses set up so that incoming mail is automatically redistributed to a list of addresses. Thus, varying degrees of editorial control are possible.

Computer conferences might seem almost by definition to be distributed creations, the product of many individuals contributing as equals, however, this is not necessarily the case. A course may be taught as a computer conference, or a research project may be conducted as a computer conference. In such cases, one or two individuals may be responsible for generating or synthesizing much of the content (but not for editing the contributions of others). A list, as opposed to a conference, may be a completely asymmetric one-to-many publication like a newsletter.

Conferences may be restricted, which is especially critical if there is an exploding list (and therefore no editorial controls). A list may be completely private, in that it is the personal creation of the "list owner," who perhaps uses it to address a few highly regarded colleagues, and no one else may even know that the list exists. Or a list may be publicly known and open for automatic subscription. There are many variants in between: The list owner may have the opportunity to review subscribers or may require an application from prospective subscribers.[11]

In all respects, the production and publication of scholarly research have differed radically from distributed computer conferencing. The production process is traditionally highly centralized, edited, and private. Even when others are brought in through the process of peer review, it is understood to be on a confidential basis. Only when a report or article has assumed a final, canonical form does it become public.

Whereas research projects contemplate the production of singular reports and articles that synthesize the work of the team, computer conferences are aggregations of discrete individual contributions, ranging from single-sentence utterances to expositions the length of journal articles. Although short comments are not considered protectable by copyright, at some ill-defined point contributions become protectable expression. Such contributions remain the property of their authors, unless they are clearly dedicated to the public domain, either by the statement of the authors or by an explicitly stated policy on contributions to the list. Since the United States acceded to the Berne Convention in 1989, the use of a copyright notice is no longer necessary to preserve copyright in a published work.

Few conferences have explicit policies on reuse of contributions. Individual contributors might reasonably be expected to label contributions as to whether and how they may be redistributed or cited. This is rarely done, although such notices could be effective public licenses, as a redistributor needs the copyright owner's permission to copy the text and so must comply with the owner's conditions.

There may also be a copyright in the computer conference as a compilation, if it is moderated and archived so that it expresses a degree of selectivity.[12] A moderator holding a compilation copyright could conceivably claim control over the archive or even sequences of interaction among the conference participants. A case could also be made, however, that the compilation copyright belongs to the contributors jointly or to the contributors and the moderator jointly. A mere "lurker," or informal participant, might have no rights to the compilation.[13] But what is the determining context? Is it a particular strand of discussion? Or is it the conference as a whole?

Ideally, conferences would have policies that would be dispositive of these issues and clearly advertised to anyone joining the conference. In addition, guidelines could be developed that reflect expectations based on the nature of the conference. In general, the more private the originating conference, the more one would expect redistribution to be restricted. Conversely, the more private the forum in which the material is redistributed, the more likely the original author would be to tolerate the redistribution.

It is less clear how the degree of editorial control or the relative role of the owner of the originating conference should affect redistribution. The degree of editorial control in the redistributing conference, however, may have serious repercussions: if the conference owner behaves more like a conventional publisher than a passive carrier and actively reviews and filters contributions, then he or she should be liable for redistributing material owned by third parties.

Anonymous FTP presents this end of the problem in a tightly focused way. Anonymous FTP is the posting of files in a publicly accessible directory, for remote retrieval (using the Internet file transfer protocol) without a password. What assumptions, if any, should be made about files posted for anonymous FTP? Can it be assumed that the files may be freely copied and redistributed by anyone? Or can one assume only that files can be retrieved by anyone but redistributed only if the file itself explicitly permits redistribution?

Anonymous FTP is a special case but an important one, because it is a frequently used mechanism for distributing large quantities of information on the Internet. Assume for the moment that the copyright owner has not given the FTP site any rights in the file, and the site nonetheless posts the file for anonymous FTP. Unlike distribution of a file in a mailing, merely posting the file for remote retrieval by others does not plainly violate the rights of the copyright owner.[14] Each retrieval creates a copy, however, which presumably infringes the reproduction right. So the posting site may well be liable as a contributory infringer, especially if the posting is truly public.[15]

But is posting for anonymous FTP completely public when the posting is tucked into an obscure directory or machine? Does this analysis change when a program such as Archie comes along, which provides for automated scanning and cataloging of anonymous FTP sites? Aside from the liability of the posting site, what implications do these circumstances have for those who retrieve the files? Does the availability of Archie in effect create an expectation that the files are in the public domain? The more liberal the assumptions about reuse, the greater the liability risks for the posting site.

Derivative and Iterative Works
A third set of problems arises from the tension between prepublication and formal publication, from the increasing numbers of sequential and variant versions, and from effects on the relationship between authors and publishers.

It is a longstanding practice for journal publishers, including most noncommercial publishers, to require a full copyright assignment from authors. In theory, publishers are better able to manage exploitation of the work, including the sale or licensing of reprints, than authors. Certainly, publishers desire as much exclusivity as they get, and a copyright assignment appears to give them all they need. But because assignment of copyright includes the right to prepare derivative works, this precludes the author from revising or republishing his or her work. In effect, the work is limited to a single canonical journal publication, although the author is often granted the right to use the article and its contents in books or lectures.

This traditional practice may be appropriate for reporting simple research projects (e.g., in which a hypothesis is tested by collection and analysis of data) within delineated specialties. But what if the research activity is complex, ongoing, and involves many participants at multiple locations? Under such circumstances, the reporting of research may be an iterative process rather than a final product. Results may be aired with the expectation that feedback from the field will contribute to the further design and conduct of the research.

Peer review normally works as a conservative force that sharply differentiates between submission and acceptance—and between unpublished and published. Whereas publication in refereed journals is important for the young scholar who is seeking tenure and promotion, it may be of less concern to established scholars, who, though as eager to advance their reputations, are free to do so in less conventional ways. It is likewise of less concern to those working outside traditional disciplines and at the fringes of academia. In newly emerging fields, timeliness, turf preemption, and visibility may be important factors in expediting publication. Patent considerations may work to either hurry or slow publication,[16] and a patent itself is also a publication that may effect promotion and tenure.

Interdisciplinary research may merit multiple publications in multiple versions in order to reach its full audience.[17] As the use of the network for scholarly communication increases, authors of specialized papers may become more expert on the potential audience for their work than publishers. The network and new software environments will invite constellations of preliminary, secondary, and tertiary publication that vary from field to field. Author-generated abstracts, synoptic publishing, and indexing will take on new forms and new significance. Authors, research programs, and scholarly organizations may find themselves negotiating with complex multipublisher systems (the next generation of online vendors) to design dissemination programs that fit the institutional landscape, culture, and other information resources of their specialty.

How much flexibility should authors (and research projects) have to recast their work in the light of new knowledge or for the benefit of new audiences? It would seem desirable to have new knowledge, or a continuing flow of related knowledge, appear in the same periodical as the original research. What claims and what obligations should the original publisher have? To what extent will different kinds of research result less in discrete occasional products and more in the form of a service? Indeed, the textbook that is reissued in new editions every year or two may be a better model for some forms of networked publication than the journal.

On close inspection, the traditional assignment of copyright may not be as effective as it appears. Under the 1976 Copyright Act, copyright inheres in a work from the moment it is fixed in a tangible medium. There is no longer any distinction between the common-law copyright in unpublished works that was determined by state law and the statutory copyright in published work determined by federal law. Instead, there is a copyright in every outline and every draft of a work as much as in the final published version. The later versions are derivative works based on underlying works, but the assignment of copyright in the final version does not automatically assign copyright in the underlying work. Thus an author may be able to go back to an earlier draft and construct another version based on the draft that does not infringe the publisher's copyright in the original published version.

This is not to suggest that such assignments are necessarily ineffective: if, as part of the copyright assignment, the author warrants that the work is original, that may be construed to mean that it does not derive from an underlying work. I mean, rather, to illustrate the complexity of determining ownership, especially when word processing programs and networks make it easy to create and disseminate variant versions. And this example also makes it clear that relationships between publishers and authors need to be recast in terms of realistic and shared expectations.

The Distribution Environment

The second set of legal and ethical issues addressed here revolves around the impact of the network on the distribution process, driven by the expected speed, functionality, and cost efficiency of electronic publication.

No more than a dozen refereed electronic journals presently exist, most of which are university-based efforts initiated by individual editors.[18] Until the mid-1990s, their development was constrained by policies on acceptable use of the academic networks, especially BITNET, that seemed to preclude charging for material sent over the network. BITNET's policies, however, were revised in November 1990 to permit fee-based services in support of "academic, research and educational purposes," provided there is no separate charge for use of the network.[19] Policies on the Internet vary, but in most cases commercial use in support of education and research is permissible and increasingly accepted. NFSNET policies were similarly relaxed in 1994–1995.

These experiments have followed the traditional scholarly journal paradigm: that is, individuals and libraries pay a fixed annual fee to a publisher who maintains an editorial apparatus, including a peer-review process, linked to a journal name. This same system could deliver an irregular stream of individual articles, as there is no compelling reason for delivering electronic articles in uniform bundles at even intervals. The continued value of journals in the digital environments is unclear, because the individual article is the fundamental unit sought by the user, and the journal is merely an organizing unit and navigation aid suited to the economics and practicalities of print publication. Nonetheless, the journal title may remain an imprimatur of editorial integrity, quality, and intellectual continuity.

But in the intelligent networked environment, the article is emancipated from its archival home in journal time and space. It is instead found and used in functional space, linked to related articles, reviews, commentary, abstracts, and references, and perhaps available in multiple forms and versions. The form and scope of the scholarly article may vary, and the traditional concept of publication as preserving an instant in time may vanish. There may well be many ways for ordering the flow of information in the conduct of research prior to publication, including new forms and procedures for peer review (Harnad 1990; Rogers and Hurt 1989, p. A56).

Electronic journals (or articles, as the case may be) also appear to offer significant cost savings by eliminating press runs, packaging, and physical delivery—short-circuiting a publication process that now almost always begins in electronic form. Accordingly, such journals are sometimes seen as a partial solution to the high prices for serials that are currently troubling research libraries. Indeed, networked digital information is sometimes envisioned as a leveling, democratizing force, capable of transcending any distance and rendering all information equally available to all points on the network.

But the network is not ubiquitous, and if access to journals is to be universal, printed versions must also be available. An electronic document that is more than a simple ASCII text may require additional processing power, software, storage capacity, graphics capability, and other end-user technology. The overall efficiency and effectiveness of electronic publication will increase, certainly relative to costs of end-user equipment; but there will be disparities, especially in functionality of the publication and the user's ability to make effective use of it, that do not exist for print.

Even people who have only the technology to use a digital document on a primitive personal computer, however, also have the power to reproduce and redistribute the document at virtually no cost. For this reason, publishers have had little interest in distributing articles in electronic form. Instead, they have focused on electronic publishing as an enhancement of bibliographic indexes. A pre-microcomputer market was developed in which computing power, intelligence, functionality, and storage capacity were centrally provided to line-oriented, character-based terminals, seldom at more than 2,400 baud. Even as PCs became ubiquitous, the old network (whether voice or X.25) remained a common low-bandwidth bottleneck, and it remained easy to assess usage charges based on connect time and to bundle in time-based telecommunications costs.

Eventually elaborate algorithms were devised to charge for CPU cycles, searches, and retrieved records in order to even things out between those logging in at 1,200 or 2,400 baud and the laggards at 300 baud. But by marketing information retrieval as a low-bandwidth metered service, publishers and distributors have been able to charge prices keyed to use and perceived value while minimizing problems associated with downloading and reuse.[20] Under the circumstances, wholesale downloading is expensive and noticeable, and anyone doing so cannot readily re-create the functionality of the vendor's software environment.

Usage-based pricing is sometimes described as desirable (especially to small users) in that users are charged only for their use of the system and no more. Flat-rate pricing, however, is much easier to budget for, whether the organization is for-profit or nonprofit. Usage-based charging also creates major disparities within the research community, within higher education as a whole, and between universities and the general public. The stratification within the research community is even more severe than it might appear: instead of being included in overhead, usage-priced information is customarily treated as a direct cost of a research project subject to overhead, typically 50–70 percent. The effect is both to discourage and limit the use of metered information services—and implicitly to cross-subsidize library services and other forms of unmetered information. Furthermore, offering information on a metered basis threatens to change the nature of the library. Instead of a public repository offering free access to resources it owns, it now becomes a mere gateway for information held by others.

Copyright has traditionally controlled the printing of texts but not the use of texts once printed. Over time, various rights have been added to the reproduction right that is at the heart of copyright; these additions include the adaptation right, the distribution right, the public performance right, and the public display right. But these additional rights still do not limit ordinary use of the text. Under the "first sale doctrine," the distribution right does not apply to owned copies, so that a book can be publicly sold, rented, or loaned without the permission of the copyright owner.[21] The first sale doctrine also limits the public display right: there is no restriction on the ordinary display of owned texts. The public display right comes into play only when a remote or multiple display is created, or if the embodiment of the text is not owned by the party creating the display.[22]

Copyright has encouraged the growth of libraries as an institutionalized system for allowing individuals the privilege of trading cost against convenience, of reading or borrowing rather than buying. In effect, this means that those who acquire and collect books and journals subsidize those who merely read them. Digital, networked information changes this, presenting a seductive vision of a library without walls but eroding the paradigms of print publishing at a basic level. As network and storage resources grow in abundance, decline in cost, and are used for an increasing variety of purposes, the medium itself becomes increasingly nonspecific, abstract, and trivial.[23] The distinction between the medium (the book) and the content (information) disappears with the dematerialization of the medium and disembodiment of information.[24]

Control of Dissemination

Although publishers fear losing control of their property in an environment where reproduction and broadcast are trivial, they also look to this environment as a unitary market where they can sell access to information—rather than sell copies into a market where the copies can be resold or loaned at will. Indeed, it offers an opportunity for marketing that eliminates all intermediaries, distributors as well as libraries. Furthermore, a direct relationship with the end user makes it easier for the publisher to rely on contracts to control access and use. Unlike copyright, which applies universally, regardless of any relationship between the parties, contracts must be individually established, and contractual controls are difficult to maintain through multiple intermediaries.

But although a direct relationship between publisher and user looks relatively secure and profitable, it may limit the publisher's market. A competitive marketplace with a full complement of distributors and retailers enables a publisher to reach the largest possible universe of users. In the networked environment, intermediaries can add value to information in many ways that are not possible in the print environment, further increasing the scope and size of the market.

Although from a private publisher's perspective this is a strategic issue, there are important policy implications, because single-channel distribution necessarily limits application and use of information. Spillover effects will be lost, as will opportunities for third-party enhancements through software and linkage to other information.

Publishers may counter arguments for efficiency, diversity, and openness with notions that data integrity and quality can best be maintained by tightly controlling dissemination. In addition, close control allows publishers to subsidize certain users, such as educational institutions or users lacking advanced telecommunications facilities, and thereby justifying controls for reasons of equity.

Two related issues have been debated. First is whether government agencies, which are not able to assert copyright in the information they generate (Sec. 105, title 17 U.S.C.), should be able to control redissemination through the use of contract. In particular, much debate has centered on the pricing policies of the National Library of Medicine, where it is linked to complex questions of what sort of cost recovery should be encouraged or permitted (U.S. Congress 1986).

More recently, similar issues have been raised in an antitrust context in Dialog's lawsuit against the American Chemical Society over (among other things) the restriction of portions of *Chemical Abstracts* to ACS's own system and network (Dialog Information Services, Inc., v. American Chemical Society 1990).[25] This case brings up policy questions about when privately created information services should be deemed "essential facilities" and therefore subject to special obligations. Also, the National Science Foundation provided initial funding for mounting *Chemical Abstracts* as a machine-readable database in the 1960s. Although this issue in the lawsuit is linked to the specific terms of the original funding agreement, it inspires questions about what the intellectual rights policies of NSF and other agencies should be when they fund the development of information resources. Finally, there is the question whether any special obligation should attach to an organization's tax status—that is, whether an educational or charitable organization exempt under Section 501(c)(3) has obligations different from a private company.[26]

Site Licensing

Although publishers have considerable power to shape their rights with distributors, the retail market depends on end users. Large institutions and corporations wield considerable buying power on behalf of their employees and students; they are vulnerable to infringement claims because they are visible targets with deep pockets and thousands of potentially disaffected employees. The Software Publishers Association has been effective in enforcing copyright compliance for microcomputer software through a program that combines the use of free auditing software, a toll-free reporting number, and litigation when necessary. The SPA now estimates compliance in major companies at greater than 90 percent (purchased software packages as a percentage of installed software). Publishers see site licensing as an opportunity to maintain such direct relationships at a reasonably high level with a responsible office.

In contrast to large firms, individuals who work alone may abuse copyright with impunity. Nobody is going to turn them in, and the cost of pursuing them in court is prohibitive. But the effect is to reinforce the hierarchy—to encourage marketing to companies and not to individuals. It even suggests that publishers should price higher for individuals to compensate for losses due to illegal "sharing."

Despite the changes in technology and the market, library operations could still be supported by taxing all potential users in order to subsidize actual users. This practice (i.e., treating library expenditures as common overhead) appeals to educational institutions because it encourages use of information resources and minimizes inequities among students. It appeals to all organizations in that it aggregates purchasing power, facilitates budgeting, and eliminates transaction costs.

At the same time, the vanishing marginal cost of digital information encourages publishers to offer institution-level site licenses.[27] Colleges and universities receive the best prices because publishers expect to win future commercial users this way. Licensee institutions, however, are typically required to restrict use by outsiders—which has not been the case for library books and journals. Users without institutional affiliations may be left to fend for themselves.

Restrictions on use by outsiders can put libraries in an uncomfortable position. Such restrictions could ultimately jeopardize a library's ability to rely on the Copyright Act's Section 108 "safe harbor" provisions for archival reproductions and interlibrary loan. Section 108 is available only to libraries and archives whose collections are either open to the public or to unaffiliated persons doing research in a specialized field (Sec. 108 (a) (3), title 17 U.S.C.). Such restrictions can also be problematic for state universities, which are often obliged to extend library privileges to all citizens of the state. Even state libraries cannot reasonably be expected to buy a site license to provide electronic information for the state as a whole. Ironically, one way to resolve the problem is to resurrect the library walls and allow unrestricted use only within the library premises.

In practice, site licensing of electronic resources is a kind of localized resource sharing. It contrasts dramatically with the technical delineation of acceptable resource sharing in the print environment. Under Section 108, the photocopying of scholarly journals for interlibrary loan must not be "systematic" or "substitute" for subscriptions (Sec. 108 (g), title 17 U.S.C.). Guidelines negotiated by librarians and publishers, promulgated by the Commission on New Technological Uses of Copyrighted Works in 1976 (United States 1978, pp. 54–55; U.S. Congress 1976, pp. 72–74) and endorsed by Congress, interpret this to mean that a library may request no more than five photocopies of articles from a given journal per year.[28]

Limitations on concurrent use can also provide an artificial constraint on "overly efficient" use of digital resources. Concurrent use limitations, supported by software lock-outs, are already becoming a standard method for licensing software programs on local area networks. Concurrent licensing is actually a step back toward the natural use limits of the book (as exemplified in reserve readings for college courses)—but without giving the library the benefit of an owned copy.

The lack of an owned copy means that if the library decides to terminate a subscription to a database service or a CD-ROM, it has nothing to offer its patrons.[29] Although libraries have not normally retained outdated reference works, librarians perceive that publishers are not interested in or capable of adequately archiving what they publish. The controversy is not fully under way because the primary literature is not yet in electronic form. But although publishers have not asked libraries to give up their archival function for journals, the precedent being set for indexes and abstracts is troubling to librarians.

International Access

The international nature of the Internet adds another dimension to the site-licensing issue. If licensing can be managed with security and confidence, each country can be treated as a separate market, so prices and terms for information services can readily be set to reflect local economic conditions and the ability to pay. Where the marginal cost of production is much lower than the average cost, the ability to discriminate in price is important to maximizing revenues, regardless of equity issues. For example, pharmaceutical drugs are typically sold at much lower prices in developing countries than in the United States. Thus, a drug available at low cost in sub-Saharan Africa may be prohibitively expensive to an uninsured American.

Lives may be less at stake in the publication of scholarly research, but the very openness of the network brings such equity issues to light. And although the network makes communication and publishing distance-independent, different intellectual property laws and practices apply in different countries. In some cases, the result may be to shift certain publishing to favorable foreign havens. In addition, precedents set for free dissemination—either of government information[30] or as charity[31]—may color expectations about the use and redistribution of proprietary information. The consequences may be a source of conflict with efforts to create a truly inclusive global Internet, where research is not disadvantaged by location.

Next Steps: Statements of Policy and Principle

In 1995 individual researchers, scholars, libraries and library organizations, journal editors, and academic societies will engage in debating the issues raised in this chapter:

Is joint authorship an appropriate paradigm for scholarly communication? Should derivative works by one of many joint authors be approved by the joint authors? Is it possible to craft policies on communication and publication of research results without appearing to infringe on freedom of speech? What would such policies look like?

Should a contribution to a public list carry a public license that allows reposting unless the contribution provides a notice to the contrary? Should similar assumptions be made of files posted for anonymous FTP—assuming that anyone can retrieve but only authorized individuals can post to the directory? How can lists and FTP sites and directories be coded to convey warranties and licensing information?

Should academic authors reserve the right to prepare and publish derivative works? What sort of exclusivity is appropriate for publishers and how should it be expressed so as not to inhibit legitimate modification of the author's work?

How should academic publishers and societies license their information

- to commercial and noncommercial information services?
- to academic institutions, other organizations, and individual users?
- for use in developing countries?

The crafting of specific policy statements requires common reference points. What is a private list? What is a public list? What is a public FTP site? We are staking out the electronic frontier. The distances fool the eye, but it is not the flat expanse we first saw.

Notes

This chapter has been prepared as a part of a joint project between the Information Infrastructure Project at Harvard and the Coalition for Networked Information. The project is partially supported by a grant from the National Science Foundation's Program on Ethics and Values Studies in Science and Technology.

1. Technically, copyright protects original expression of information (including selections or arrangements of facts), not facts or ideas.

2. Concerns are frequently voiced that copyright law has been antiquated by technology, but these concerns often reflect problems of enforcement or of the complex private arrangements that overlay copyright. In any case, no convincing alternative to copyright law for digital information has yet been proposed. One of the few attempts to do so was presented to the Library of Congress

Network Advisory Committee (Kost 1989, pp. 71–76). The committee concluded, however, that the copyright system did not require radical revision.

3. Thus, the network can extend the boundaries and functions of the traditional laboratory to encompass a national or international "collaboratory." See Wulf 1988.

4. Clinical research and policy research might seem to present worst-case scenarios because they involve both practitioners and academics. Professional codes and practices, however—and learned discretion of policymakers—presumably work to limit dissemination by the practitioner. In any case, the use of electronic mail is much less commonplace outside of higher education.

5. Industrial sponsors reserve the right to delay publication in order to perfect patent filings abroad. Although U.S. patent allows inventors who publish information about an invention a one-year grace period in which to file a patent application, in most countries a patent application cannot be filed once the invention is publicly disclosed.

6. Another notable exception is research on human subjects where privacy is an issue.

7. From the institution's perspective, it is desirable that the contractor's contribution be considered "work made for hire." But this can only be achieved if the contractor agrees in writing and the work is specially ordered or commissioned for use as: a contribution to a collective work, a part of a motion picture or other audiovisual work, a translation, a supplementary work, a compilation, an instructional text, a test, answer material for a test, or an atlas (Sec. 101, title 17 U.S.C.). A stand-alone report does fall into any of these categories. Nor does a jointly authored paper that is not written for a particular anthology or collection. Because the limited definition of work made for hire could possibly operate as a trap, it is considered sound legal practice to include an assignment of copyright in the contract in case the assertion that the work is made for hire is ineffective. An assignment is less desirable to the institution because it is subject to the author's termination rights after 35 years (see Sec. 203, title 17 U.S.C.).

8. Many universities permit graduate student research assistants to retain ownership of their writings.

9. An exclusive license to all the rights inherent in the copyright (i.e., the rights of reproduction, adaptation, distribution, public performance, and public display) is treated as equivalent to an assignment of copyright.

10. However, an assignment of copyright does not necessarily mean that one of the joint owners has not already licensed the work for publication elsewhere, and a careful publisher will want some assurance that this is not the case. Naturally, such assurance must come from all the joint owners.

11. A related matter is whether the individual subscribers are aware of who the other subscribers are. In many cases there will be a publicly available subscriber record, but subscribers may suppress their names from the public record.

12. Feist Publications, Inc. v. Rural Telephone Service Co. (1991) dispensed with the controversial "sweat of the brow" doctrine which permitted compilation

copyright based on no more than industrious collection of facts. Some selectivity or arrangement is required to meet a threshold requirement of originality. Archiving may be necessary to establish a fixation of the compilation, which is required to support a copyright (Sec. 102 (a), title 17 U.S.C.)

13. The lurker might argue that the discussion sequence is not a product of selection but a historical fact and therefore not subject to copyright.

14. This is not clearly a violation of the distribution right, because there is no delivery of a copy, nor of the display right, because the content of the file is not visible.

15. Contributory infringement is not defined in the Copyright Act but was discussed at length in the Betamax case; Sony v. Universal Studios 1984. It could also be argued, however, that anonymous FTP is equivalent to placing a journal in the library. It provides an opportunity for anybody to make photocopies, but that does not amount to contributory infringement.

16. Industry-funded research often provides that publication may be postponed to enable the preparation filing of patents before publication. Although there is a 12-month grace period in the United States, there generally is no grace period in other jurisdictions, yet it may be advisable to publish rapidly to ensure that nobody else is able to secure a patent that might jeopardize further funding or otherwise inhibit future research.

17. The cross-fertilization that can result from divergent publication is a strong argument for networking infrastructure. Lewis M. Branscomb, "Information Infrastructure for the 1990's: A Public Policy Perspective," paper presented at the Kennedy School symposium, "Information Infrastructure for the 1990s," November 29, 1990.

18. Representatives of eight of these journals met at the Association of Research Libraries in October 1990 and established themselves as the Association of Electronic Scholarly Journals.

19. There was considerable discussion on the POLICY-L electronic mailing list in early 1990 concerning subscription fees for a proposed electronic journal on research in hotel administration. Many of the participants in the discussion would have preferred a membership arrangement (wherein the members of the organization received a "free" journal) to a straightforward subscription fee. NSF, by contrast, has been very liberal in permitting use of the NSFNET backbone for any service that supports education and research. Charging is not an explicit factor, and even qualifying for-profit uses have been permitted on an experimental basis. Furthermore, NSF-funded mid-level networks have been free to set their own policies.

20. Publishers may be schizophrenic about downloading, however. See Hearty and Polansky (1987), who contrast legal and marketing perspectives within the same organization.

21. The 1976 Copyright Act codified the first sale doctrine as Sec. 109, title 17 U.S.C. The first sale doctrine has been modified with respect to phonorecords (1984) and computer programs (1989). Some European countries have limited

the application of the first sale doctrine to libraries by creating a public lending right.

22. Thus, the copyright owner's permission is required in order to put a CD-ROM on a network because a remote display is created. In addition, many CD-ROMs are leased rather than sold, so that even a local display requires permission from the copyright owner.

23. Or, to look at it another way, the medium becomes the network—an increasingly transparent, ubiquitous network—and any storage device or display facility is merely an extension of the network.

24. In the copyright context, it is the distinction between the copy and the protectable expression that is disappearing. This means that prerogatives inherent in copies are disappearing. Special provisions for copies are found in Sections 110(1) ("lawfully made copies" under the "face-to-face teaching exemption") and 117 (owned copies of computer programs) as well as Section 109 (owned copies under the first sale doctrine).

25. ACS's counterclaim for unpaid royalties illustrates the anxiety that publishers feel toward vendors in the online environment.

26. Although ACS is recognized as a 501(c)(3) organization, exemptions for professional societies are currently granted under 501(c)(6), the category that applies to trade associations and business leagues. 501(c)(6) organizations are tax-exempt but not "tax-deductible"—that is, donations are not tax-deductible as charitable contributions, and foundations cannot ordinarily make grants to 501(c)(6) organizations. Academic societies are more likely to qualify as 501(c)(3) organizations.

27. A pure site license permits unrestricted copying and use at a given site, however, site licenses often limit the number of copies or, in the case of network licenses, concurrent users.

28. For the sixth and subsequent copy, many libraries pay the Copyright Clearance Center the fee indicated on the article. Some libraries feel that the fair use provisions in Section 107 of the Copyright Act cover at least some copying beyond that permitted under Section 108. In any case, the five-article limit, while cited approvingly by Congress, does not actually appear in Section 108. It is important to note that these guidelines constrain only requests by libraries. Individuals may request copies directly from the library holding the journal without any limitation on the number of times that journal articles are copied.

29. CD-ROM licenses typically require the return of outdated CD-ROMs as new ones are received.

30. Although not subject to copyright within the United States, works of the U.S. government are protectable by copyright elsewhere. See U.S. House, Committee on the Judiciary, Copyright Law Revision: Report Together with Additional Views to Accompany S. 22, 94th Cong., 2d sess., 1976, Report 1476, pp. 58–60. Virtually all other countries protect government works by copyright, so under the reciprocity principles of the Berne and UCC conventions, those countries are obligated to provide protection to U.S. government works on the

same basis. In practice, international exchange agreements negotiated by NTIS often end up providing the information at no cost.

31. The United States Information Agency and private foundations, such as the Carnegie Corporation, have supported dissemination of print materials to countries in the developing world. There has yet been little concerted effort to make electronic information available on special terms, although Cornell University has a project under way to provide core agricultural literature to the developing world on CD-ROM.

References

Byrd, Gary D. (1990). "An Economics 'Commons' Tragedy for Research Libraries: Scholarly Journal Publishing and Pricing Trends." *College and Research Libraries* (May).

Dialog Information Services, Inc., V. American Chemical Society. (1990). Docket no. 90–1338, U.S. District Court for the District of Columbia.

Feist Publications, Inc., vs. Rural Telephone Service Co., Inc., 113 S. Ct. 1282 (1991).

Harnad, Stevan. (1990). "Scholarly Skywriting and the Prepublication Continuum of Scientific Inquiry." *Psychological Science* 1 (November): 342–344.

Hearty, John A., and Barbara F. Polansky. (1987). "ACS Chemical Journals Online: Is It Being Downloaded, Do We Care?" In *Intellectual Property Rights in an Electronic Age*. Network Planning Paper No. 16. Library of Congress Network Advisory Committee.

Kost, Robert J. (1989). "Useright." In *Intellectual Property Issues in the Library Network Context*, by the Network Advisory Committee, pp. 71–76. Washington, D.C.: Library of Congress.

Merton, Robert K. (1988). "The Matthew Effect in Science, II: Cumulative Advantage and the Symbolism of Intellectual Property." *ISIS* 79.

Nelkin, Dorothy. (1984). *Science as Intellectual Property: Who Controls Research?* New York: Macmillan.

Rogers, Sharon J., and Charlene S. Hurt. (1989). "How Scholarly Communication Should Work in the 21st Century." *Chronicle of Higher Education* (October 18).

Rushing, Francis W., and Carole Ganz Brown. (1990). *Intellectual Property Rights in Science, Technology, and Economic Performance: International Comparisons*. Boulder: Westview Press.

Sherwood, Robert M. (1990). *Intellectual Property Economic Development*. Boulder: Westview Press.

Sony v. Universal City Studios, Inc. (1984). 464 U.S. 417, 104 S. Ct. 774.

United States. (1978). National Commission on New Technological Uses of Copyrighted Works. (1978). Final Report. Washington, D.C.: Library of Congress, pp. 54–55.

U.S. Congress, House of Representatives. (1976). Conference Report, Report No. 94-1733, September 20, pp. 72–74.

U.S. Congress, House Committee on Government Operations. (1986). Electronic Collection and Dissemination of Information by Federal Agencies: A Policy Overview. 99th Cong., 2d sess., House Report 99–560.

Weil, Vivian, and John W. Snapper, eds. (1989). *Owning Scientific and Technical Information: Value and Ethical Issues.* New Brunswick, N.J.: Rutgers University Press.

Weismann v. Freeman. (1989). 868 F.2d 1313 (CA2 1989).

Wulf, William. (1988). "The National Collaboratory: A White Paper." National Science Directorate for Computer and Information Science and Engineering, December 20.

18

Where Electronic Publications and Television Programs Are Really Computer Programs: Some Copyright Implications

Patrice A. Lyons

In this chapter I address some of the fundamental copyright-related issues involved in providing interactive access to computer programs over communications systems—issues that will challenge the print-on-paper industry for years to come. Many information resources now accessible to the public over computer networks may appear to look and sound like conventional copyright works. Often, the term *multimedia* is applied to these capabilities, as if such resources were simple compilations of traditional works such as music, video, or text to be treated as what might loosely be called "data." In fact, the work as a whole is almost always a computer program and may have the capability to be used interactively over a network or other communications pathway. The output of the program for purposes of copyright is a performance of the program. The issue of performance rights has been widely addressed in the copyright-dependent industries, particularly music, but the key open issue here is the nature and scope of the application of the public performance right to computer programs. There are also related matters to consider, dealing with the concept of derivative works.

Considerable attention has been paid over the past 25 years to the protection for computer programs and databases under U.S. copyright law and to the retransmission of performances or displays of television programs by cable systems and satellite carriers. Although both computing and communications come into play here, it is unfortunate that, in most instances, they have been considered in isolation. Considerable evidence suggests that the experience of the broadcast, cable, and other communications industries needs to be considered in tandem with progress in the computer industry in the context of communications to the public embodying performances of computer programs.

We are at the early stages of a convergence between computers and communications that continues to make a wide range of products and services available to the public. Unlike traditional television or radio programming, where analog signals are tightly bound to the hardware of display or rendering systems, typical computer communication practices involve formats that are open to a variety of presentations, often determined at the receiving end. For example, the pace, positioning, appearance, and content of a presentation may be altered by programs resident in a remote computer. In this role, computer programs are more than just tools; they are active participants in the process. The intervening network and computing environment may include databases, knowledge-based systems, brokering systems, gateways, conversion systems, and software agents such as Knowbot programs.[1]

At the present stage of development, many of the computer program cases that come before the courts are in the video game industry and involve competing claims to copyright in computer programs. Complex computer programs such as knowledge-based systems are beginning to appear outside research circles, but among the most ubiquitous computer programs in commercial distribution today are video games. It is in the context of such relatively simple programs that the courts are grappling with the application of the copyright law. However, such issues as the scope of protection for the dynamic behavior of computer programs or, to use the terminology of the copyright statute, the public performance of programs, particularly in connection with computer networking, have received little attention.[2] This topic will undoubtedly undergo considerable examination and scrutiny as complex computer programs continue to find their way into the marketplace.

Information resources accessible over advanced communications systems include a wide range of digital object types such as printable material, viewable material, and executable material. The nature and amount of this material available in the future will be limited only by the willingness and desire of authors and other copyright owners to make them available, the ability of users to retrieve them straightforwardly over networks, and the capability of information technology to provide adequate protection, including capabilities for authentication and integrity.

The diversity of information resources potentially accessible through such systems may require certain changes in the way the rights and interests under copyright are managed today. There is an emerging realization that the copyright-dependent industries need to understand that the way they have formerly done business may not be adequate for them to take advantage of and develop many of the emerging opportunities in the digital marketplace. When a variety of copyrighted material may be accessed by users over the same or similar communications pathways (using computer-mediated search and retrieval mechanisms), it is reasonable to assume some common level of understanding and technical interoperability among the various users, providers, and their systems. This will be particularly evident in the case of knowledge-based systems where computer programs may interact with users to provide guidance, advice, or direct assistance on a wide range of subjects or actions.[3]

Public Performance of Computer Programs

Let us now consider in greater detail the application of the copyright right of public performance to interactive access to computer programs, and the communication to the public, over computer networks and other communications pathways, of performances of computer programs. In the case of interactive access to computer programs, the performances generated by the programs usually take the form of sets of sequences of bits that may be communicated to the public. Unlike the case for analog transmission, performances of computer programs embodied in digital communication systems are sent and received as bits, rather than as images or sounds. At the point of reception, programs or hardware resident in a remote computer may interpret the bits received and manifest images or sounds.

Roughly speaking, the copyright law defines transmission of a performance in such a way as to require that images or sounds be communicated to a remote location.[4] Ordinary analog communications systems, such as AM or FM broadcasting, would appear to meet this definition, because they send a modulated representation of a performance embodied in a signal essentially unchanged from the form in which it occurred or was generated. For communication over digital communications systems, a performance of a computer program is initially generated in the form of binary digits according to some format or algorithm. The performance need never have existed outside the computer environment. No images or sounds would appear to be communicated in this situation. When repositories containing computer programs are invoked interactively by users over a network, the sets of sequences of bits sent from those repositories would likewise constitute the communication of the performance of the program, which takes the form of bits rather than images or sounds. Images and/or sounds may still be generated by programs resident at the point of reception; however, no "transmission" of them would have occurred.

It may be helpful at this point to develop an example of the concept of computer program. The Copyright Act of 1976, as amended by Congress in 1980, defines "computer program" for purposes of copyright in section 101, title 17 U.S.C., as a "set of statements or instructions to be used directly or indirectly in a computer in order to bring about a certain result." There is within this definition a notion of use, or what is often referred to as program execution. It is generally understood that a computer program has the capability of changing its internal state when executed. In fact, that is one definition of what it means to execute a program.

By contrast, a computer database in digital form is a set of bits that just sits there doing nothing until acted upon by a program for some purpose. Although elements of both a computer program and a computer database may be considered "data," the presence or absence of data elements in a computer program does not alter the basic characteristic of the program. It is the essentially dynamic character of a computer program that differentiates it from a computer database. Whether elements of a given program are viewed as simple numbers or "data" should not, as such, restrict the exercise of the right of public performance in the computer program as a whole. Where such performances are embodied in communications to the public, sometimes called data flows or data stream, this may constitute a public performance for copyright licensing purposes.

There is a growing recognition that the distinction between data and program in this context is not an acceptable or technically accurate way to categorize what is happening. Take an example from the video games industry. If a musical work is converted into an interactive digital form and integrated with other elements to create a video game computer program, and the program is accessed from a remote computer using an intelligent search engine, the performance of the program would be communicated to a user in the form of a set of sequences of bits. The unauthorized interception and use of these numbers in the course of a communications pathway may give rise to liability, not just under copyright law, but also under relevant provisions of the Communications Act of 1934. There may also be rights under patent law theories. As suggested in an American Bar Association report on performance rights in computer programs, "to the extent that the formation or communication of 'sets of sequences of bits' is in any way related to patented formats for data, i.e., the way in which bits are organized, or the processing of bits, issues related to the overlap of patent and copyright laws may need to be addressed."[5]

There has been some confusion about the scope of protection for "data" that may be present in a computer program. This is particularly relevant where a program performance is embodied in a communication to the public. Where such a performance is further performed in the course of communication to a remote user, this may constitute a secondary performance of the program that needs to be taken into consideration for licensing purposes.

An order in a case involving security measures for a video games system, *Atari Games Corp. v. Nintendo of America, Inc.*, may be of interest in this context. The court attempted to view "program data" as somehow separable from the program itself for purposes of copyright protection. With respect to the definition of computer program, the court noted that the "definition indicates that protection for computer programs includes program instructions, or the software code that tells the microprocessor what to do, but not program data which is stored in memory and often changes as the program instructions are being executed by the microprocessor."[6] There was even a reference to program data as "nothing more than specific numbers or specific series of numbers" and copyrightable, if at all, "only in the context of a substantial computer database and, even then, only if the arrangement, selection, and coordination of the data" can overcome the requirements of the Supreme Court's decision in *Feist Publications v. Rural Telephone Service Co.*, 111 S.Ct. 1282 (1991).[7]

In the *Atari* case, the court viewed program data as the "result sought by execution of the program instructions. Thus, the statements that manipulate the data would fall within the statutory definition [of computer program], while the data that result from those calculations would not." Construing the definition of computer program in the copyright law, the court would cover program instructions as subject matter of copyright, but it would appear to limit protection for what it terms program data. Fortunately, this decision is not the only guidance available in sorting out the status of program statements, that is, program data.[8]

Another interpretation of the law may be found in the February 1992 decision of the Copyright Office on registrability of computer programs that generate typefaces. It had been the policy of the Office, first enunciated in 1988, that, where a "master computer program includes data that fixes or depicts a particular typeface, typefont, or letterform, the registration application must disclaim copyright in that uncopyrightable data."[9] On the basis of testimony at a public hearing and written comments received, the Copyright Office was persuaded that "creating scaleable typefonts using already-digitized typeface represents a significant change in the industry since our previous Policy Decision. . . . [and] that computer programs designed for generating typeface in conjunction with low resolution and other printing devices may involve original computer instructions entitled to protection under the Copyright Act."[10]

An interesting line of reasoning that emerged at the Copyright Office public hearing on the typeface design matter was the growing realization that it may not be realistic to distinguish between data and program in the case of computer programs. The discussion called to mind a comment made by the late renowned computer scientist Allen Newell of Carnegie Mellon University. When addressing the form of algorithms, he observed, "As anyone in computer science knows, the boundary between data and program—that is, what is data and what is procedure—is very fluid. In fact, . . . there is no principled distinction in terms of form or representation of which is which. What counts is the total body of knowledge represented somehow in the assembled symbolic expressions. This totality determines the ultimate behavior of the machine."[11] This issue will arise with increasing frequency when large amounts of what may be termed knowledge or heuristics are incorporated into computer programs.

From a legal perspective, because Congress has specifically brought computer programs within the U.S. copyright law, it is necessary to consider the nature and scope of protection, not just for the static elements of a program, but also for its execution. This is particularly important where sequences of binary digits representing the dynamic elements of program execution, or in copyright terms, performances of programs, are embodied in communications to the public. The performance of a program that results in the generation of a set of sequences of bits may be viewed as subject to authorization by a copyright owner. There may also be rights in the performance itself as a derivative work.

The state of a computer program in the form of the binary digits that represent its performance at any point in time during execution will generally differ from the state of the program in its static form. The different aspects of a computer program relate to what has been termed the program's behavior. It has been noted that the "behavior of programs is not necessarily linear, that is, the order in which the instructions appear on the page is not necessarily the order in which they are in fact executed. Put slightly differently: *the sequence in which a program does things when running may be quite different from the sequence in which those things occur in the program text.*"[12]

The courts are just beginning to analyze the extent of copyright protection for the execution of computer programs, or what has been termed the program's behavior. An illustration from a court in Colorado may help to clarify this point. In *Gates Rubber Co. v. Bando American, Inc.* the computer program in question, called Design Flex 4.0, was designed as an aid in the selection of replacement belts for industrial customers. The program has an interactive capability: a user answers relevant questions and provides other information for use by the program, which assembles the information necessary for the program to perform its calculations.

With respect to the execution of the program, the district court considered this to be a protected element under the copyright law. The court held that "a program's behavior can be protected by copyright law. A particular example of common error concerns the minimum/maximum error where both programs, upon receiving a particular answer, erroneously take the user back to another part of the program. In this example, the commonality of this error denotes 'behavior' as to how one part of the program works with another. This is part of the creative expression of the program itself."[13] On appeal, the court took a narrower view of the significance of the actual misbehavior or faulty operation of the computer program, and remanded the issue to the district court for further analysis.[14]

Multimedia Works and Other Computer Programs

Where digital representations of video, text, audio, database, graphic, and other information, whether preexisting or created directly in digital form, are converted into computer executable form so as to be indistinguishable in practice from what are usually viewed as computer programs, it would be helpful to agree that they are in fact computer programs for purposes of copyright in order to facilitate the drafting of licensing agreements. Unlike "pay per view" (as it is now known in the entertainment industry), where a customer provides a simple request to the system, in the case of complex computer programs the user may eventually provide large amounts of information to the program on an interactive basis. Whereas books and other similar works derive their value when read by the user, such computer programs will be valued for the information or service provided when they are executed. This behavior of the program may be covered by the copyright right of performance. Further, where the output of computer program execution in the form of a set of sequences of bits is embodied in a communication to a remote computer, this may constitute a "public" performance for copyright licensing purposes. Although certain performances will be public and thus subject to copyright, many will be private and fall outside the scope of the exclusive right under copyright. This does not mean, however, that they will not be protected under other legal theories, such as communications or privacy.

The performance of computer programs was anticipated by Congress when it revised the copyright law in 1976. The legislative history of the law notes that a performance of a copyrighted work "may be accomplished 'either directly or by means of any device or process,' including all kinds of equipment for reproducing or amplifying sounds or visual images, any sort of transmitting apparatus, any type of electronic retrieval system, and any other techniques and systems not yet in use or even invented."[15] This language is rather comprehensive.

Distributed Performance

Let us now suppose that a program is composed of many distributed elements running on different machines on a network: a complex multi-party distributed application. The previous issues relating to program performance become increasingly complex in this new context, because many of the instances of a performance are internal to the execution of the system. To take an example from the entertainment world, let's assume there is a computer program called Football. The program allows individual players to be implemented as separate but interactive program elements at widely rembte locations, and they interact over the network to play a game of football. There are many ways in which such a program could be implemented. For example, all the program elements could report back to a central computer location, which keeps track of the game or even manages it. Or there may not be any such central control. It is possible to think of this program as a single computer program composed of distributed program elements, each of which carries out its part of the program running at different locations, that is, a distributed execution.

The Football program may be based on or incorporate works of the visual arts, audiovisual works, music, databases, and even other computer programs. For example, a database of football plays may be incorporated in one of the elements or redundantly distributed among all the elements. Although some people may refer to the program as a "multimedia" work, this may be the result of the past segmentation of the computer, communications, and entertainment industries. It is preferable to view the work *as a whole* as a computer program for purposes of copyright.

Derivative Works

At what point in the continuum between the originator of interactive programming and the user would derivative works come into play? What happens in the original computer? What happens in the communications pathway where the computer programs in transit in the network (sometimes called intelligent agents) may access other computer programs or computer databases on behalf of a user to answer a query, provide advice, or perform some other service? What happens in the destination machine?

Apart from the normal execution of a program, which changes the internal state of the program itself, there may be instances where a program is performed by another program; the resulting performance may contain elements derived from both the underlying program and the program carrying out the performance. Or both could equally participate in creating a performance. This may be the case where intelligent agents interact over a communications pathway in order to provide advice or guidance for a remote user.

Would the right to prepare derivative works be infringed by the performance of a work without any new fixation being made? Some guidance may be found in the legislative history of the Copyright Act of 1976, where it is noted that "[t]he exclusive right to prepare derivative works . . . overlaps the exclusive right of reproduction to some extent. It is broader than that right, however, in the sense that reproduction requires fixation in copies or phonorecords, whereas the preparation of a derivative work, such as a ballet, pantomime, or improvised performance, may be an infringement even though nothing is ever fixed in tangible form."[16] This issue is particularly interesting when computer programs are performed on an interactive basis to provide services within a computer network or other communications pathway.

For example, suppose that you are the developer of an interactive computer program that contains one or more databases pertaining to the analysis of stock portfolios, as well as other programs containing rules or other expertise on the financial markets. If you allow other programs resident on a network to access your program on behalf of customers, licensing of a derivative work right, as well as the performance right, may be required. If a mere instruction to buy or sell is retrieved and the information is not combined or integrated with other information, would this be a fair use? Because something of value has been obtained by the user, it is not likely that an equitable argument of fair use would be successful. This is also evident where there is an attempt to redefine computer programs, such as the knowledge-based systems under development, as somehow merely compilations of data. This approach would be particularly problematic where such works are made subject to compulsory licenses or arbitrary extraction rights, which may be the case with the proposed European Community Database Directive.[17]

Identification of Copyright

What constitutes a computer program has important implications for purposes of identifying who is the author or other copyright claimant. It is necessary to determine what the work is before it is practical to identify who has claims to rights or interests in the work. What's the "what" that is the basis of any claims? Although the importance of the copyright notice has been considerably attenuated following entry of the United States into the Berne Convention, there is a need for agreed ways to identify copyright ownership claims in a network environment. How to reinvent a copyright notice system that will be flexible and effective for implementation in advanced communications systems is a complex, but not impossible, task.

A type of notice system would be helpful, not just for purposes of identifying claimants for purposes of payment of royalties, but also for determining when a work is in the public domain and freely accessible to the public. This element of public access was an important aspect of the copyright notice as it was originally conceived in the United States. For example, under the 1909 law, a work published without notice of copyright was deemed to be dedicated to the public domain.

The copyright notice requirement in the United States has changed over the years and is no longer an effective mechanism for purposes of determining ownership or providing guidance on when a work may be deemed freely accessible to the public. In its current form, the notice does little more than alert the public that there may be a claim to copyright. Where works, or performances of works, are expressed as binary digits, even this simple notice function appears to be relatively useless. For example, the conventional copyright notice is of little or no importance where a computer program incorporating thousands of discrete preexisting works is accessed on an interactive basis to obtain an answer to a query. No specific elements from any of the preexisting works need appear in the reply in any form; for example, a medical diagnosis program may simply reply: the patient does not have cancer.

Some people argue that, following its entry into the Berne Convention, the United States should abandon any type of copyright notice system. It has long been a principle of the Berne Convention that the enjoyment and exercise of rights under the Convention may not be made subject to the observance of any formality; however, this prohibition is understood to cover only formalities that are required as a condition of copyright.[18]

The Paris Act (1971) of the Berne Convention on Protection of Literary and Artistic Works does continue to provide for what may be considered a type of formality. In its Article 15 on presumptions of authorship, the Convention provides that: "In order that the author of a literary or artistic work protected by this Convention shall, in the absence of proof to the contrary, be regarded as such, and consequently be entitled to institute infringement proceedings in the countries of the Union, it shall be sufficient for his name to appear on the work in the usual manner." It does not specify how this provision should be implemented but leaves member countries free to make their own rules on the subject. Article 15 also contains special provisions for cinematographic works, anonymous and pseudonymous works, and unpublished works generally considered folklore (the concept of unpublished works may require clarification, because many works accessible over networks may be unpublished).

A system of presumptions of authorship and other copyright owner-ship would fulfill several important functions in a rights management system: it could provide a basis for identifying whether a work, or parts of a work, is subject to copyright rights or interests and could provide for a widely understood means of contacting copyright owners or their representatives in a dynamic, interactive manner for purposes of obtain-ing any required permissions. Further, standard ways of clearing rights in a network environment could be developed, based on such a system of presumptions. If a time and date stamp are also standardized as part of a system of presumptions of authorship, it would fulfill a useful part of the current copyright notice: the indication of the year date of publi-cation, and, presumptively, that the work has been published. This will be particularly important, as it is generally agreed that performance of a protected work in itself does not serve to publish the work in a techni-cal copyright sense, and a concept of public dissemination may be devel-oped as an equivalent act.[19]

A key element to bear in mind in developing a standard manner of identifying ownership of rights and interests in computer networks and other communication pathways is that any such standard should be vol-untary and not deemed a condition of copyright. As such, it would not be a prohibited formality under the Berne Convention.

In conclusion, the convergence between communications and com-puters has become an important subject for discussion and research; however, incentives for creativity established under the copyright law should not be neglected in the process. Interactive computer programs will play a critical role in the communications environment of the future; however, the tendency to look to past practices as a basis for identifying, securing, and otherwise managing rights in programs may not be ade-quate for purposes of providing interactive access to these important new works of authorship.

Notes

1. "Knowbot" is a registered trademark of the Corporation for National Research Initiatives.

2. *Red Baron-Franklin Park, Inc. v. Taito Corp.*, 883 F.2d 275 (4th Cir. 1989), *cert. denied*, 110 S. Ct. 869 (1990) (right of public performance not waived by sale of copies of program; section 109(e), title 17 U.S.C., subsequently amended,

effective Dec. 1, 1990, to provide an exception to the rights of public performance or display in the case of video game computer programs intended for use in coin-operated equipment); *see also Gates Rubber Co. v. Bando American, Inc.*, 1992 Copyright L. Dec. (CCH) ¶27,000, at 25,864 (D.Col. 1992) ("[e]ven if this [running of the program] is termed a public performance which makes the program public, there is little doubt that such performance does not amount to a [more than a limited] publication under §101 of the Copyright Act").

3. For purposes of this discussion, knowledge-based systems are considered to be either conventional databases with smart retrieval software, where the output is more than simply information stored in the database, or knowledge bases in the more usual sense of artificial intelligence (AI), where rules, facts, heuristics, and other forms of experiential knowledge are embedded in a computer program. A knowledge-based system in an AI sense may or may not have a separable and distinguishable database system associated with it. *See generally* Lyons 1992; *see also* "Databases with Artificial Intelligence: Proprietary Protection," ABA Sec. of Patent, Trademark & Copyright Law, Comm. 702, Subcomm. F, 1991–1992 *Annual Report*, at 387 (1992).

4. In light of the definition of "transmit" in the copyright law, a performance of a computer program may be embodied in "communications," but not "transmissions," since binary digits but not images or sounds are received beyond the place from which they are sent. For purposes of copyright, "to 'transmit' a performance or display is to communicate it by any device or process whereby images or sounds are received beyond the place from which they are sent." Sec. 101, title 17 U.S.C.

5. "Network Access to Computer Programs," ABA Sec. of Patent, Trademark & Copyright, Comm. 702, Subcomm. F, *1993–1994 Annual Report*, at 419 (1994).

6. *Atari Games Corp. v. Nintendo of America, Inc.*, No. C 88-4805 FMS, C 89-0027 FMS, 1993 U.S.Dist. LEXIS 8183, Dialog Search Report, at 7 (N.D.Cal.1993) (redacted version of order filed under seal, April 15, 1993).

7. *Id.* at 8.

8. *See Stern Electronics v. Kaufman*, 669 F.2d 852 (2d Cir. 1982) ("[a] program is simply 'a set of statements (i.e., data) or instructions to be used directly or indirectly in a computer in order to bring about a certain result'").

9. Policy Decision on Copyrightability of Digitized Typefaces, Notice of Policy Decision, 53 *Fed. Reg.* 38110 (1988).

10. Registrability of Computer Programs that Generate Typefaces, Final Regulation, 57 *Fed. Reg.* 6201 (1992).

11. Newell 1986; *see also* Reconsideration of 1988 Policy Decision on Copyrightability of Digitized Typefaces, Library of Congress, Copyright Office Doc. No. RM 91-6, *Statement of Adobe Systems Incorporated*, at 13 ("[d]ata and instructions are coordinated and combined inseparably in recent programs, making the use of disclaimers difficult if the purpose of the disclaimer is to enable others to readily distinguish between data and code").

12. Davis 1992.

13. *Gates Rubber Co. v. Bando American Inc.*, 1992 Copyright L. Dec. (CCH) ¶27,000, at 25,879 (D.Col. 1992), *aff'd in part, rev'd in part, and remanded,* 1993 Copyright L. Dec. (CCH) ¶27,158 (10th Cir. 1993).

14. *Id.* ¶27,158, at 26,891.

15. H.R. Rep. No. 94-1476, 94th Cong., 2d Sess., at 63 (1976).

16. *Id.* at 62; *see also* Goldstein 1983; *see generally* Lyons 1991, p. 265.

17. *See* European Commission's Proposal for a Council Directive on the Legal Protection of Databases, Commission Document COM (92) 24 final, dated May 13, 1992. For discussion of proposed Council Directive, see Hupper 1994.

18. It is generally agreed that, under the Berne Convention, "protection may not be made conditional on the observance of any formality whatsoever. The word 'formality' must be understood in the sense of a condition which is necessary for the right to exist—administrative obligations laid down by national laws, which, if not fulfilled, lead to loss of copyright." *Guide to the Berne Convention for the Protection of Literary and Artistic Works (Paris Act, 1971)*, World Intellectual Property Association, at 33 (1978).

19. Copyright Reform Act of 1993, H.R. Rep. No. 103-833, 103d Cong., 1st Sess., at 25 (1993) (proposed study "to determine how to implement an amendment to that section [407] extending the mandatory deposit provisions to unpublished, but publicly transmitted works, including computer programs and online databases"); *see also* Report of the Advisory Committee on Copyright Registration and Deposit, Co-Chairs R. Wedgeworth and B. Ringer, 86 Copyright L. Rep. (CCH), at 55, n. 14 (1993).

References

Davis, R. (1992). "The Nature of Software and Its Consequences for Establishing and Evaluating Similarity." *Software L. J.* 5: 299, 306.

Goldstein, P. (1983). "Derivative Rights and Derivative Works in Copyright." *J. Copr. Soc'y* 30: 209, 231, Item 442.

Hupper, G. J. (1994). "Forum on European Community Database Directive." Summary of Proceedings (9 December 1992), European Law Research Center. Report issued August 1994.

Lyons, P. A. (1991). "Copyright Considerations of Hypertext Producers: Imaging and Document Conversion." In *Hypertext/Hypermedia Handbook*, chap. 17.

Lyons, P. A. (1992). "Knowledge-Based Systems and Copyright." *Serials Review* 18: 88.

Newell, A. (1986). "The Models Are Broken, the Models Are Broken." *U. of Pittsburgh L. Rev.* 47: 1023, 1033.

19

TeleRead: A Virtual Central Database without Big Brother

David H. Rothman

Pity the journalist who must decode the jargon of lawyers or pharmacists; the science teacher who knows that he or she is teaching obsolete theories; the congressional aide curious about health care in Sweden or the psyche of North Korean leaders; or the average voter who can't fathom most government news, and who then retreats to the sports section.

Even scholars can feel cut off from their specialized peers. In "As We May Think," a classic essay in the *Atlantic Monthly* of July 1945, Vannevar Bush (1945) called for technology to help consolidate knowledge. "Mendel's concepts of the law of genetics was lost to the world for a generation because his publication did not reach the few who were capable of grasping and extending it," Bush wrote, "and this sort of catastrophe is undoubtedly being repeated all about us, as truly significant attainments become lost in the mass of the inconsequential (p. 101)." His observations are even truer today—given the many more words churned out each year by modern academia, and the fact that the full texts of most books are not available in electronic form through computer networks. Simply put, we need a virtual central database online, melding wisdom from many subjects and fostering mass enlightenment.

The real value of knowledge is not in dollars and cents but in the potential to help give us a cancer cure or a 175-mpg automobile. The easier it is for a medical researcher or engine designer to explore other fields, the more they can accomplish in their own; the cancer researcher, for example, might benefit from the most arcane of papers on DNA, and the designer might hasten the coming of the 175-mpg car if he or she saw the right paper in metallurgy. A virtual central database with powerful search capabilities would enrich U.S. citizens both intellectually and financially. (The ideas in this chapter, although discussed in U.S. terms, might also apply to other countries, such as Canada.)

Such a national information system could even be part of our schools. American students could grow up with computers that could tap into well-stocked databases from home; they would spend more time reading the most appropriate books and other items, and less time searching for them—assuming they could even afford the materials in the first place without such a system. Teachers, of course, would be able to prepare for classes more efficiently. Such a program could help address some of the major concerns in the "Prisoners of Time" report from the National Education Commission on Time and Learning, which was distributed on Internet discussion groups in 1994.

We could serve other needs simultaneously if the federal government used a focused procurement program to drive down the cost of tablet-style computers for reading, writing, other school-related uses, and civic networking. The same machines would be just right for smart electronic forms. In small ways and large, then, we would be more efficient. So businesspeople would spend far less time meeting the paperwork needs of federal, state, and local governments. Likewise, TV watchers could use the forms for ordering goods and services more easily than they could with regular remote controls.

The total savings in time and money would reach tens of billions of dollars a year—an unscientific but conservative estimate for a $6-trillion-plus economy. Benefits would easily justify a virtual central database consuming about half a percent of the gross domestic product as envisioned here. In effect we would be shifting billions of dollars from bureaucracy to knowledge.

When, in the issue of April 4, 1994, the *New Yorker* ran a significant but flawed article about electronic library catalogs (Baker 1994), it unwittingly showed the need for a better information system than we have today. The *New Yorker* is the Tiffany of magazines. It has long prided itself on popular writing that offers the authority of experts and that can sway policymakers. Despite gossip about the weaknesses of this or that editor, the magazine is among the more prestigious of lay periodicals. But even at the *New Yorker*, articles may contain striking omissions, as in the case of the long piece by Nicholson Baker (1994).

The *New Yorker* complained that new computerized catalogs were replacing the venerable stacks of cards in wooden trays. Rather astutely, Baker pointed out the large number of errors in the electronic versions put together by cheap labor. He also praised the value of the handwritten cross-references and other informal annotations that libraries make on card catalogs. So far, so good; major libraries indeed are foolish to throw out the cards without preserving the notes electronically.

Not once, however, did Baker allude by name to the World Wide Web (WWW), the talk of the Internet. The article mentioned hypertext only in a generic way. Either the writer did not know of the Web, or he failed to grasp how germane it was to his article.

Using technology like the Web, not only librarians but also others could create cross-references and annotations. A Web-style approach, especially one with improved search capabilities, would be far superior to the old paper catalogs. That is no piddling detail. Granted, the *New Yorker* article served up its share of useful facts, such as the premature destruction of the cards blessed by the annotations. But a picky professor of information science would have flunked him for overlooking the full potential of the Web.

Still, for reasons that Baker failed to explore adequately, he is right in his gut feeling that today's electronic libraries are a long way from the paper equivalent. And this is not just for want of enough books online. Consider the shortcomings of popular search tools on the Internet, such as the Gopher-Veronica combination.

When an Internaut looks for items on a specific topic, dozens of seemingly duplicate entries may pop up on the screen. And yet the actual documents may differ. Casual researchers will not be able to verify which entries are most up-to-date. The remote chance even exists that some versions are frauds. What's more, it may be hard to learn the identities of the authors or when the documents were first electronically published. The Web poses similar problems for serious, library-trained researchers.

Moves are under way to correct many shortcomings of the Web, Gopher, and other Internet tools for locating and displaying information. Web browsers such as Mosaic and Netscape are key. Via the Web and programs in the Mosaic vein, users can apply a graphical interface to many other resources on the Internet; suddenly the Net looks more like the CompuServe or Prodigy commercial services and less like one big UNIXfest. It should also be easier in the future to establish the authenticity of text and other material on the Web. Readers eventually should be able to identify authors, publishers, and dates of publication in a systematic way. Another of the major network tools, WAIS (Wide Area Information Servers) is already geared in some respects to the needs of serious researchers and publishers. But it is harder to use than the Web and Gopher.

All those tools share a trait that is both a flaw and a strength. The accompanying resources are distributed, and potentially each may vanish in a flash; there is no reliable, central library on the Internet, not even of a virtual kind. Granted, wonderful collections do exist of some categories of information. One of the best examples is the CICNet project at the University of Michigan, which brings together hundreds of electronic serials. Also, the independent E-Text Archive, started by a CICNet staffer, collects such material as underground magazines and the writings of political activists. The Internet teems with gems of this kind. The E-text archives are a labor of love and are not under the thumb of Big Brother; material can originate from groups ranging from Maoists to libertarians—that is the glory of a distributed system of information.

A curse, however, comes with the glory: the pointer dilemma. True, an archivist, publisher, or writer might ask sites on the Internet to point only to a certain Gopher or Web site to guarantee authentic, up-to-date documents, but some recalcitrants might ignore the originating site's request. That is Threat A. Threat B is that if everyone pointed and backups did not exist elsewhere, the whole network community would lose if a fire destroyed the hard drives and tapes of the originating server. Of course, Internet sites can mirror parts of each other's disks, but this approach is hardly consistent or reliable. Suppose, too, that a site on the present Web closed for financial reasons, especially if it were a publishing house. The situation would be much less tidy than those involving traditional publishers and libraries. If a paper publisher goes belly up then a book will not vanish into the ether; the work will still be on library shelves.

Paper books fall apart over time, but libraries are accustomed to this problem. Thousands of electronic books, however, might be lost at once if magnetic and optical media proved less reliable than anticipated, and if a systematic system of monitoring and backups did not exist. Copyright law emphasizes the need to spread knowledge, including that of the past. We need a good, sound archival system if we are to entrust our electronic books to the new, unproven media—in an era when copyrights are to last for decades.

The potential fragility of e-texts illustrates one of the main differences between the worlds of computers and libraries. So does the issue of user friendliness. Computer programmers have come up with basic building blocks of new technologies, such as the Web. Their work is invaluable. But the ethos of computer science, which places a premium on change, prevails above all. Computer museums exist, but, as a rule, people in this field are unsentimental about information that can no longer earn its keep. Also, it seems many computer scientists may esteem performance of their pet hardware or software above all else—even its usability to the rest of the world.

Librarians are different. They care more about the permanence and overall friendliness of information systems than do most computer professionals. Although many library administrations have embraced electronic information retrieval as a nice, neat alternative to paper—and many librarians thrive on the new complexity—thousands of librarians are resisting.

Many journalists, too, have balked. Some may just be gadget-fearing holders of liberal arts degrees; others may be mavericks by nature and may worry about repressive uses of the technology. Also, like Baker and many working librarians, they dread the loss of historically valuable material. They are even prepared to defend the old ways partly on aesthetic grounds, as Baker (1994) did when he approvingly quoted a Cornell librarian's praise of the "brown and beautiful and round" card catalog at the Library of Congress that "could bring tears to your eyes." The librarian said that her own cards "have to be burned," but it was clear where Baker's sympathies were. He himself longed for Philistines to show more respect for wood-and-cardboard information systems.

Information professionals can at least be grateful that he did not report his present-day Gopher experiences in detail and spend several pages describing the chaos on the Internet. Compared to today's Gopher and Web, electronic card catalogs are models of accuracy and organization. When I searched for librarians' comments on the Baker article, Gopher acted entirely in character. I found not only legitimate items but also such entries as, "This Item has been moved to tape and cannot be accessed via GOPHER. Unable to find the body of requested item 333963. Trying method PNMIASPR PACS-L PAC94086 (FROM 2246 FOR 35 ON IDS 4FF)." I might as well have been searching an old catalog that forced me to dawdle in front of almost-blank cards.

Expensive databases are not the ultimate solution for information seekers like Baker or, for that matter, me. A journalist may end up paying hundreds of dollars to receive articles from Nexis for just one story. Such resources are but a dream to most teachers in elementary and high schools. Besides, many of the commands are just too complex, and even if we rely on collections of collections such as Lexis-Nexis, we may still see knowledge balkanized for business reasons. Until recently, for example, if a researcher wanted a comprehensive search to yield full-text versions of *New York Times* stories, he or she had to pay. The goals of today's commercial databases can clash directly with those of the research community. Businesses pride themselves on offering unique information, but many researchers would love one-stop shopping that was even more inclusive than databases such as Lexis-Nexis and Dialog. Perhaps the original owners of Lexis-Nexis grasped this paradox when they decided to leave the database business.

Certain network-aware librarians, of course, are benefiting from the complexities and wildly differing commands of the Internet and commercial databases. Such chaos is even a form of job security. A common prediction is that the online world will teem with libraries, and experts will guide civilians to the proper collections. There is some truth in this vision. Even under the plan I am about to describe, the need for such professionals would persist and probably even grow. Intelligent agents will always have limits. And no database will be perfectly logical.

Nevertheless, a virtual central database, well organized, is a must if we want to avoid a multidisciplinary Tower of Babel and maybe even convert intelligent skeptics. The word *central* appears here with some qualification. Far from killing off the anarchy of the present Internet, we should expand the Net: as a way for researchers to spread knowledge without commercial considerations gnawing away at scholarly ones; as a petri dish for ideas, popular and unpopular; and as an alternative for writers and publishers whom censors keep out of the central database.

Visionaries designed the Internet to allow packets to be routed around bad connections, and planners of a virtual central database could do likewise to help users circumvent censors by turning instead to the Internet and other paths, including commercial services. Such an approach would give us the best of several worlds. We could enjoy the order and quality control of a virtual central database, the freedom of the Internet, and the slick packaging of proprietary networks for those who wanted them. The central database could pick up not only direct submissions but also much of the best technology and content from the Internet, and could perhaps share some network resources with the Net.

Electronic federalism is the operative term here, with the U.S. political system very much in mind. Washington is more powerful than each state alone, but it does not run everything. And it freely borrows ideas at times from Montana or New York. The federalism metaphor is not perfect, of course; Internet sites do and should enjoy more freedom from central authority than states and localities do. But the parallels between the electronic and political forms of federalism are indeed striking. The virtual central database need not be just a creature of Washington; instead it could reflect the wishes of many academic and public librarians in many locations. What counts in the end isn't whether one database exists but where its managers are, and for whom they work.

Moreover, keep in mind the use of the word *virtual* in front of "central database." The information system should not rely on one bank of machines in one city. Computer-oriented subject matter might be physically stored in California, for example, and government-related books might be in Washington, D.C.; in both cases, librarians across the country could make acquisitions. Other databases could back up the contents of sites focused on specific subjects, with real-time replication used as soon as it was technically feasible. And if universities and other responsible institutions wanted to make copies of their own, so much the better. Moreover, although academic and public librarians would choose the contents of the databases, private companies could own most of the actual physical facilities and lease them to the government—yet another way to diffuse power.

Following is a four-part plan for this system, which I call TeleRead. It would help students and other readers, writers, and the U.S. computer industry.[1] TeleRead would also save Americans money through its electronic forms capability. What's more, TeleRead would be Big Brother-proof, offering more freedom of expression for writers and more privacy for users than do libraries of the paper era.

Part One: Make Powerful, Affordable Computers Available to All

The student-computer ratio in American public schools is about 16 to 1; imagine a bureaucrat at Agriculture or Exxon sharing a PC with 15 colleagues. So let's start a long-range program to buy portable computers that schools and libraries can lend to students and the public at large. Eventually the schools could even give away TeleReaders to many students from low-income families. By encouraging mass production, the TeleRead program in the future would make computers almost as cheap as calculators, so that middle-class children could buy them without any subsidies.

Using TeleReaders or substitute machines, students would learn word processing, swap electronic mail, and work with personal databases, spreadsheets, and other applications, such as educational software. They and their parents could also use TeleReaders for applications such as electronic forms, community networking, and home shopping. Especially, however, TeleReaders would promote reading, the most vital skill. They would be small, rugged, and affordable and would boast sharp screens that you could read more easily than a paper book.

The screens would be flickerless; you could adjust the size and style of the type, and perhaps the screen colors, too. If you wanted, you might even detach your TeleReader's keyboard and curl up in bed with just the thin, light screen. You could move on to other "pages" or reach other chapters by pressing a button or by touching the appropriate part of the screen with a penlike device. Knight-Ridder, the newspaper publisher, has already described a tablet-style computer that lets readers browse freely through electronic newspapers. And some of the same basic principles could be applied to books. A bar at the bottom of the screen might be divided into sections that represented chapters or sections. By touching the proper section with the "pen," you could go immediately to the appropriate location in the book you were reading.

Needless to say, the same pen-type device could allow you to wander more easily through virtual libraries, not just individual books. Many people would rather work with lists of titles, but others might want to zoom in on shelves and then on icons that looked like the spines or covers of books. In fact, researchers at the University of Maryland have already developed virtual library software that offers these basic capabilities

Furthermore, the same pen devices could also let you jot notes electronically, or underline or highlight key sentences in books or articles. You could use the pen device to develop hypertext links within books or between different ones.[2] You might even be able to split the screen and draw lines between the halves—or thirds—showing different texts.

What about keyboards and alternatives? As a rule, good typists are far more productive on computers than nontypists are. This may change somewhat, but even then TeleReaders could allow the use of keyboards for those needing them. At the same time we could also provide for other options. The era of practical speech recognition for the mass market is much closer than many would think. Using a TeleReader, you might dictate the bulk of a report and pen in alphanumeric corrections with a stylus; for original composition or extended cleanup work, you could, if you wanted, rely on a keyboard.

Needless to say, we could design the TeleReaders to be comfortable for extended periods of writing—with or without keyboards. You could use a pull-out wire stand to prop up your screen on your desk. The stand could even help you position the screen at the best angle and height.

Different TeleReaders might serve different needs, with small, plug-in cards used for customization. Many machines might be able to read material aloud in the most natural of voices and highlight the spoken words on screen—one way to help bring books to the very young, the vision-impaired, and the semiliterate. Even early on, we could make TeleReaders with voice recognition that could pick up commands from the handicapped. The basic TeleReader, then, might work with many different modules, and besides, this effort could be a multivendor program offering many flavors of hardware. TeleReaders could even turn into computer-televisions in the future, but the promotion of literacy should come first.

What about printers? Because the screens on TeleReaders would be so good, you normally would not have to print out books or magazines. Why clutter up your house? If need be, however, TeleReaders could work with low-cost inkjets, lasers, or other printers.

TeleRead would not just promote the production of low-cost portable computers. The program could also make certain that machines were used regularly and well; it could help pay the salaries of computer instructors to bring teachers and librarians up to speed. Let's not turn teachers into programmers, however. Rather, instructors could show teachers how to employ high tech in their disciplines. Teachers should be able to tell students how to write clear, well-organized prose with a word processor, use spreadsheets, dissect electronic frogs, retrieve facts on a proposed national budget, or send e-mail notes to local members of Congress. And the resources should be there for librarians, as well, to receive the requisite training for the era of digital books. Praising TeleRead's educational potential, Vicki Hancock, an educational technology expert at the Association for Supervision and Curriculum Development in Alexandria, Virginia, says, "This program would benefit average students as well as gifted ones, and it would better prepare Americans for work in an information-dependent society" (personal communication, 1993).

While aiding schools and libraries, the TeleRead program would also be a boon to Silicon Valley and other high-tech areas. Flat screens, new kinds of memory chips, and other technologies would grow more attractive to our oft-skittish venture investors. TeleRead would not ban the use of foreign parts but, within reason, would favor computers with a high American content. TeleRead would thus be a sane alternative to mindless tariffs such as the duties that the United States once imposed on some foreign-made screens for laptops.

Moreover, because the government would buy finished equipment, Washington would not need to set up a big research and development bureaucracy for TeleRead. Rather, the taxpayers could benefit from competition for TeleRead contracts, and Silicon Valley could do its own R&D, taking advantage of existing federal programs such as the Defense Department's massive efforts to improve flat-panel displays.

What's more, Washington would issue clear-cut standards for equipment, so that many vendors could compete on the basis of price, equipment capabilities, and past performance. A TeleRead agency could encourage small companies to team up with larger ones if doubts existed about their abilities to meet the demands of major contracts. To protect the taxpayers, the program would not buy scads of portable computers at once; it would wait until the technology improved enough to justify truly large purchases. Even then, the program could send out requests for proposals on an ongoing basis to avoid overcommitment to outdatable technology.

Part Two: Set Up a National Database as Soon as Possible

TRnet, part of the TeleRead program, would offer an electronic cornucopia. Like most public libraries, it would normally avoid pay-per-read books. TRnet would be free or would charge low subscription fees based on annual family income, and perhaps would be included as an option on federal tax forms. The poorest Americans, of course, should be able to dial up TRnet without paying a penny. Think of the "I" word: consider TRnet an investment in our economic and intellectual development, and use general revenue money to make the network affordable to all.

Reachable from anywhere in the United States, TRnet would try to carry the full texts of all new books and other publications. How? Material longer than ten thousand words, and intended for publication, would have to be in digital form on TRnet for a copyright to stick. Existing domestic copyright law would be changed as needed. We mustn't split hairs at the expense of creators, so, certainly, exceptions could exist. For instance, if a plagiarist stole from an unfinished novel before the author had a chance to publish it, the writer would still enjoy full protection. So would a writer shopping around for a publisher of a book or article. What's more, originators of informal postings on BBS systems, the Internet, and other networks would not have to register material to enjoy copyright protection.

Some may ask, "Well, what is the difference between formal and informal postings?" The most conspicuous one is that formal material has value added. Only a fraction of items on the Internet have been reviewed by a publisher or a committee of scholarly peers. Commercially and academically, the material is worth less, as a rule, than is the edited writing in published books and paper journals. It may not be as factual or as easy to digest. What the reader saves in money, he or she might make up in time to allow for the raw material's failings.

Even now, in the case of informally posted items, copyright isn't necessarily surrendered. Although CD-ROM collections of Internet-related material have reached the market without permission from individual contributors, the legal issues are fuzzier than many would think. For example, if I write an Internet cookbook and am prudent about it, I may have to contact scores of authors of recipes for permission. If anything, TeleRead could somewhat lessen the ambiguities of the present law in favor of creators of informally posted material such as the recipes. Should an author and publisher be able to make money off a cookbook without paying a penny for the material?

The formal registration requirement, however, would indeed apply to publishers and writers who deemed their work to be ready for formal publication. If someone copy-protected an e-book and were about to offer it for sale in a polished format, then clearly the person would need to register.

What about undigitized articles? If the material were shorter than ten thousand words, then scanners could pick up the images, either for conversion to computer text or as pictures to be dialed up on TRnet. Video or audio material—whether TV series or radio broadcasts—would require registration with TeleRead. Unlike e-books, however, this material would not necessarily need to be posted on TRnet itself. Instead, copyright holders would supply brief descriptions and ordering information—similar to what the Vanderbilt archive provides for people desiring to track down old news programs. Maybe video and audio material from commercial sources like Paramount or CBS might be part of TeleRead's actual collection someday, but not at the start. Movie properties and the like would cost more to buy than books do, and the written word is normally the most efficient way to impart knowledge. So although films and tapes would need to be registered, they would not be available free, as books might be. (Pointers, of course, could eventually guide you from TeleRead to the video and audio databases of the commercial providers such as TV networks.)

Washington would phase in the registration requirement with a voluntary program. Technophobic publishers would have plenty of time to learn to convert their material to the proper format. To make these massive but needed changes possible within copyright law, the United States would work closely with other countries. Already TeleRead is in keeping with the Berne Convention's intent to protect creators; most writers would fare much better under TeleRead than under the present system. Still, TeleRead should be within the letter of international law, not just the spirit, and the solution is obvious: change the laws. The task isn't so formidable as it might seem. The whole world is asking the same questions that we in the United States are: Just how can society compensate creators fairly and also make information affordable to rich and poor? And what to do about the flow of intellectual property across national borders by way of computer networks? With TeleRead-style arrangements to discourage piracy, might it not be easier to guard against the international variety? Wealthy countries could help poorer ones develop TeleRead-style libraries over the years, as an incentive for poorer countries to respect copyright laws. Indeed, an international electronic peace corps might be started to improve telecommunications infrastructures, enable nations to share technical knowledge, and work on other communications-related goals that advance such basics as agriculture and public health.[3] Developing countries will never respect the intellectual property of wealthy nations unless the latter offer suitable incentives.

In the United States and elsewhere, debates are also heating up over the technologies that information networks could employ to transmit books and other material. No single solution needs to prevail. TRnet could use old-fashioned phone lines, fiber optic cables, or radio, whatever cost the least. No matter what the technology, the results would be impressive. *The Great Gatsby* could reach you in a fraction of the time it took to watch a rerun of "I Love Lucy."

Before you hooked into TRnet, you would answer a series of easy questions to pinpoint exactly what you needed. Your might punch in the name of an author, dial up the network, and instantly get a list of all of the author's works, with quick descriptions. Then the TeleReader would disconnect you from the network. At your leisure, without tying up the phone lines, you would go on to choose which books you wanted sent into your computer when you logged on a second time. This would be the most expedient scenario at the start. More and more, however, especially in areas with cable TV lines connected to computer networks, users would be able to stay online hour after hour at much less expense than now.

Even then, TeleRead could minimize the amount of time needed to find information. You could select books not only by author but also by publisher, your own predesignated groups of publishers, editor, general category, subject, search words, geographical setting, academic level, the number of retrievals, time of publication, or other criteria. If you were a sixth-grader curious about airplanes, you would not be swamped by hundreds or thousands of titles; you could limit your searches just to books for your age group. And if you were in high school and keyed in "Washington" and "novels," you would see everything from *Democracy* to *Washington, D.C.* Then if you added the words *black literature* to your search, you could call up Afro-American fiction from the local writers. Inner-city teachers could easily track down books that meant thousands of times more to bright teenagers than anything on television. In fact, they could tailor reading assignments to individual children.

Electronic indexes needn't be the only technique with which TeleRead might eventually direct users to the right material. You might also browse through images of book covers, or at least well-designed lists of books; just as at real libraries, serendipity could reign supreme. And what better way to foster serendipity and curiosity than hypertext? You could highlight a word or phrase and be referred to another place in a text, or even to another book or article. Clearly TeleRead could benefit from much of the same technology found on the Web in 1994, where CommerceNet, MecklerWeb, and similar areas serve as test cases.

TeleRead would also go beyond indexing and hypertext alone and would use intelligent agents, sometimes described as electronic butlers. Intelligent agents could prowl networks, looking for material of greatest interest to you, even while you slept. As telecommunications costs shrank, the agents could grow in importance. If we trusted agent-style software to ferret out books for us, a centralized subscription arrangement such as

TeleRead would make more sense than a motley series of collections from providers of often-pricey information. What if an agent accidentally downloaded megabyte after megabyte of material from a commercial library that charged outrageous fees? Or suppose that an agent-created summary misled you into thinking that an expensive e-book was much more valuable to you than it actually was. A truly centralized TRnet—free, or with low-cost, flat-fee subscription rates—would end such risks.

Although I have mentioned books and articles in examples, TRnet could carry educational software, too, from which teachers and students could choose the best programs for them. Math and science students could especially benefit. And young immigrants could use software rich in moving images and synthesized speech to help them learn English. In addition, TRnet might carry business and entertainment programs from people who now distribute their work as shareware. Let the software community help decide if TeleRead should include shareware of a noneducational nature. Certainly, given the high rate of piracy at many schools, TeleRead should cover educational software at the very least.

Educational videos also might be included eventually, and perhaps digitally transmitted radio programs of National Public Radio or similar networks. If NPR wanted, it could send out computer files of "All Things Considered" to be retrieved at the recipients' convenience. (A private service called Internet Radio already offers digitized interviews for technically oriented people. The service even features a "Geek of the Week" spot.)

TeleRead might also offer electronic reproductions of art. That is exactly what the Library of Congress is already trying in a small way, through a noteworthy experiment on the Web and on the America Online commercial service. Multimedia experts at the library look forward to the time when people at home could routinely take virtual reality tours through great art galleries of the world.

The main purpose of TRnet, though, should be to preserve the written word. Often written language is the best way to pass on detailed instructions, tell stories, and convey abstract idea and feelings. Powerful interests are aggressively promoting the growth of multimedia; now we need TeleRead to protect the survival of text.

Whatever the medium, TRnet would pay fairly. For example, software houses or independent programmers would receive fees based essentially on the number of times the public dialed up their creations (perhaps even individual, Web-style pages in some cases). And the same arrangement could apply to individual articles from newspapers and other publications. When writers kept rights to the articles, then payment would go to them.

TRnet would allow publications a delay—maybe four weeks for daily newspapers and sixteen weeks for monthly periodicals—before the network posted issues online for all to see. The online editions could be highly customized for individual subscribers, just as some experts now foresee. These electronic periodicals could even offer interactive ads through which subscribers could order merchandise, which TeleReaders eventually would be able to display in color and with moving images. Newspapers and magazines could run not only their normal ads but also AdLinks to archives with further information about goods or services. Ad-focused newsgroups are already sprouting on Usenet, and electronic malls have proliferated on the World Wide Web. Publishers could rent out AdLinks from their electronic publications to these areas and equivalents, which, in the future, could offer lively, specialized editorial matter to encourage readers to visit. Such areas could even take the form of imaginary online worlds. Witness MCI's recent creation of a fictitious publisher online, to which readers can submit manuscripts and send e-mail messages. The next step, logically, would be entertaining games in which people used virtual versions of the advertised products to win prizes. Ad areas—or AdWorlds—would be to electronics periodicals what independently published Sunday supplements are to present-day newspapers, except that they could be much more narrowly targeted for the appropriate readers. Simply put, nonintrusive advertising online could be just as lucrative as ads in traditional newspapers and magazines, and maybe even more so. What's more, unlike traditional periodicals, the electronic versions could offer readers the choice of paying extra to avoid ads.

Electronic periodicals could rely directly on phone companies and cable systems to speed current editions to paid subscribers, but often TRnet might make more sense. Understandably, many newspapers see phone companies as rival publishers. Suppose, however, that telecommunications firms signed long-term contracts with TRnet; then the network could act as a buffer between them and the newspapers that subleased the lines at discount rates.

What about TRnet's compensation for professional writers of books and for their publishers? Authors could sell to TRnet directly, or, armed with this new bargaining power, they could sign contracts with publishers. Without heavy production and distribution costs, writers' pay would be far better. Writers and publishers would earn fees based on how often people retrieved books, and on other criteria such as length and subject matter. As a mass purchaser of material, TRnet could pay de-escalating royalties on best-sellers to discourage publishers from overhyping "big" books at the expense of midlist titles. Publishers could set advances by the expected number of dialups. Businesspeople could pay authors and publishers for rights to anticipated dialup fees; let Wall Street invest in literary futures.

If TRnet gouged readers, then the public would bootleg books electronically and cheat authors, publishers, and literary investors; but if network use were free or cheap, piracy just would not be worth the trouble. Electronic books especially demand protection of this nature. Aging better than most newspaper and magazines, they can be excellent prey for bootleggers.

Even paper books will no longer be safe in the future. The Authors' Guild has protested against an experimental photocopier from a Japanese company. The troublesome machine can automatically turn pages of a book. With a scanner, the machine could translate a long book into ASCII within hours. Mary Pope Osborne, guild president, complained to *SIMBA Media Daily* (May 23, 1994), "An infringer could then post the electronic version on the Internet, where thousands of illegal copies could be made."

TeleRead could rely on a protection scheme similar to those proposed for pay-per-read. In other words, the books and other material would be everywhere. But you could not read the text in full without a decryption device that used up "credits" that you obtained by modem. All this sounds like pay-per-read—or pay-per-download, as some p-p-r advocates might prefer to call it. But a major difference would exist. The credits would be free. You would amass them whenever you logged on to record your past downloads of material. And just as in pay-per-read schemes, the reporting would be painless and automatic, through a quick modem or network call to a central reporting bureau.

Under such a plan, most people would not *have* to dial up TeleRead books directly from the virtual central database; instead they could log onto the servers of local and university libraries and other organizations. Libraries could offer their own hypertext links of material in the virtual central database. So could individual professors, even, customizing the reading for Sociology 101 or Philosophy 212. And, of course, so could Net providers and other businesses. Services such as CompuServe could sell additional value-added features; they could start online conferences centered on TeleRead books and authors, for example, and sell fresh articles from newspapers and magazines. Remember, TeleRead would not provide *fresh* articles from commercial publications for free.

The AT&T Interchange Online Network, started by Ziff-Davis, is a good example of the potential for the private sector to add value. If you retrieve a new story on Interchange, you may benefit not only from links to other articles but also from links to downloaded files and a related forum. Moreover, if the virtual central database ever were to censor a book, nothing would prevent services such as Interchange from offering it on their own. In fact, censored works might even enjoy extra appeal on the commercial side. Meanwhile, commercial services from CompuServe to local BBSs would be earning money from books already in the database.

Online services wouldn't be the only businesses able to benefit from TeleRead's databases. Bookstores and copy shops could print out material distributed on the network. The book industry has long talked about paper books on demand as a way to reduce inventory problems. Trnet might electronically transmit eye-appealing covers and page layouts; and with the high-resolutions color printers of the future, these books-on-demand could win over even the most diehard technophobes. Each time a store downloaded a book, the author or publisher could receive a dial-up fee, as if a reader had logged on to TRnet directly. Metering devices, perhaps tested at random by Washington, would keep track of the number of copies printed out. But because the stores were obtaining the material so inexpensively from TeleRead, they would lack much temptation to cheat.

What about cheating by contributors to the database, however? Could the unscrupulous type their names over and over again, go on for 60,000 words, and have friends dial these nonbooks at public expense? Unlikely. Anyone could post almost anything on TRnet, after storage costs dropped sufficiently, but professional librarians or committees, each working within limits on the number of books selected, could help decide which works merited royalties from the national library. The librarians would be at national, state, and local levels, and they would regularly monitor a central database for new submissions in their specialties.

After a certain number of dialups, almost any book or program could earn fees, regardless of the wishes of the librarians. Moreover, writers and publishers would also be able to bypass librarians by gambling a certain amount of money up front to reduce the number of dialups required for royalties. The TeleRead laws might require TRnet to reserve maybe a quarter or third of its acquisitions budget for "bypass books," as I'll call them: books that librarians did not approve. By raising or lowering the fees charged authors or publishers, the network could help control the total bypass expenditures. De-escalating royalties on the biggest best-sellers, and only on them, would also keep a lid on costs. Even those limits, in fact, might not be necessary if Lloyd's-of-London-style risk pools from the private side were used to cushion the library system against expensive surprises.

TeleRead could reduce costs, as well, by encouraging copyright registrants to do much of the work themselves. For example, publishers of popular books could build in links to specialized works that their writers used in research. If TeleRead's librarians considered the links to be useful, the publishers or writers might receive higher compensation than otherwise.

So what would TeleRead's expenses total? To be hypothetical, suppose we could immediately put all paper books and some other material on TRnet. When I researched this question in 1993, my tentative estimates added up to $30.05 billion:

• $10 billion for online books, which would be more appropriate than the less than $5 billion that book publishers were spending on writers and editorial employees as of 1993. The $5 billion is my estimate based on a book industry study and on informal talks with publishing authorities. In a nation with a Gross Domestic Product of more than $6 trillion a year, it is an outrage that so little now goes for editorial expenses associated with books. All of society suffers when book writers—major disseminators of knowledge—do not receive fair compensation for their work.

If you want to place the present $5 billion in context, then consider the sales of just one technology company, Hewlett-Packard. In the six month period ended April 30, 1995, or within two years of 1993, it enjoyed some $14.7 billion in net revenue—and net earnings of $1.2 billion, according to a press release dated May 16, 1995. The problem isn't that HP is making too much, just that writers and editors are receiving too little. Yes, writers could publish directly, but good publishing houses that added value—for example, through editing and proper promotion—would fare very well in a system where librarians enjoyed more influence than today.

• $0 for fresh editions of newspapers and magazines, including academic journals, because TRnet would be a mere conduit in those cases. TRnet would drive down the cost of communications and allow readers to access the new material more easily.

• $5 billion for past editions and old articles. That's a fifth of the approximately $25 billion that American readers paid each year for newspapers and the magazines for 1993, according to Commerce Department figures. Adding to TeleRead's appeal for publishers, the library versions of electronic periodicals could feature automatically updated links to current advertisements. The editorial content of a two-year-old electronic newspaper would be the same as the original, but the ads would be today's.

• $50 million for articles and papers that TRnet bought directly. As any professional writer or academic can tell you, some of the most valuable writing will never find readers because it is outside the commercial or academic formats of existing publications. Granted, thousands of Americans would contribute material to TRnet without counting on financial rewards. But TRnet could at least hold out a slim possibility of pay. The amount of money in this category would be kept small, so that TRnet was not competing with commercial newspapers and magazines.

• $3 billion for educational software, or about three times the amount that schools and families now spend if you extrapolate from 1993–1994 statistics of the Software Publishers Association.

• $2 billion for computers for libraries, schools, and some low-income people, and some computer training programs for librarians and teachers. A billion dollars could buy a million TeleReaders at $1,000 each, or, eventually, 10 million computers at $100 each. Again, however, the idea is not to give every American a machine but rather to spur production of good, affordable portables for reading. Skillful jaw-boning by politicians—not just a procurement program—could work miracles. The Valley would be much more likely to produce TeleRead-style machines if Washington spoke up. Without this mix of talk and *focused* procurement by the Valley's largest customer, the industry will remain too oriented toward entertainment and not enough toward enlightenment.

• $10 billion for staffers, telecommunications and leasing of computer facilities. Many would consider the $10 billion to be far too high. I've tried to err on the cautious side, extrapolating from figures for present online services, which lack TeleRead's economies of scale. Staff costs would be low, because TRnet would rely mostly on existing librarians, who are already accustomed to choosing books for public use. Telecommunications might well be the biggest cost. Rather than squander tax money on rapidly outdatable technology, the government could rely on cable systems and private phone companies. As much as possible, TeleRead could take advantage of the infrastructure of existing networks. The system might even offer bargain subscriptions to users willing to dial up their books outside peak times. Also, TeleRead could lease private computer facilities to avoid technolock (technolock: n. A tendency of many large bureaucracies to keep using antique equipment to justify past investment).

The hypothetical $30.05 billion is about 2 percent of the federal government's 1993 budget, or around half a percent of the gross domestic product. What's more, Washington could scale down a pilot project to suit a national mood of austerity. The actual first-year expenses of TeleRead's database and related activities could be in the tens of millions, and perhaps much less. Only a minority of Americans would sign up in the beginning if we limited the first users to public domain material and specialized books and articles of a scientific, technical, medical, or educational nature.

Moreover, as suggested by an acquaintance of mine, the program could include only older books at the start—works that publishers otherwise would simply remainder. And it could be voluntary for the publishers at first. Modest subscriptions fees, perhaps $50–$100 per year for an average family, could help pay for this scaled-down program. In addition, we could reduce initial expenses by using existing resources on the Internet as much as possible. Areas of the Web might be excellent as a test not just for the electronic books but also for the electronic forms. Let a lean TeleRead sell itself. Then, as the economy picked up and reading computers grew more powerful, support would grow for an expanded program.

Of course, an early TeleRead could avoid subscription requirements and metering of any kind and simply put material on the Web to encourage hardware vendors to spend more R&D money on equipment for reading electronic books in style. Counting WWW accesses wouldn't be as precise a measurement for compensation purposes. But it would reduce technical requirements at this early stage.

Part Three: Cost-Justify TeleRead by Encouraging the Use of TeleReaders for Government-Related Paperwork and for Commerce

Many in the public interest community love the idea of taking money from rich users of high-tech services to pay for the database require-ments of the poor. User-to-user subsidies are laudable for purposes such as assuring universal telephone service. This regulatory model, however, is wrong in a database context; the money just will not be there. Subsidizing databases is different from subsidizing telephone service. If our schools are fair to the children of the poor, their database needs will be too extensive and too unpredictable. The rich will give up only so much to the youngsters from poor and working-class families. Meanwhile, demographic trends will only worsen the problem; in California, for example, well-off white people hate to spend money on schools and libraries for black- brown- and yellow-skinned children. Given the increases expected in minority populations, California could be a forerunner for many other states. What applies to tax money will apply to user-to-user subsidies, and despite the Robin Hood talk, the poor will only lose in the end.

Suppose, however, that we use a new model. What if high tech can transfer resources from bureaucracy to knowledge? Visit a government office, and you'll see batteries of clerks typing away, tapping out data from citizens and businesses. What a waste! Paperwork is not just expensive for the government; it diverts citizens from more productive activities. But let's say that you could fill out smart forms on TeleReaders or equivalent machines, then send the information over the phone lines—directly to government-run computers. Easy-to-use software could guide you as you worked on your taxes or otherwise engaged in an official transaction.

These programs would be no dummies. You would supply the rele-vant facts about your family or business, and then the software would tailor the questions to you and discard irrelevant ones. The programs might tie in with commercial software, meeting specifications such that, for example, you would not have to re-enter items from your electronic checkbook. Indeed, private industry could supply TeleForm programs of its own for people not wanting to use the official software. Corporations already have come up with tax software. But TeleRead would encourage the development of programs that were much easier to use. Public or pri-vate, the software would let you know how it toted up your taxes—and would let you change any entry if you disagreed. The Internal Revenue Service might challenge your return later on, but at least you would still enjoy just as much control over the tax form as you do now.

Working with these TeleForms, we would all come out ahead. We would spend less time and money keeping the government happy. Small businesses, especially, would welcome the reduction in paperwork, which is as much a cost of government as taxes are. And the bureaucracies could more easily digest the information—without any need to rekey it, and with less need to pester citizens about errors or missing facts. Moreover, TeleRead's forms would be well structured enough to encourage more responsive answers. Because TeleReaders would use pen interfaces, not just keyboards, citizens could sign tax papers and augment digital identification the old-fashioned way.

Tax forms are one example of how TeleRead could help Americans in areas besides reading. What about Social Security forms? Software could deal with all kinds of "ifs" when Americans applied for benefits. We could reduce the staffs of hundreds of local Social Security offices—doing this slowly over a period of time to cushion effects on workers. Similarly, government at all levels could use TeleForms to handle matters ranging from drivers' licenses to unemployment compensation, health-care claims, and applications for government-backed loans. E-forms and databases could help match up workers and jobs in a truly massive but cost-effective way. Imagine the benefits for small business.

Computerized forms, of course, are hardly a revolutionary idea. Even now, with inexpensive software, you can create a paper tax return or even an application to work for the government. And the IRS has experimented with electronic filing of returns from ordinary citizens, not just from tax-preparation firms. The IRS also plans to spend a fortune on scanners to pick data from paper returns. But direct filing by computer is the future, and TeleRead would dramatically advance such goals.

Furthermore, TeleRead could also contribute to knowledge about government via government-related databases. With a tax system built around electronic forms, you could much more easily plug in facts from a tax proposal in Congress and see how it would affect you.

TeleRead would also aid transactions on the consumer side, such as home shopping. More than a few people think of data highways in terms of Macy's department stores online, five hundred channels, violent *Terminator* films on demand, and the other pinnacles of modern civilization. Yet we need machines to promote literacy. How to reconcile the two visions to further cost-justify TeleRead? Suppose that we could buy some TeleReaders with radio links to remote boxes on our televisions or to circuitry in the TVs themselves. We could actually use the forms capability of the TeleReaders to program the televisions and order airplane tickets, pizzas, designer clothes, and so on. People could reach for tiny remote controls to scoot from channel to channel. When they want to record future programs, configure their TVs in intricate ways, or order merchandise, movies, and the rest, their TeleReaders would help out. Consider the fashion industry. Recently the *New York Times* quoted an expert as saying that it could be a decade before people tried clothes on virtual versions of themselves on computer screens. With TeleRead, such wizardry might happen much sooner; the pen-style interface would easily allow consumers to specify the right colors, measurements, and the like.

Standard network interface devices—perhaps PCMCIA-style cards—could add the necessary radio-frequency links between set-top boxes and TeleReaders or other computers. These linking devices could be optimal. But many if not most people might want the links eventually. With them, TeleReaders could control TVs in fancy multimedia applications that used televisions more than as computers than as one-way pacifiers. The same radio links with the televisions could be one of the ways used to download books and narrow-bandwidth educational software into TeleReaders themselves.

The radio links to televisions could be one of the paths used to download books and narrow-bandwidth educational software into TeleReaders. Intellectual snobbery notwithstanding, these radio links would not lessen the value of TeleReaders for reading, writing, government forms, civic and educational networking, and other serious uses. Quite the contrary. The links could be used not just with TV but also for exchanging material in the classroom, including copyrighted works—with an appropriate reporting system. Furthermore, TeleRead's radio links could be used in some business applications, especially video conferencing. An executive could work with just a tiny camera and a TeleReader nearby—and use the latter to tweak charts and otherwise control images on a huge wall-mounted screen. On top of everything else, TVs or other large devices could offer auxiliary storage or backup for TeleReaders. They could house printers, so consumers could print either articles or other materials, such as coupons for shoppers.

Clearly, the TeleRead vision could coexist well with a TV-based system at home and in the office. The philosophy of this plan is to make book-optimized machines attractive to as many people as possible. If TV links or teleputer-style TeleReaders furthered this goal, so much the better. TeleReaders could remain valuable for their original uses as well.

Part Four: Consciously Work to Keep Big Brother Out of TeleRead

Electronic federalism—and the strengthening of the Internet, along with value-added opportunities for CompuServe-style services and local BBS systems—would promote the freedom of ideas and avoid the tyranny of a government monopoly. Commercialization of the Internet would help greatly. The more the Internet gears up for high-bandwidth, business-related applications, the more cheaply the Net will transmit low-bandwidth material such as list mail and electronic books. The only proviso here is that precautions must be taken to assure that the commercial side would pay its true costs.

Balance is the goal. A national library would be less vulnerable to the marketplace values that so often dominate popular culture and that might distort academic and scientific literature. Private information providers, however, are needed to expose abuses of government and to avoid bureaucratic rigidity. That is why the book side of TeleRead should allow publishers to gamble money up front against future royalties from the national library if TeleLibrarians did not chose their offerings. It is also why the virtual central database ideally would be able to handle newspaper and magazine ads, not just editorial matter. The old cliché is true—advertising is indeed the mother's milk of newspapers—and if we did not let newspapers support themselves, then we would throw the balance between government and the press out of kilter.

In other ways, too, TeleRead would guard against Big Brother. George Orwell's bureaucrats rewrote old stories in the *London Times* to suit the whims of the moment, but that would be inherently impossible with TeleRead. The same technical precautions used to safeguard data would also serve as political precautions. Questions still exist about the permanence of various storage methods, and with that in mind, TeleRead might provide for constant backups on read-only media of different kinds—and constant monitoring of the integrity of the material at different locations. Also helpful would be the use of different contractors to run databases, not just the use of many librarians at different locations. With so many people involved, and with an Internet-style, anticensorship ethos, bureaucratic meddling with old material would be impossible. Contractors might even be required to monitor the integrity of rivals' databases.

Moreover, TeleRead could hasten the coming of machines for the masses that included enough storage to preserve almost everything that users dialed up. So no changes could be made to books in the central database without the risk of howls from thousands of TeleRead users. Still another safeguard would be for TeleRead to be an independent agency with long-range funding, or, at the very least, a part of the Library of Congress that was as insulated as much as possible from political influence. TeleRead's directors could be appointed for long terms.

Another way to preserve free expression would be to allow parents to restrict the information choices of young children. That sounds paradoxical and may even violate the professional codes of some library groups, but think of it from this perspective: most book censorship happens in the name of child protection. By allowing parents to choose books for their children, much of the wind would be taken out of the censors' sails.

All in all, freedom of expression under TeleRead would be far greater than today, because readers in every city could dial up virtually every book. The dirty secret of U.S. libraries is that despite all the talk about freedom to read, their shelves reflect just the taste of local librarians and their publics. In Fairfax County, Virginia, for example, which boasts one of the nation's largest public library systems, I cannot find a single item by the late Saul Alinsky—among the country's most notable community organizers. The neglect of Alinsky's writings is not censorship per se. But the effect is the same.

Beside assuring a truly national audience for books of all kinds, TeleRead should increase privacy for all readers. If the program charged nothing or just flat subscription fees, there would be no need to keep permanent records on the reading choices of individuals. When you retrieved a controversial political work—your machine would tell TRnet to pay the author or publisher. But the library's computers would be programmed to forget your personal selections in a short time. TRnet would keep the temporary records only as a way to guard against constant dialups by those profiting off them.

For the really worried, private companies such as Barnes & Noble could set up vending machines that would accept old-fashioned, untraceable paper money and nameless debit cards. The machines would copy books onto a tiny memory card that plugged into your computer and held many volumes. Bearing bright logos, such machines could be a fixture at malls, airports and other public areas. They could serve both the privacy-minded and people who just did not want to become regular subscribers. Revenue would go both to TRnet and operators of the vending machines.

The possibility even exists that with enough protection against fraud, TeleRead could use nameless, debit-style cards without any money involved. Citizens could not receive new cards from the private contractors' machines unless they reported past usage, via the old cards they turned in. Still another possibility would be the use of private companies—selected from among certified possibilities by individual citizens—to serve as buffers and isolate individual accounts from government scrutiny.

Needless to say, TeleRead's forms capabilities, not just the library features, should respect privacy. Like it or not, the move in government is to automate and consolidate as many databases as possible. TeleRead has a major advantage in privacy over some other approaches. Certain officials have been talking about using just one card to serve many needs and streamline citizens' dealings with the government. That could mean that government databases would exchange information even more than they do today. TeleRead, however, would give more processing power to individual citizens, so that, for example, they could more easily handle their own tax returns; they would not have to entrust as much raw data to the IRS.

Conclusion

Even with financial benefits and Constitutional protection, skeptics might dismiss TeleRead and its TRnet as socialistic; but they are no more socialistic than a public library. If Andrew Carnegie—the nineteenth century capitalist extraordinaire—were alive today, he would be probably be funding demonstration projects, just as he helped small-town libraries across the United States, hoping that ambitious Americans could use the technology of the day to better themselves. If we could break down barriers between experts and the rest of us, and if even the technophobes at the *New Yorker* could understand the Web, all would benefit from this future vision of electronic publishing.

Notes

1. TeleRead is an evolving proposal. Related writings by its author are Rothman 1992a, 1992b, and 1993. TeleRead has also been discussed in other articles such as Barron 1993. William F. Buckley, Jr. (1993) endorsed the TeleRead concept.

2. TeleRead could be designed with many and perhaps all the hypertext-related wrinkles of Ted Nelson's Xanadu publishing system. At the same time TeleRead would offer a much more comprehensive collection of works than Xanadu would. Nelson is far too sanguine about the willingness of writers and publishers to participate in his project. TeleRead would require electronic books to be made available to a national library—while providing for fair compensation to writers, as well as to publishing houses that added value.

3. See "Building an Electronic Peace Corps," *International Health News*, November 1987, p. 4. The proposal is mentioned as an option in a report from the Office of Technology Assessment, *Perspectives on the Role of Science and Technology in Sustainable Development*, September 1994, p. 55. For more details on the EPC, including citations of past articles from the *Washington Post* and elsewhere, see the following address on the World Wide Web: http://www.clark.net/pub/rothman/epc.html.

References

Baker, Nicholson. (1994). *New Yorker,* April 4.

Barron, Billy. (1993). "TRNet: A Possible Future Use of the Internet." *ConneXions*: The Interoperabiliity Report (December), p. 25.

Buckley, William F., Jr. (1993). "On the Right," May 17.

Bush, Vannevar. (1945). "As We May Think." *Atlantic Monthly*, 176: 101–108.

Rothman, David H. (1992a). "Americans Could Dial Up Books from Home—and Help Industry." *Baltimore Sun*, August 9, Perspective Section, p. 4G.

Rothman, David H. (1992b). "Information Access for All." *Computerword*, July 6, p. 77.

Rothman, David H. (1993). "The World at Your Figertips." *Washington Post Education Review*, April 4, p. 3.

Contributors

Janet Fisher
Journals Manager
The MIT Press
55 Hayward Street
Cambridge, MA 02142
fisher@mitvma.mit.edu

Lisa Freeman
Director
University of Minnesota Press
2037 University Avenue, SE
Minneapolis, MN 55455
lfreeman@maroon.tc.umn.edu

Ira H. Fuchs
Vice President for Computing and
Information Technology
Princeton University
Nassau Hall
Princeton, NJ 08544
fuchs@tsar.princeton.edu

Jean-Claude Guédon
Departement de littérature comparée
Université de Montréal
C.P. 6128, Succursale "A"
Montreal, H3C 3J7,
Canada
guedon@ere.umontreal.ca

Rebecca S. Guenther
Network Development and MARC
Standards Office
Library of Congress
101 Independence Ave at First Street, SE
Washington, D.C. 20540
rebecca@rgue.loc.gov

Stevan Harnad
Department of Psychology
University of Southampton
Highfield, Southampton
SO9 5NH
United Kingdom
harnad@soton.ac.uk
ftp://ftp.princeton.edu/pub/harnad/
http://cogsci.ecs.soton.ac.uk/~harnad/
http://www.princeton.edu/~harnad/
gopher://gopher.princeton.edu/11/.libr
aries/.pujournals

Brian Hayes
211 Dacian Avenue
Durham, NC, 27701
bhayes@mercury.interpath.net

Larry W. Hurtado
Department of Religion
University of Manitoba
Winnipeg, Manitoba, R3T 2N2
Canada
hurtado@cc.umanitoba.ca

Brian Kahin
Director
Information Infrastructure Project
Science, Technology and Public
Policy Program
John F. Kennedy School of
Government
Harvard University
79 John F. Kennedy Street
Cambridge, MA 02138
kahin@harvard.edu

Rob Kling
Department of Information and
Computer Science
University of California, Irvine
Irvine, CA 92717
kling@ics.uci.edu

Roberta Lamb
Department of Information and
Computer Science
University of California, Irvine
Irvine, CA 92717
rlamb@binky.ics.uci.edu

Clifford A. Lynch
Director DLA
University of California
Office of the President
300 Lakeside Drive, 8th Floor
Oakland, CA 94612-3550
clifford.lynch@ucop.edu

Patrice A. Lyons
Law Offices of Patrice Lyons,
Chartered
1401 16th Street, NW
Washington, D.C. 20036

Marlene Manoff
MIT Libraries, 14S–222
Cambridge, MA 02139-4307
manoff@mit.edu

Gregory B. Newby
Graduate School of Library and
Information Science
University of Illinois at Urbana-
Champaign
501 E. Daniel Street
Champaign, IL 61820
gbnewby@uiuc.edu

Andrew M. Odlyzko
AT&T Bell Laboratories
600 Mountain Avenue
Murray Hill, NJ 07974
amo@research.att.com

Ann Okerson
Director, Office of Scientific and
Academic Publishing
Association of Research Libraries
Dupont Circle, NW
Suite 800
Washington, DC 20036
ann@cni.org

Robin P. Peek
Graduate School of Library and
Information Science
Simmons College
300 The Fenway
Boston, MA 02115
rpeek@vmsvax.simmons.edu

David H. Rothman
805 N. Howard Street, #240
Alexandria, VA 22304
rothman@clark.net
http://www.clark.net/pub/telhome.html

Fytton Rowland
Department of Information and
Library Studies
Loughborgough University of
Technology
Leicestershire, LE11 3TU
United Kingdom
j.f.rowland@lut.ac.uk
http://info.lut.ac.uk/departments/dils/s
taff/frowland.html

James E. Rush
Executive Director
PALINET
3401 Market Street, Suite 262
Philadelphia, PA 19104-3374
rush@shrsys.hslc.org

Robert J. Silverman
301 Ramseyer
29 W. Woodruff
Columbus, OH 43210
rsilverm@magnus.acs.ohio-state.edu

Index

ASIS and Its Members

For over 50 years the leading professional society for information professionals, the American Society for Information Science is an association whose diverse membership continues to reflect the frontiers and horizons of the dynamic field of information science and technology. ASIS owes its stature to the cumulative contributions of its members, past and present.

ASIS counts among its membership some 4000 information specialists from such fields as computer science, management, engineering, librarianship, chemistry, linguistics, and education. As was true when the society was founded, ASIS membership continues to lead the information professional in the search for new and better theories, techniques, and technologies to improve access to information through storage and retrieval advances. And now, as then, ASIS and its members are called upon to help determine new directions and standards for the development of information policies and practices.